# Charisma's BIBLE HANDBOOK on the HOLY SPIRIT

JOHN REA

Contributing Editor,
*Holy Spirit Encounter Bible*

CREATION HOUSE
Orlando, FL

CHARISMA'S BIBLE HANDBOOK ON THE HOLY SPIRIT by John Rea
Published by Creation House
Strang Communications Company
600 Rinehart Road
Lake Mary, FL 32746
Web site: http://www.creationhouse.com

Unless otherwise noted, all Scripture quotations are from the New American Standard Bible. Copyright © 1960, 1962, 1963, 1968, 1971, 1972, 1973, 1975, 1977 by the Lockman Foundation. Used by permission.

Scripture quotations marked AMP are from the Amplified Bible. Old Testament copyright © 1965, 1987 by the Zondervan Corporation. The Amplified New Testament copyright © 1954, 1958, 1987 by the Lockman Foundation. Used by permission.

Scripture quotations marked TEV are from the Good News Bible, in Today's English Version. Copyright © 1966, 1971, 1976 by American Bible Society. Used by permission.

Scripture quotations marked JB are from the Jerusalem Bible. Copyright © 1966, 1967, 1968 by Darton, Longman & Todd Ltd. and Doubleday, a division of Bantam, Doubleday, Dell Publishing Group Inc. Used by permission.

Scripture quotations marked KJV are from the King James Version of the Bible.

Scripture quotations marked TLB are from The Living Bible. Copyright © 1971. Used by permission of Tyndale House Publishers Inc., Wheaton, IL 60189. All rights reserved.

Scripture quotations marked NEB are from the New English Bible. Copyright © 1961, 1970 by the Delegates of the Oxford University Press and the Syndics of the Cambridge University Press. Used by permission.

Scripture quotations marked NKJV are from the New King James Version of the Bible. Copyright © 1979, 1980, 1982 by Thomas Nelson, Inc., publishers. Used by permission.

Scripture quotations marked NIV are from the Holy Bible, New International Version. Copyright © 1973, 1978, 1984, International Bible Society. Used by permission.

Scripture quotations marked RSV are from the Revised Standard Version of the Bible. Copyright © 1946, 1952, 1971 by the Division of Christian Education of the National Council of the Churches of Christ in the USA. Used by permission.

Scripture quotations marked TAN are from The Tanakh: The New JPS Translation According to the Traditional Hebrew Text. Copyright © 1985 by the Jewish Publication Society. Used by permission.

Scripture quotations marked WILLIAMS are from the Williams New Testament: The New Testament in the Language of the People, by Charles B. Williams. Copyright © 1937, 1966, 1986 by Holman Bible Publishers. Used by permission.

Scripture quotations marked WUEST are from the Wuest New Testament: An Expanded Translation, by Kenneth S. Wuest. Copyright © 1961 by Wm. B. Eerdmans Publishing Co., Grand Rapids, Michigan. Used by permission.

Produced with the assistance of The Livingstone Corporation.
Design and composition by Design Corps.

**Library of Congress Cataloging-in-Publication data**
Rea, John, 1925–
    Charisma's Bible Handbook on the Holy Spirit/John Rea.
    p.    cm.
    Includes bibliographical references.
    ISBN 0-88419-566-X
    1. Holy Spirit—Biblical teaching.    I. Title
BS860.H56R43        1998
231'.3—dc21                98-28753
                      CIP

This book previously published as The Holy Spirit in the Bible, copyright © 1990, ISBN 0-88419-261-x.
89012345 87654321
*Printed in the United States of America*

*To*
**Hubert and Rachel Mitchell**

*Living demonstrations of the fruit and power of the Holy Spirit in their many decades of dedicated service in missions at home and abroad*

# CONTENTS

# FOREWORD

I am grateful for the appearance of *Charisma's Bible Handbook on the Holy Spirit*. This book by John Rea fills an important place in the study of the Holy Spirit in the Scriptures. To my knowledge there are no other books for lay people that cover the biblical data on the Holy Spirit as comprehensively as this volume does.

A number of years ago Dr. Rea wrote a book entitled *The Layman's Commentary on the Holy Spirit*. That book, however, dealt only with the New Testament material. As one of the consulting editors I was afforded the opportunity to read and make comments on the material as he wrote it. I was again and again delighted with his astute and penetrating biblical presentation. My only wish at the time was that he had also written on the Old Testament.

Nevertheless, I am glad he waited until now, for over the years as an Old Testament professor he has had opportunity many times to teach basic courses on the whole Old Testament as well as a course entitled "The Spirit of God in the Old Testament." Thus the author has become increasingly prepared for the task of also elucidating the Old Testament materials on the Holy Spirit. Now at last the task is complete with introductory teaching about the nature of the Spirit of God and Old Testament sections prior to the New Testament material. This is truly a commentary on the Holy Spirit in the whole Bible.

Dr. Rea represents a very fine combination of conservative biblical scholarship with a lively sense of the Person and work of the Holy Spirit. He also writes with a lucid style that makes for challenging and exciting reading.

*Charisma's Bible Handbook on the Holy Spirit* is an important contribution to the Charismatic Renewal in our time. Again I am thankful for its publication and know it will be a blessing to all who read it.

—*J. Rodman Williams*

# AUTHOR'S PREFACE

I have been directly involved in the charismatic renewal since 1962. In that year, when I was teaching at a prominent evangelical Bible institute in the Midwest, the Lord sovereignly healed my wife of a long-standing kidney blockage and touched both of us in a new way by His Spirit. I began to study the Word with fresh intensity regarding the Holy Spirit and His work in the church.

In the early 1970s I was asked to write notes on the Holy Spirit in the New Testament for the Logos Study Bible. These were also published in 1972 under separate cover as *The Layman's Commentary on the Holy Spirit* and in revised form in 1974. For the past several years the book has been out of print. The present book incorporated most of that New Testament material but with numerous revisions and additions. Meanwhile it has become increasingly apparent that there is a dearth of comprehensive studies in book form on the passages about the Spirit in the whole Bible, especially in the Old Testament.

Leon J. Wood's fine book *The Holy Spirit in the Old Testament* is now out of print. Lloyd Neve's work *The Spirit of God in the Old Testament* was published in Tokyo, Japan, where he taught as professor of Old Testament in the Lutheran Theological College; it is practically unobtainable in the United States. Canadian Roman Catholic scholar George Montague has written a penetrating work, *The Holy Spirit: Growth of a Biblical Tradition*. As a commentary on the principal texts of the Old and New Testaments it is similar to my book; however, it is organized differently, since it follows higher critical theories, and it lacks a Scripture index. Stanley M. Horton's *What the Bible Says About the Holy Spirit* remains the best popular book in print covering the entire Bible.

On each of these works I have drawn heavily as well as on my classroom teaching. From the great volume of literature in the last two decades on the Holy Spirit and charismatic experience I have selected additional insights which I believe will be helpful to the reader.

The book has been written especially for those whose lives, like mine, have been touched by God in the modern spiritual renewal. In this movement there is a continuing need for indepth instruction in the biblical doctrine of the Holy Spirit from an evangelical standpoint. I approach the Bible with full assurance that the canonical writings of both Old and New Testaments are the authoritative Word of God, written under the supervision of the Holy Spirit.

My desire is to reach as wide a readership as possible, lay people as well as scholars trained at Bible schools and seminaries. Therefore the biblical exegesis and exposition are treated in semi-popular style rather than as an academic treatise. Complete data for references given in the endnotes can be obtained by looking up the relevant author's name in the bibliography. In some cases poetic lines from Scripture have been rearranged for clarification.

Humanly speaking, the incentive to write this book has come from my colleague and friend Professor J. Rodman Williams. It was his frequent encouragement that stirred me to add the Old Testament section to the former book. He has read the entire manuscript and has made many valuable suggestions. Likewise Charles L. Holman, professor of biblical interpretation and New Testament in the department of biblical studies, has kindly helped me to clarify a number of passages. Without the diligent work and technical skill of my fine graduate assistant, Les Ballard, who typed and revised the manuscript on a word processor, this book could not have come to publication; my sincere appreciation goes to him.

I am indebted to Regent University for the sabbatical leave that gave opportunity for the writing of this book and for providing the graduate student assistance. In this regard I express special thanks to Bob Slosser, president; Carle Hunt, vice president for academic affairs; and Jerry Horner, dean of the College of Theology and Ministry.

Also I extend my gratitude to Bert Ghezzi, former editorial director of Creation House, for initially taking my manuscript for publication; to John Archer and Paul Thigpen for their diligent editorial work; and to Deborah Cole for her keen, warmhearted interest in details of the manuscript and her competent supervision of the publication process.

Above all, I am deeply grateful to my wife, Elaine, for her many helpful ideas and practical suggestions for elucidating various parts of the manuscript.

My prayer for you, the reader, is that the Lord, who is the Spirit, may continually transform you into His likeness with ever-increasing glory (2 Cor. 3:18, NIV) and empower you as His witnesses (Acts 1:8).

—*John Rea, Th.D.*
*Professor Emeritus, Regent University*

# ABBREVIATIONS

## Bible Versions

| | |
|---|---|
| AMP | The Amplified Bible (1965) |
| ASV | American Standard Version (1901) |
| BERKELEY | The Berkeley (or Verkuyl) Version (1959) |
| GNB | Good News Bible (formerly Today's English Version), by Robert G. Bratcher (1976) |
| JB | Jerusalem Bible (1966) |
| JPS | The Holy Scripture, Jewish Publication Society (1917) |
| KJV | King James Version (1611) |
| NAB | New American Bible, Catholic Biblical Association of America (1970) |
| NAS | New American Standard Bible, Reference Edition (1971) |
| NEB | New English Bible (1970) |
| NIV | New International Version (1978) |
| NIV STB | The NIV Study Bible (1985) |
| NKJV | New King James Version (1979) |
| RSV | Revised Standard Version (1952) |
| TAN | Tanakh, Jewish Publication Society (1985) |
| TCNT | Twentieth Century New Testament (1904) |
| TEV | same as GNB above |
| TLB | The Living Bible, by Kenneth N. Taylor (1971) |
| WILLIAMS | The New Testament: A Translation in the Language of the People, by C.B. Williams (1937) |
| WUEST | The New Testament: An Expanded Translation, by Kenneth S. Wuest (1961) |

## Bible Commentaries, Dictionaries, Encyclopedias, Journals and Lexicons

| | |
|---|---|
| BDB | Brown, Driver, Briggs—Gesenius, *Hebrew-English Lexicon* (1907). |
| EGT | *Expositor's Greek Testament.* 5 vols. Ed. by W. R. Nicoll (1897). Reprint. Grand Rapids: Eerdmans, 1961. |
| ICC | *International Critical Commentary.* 51 vols. Edinburgh: T. & T. Clark, 1896–. |
| ISBE | *International Standard Bible Encyclopedia.* 5 vols. Ed. by James Orr (1939). Revised; ed. by G. W. Bromiley. Grand Rapids: Eerdmans, 4 vols., 1979–1988. |
| JBL | *Journal of Biblical Literature* |
| JETS | *Journal of the Evangelical Theological Society* |
| JFB | Jamieson, Fausset and Brown, *Commentary on the Whole Bible.* 6 vols. (1871). 1 vol. ed. Grand Rapids: Zondervan, 1962. |
| NBD | *New Bible Dictionary.* Ed. by J. D. Douglas. Grand Rapids: Eerdmans, 1962. |
| NICNT | *New International Commentary on the New Testament series.* F. F. Bruce, general editor. Grand Rapids: Eerdmans, 1953–1988. |
| NICOT | *New International Commentary on the Old Testament series.* R. K. Harrison, general editor. Grand Rapids: Eerdmans, 1976– . |
| RT | *Renewal Theology* by J. Rodman Williams. Vol. I, 1988; vol. II, 1990. |
| TDNT | *Theological Dictionary of the New Testament.* Ed. by Gerhard Kittel and Gerhard Friedrich. Trans. by G. W. Bromiley. 9 vols. Grand Rapids: Eerdmans, 1964–1974. |
| TWOT | *Theological Wordbook of the Old Testament.* 2 vols. Ed. by R. L. Harris, G. L. Archer and B. K. Waltke. Chicago: Moody Press, 1980. |
| VT | *Vetus Testamentum* |
| WBC | *Wycliffe Bible Commentary.* Ed. by C. F. Pfeiffer and E. F. Harrison. Chicago: Moody Press, 1962. |

# Books of the Bible

| | | | | |
|---|---|---|---|---|
| Genesis | Gen. | Habakkuk | Hab. |
| Exodus | Exod. | Zephaniah | Zeph. |
| Leviticus | Lev. | Haggai | Hag. |
| Numbers | Num. | Zechariah | Zech. |
| Deutoronomy | Deut. | Malachi | Mal. |
| Joshua | Josh. | Matthew | Matt. |
| Judges | Judg. | Mark | Mark |
| Ruth | Ruth | Luke | Luke |
| First Samuel | 1 Sam. | John | John |
| Second Samuel | 2 Sam. | Acts | Acts |
| First Kings | 1 Kings | Romans | Rom. |
| Second Kings | 2 Kings | First Corinthians | 1 Cor. |
| First Chronicles | 1 Chron. | Second Corinthians | 2 Cor. |
| Second Chronicles | 2 Chron. | Galatians | Gal. |
| Ezra | Ezra | Ephesians | Eph. |
| Nehemiah | Neh. | Philippians | Phil. |
| Esther | Esther | Colossians | Col. |
| Job | Job | First Thessalonians | 1 Thess. |
| Psalms | Ps. | Second Thessalonians | 2 Thess. |
| Proverbs | Prov. | First Timothy | 1 Tim. |
| Ecclesiastes | Eccles. | Second Timothy | 2 Tim. |
| Song of Solomon | Song of Sol. | Titus | Titus |
| Isaiah | Isa. | Philemon | Philem. |
| Jeremiah | Jer. | Hebrews | Heb. |
| Lamentations | Lam. | James | James |
| Ezekiel | Ezek. | First Peter | 1 Pet. |
| Daniel | Dan. | Second Peter | 2 Pet. |
| Hosea | Hos. | First John | 1 John |
| Joel | Joel | Second John | 2 John |
| Amos | Amos | Third John | 3 John |
| Obadiah | Obad. | Jude | Jude |
| Jonah | Jon. | Revelation | Rev. |
| Micah | Mic. | | |
| Nahum | Nah. | | |

# TRANSLITERATION TABLE

Hebrew and Greek words have been transliterated according to the following form:

## Hebrew Alphabet (consonants)

| א | aleph | = | ʾ |
|---|---|---|---|
| ב, בּ | beth | = | b |
| ג, ג | gimel | = | g |
| ד, דּ | daleth | = | d |
| ה | hē | = | h |
| ו | waw | = | w |
| ז | zayin | = | z |
| ח | ḥeth | = | ḥ |
| ט | ṭeth | = | ṭ |
| י | yōd | = | y |
| כ, בּ, ךּ | kaph | = | k |
| ל | lamed | = | l |
| מ, ם | mem | = | m |
| נ, ן | nun | = | n |
| ס | samek | = | s |
| ע | ʿayin | = | ʿ |
| פ, פּ, ףּ | pē | = | ʾ |
| צ, ץ | ṣadhe | = | ṣ |
| ק | qōph | = | q |
| ר | resh | = | r |
| שׂ | śîn | = | ś |
| שׁ | shîn | = | š |
| ת, תּ | tau | = | t |

## Hebrew Vocalization

| רָ | = | rā |
|---|---|---|
| רוֹ | = | rô |
| רוּ | = | rû |
| רֵי | = | rê |
| רִי | = | rî |
| רֵ | = | rē |
| רֹ | = | rō |
| רֻ | = | ru |
| רַ | = | ra |
| רֶ | = | re |
| רִ | = | ri |
| רָ | = | ro (in closed syllables) |
| רֲ | = | ră |
| רְ | = | re |
| רֱ | = | rě |
| רָה | = | rāh (as in tôrāh) |
| רָה | = | rāh |
| רָא | = | raʾ |
| רֵה | = | rēh |
| רֶה | = | reh |

**Note:** *Dagesh lene* is not indicated; *dagesh forte* is represented by doubling the consonant

## Greek Alphabet

| | | | |
|---|---|---|---|
| α | alpha | = | a |
| β | beta | = | b |
| γ | gamma | = | g |
| δ | delta | = | d |
| ε | epsilon | = | e |
| ζ | zeta | = | z |
| η | ēta | = | ē |
| θ | thēta | = | th |
| ι | iota | = | i |
| κ | kappa | = | k |
| λ | lamda | = | l |
| μ | mu | = | m |
| n | nu | = | n |
| ξ | xi | = | x |
| o | omicron | = | o |
| π | pi | = | p |
| ρ | rho | = | r |
| σ, s | sigma | = | s |
| τ | tau | = | t |
| υ | upsilon | = | (u), y |
| φ | phi | = | ph |
| χ | chi | = | ch |
| ψ | psi | = | ps |
| ω | omega | = | ō |

## Greek Vocalization

| | | |
|---|---|---|
| ' | = | h |
| 'ρ | = | rh |
| γγ | = | ng |
| ᾳ | = | â |
| ῃ | = | ê |
| ῳ | = | ô |

# INTRODUCTION

As we begin the new millennium, think of all that humankind has accomplished in the last one hundred years. Things unimaginable to our forebears have startled the world in the twentieth century and have even become routine—radio communication, television, atomic explosions, supersonic air travel, laser surgery, intercontinental ballistic missiles, microcomputers, journeys to the moon, space stations, the Hubble space telescope. The list of scientific achievements could be extended almost *ad infinitum*.

Humankind, however, seems further from moral and ethical perfection than ever. The record of wars, genocide and human misery multiplies. As a result many are filled with despair and others with grave apprehension about our chances of survival on this planet. A sense of urgency if not foreboding looms as the end of this century draws near.

The Holy Spirit has not been silent during this century of tumultuous change. Revivals greater than any known previously in the history of the church have broken out all over the world. Spiritual renewal movements of the twentieth century have touched every facet of Christianity. Charismatic manifestations reminiscent of the Book of Acts have startled believer and skeptic alike.

Beginning at Azusa Street in Los Angeles in 1906 the modern-day outpouring of the Holy Spirit spread rapidly to thirsty Christians in North and South America, Europe, Asia and Africa. Pentecostal churches sprang up, and new denominations were formed. Thousands were touched by God's healing power in the tents of traveling evangelists as well as through prayer meetings in more formal church settings.

Around the middle of the century in America a new wave of the Spirit's power began surging into long-established Protestant denominations and eventually into the Roman Catholic church in 1967. Some believe a new spiritual movement began among traditional evangelicals in the 1980s, a "third wave" of the modern outpouring of the Spirit, character-ized by signs and wonders. Overseas in the past four decades major ongoing revivals have affected Korea, Indonesia, Kenya, Uganda, Zaire, Guatemala, Argentina and Brazil, to name only a few countries. The persecuted church has not only survived in communist lands but has even expanded tenfold since 1950 in lands such as China. A recent survey of the twentieth-century Pentecostal/Charismatic Renewal reports more than 300 million church mem-bers in its ranks, over 20 percent of the world's church-member Christians.[1]

What are the earmarks of this modern renewal in the Holy Spirit? We can note several. There is no one outstanding human leader, such as Martin Luther, after which it could be called. Miracles in the name of Christ not only corroborate the preaching of the gospel but also bless and help countless thousands of individuals. Churches where faith had grown cold and dormant are witnessing new reverence for the Lord Jesus and a resurgence of sound doctrine. Both clergy and laity give spontaneous vent to exuberant praise and worship, often with accompanying gifts of the Spirit. Renewed interest in the Bible is evidence of great hunger to know God's Word.

Of course, as in any revival movement, excesses, counterfeits and failures have littered the trail. But these do not invalidate the new life, joy and hope that the Holy Spirit has clearly brought to millions of people in this century.

What strategy will ensure the continuing growth and vitality of the Charismatic Renewal on into the twenty-first century? The Book of Acts pre-sents a general pattern for us to follow as well as for Theophilus, to whom it was addressed (1:1), and other readers in the first century. Acts was written not merely to be an historical account but to demonstrate God's abundant resources available to His people until Jesus comes back in glory (1:8, 11).

Christ has not yet returned, however, and Spirit-filled Christians have not yet "arrived" (Phil. 3:12–14). But, like Paul, we must be continually commit-ted to God's authority and the lordship of Jesus Christ (Acts 24:14–16; 26:15–19). We must "obey God rather than men" (5:29) and stay obedient to the Holy Spirit (5:32).

As the first Christians in Jerusalem did, we must devote ourselves to bibli-cal teaching, to corporate fellowship with other believers, to the breaking of bread together in frequent observance of the Eucharist or Lord's Supper, and to prayer and praise in public as well as in private (2:42–47). For it is in assem-bling together regularly (Heb. 10:25) that we receive the renewing and strengthening fellowship of the Holy Spirit, our Comforter and helper (2 Cor. 13:14; John 14:16). Thereby we are enabled to maintain the unity of the Spirit (Eph. 4:3–6) and to encourage one another (Acts 11:23; Phil. 2:1; Heb. 3:13; 10:25).

We must endeavor to fulfill Christ's commission for His church in this age (Matt. 28:18–20). To that end we must give witness to what He has done for us, confident that the Holy Spirit will empower us to speak boldly in Jesus' name just as He empowered the early disciples (Acts 1:8; 4:31, 33; 10:41–42; 22:15; 26:16). Every nation and tribe, language and hidden people group must hear the gospel before our Lord will return (Matt. 24:14).

Finally, we must study to know the Word of God and proclaim it courageously (Acts 4:29, 31; Eph. 6:19; Phil. 1:14). Because the Word is living and active (Heb. 4:12), it remains authoritative to us; it is still *God* instructing and exhorting and directing us. He works in and among us by His Spirit in accordance with His revealed Word. His Spirit is the locomotive; His Word is the railroad—the tracks—to keep us on course.

Therefore we must handle the Word of truth correctly (2 Tim. 2:15). But *how* can we read it effectively and interpret it properly? How can we know which parts are applicable for us to obey?

## How to Read the Bible

First, read the Bible believingly, with the assurance that it really is the Word of God. "All Scripture is inspired by God and profitable for teaching, for reproof, for correction, for training in righteousness; that the man of God may be adequate, equipped for every good work" (2 Tim. 3:16–17). The Bible is God breathing forth His Word by His Spirit, speaking through His apostles and prophets.

God furthermore directed that His revelations to His chosen servants of old be recorded (Exod. 17:14; Deut. 31:19; Isa. 30:8; Jer. 30:2; Hab. 2:2; Rev. 1:11). His Spirit so moved those men (2 Pet. 1:21) and inspired and superintended the writing-down process that the final product was what God intended it to be. Therefore we can confidently make the claim that all Scripture was infallible and without errors in the original manuscripts and that it bears the full authority of God Himself.

In giving the world His written Word, God is like a great composer who also directs His own symphony. He originated the score, and He selected and directed the musicians of the orchestra—the human authors of the Scriptures—each with his own virtuoso style, to play it harmoniously so that what we hear is a beautiful masterpiece.

Second, read the Bible with the Holy Spirit to illuminate your mind. The Bible is God's Word, originating in His infinite, omniscient mind. Thus it is a spiritual book and needs to be discerned spiritually.

Many parts of God's Word simply cannot be comprehended fully by the natural, secular mind. Such a person does not receive the things of the Spirit of God favorably or appreciatively (1 Cor. 2:14, KJV; compare Luke 8:13; Acts 8:14; 17:11; 1 Thess. 1:6; 2:13). Therefore to read the Scripture properly you need to be born again, spiritually alive. You need to have the Holy Spirit. He alone can reveal to you the deep things of God (1 Cor. 2:10–14), God's secret wisdom "which God decreed before the ages for our glorification" (2:7, AMP). As a believer you can be assured that you have available to you the mind of Christ (2:16; compare John 15:15).

Third, read the Bible devotionally. As a Christian you should feed on God's Word for spiritual nourishment. Be like a newborn baby craving the pure spiritual milk of the Word "so that by it you may grow up in your salvation, now that you have tasted that the Lord is good" (1 Pet. 2:2–3, NIV). For as Jesus reminded Satan during His temptation, "It is written, 'Man shall not live on bread alone, but on every word that proceeds out of the mouth of God'" (Matt. 4:4, quoting Deut. 8:3). Each of us needs the Scripture as a regular diet in order to grow in grace and knowledge of our Lord and Savior Jesus Christ (2 Pet. 3:15–18).

Fourth, read the Bible therapeutically. Ask the Holy Spirit to convict you of sin (John 16:8) and to sanctify you (1 Cor. 6:11), teaching you how to control yourself in a way that is holy and honorable (1 Thess. 4:3–8, NIV). Make the commitment of Psalm 119:11 your very own: "Thy word I have treasured in my heart, that I may not sin against Thee."

The Word can warn you and help you discern your errors and keep you from willful sins so that the meditations of your heart will be pleasing to the Lord (Ps. 19:11–14). And "let the word of Christ dwell in you richly" (Col. 3:16, KJV), enabling you to rid yourself of the sins of your earthly nature and to clothe yourself with love so that you may forgive others as the Lord forgave you (3:5–14).

Fifth, read the Bible prayerfully, adoringly, worshipfully. Ask the Holy

Spirit to open your eyes to behold wonderful things in God's law (Ps. 119:18). Look for Christ in every part of the Bible, for He is the central theme of Scripture (Matt. 26:24; Luke 24:27, 44; John 5:39; 1 Cor. 15:3).

Make Paul's reason for living yours: "For to me, to live is Christ" (Phil. 1:21). Make his ambition yours: "that I may know Him"—in actual experience—"and the power of His resurrection and the fellowship of His sufferings" (Phil. 3:10). Adore Jesus not only as your Savior and Lord but also as the eternal Son, the living Word and creator of all things (John 1:1–3; Col. 1:13–18; Heb. 1:1–3).

Recognize the preincarnate Christ as the Lord Himself coming to Abraham's tent at Mamre and promising a son to aged Sarah (Gen. 18), or as the angel of the Lord visiting Samson's parents (Judg. 13:2–23). Praise David's Lord in the Psalms (110:1; compare Matt. 22:41–45), and worship the Lamb with the twenty-four elders and the angels surrounding the throne of heaven (Rev. 4:9–11).

## How to Study the Bible

The twofold purpose of Bible study is to understand the original intent of a passage and to seek its relevance for today. To interpret Scripture properly and apply it successfully, you must follow some basic principles and guidelines. Be assured that God wants you to know what His Word means. For instance, the Scripture tells us that He intended Christians to read about the Israelites in order to avoid repeating the Israelites' sins (1 Cor. 10:6, 11). You can read most parts of the Bible and find the plain meaning of the text by using good common sense.

Like most readers, you may not have opportunity to master the original languages of the Bible, so you will need to depend on a reliable English translation or version. Better yet, you should have several good translations to compare with one another when studying a difficult passage.

The more recommendable English Bibles for study as well as for reading are the Revised Standard Version (RSV), the New American Bible (NAB), the New American Standard Bible (NAS), the New International Version (NIV) and the Tanakh. The RSV and the NAS are revisions of the King James Version, making use of modern linguistic studies and Hebrew and Greek manuscript copies discovered since A.D. 1611. The RSV achieves more refined literary quality but clouds a few Old Testament messianic passages.

The NAS is more literal. Biblical quotes in this book *will* be from it, unless otherwise noted.

The NAB admirably upgrades the Roman Catholic Confraternity Edition. The NIV is newly translated from the original languages by evangelical scholars. It follows the policy of dynamic equivalence (as distinct from more literal word-for-word equivalence), giving an English expression of the same *meaning* as that intended by the original word or phrase. The Tanakh is a new idiomatic translation of the Old Testament by Jewish scholars according to the traditional Old Testament (Masoretic) Hebrew text.

Those Bibles not as helpful to the modern reader for careful study purposes are the King James Version (KJV—very literal but old-fashioned language; modernized in the New King James Version, NKJV); the Living Bible (TLB; a paraphrase rather than a translation); the Good News Bible (GNB) and the New English Bible (NEB)—both are rather free translations which frequently adopt an unwarranted textual emendation or change; the Jerusalem Bible of the Roman Catholic church (JB—a rather idiomatic translation often based on ancient versions or emendations); and the Amplified Bible (AMP—often confusing because it expects the reader to choose between several suggested meanings).

For more intensive Bible study you may employ a great variety of fine helps. I would recommend the NIV Study Bible as the best of its kind because of the excellent introduction to each book of the Bible plus the cross references and the brief but helpful footnote comments on each page of the text. For comparative word studies you should have a complete concordance to the Bible to look up all the occurrences of an English word, with an indication of the original word it translates. An up-to-date Bible dictionary or encyclopedia will enable you to research the historical and cultural background of a passage. A reliable commentary on the Bible book you are studying should help explain difficult problem passages.

In all of your study, however, maintain a balance between depending on the work of others and feeding yourself by your own diligent effort. The Spirit will strengthen and guide you most often through what you yourself read and study in the Word of God.

Keep in mind the three basic principles of sound interpretation of the Bible: the grammatical, the contextual and the theological. By following these principles you, the reader, are better enabled to decide on the sense intended by the original author. He had only one thought in mind when he wrote that passage. Therefore no statement may be considered to have more than one meaning for the original readers, although it may have various *applications* for us today. No word can mean two different things at the same time.

Scripture should normally be taken literally unless the context clearly indicates otherwise. These principles guard against fanciful allegorical interpretation, a method that delves behind the actual wording looking for deep hidden meanings, usually of a devotional or theological nature. The allegorical method, which prevailed in the church for twelve hundred years from Origen to the Reformation, depends on the whim of the reader's imagination instead of being controlled by the grammar and context of the passage.

The *grammatical principle* observes the actual linguistic structure and verbal content of a passage. It is concerned with grammatical relationships in sentences as well as with the meaning of words, phrases and idioms at the time of writing. For instance, grammatical interpretation notes that the biblical statement "all men are liars" was not intended to be an absolute truth, because it is part of the distressed psalmist's confession: "I said in my alarm, 'All men are liars'" (Ps. 116:11). Another example is found in Psalm 34:6, where the Hebrew word *'ānî* for "poor man" meant someone needy because defenseless and oppressed, not necessarily financially stricken.

Proper grammatical interpretation also recognizes the presence of figurative language that was never intended to be taken literally. For example, James, Peter and John were reputed to be "pillars" in the Jerusalem church (Gal. 2:9). Jesus dubbed the ruler Herod "that fox" (Luke 13:32). Trees of the forest "sing for joy" (Ps. 96:12) and "clap their hands" (Isa. 55:12), expressing unparalleled happiness and prosperity.

The *contextual principle* steers you to look at the portion of Scripture within both its immediate and its broader context. The context is the final determinant of the proper meaning of a word or phrase in a verse. For example, "law" in Romans 2:12–27 and 3:19–20 is the Jewish Old Testament, whereas in Romans 7:23, 25 and 8:2 "law" is a dominating power or impulse (to commit sin).

The type or genre of literature to which the passage belongs is an important aspect of the context. If the section you are studying is Hebrew poetry, you will come across much thought repetition (parallel statements) and figurative language. If it is narrative history, investigate the names of the actual persons, places, battles or disasters, and the lengths of time.

If it is covenant law, such as in Deuteronomy, you will find promises and exhortations as well as commandments. If the passage is teaching by proverb or parable, detect the one key point or lesson. If it is apocalyptic revelation of End-Time events, expect dreams and visions, supernatural creatures, cataclysmic judgments and extensive symbolism.

In addition to the context of the passage in the Bible itself you should consider the larger background of the historical and cultural setting. You should be aware of changing social customs: ancient clay tablets and Hammurabi's law code reveal that Mesopotamian law in the patriarchal period required the husband of a barren wife to beget a child for her by the wife's maidservant (compare Gen. 16; 30:1–7); but this was not so under the Mosaic law. By means of ancient history, archaeological discoveries and geographical surveys, we can recreate much of the political and sociological world of Bible times.

For example, encyclopedia articles on Assyria will throw much light on whole chapters in 2 Kings plus the Books of Jonah and Nahum. The voluminous writings of the Jewish historian Josephus give extensive detail about wicked King Herod and his descendants, who appear often in the Gospels and the Book of Acts.

The third principle of sound biblical interpretation embraces the *theological unity* of God's Word. The Bible has one ultimate author who cannot lie (Titus 1:2). He Himself does not change (Mal. 3:6), and He does not change His mind (Num. 23:19, NIV; 1 Sam. 15:29; Ps. 110:4). God does not contradict Himself nor use double-talk.

In saying this we do not deny the paradox of divine sovereignty and human responsibility. But with assurance we can assert that the Bible contains only one system of doctrine. We recognize a *progress* of doctrine in Scripture, as God continued to reveal more and more of Himself and His great plan of salvation. Yet salvation has always been by grace through faith, not by works (Gen. 15:6; Hab. 2:4; Rom. 1:16–17; 4:1–25; Eph. 2:8–9).

God's Word remains theologically consistent, even though He made various covenants with people. The later covenant does not annul or countermand the earlier (Gal. 3:17). Rather each successive covenant builds on the previous one to bring them all to fulfillment in Jesus Christ. True, there are at least two major dispensations—the Old Testament (Mosaic covenant) and the New Testament (Christ's covenant). Certain Old Testament practices such as the offering of animal sacrifices were cancelled by the New Covenant, but that is only because they were fulfilled in Christ. The New Testament does not contradict the Old Testament.

Because of the continuity in the cumulative revelation of God's will, Scripture possesses an underlying unity. For example, in the Sermon on the Mount Jesus declared that unless your righteousness surpasses that of the Pharisees you will not enter God's kingdom (Matt. 5:20). His use of the term "righteousness" does not refer to an individual's good works. Instead its meaning is established by the sense of that significant word as set forth in the Old Testament prophets. Righteousness is linked to a salvation relationship with the Lord who bestows righteousness through the Messiah (Isa. 45:24; 46:13; 51:5–8; 54:14; 61:10; Jer. 23:6; 33:15–16; Hos. 2:19).

Again, the moral law of God expressed in the Ten Commandments is not abrogated but reiterated in the New Testament law of love (Matt. 7:12; 22:36–40; John 13:34; Rom. 13:8–10; James 2:8) and shown to be still relevant to the Christian. God's precious threefold promise — "I will be your God, and you shall be My people, and I will dwell among you"—is repeatedly stated and unites the entire Bible (Lev. 26:11–12; Jer. 32:38; Ezek. 37:27; 2 Cor. 6:16; Rev. 21:3).

Consequently, you should never interpret a passage so that it would contradict God's intent in the rest of the Bible. If you follow this principle you can check the correctness of your interpretation by the theological harmony of Scripture.

Several guidelines based on these principles of interpretation will round out our discussion of how to study the Bible:

*(1) Interpret Scripture by the rest of Scripture.* The Bible is its own best interpreter. The *whole* of Scripture should be considered as relevant in explaining a *part* of Scripture. For instance, look in the New Testament for fulfillment of Old Testament prophecies, such as those foretelling the appearance and work of the Messiah.

On the other hand, be aware that various biblical writers may emphasize different aspects of a truth. For example, Paul stressed that we cannot save ourselves by doing works of the Law (Gal. 2:16; 3:11), whereas James discussed works as evidence of the genuineness of the faith we already have (James 2:14–26). Luke in his Gospel and Acts used distinctive Old Testament terminology to describe the charismatic activity of the Holy Spirit that enables the Christian community to carry out its mission. But it is usually the more personal inner working of the Holy Spirit in regeneration, sanctification and fruit bearing that was discussed in the writings of John and Paul (except in 1 Cor. 12–14).

The principle of the theological unity of the Bible thus keeps us from interpreting any passage in a way that would twist the basic teaching of the whole of Scripture. We must explain a difficult text in the light of others that are clear.

Interpret according to the context and with the aid of cross-references and parallel or closely related passages. As an example, we can explain the meaning or purpose of Christian baptism in Acts 2:38 by observing that Cornelius and his household heard the message of forgiveness, believed in Jesus and received the Holy Spirit before they were baptized in water (Acts 10:43–48; 11:15–18). Thus we can conclude that baptism is not necessary for regeneration.

Biblical symbols can usually be interpreted by finding the key in the near-at-hand context or by their use in other Scripture passages. The seven hills or mountains in Revelation 17:9 on which the woman Babylon sits are explained in verse 10 to be seven kings or rulers (not the seven hills on which Rome was built as some scholars have suggested). That political powers are meant is in keeping with the Old Testament concept of mountains representing world powers (Isa. 2:2, 14; 41:15; Jer. 51:25; Dan. 2:44–45; Zech. 4:7). In fact, most of the symbolic language in the Book of Revelation is taken from the Old Testament (especially from Isaiah, Ezekiel, Daniel, Joel and Zechariah). Thus the various occurrences of a symbol in different parts of the Bible all help to explain that symbol.

*(2) Seek to discover the original intended meaning.* God does not expect you to find a meaning in a biblical text that it never could have had for its human author or its first readers. A verse cannot mean now what it never meant in the first place. "The Holy Spirit cannot be called to contradict Himself, and He is the one who inspired the original intent. Therefore His help for us will be in the discovering of that original intent, and in guiding us as we try faithfully to apply that meaning to our situation."[2]

Seek to obey those statements of the Bible which deal with timeless moral issues. The Word of God—both Old Testament and New Testament— takes a clear-cut, consistent stand on many ethical and religious matters:

worship of God alone; love for our neighbor; the duty of children to obey their parents; the command to be holy; the sinfulness of quarreling, hatred, murder, stealing, filthy joking, drunkenness and sexual immorality of all kinds.

But what about the many other laws and commands in the Bible? The Old Testament ceremonial laws became obsolete when the Levitical ceremonies and sacrifices were fulfilled in Christ's atoning death (Heb. 8:13). Certain directives may not apply to you at all, because they were given to individuals on a specific occasion: for example, Jesus' command to His disciples not to leave Jerusalem until the Holy Spirit was poured out (Luke 24:49; Acts 1:4).

Some injunctions you may not be able to carry out, because they dealt with localized situations in another culture long ago: for example, the command to make a parapet around your flat roof so no one falls from it (Deut. 22:8). It was only Jesus' twelve apostles, on their first preaching mission, who were required to take no supplies with them (Matt. 10:5–14). No universal moral principle is involved in that directive, although you may draw from it a lesson of simple trust in God's provision.

Furthermore, you as a Christian are no longer *obligated* to keep the laws of the Old Covenant that are not repeated in the New Testament. At the cross Christ canceled our indebtedness (Col. 2:14) and redeemed us from the condemnation of the Law (Gal. 3:13). The Law and the Prophets stopped being proclaimed authoritatively, Jesus said, when John the Baptist began preaching the kingdom of God (Luke 16:16). Jesus came to fulfill the Old Testament Scriptures in Himself, in the sense of bringing them to completion and demonstrating their true meaning (Matt. 5:17). He was "the end" or the culmination of the Law by His provision of righteousness for every believer (Rom. 10:4, NIV).

Nevertheless, we must recognize the function of commandments and laws in the Bible. The Hebrew word for "law" is *tôrāh*, primarily meaning instruction, direction and teaching, not a code of laws and regulations. God gave the Law, His *tôrāh*, to train and guide the Israelites for long, productive lives (Deut. 5:33), not to restrict them arbitrarily. They were a people He had already redeemed from bondage and brought into covenant relationship with Himself. The Law therefore was not intended to be the means of their gaining access to His favor.

The Lord first presented to Moses the essence of the entire *tôrāh* on two stone tablets. All the subsequent laws are rooted in the theological and moral absolutes of the Ten Commandments. The first four commandments pertain to God (Exod. 20:3–11; Deut. 5:7–15) and are summarized in what Jesus called the first and great commandment: You shall love the Lord your God with all your heart, soul, mind and strength (Matt. 22:36–38; Mark 12:28–30; Deut. 6:5). The final six commandments pertain to people (Exod. 20:12–17; Deut. 5:16–21) and are summarized in the second most important commandment: Love your neighbor as yourself (Matt. 22:39–40; Lev. 19:18).

The case laws (Exod. 21–23; Deut. 6–25) that follow the listing of the Ten Commandments, plus the laws of the holiness code (Lev. 18–20), demonstrate in specific real-life situations how the universal moral principles were to be practiced. The civil laws take the Ten Commandments out of the realm of the abstract and place them "in the real world of concrete illustration and personal attachment."[3] While not binding upon Christians, these stipulations, along with the narrative sections and the prophetic exhortations of the Old Testament, are nevertheless beneficial to us. They are "useful for teaching, rebuking, correcting, and training in righteousness" (2 Tim. 3:16, NIV).

Paul, for instance, applied the civil ordinance that prohibited the muzzling of an ox by an Israelite farmer (Deut. 25:4) to the right that Christian ministers have to earn their living from the gospel (1 Cor. 9:9–14). James, in his very practical epistle, used the injunctions of Leviticus 19:12–18 as his basis in explaining the "royal law" of love (James 2:8), the perfect law that gives liberty (1:25; 2:12).

The Law will always stand as part of the revelation of God's holy will (Matt. 5:18; Rom. 3:31; 1 Pet. 1:14–16). So you need to study the Law and the Prophets as well as the Gospels and the Epistles to apply their directives and examples in your life.

*(3) Exercise humility and avoid being dogmatic.* Especially with regard to a problem passage, do not insist that yours is the only possible correct solution. Be willing to admit that you really don't know what a difficult text meant to its original readers and that you cannot be sure whether it has any relevance for you. Such a verse is 1 Corinthians 15:29, which refers to baptizing for the dead. Paul was writing to the Christians in Corinth who could understand his reference, but we today simply do not have the detailed information needed to understand it. "We do not know and probably never will know *who* was doing it, *for whom* they were doing it, and *why* they were doing it. The details and the meaning of the practice, therefore, are probably forever lost to us."[4]

Expect to come upon some passages in God's Word too deep to fathom. If Job could not understand the mysteries of nature (Job 38:1–42:6), how could he or we expect to comprehend the ways of the Almighty (Ps. 131:1; 139:6; Isa. 55:8–9; Rom. 11:33–36)? "Answers to some questions will come later, like finding the missing piece in a jigsaw puzzle. Some will never be answered this side of heaven. An appreciation for the mysteries in the Christian faith is in itself a sign of maturity."[5] God's ways are higher than our ways and His thoughts than our thoughts (Isa. 55:9).

Check your interpretation with the conclusions of others. Recognize that godly Bible teachers and commentators of past and present generations are Christ's gifts to His church (Eph. 4:11–13). Do not seek the thrill of merely being different, of promoting some "new" truth. Do not interpret a passage in such a way that it is made to contradict other passages, just so that you might support a pet theory or doctrine of your own.

On the other hand, you are responsible for weighing biblical truth and for forming your own convictions. Follow the noble example of the Bereans who received Paul's message "with great eagerness and examined the Scriptures every day to see if what Paul said was true" (Acts 17:11, NIV).

Show charity toward those who take a different position from yours. For example, on the basis of a hard-to-understand text such as 1 Timothy 2:9–15 some argue against its ever being right for women to teach men in churches. Others honestly believe Paul was speaking to a local problem in Ephesus, and therefore the prohibition in verses 11 and 12 is culturally relative, not universal.

Because of such differences of opinion many biblical scholars urge that Christians recognize the difficulties of proper interpretation, discuss the issue openly with those holding an opposite view and love those with whom they differ.

# ONE

# The Nature of God's Spirit

The Holy Spirit is the eternal Spirit of God—God Himself. God is always God, and He does not change (Mal. 3:6; James 1:17). The Spirit is the same in the Old Testament as He is in the New Testament. As Jesus clearly taught, God in His essential being is spirit (John 4:24). God's Spirit, the Holy Spirit, is His very self, not merely an attribute or function of God.

## The Meaning of the Biblical Terms

In both Hebrew and Greek, the two principal biblical languages, the basic meaning of the terms for "spirit," *rûaḥ* (Hebrew) and *pneuma* (Greek), is "breath, strong breathing through the mouth or nostrils." In the Old Testament, *rûaḥ* is distinguished from Hebrew *hebel*. This latter word means a mere transitory, fleeting puff of breath or vapor (Prov. 21:6); figuratively it speaks of the vanity, futility or meaninglessness of life apart from the Lord (for example, Eccles. 1:2, 14; 2:1, 17, 19, 21; 3:19; 6:2, 4, 12). On the other hand, *rûaḥ* is powerful and continuous; for example, "the breath (*rûaḥ*) of the ruthless is like a storm driving against a wall" (Isa. 25:4, NIV).

Breath is air in motion. Strong prolonged breathing easily suggests the wind. Jesus explained the mysterious operation of God's Spirit by this analogy: "The wind (*pneuma*) blows (*pnei*) wherever it pleases. You hear its sound, but you cannot tell where it comes from or where it is going. So it is with everyone born of the Spirit (*pneuma*)" (John 3:8, NIV).

In the Old Testament, *rûaḥ* is used some 377 times. It designates breath of the mouth or nostrils (more than thirty times), wind and air (about 115 times), the four directions or sides (six times), the human spirit with attending thoughts and emotions (about 100 times), God's Spirit (nearly 100 times), angels and evil spirits (more than twenty-five times). The common denominator of these is their vitality and invisibility.

Rapid, animated breathing in humans is proof of the presence of life. Therefore *rûaḥ*—in its various active manifestations such as vivacity or strength (Gen. 45:27; Judg. 15:19; 1 Kings 10:5), courage (Josh. 2:11), temper or anger (Judg. 8:3; Eccles. 7:9), heaviness or depression (Isa. 61:3), grief or rejection (Isa. 54:6), mental or emotional disturbance (Gen. 41:8), thoughts of the mind (Ezek. 11:5)—is an apt term for the living spirit residing in humanity. The human spirit may be considered the seat of our attitudes, emotions, passions and intellectual functions. It is the seat of our moral character (Ps. 32:2), yes, of our very personality. The Bible makes it clear that this invisible life-force in humans is from God (Job 27:3; Ps. 104:29; Isa. 42:5; Zech. 12:1) and returns to Him at death (Eccles. 12:7; Acts 7:59).

As in the case of the human spirit, God's *rûaḥ* or *pneuma* is likewise the expression of His personality. The *rûaḥ* of God is the very living personal presence of God Himself (Ps. 139:7–8) breathing or blowing mightily upon a situation or individual to create or effect change. God's Spirit is God revealing Himself in ongoing power. The Spirit is God manifesting Himself as transcendently glorious and yet at the same time wonderfully and mysteriously immanent, present with us.

The divine Spirit is the presence of the infinite, eternal God always proceeding to make Himself known and to act in His created universe in the exercise of His sovereignty. Psalm 104:30 says, "Thou dost send forth Thy Spirit, they are created." This idea is also found in John 15:26, which speaks of "the Spirit of truth, who proceeds from the Father."

"This powerful, mysterious Spirit belongs to God, and to God alone. It is essentially the personal God, Yahweh, in action."[1] The acts of the Spirit described most frequently in the Bible concern His work to fulfill God's redemptive plan for sinful humanity.

### The Deity and Personhood of God's Spirit

In revealing Himself to fallen humanity God chose first to make known what we might call His "oneness." In the face of the prevailing polytheism of Egypt and Canaan, God, using His covenant name Yahweh, stressed to His chosen people that He alone is the one true living God. Moses declared to Israel, "There is no other besides Him" (Deut. 4:35). In fact, the great statement of Israel's faith, the nation's rallying cry of old and Judaism's motto today, is the *shema*ʿ: "Hear, O Israel [*shĕma*ʿ *yisrā'ēl*]! Yahweh is our God, Yahweh is one!" (Deut. 6:4, author's translation).

These words could equally well be translated, "Yahweh is our God, Yahweh alone!" The Hebrew *'eḥād,* "one" or "alone," in this context also con-notes Yahweh's integrity and unswerving dedication to His covenant (Deut. 7:9).[2] Therefore God's people can love Him and worship Him with undivided loyalty, with their total being (Deut. 6:5), because there are no other true gods to worship and never will be (Zech. 14:9). To love Him is our foremost com-mandment, as Jesus stressed (Mark 12:28–30).

Not until centuries after Moses did God begin to make clear what we might call the "threeness" of His divine nature. True, intimations appear early in the Old Testament that there is more than one Person in the Godhead. In the work of creation God said, "Let Us make man in Our image, according to Our likeness" (Gen. 1:26; compare 3:22; 11:7). Isaiah heard the voice of Yahweh saying, "Whom shall I send, and who will go for Us?" (Isa. 6:8). Later, that same prophet received perhaps the clearest revelation in the Old Testament concerning three Persons who could rightfully be called deity: "And now the Lord GOD has sent Me and His Spirit" (48:16; see the comment on Isaiah 48:16).

But it remained for Jesus and the apostles to explain more clearly that God is triune. The one God has always existed in three distinct Persons—God the Father, God the Son and God the Holy Spirit—coequal in honor and power. While the word "trinity" appears nowhere in the New Testament, New Testament texts affirm that there is only one Supreme Being (1 Cor. 8:4–6) of only one divine essence or nature (John 10:30; Heb. 1:3), yet eternally exist-ing in three distinct Persons (John 1:1; 5:17–23; 17:3, 5; Matt. 28:19; 1 Cor. 12:3–6; 2 Cor. 13:14; 1 Pet. 1:2).

Consequently, the orthodox leaders of the early Christian church used the term "trinity" from the second century onward in their writings and creedal statements. As Christian believers today we must hold tenaciously both to the "oneness" *and* to the "threeness" of God. Every cult and heresy of our time fall short in believing both aspects of this biblical revelation of God's nature.

The overall teaching of the Bible about the Holy Spirit shows that He is fully deity, not simply an apparition of God and not a subordinate spirit such as an angel or demon. By poetic parallelism Isaiah appears to equate the Spirit with God: "The Egyptians are human ['ādām] and not God ['el], and their horses are flesh [bāsār] and not Spirit [rûaḥ]" (Isa. 31:3, author's translation). The identity of the Spirit with God is more certain in Acts 5:3. There Peter confronted Ananias with the sin of lying to the Holy Spirit and ended his accusation by charging, "You have not lied to men, but to God" (5:4). Paul asked, "Do you not know that you are a temple of God, and that the Spirit of God dwells in you?" (1 Cor. 3:16), and further in the same epistle, "Do you not know that your body is a temple of the Holy Spirit who is in you?" (6:19).

The Bible also indicates that the Holy Spirit has personality. That is, He is a Person. He is not a mere influence, force or power. He has intelligence—He can hear and speak and teach (John 14:26; 16:13–14). He has feelings or emotions, for He can be grieved (Isa. 63:10; Eph. 4:30).

It is true that the Greek expression *to pneuma* for "the Spirit" is neuter in gender and grammatically requires a neuter pronoun. Nevertheless, the masculine demonstrative pronoun *ekeinos* ("that one" or "he") is used repeatedly in Jesus' statements as recorded by the apostle John to refer to the Comforter, the Holy Spirit, the Spirit of truth (John 14:26; 15:26; 16:8, 13–14). Meanwhile, the New Testament makes a distinction between divine power and the Holy Spirit as a Person: "God anointed Him [Jesus] with the Holy Spirit and with power" (Acts 10:38); and "our gospel did not come to you in word only, but also in power and in the Holy Spirit and with full conviction" (1 Thess. 1:5).

In the Old Testament as well, we may infer that the Spirit is a divine Person because He identifies Himself with the Lord Yahweh. The prophet Ezekiel described how God's Spirit entered him and spoke with him and ended by saying to him, "But when I speak to you, I will open your mouth, and you will say to them, 'Thus says the Lord GOD'" (Ezek. 3:24–27; compare 2:2–4).[3] Hence Scripture in the Old Testament and in the New Testament affirms the Spirit's personhood as well as His deity.[4]

## Symbols of the Spirit

The Bible portrays the Holy Spirit by a number of different images and symbols. The term "type" should not be employed here, because a true biblical type involves specific *historical* correspondence between two biblical events, persons or objects. For example, Melchizedek is considered in Hebrews 7 to be a *type* of Christ because of the parallel between Melchizedek, who combined royal and priestly functions (Gen. 14:18–20), and Jesus, our high priest and coming king. The sacrifice of the passover lambs in Egypt, an historic act that spared Israelites from the tenth plague (Exod. 12:1–28), is a *type* of Christ's atoning death at Calvary (1 Cor. 5:7).

In contrast, a symbol or emblem metaphorically represents an abstract concept or something invisible and helps to define its general ethical or spiritual meaning. For instance, the cross is a timeless *symbol* of Christianity, the American flag the *emblem* of the United States.

The *dove* is a symbol of the Holy Spirit. At Jesus' baptism heaven was opened, and John the Baptist "saw the Spirit of God descending as a dove, and coming upon Him" (Matt. 3:16; compare John 1:32–34). Luke described the event: "The Holy Spirit descended upon Him in bodily form like a dove" (3:22). It was "not a mystical or visionary experience. It was, rather, an objective, externalized, and physical manifestation of the Spirit."[5]

In all probability this comparison of God's Spirit to a dove is meant to draw our attention to the dove that Noah sent out from the ark after the great flood (Gen. 8:8–12). Noah's dove in turn reminds us of the Spirit of God hovering over the waters of the initial creation (Gen. 1:2). The first-century rabbi Ben Zoma referred to a rabbinic tradition that "the Spirit of God was brooding on the face of the waters like a dove which broods over her young but does not touch them."[6]

As God's Spirit actively worked to achieve form and life in the original creation, and as the dove and olive leaf heralded the restoration of peace to earth after the watery destruction, so the Spirit descending at Jesus' baptism was God's announcement of the beginning of the new creation (2 Cor. 5:17; Gal. 6:15). A new springtime was here, just as the voice of the turtledove heard in the land signals that winter is past (Song of Sol. 2:11–12). The song of the dove was identified in the Jewish Targum as "the voice of the Holy Spirit of salvation."

Scripture also uses *fire* as a symbol of God's Spirit. John the Baptist foretold the purifying, sanctifying and judging ministry of the Holy Spirit when he proclaimed that the coming Messiah would baptize repentant sinners "with the Holy Spirit and fire" and that He would "thoroughly clean His threshing floor" and "burn up the chaff with unquenchable fire" (Matt. 3:11–12). In an eschatological passage (that is, a passage dealing with the end of the world), Isaiah had prophesied of the spirit (or Spirit) of judgment, the spirit of burning that Yahweh would employ to "cleanse the bloodstains from Jerusalem" (Isa. 4:4, NIV). At Pentecost, along with the audible sign of a rushing mighty wind accompanying the outpouring of the Spirit, was the visible sign of tongues of fire resting on the 120 Jewish disciples (Acts 2:3). Significantly, Malachi had announced that the Lord coming to His temple as messenger of the (new) covenant would "purify the sons of Levi and refine them like gold and silver" (Mal. 3:1, 3).

Anointing *oil* or unguent is another well-established emblem of the Spirit of God. In the Old Testament Israelite priests were installed in office by anointing them with a holy anointing oil consisting of a perfumed mixture of olive oil and various spices (Exod. 29:7, 21; 30:23–25, 30; Ps. 133:2). Likewise the kings of Israel and Judah were appointed by pouring oil on the head (Saul, 1 Sam. 10:1; David, 1 Sam. 16:13; Jehu, 2 Kings 9:3, 6; the messianic king, Ps. 2:2; 45:7); and on at least one occasion a prophet was designated in this way (Elisha, 1 Kings 19:16–21). The very word *messiah* (Hebrew *māšîaḥ*) means "anointed one," as does the title "Christ" (Greek *christos*).

That the fragrant anointing oil symbolized the "sweet Holy Spirit" may be clearly inferred from Peter's testimony regarding Jesus of Nazareth: "God anointed Him with the Holy Spirit and with power" (Acts 10:38). This statement may be coupled with Isaiah's prophecy about the Servant of Yahweh—"The Spirit of the Lord GOD is upon me, because the LORD has anointed me" (Isa. 61:1)—which Jesus appropriated for Himself (Luke 4:16–21). Furthermore, Christians are said to have an "unction" (KJV) or anointing from God, the Holy One, that abides in them (1 John 2:20, 27), an obvious reference to the indwelling Holy Spirit.

*Water is* perhaps the most frequently used symbol of the Holy Spirit in the Scripture. The concept is found in direct comparisons to water or in allusions to rain (Ps. 72:6); wells and fountains (Num. 21:16–18; Song of Sol. 4:15; Jer. 2:13); and rivers and streams (Ps. 46:4; Isa. 43:19–20; Joel 3:18). Numerous analogies can be drawn between water and the Spirit, chiefly in the ability of each to renew, refresh and sustain life (Ps. 36:8–9; Isa. 55:1; John 4:14 with 6:63; Titus 3:5), as well as to cleanse, heal and sanctify (Lev. 14:50–52; Ezek. 36:25; Amos 5:24; John 5:1–9; 1 Cor. 6:11).

Jesus promised that rivers of living water would flow from the inner being of His followers, and John the evangelist explained that by this metaphor He spoke of the Spirit (see the comment on John 7:37–39). Isaiah may have been the first to foretell the outpouring of God's Spirit: "Until the Spirit is poured out upon us from on high" (Isa. 32:15) and "I will pour out water on the thirsty land and streams on the dry ground; I will pour out My Spirit on your offspring" (Isa. 44:3). Ezekiel (39:29) and Joel (2:28–29) employed the same figure of outpouring, and the latter also seems to have referred to the Spirit as rain (Joel 2:23; see the comment on Joel 2:28–32).

A highly meaningful image of the Spirit of God is the *glory cloud,* the cloud of the Lord which escorted the people of Israel on their journey from Egypt. It signified the very presence of God, as Exodus 13:21 explains: "The LORD was going before them in a pillar of cloud by day to lead them on the way, and in a pillar of fire by night to give them light, that they might travel by day and by night." Yahweh in the cloud also protected the fleeing Israelites from the pursuing Egyptian army (Exod. 14:19–24). Whenever the Israelites complained against Moses' and Aaron's leadership (and thus against the sovereign authority of Yahweh), He would appear in the cloud to manifest His glory and thereby vindicate His honor (Exod. 16:10; Lev. 10:2 with 9:23–24; Num. 14:10; 16:19, 42; 20:6).

The glory cloud, accompanied by thunder, lightning, fire and trumpet blasts, covered Mount Sinai at the giving of the Law (Exod. 24:16–17 with 19:16–20). In this event the Israelites recognized that Yahweh had shown them "His glory and His greatness" (Deut. 5:24)—"His majestic Presence," as the Tanakh translates it. Later, the Lord descended in the cloud to reveal His divine glory to Moses alone (Exod. 34:5–6 with 33:18, 22).

God had promised to consecrate the tabernacle by His glory—by His glorious presence and to meet and speak with Israel there: "I will dwell [Hebrew *šākan*] among the sons of Israel and will be their God" (Exod. 29:43–46). When Moses finished the work, "the cloud covered the tent of meeting, and the glory of the LORD filled the tabernacle [*hammiškān*]. And Moses was not able to enter the tent of meeting because the cloud had settled [*šākan;* 'abode' in KJV, RSV] on it" (Exod. 40:34–35).

That event provides the origin of the Jewish term *shekînah,* which signifies the abiding glory-presence of God. (The word *shekînah* is not actually found in the Bible.) Exodus 40:36–38 and Numbers 9:15–23 go on to tell how the cloud of the Lord led the nation through the wilderness for forty years.

Centuries later Isaiah, in reflecting on these outstanding events, explained that whenever God's people rebelled in Moses' time they "grieved His Holy Spirit." He also stated that God "put His Holy Spirit in the midst of them," and that it was "the Spirit of the LORD" that "gave them rest" (Isa. 63:10–11, 14). In Exodus 33:1–3 Yahweh had said to Moses, "I will send an angel before you . . . for I will not go up in your midst, because you are an obstinate people." But when Moses interceded, God promised, "My presence shall go with you, and I will give you rest" (33:14). Moses replied, "Is it not by Thy going with us, so that we, I and Thy people, may be distinguished from all the other people who are upon the face of the earth?" (33:16).

By comparing Exodus 33:1–3 with 33:14–16, we may differentiate between the angel of Yahweh and Yahweh's personal Spirit-presence. It seems clear that Isaiah saw in the glory cloud of old—but not in the angel—an equation with God's Spirit. In reviewing the wilderness journey of the Israelites Psalm 106 confirms Isaiah's understanding: "They were rebellious against His Spirit" (v. 33).

Comparisons of the activity of the cloud with the ministry of the Holy Spirit today are numerous, especially in such matters as illumination, guidance, provision, instruction and revealing God or Christ to us (Neh. 9:12–13, 19–20; John 14:16–17, 26; 16:13–14). The Spirit's arrival with wind and fire at Pentecost was divinely ordered to be reminiscent of the Lord descending upon Mount Sinai and Mount Carmel in fire (Exod. 19:18; 1 Kings 18:38) and of His glory cloud filling the tabernacle and Solomon's temple (Exod. 40:34; 1 Kings 8:10–11). Those events in turn prefigured the Spirit's coming to indwell Christian believers as the present-day temple of the living God (1 Cor. 3:16; 6:19; 2 Cor. 6:16).

# TWO

# The Spirit of God in Creation and the Patriarchal Age

## (Creation–1500 B.C.)

The Book of Genesis is the primary place where we read about the cosmic activity of God's Spirit in the creation of the universe as well as of humankind. Yet there are various references in Job, the Psalms and Isaiah that also speak of the living breath or Spirit of God in His creating and sustaining work worldwide. A rather wide spectrum of the Spirit's activity is visible in Genesis, from creating to judging and restraining people from sin to providing leaders with wisdom and discernment. From the time of the Exodus onward biblical references to God's Spirit pertain mainly to His working in connection with God's chosen people.

### The Spirit of God in Creation—Genesis 1:2

The very first mention of the Spirit of God in the Bible is in the second verse. Verse 1 of Genesis seems to be a superscription or opening summary statement about God's creation of the entire universe. Verse 2 describes the earliest condition of the earth as *tōhû* and *bōhû*, shapeless and uninhabited, before God spoke His series of creative commands (1:3–31). At that initial stage "the Spirit of God (*rûaḥ 'elōhîm*) was moving over the surface of the waters."

What is the proper translation of *rûaḥ 'elōhîm* in verse 2? Various Jewish and Christian scholars for many centuries have rendered this phrase as "a wind from God" (TAN), a "divine wind" or "mighty wind."[1] But the emphasis of the entire passage (1:1–2:4a) is theological, not scientific. The traditional translation, "the Spirit of God," is more in keeping with this emphasis. Furthermore, in no other Old Testament passage is *rûaḥ 'elōhîm* used to mean a powerful wind. Also, the author would never have used *'elohim* in verse 2 with a meaning different from its many other occurrences throughout 1:1–2:4a.[2]

Genesis 1:1–2:4a is a carefully constructed and unified passage, a literary masterpiece. Written originally for the Israelites in order to reveal God to them as the sole creator and sovereign of heaven and earth, it served as a polemic against the contemporary pagan creation myths originating among the Sumerians in ancient Mesopotamia. Those stories, usually involving sea dragons or chaos monsters, pitted so-called good and evil gods and goddesses against one another in violent conflict. The Genesis account, on the other hand, depicts God in total control with no opposing forces at work. Even the great sea monsters (Gen. 1:21) are part of His good creation.

The fact that the initial watery mass is unformed (*tōhû*) does not mean that it is evil. "There is ... no hint of cosmic struggle. The chaos here is not an enemy to be overcome and trampled upon [as in the Babylonian creation legend describing how the hero god Marduk slays the chaos goddess Tiamat]; it is rather raw material to be lovingly yet powerfully blown into life."[3] Thus God's Spirit appears to be bringing forth order by preparing "the primeval formlessness" to hear the shaping word of God. This idea is more in keeping with the doctrinal thrust of the whole chapter than the passing mention of a hostile mighty wind supposedly linked with primeval chaos.[4]

The movement of the Spirit of God over the waters (Gen. 1:2) is described by the Hebrew word *meraḥepet*. The verbal form is a participle denoting continuous action. The verb in this particular stem (the *pi'el* stem) is used elsewhere in the Old Testament only in Deuteronomy 32:11, to describe the hovering flight of an eagle over her nest in providing for her young. (The meaning of "hovering" is confirmed by the use of the cognate Semitic word *rḥp* in Ugaritic to tell of the soaring of a vulture.) In his song in Deuteronomy 32 Moses was evidently making a comparison with the Spirit's hovering over the primal waters. He portrayed Yahweh as hovering over the Israelites in His glory cloud and protecting them to bring them through the howling waste (*tōhû*) of the desert (32:10) and thereby to create a new nation.

By analogy in Genesis 1:2 we see God as the divine energizer extending Himself in His creating power to bring order and design to shapeless substance. He is beginning to perfect "a nonfunctioning universe" into "one that could operate and display the glory of God," as Leon Wood stated it so well.[5]

A similar Old Testament illustration of God's care, but with different Hebrew vocabulary, appears in Isaiah 31:5: "Like birds hovering overhead, the LORD Almighty will shield Jerusalem; he will shield it and deliver it, he will 'pass over' it and will rescue it" (NIV). Psalm 104:3 (NIV) states, "He ... rides on the wings of the wind [*rûaḥ*]" (compare Deuteronomy 33:26; Psalm 68:33–34, NIV). The sovereign divine glory was often depicted in the ancient Near East by a winged sun disk, which represented the canopy of heaven. Malachi 4:2 employs this symbol: "But unto you that fear my name shall the Sun of righteousness arise with healing in his wings" (KJV).

In the New Testament it is highly significant that the concept of God's hovering presence occurs in the angel's birth announcement to Mary: "The Holy Spirit will come upon you, and the power of the Most High will over-shadow [*episkiasei*] you" (Luke 1:35). The conception of Jesus is the first act of the new creation.[6] The Greek verb *episkiazō* is also used in describing God's glory cloud that covered the tabernacle (Exod. 40:35 in the Septuagint, the ancient Greek translation of the Old Testament hereafter designated in notes as "LXX") and the cloud that overshadowed the Mount of Transfiguration (Matt. 17:5; Mark 9:7; Luke 9:34). By this common figure of the hovering and overshadowing presence of God's Spirit, the original creation, the creation of God's covenant, nation and the new creation in Christ are linked together.

The creative activity of the Spirit of God (Gen. 1:2) is continued and ful-filled in the divine word of 1:3–26. Psalm 33:6 makes this connection explic-it: "By the word of the LORD the heavens were made, and by the breath [*rûaḥ*] of His mouth all their host." Hebrew *rua* could just as well be translated "Spirit" here. Psalm 33:6a may allude to the work of the eternal Son of God in creation, speaking of Him as "the word." Note that the Son is referred to as "the Word" (Greek *logos)* in John 1:1–3, where the context again concerns cre-ation. So understood, Psalm 33:6 would infer "that all the heavenly bodies were made by a combined effort of the Son and the Spirit."[7]

Several other references to God's creative decrees or fiat commands (Latin *fiat,* "let it be done") in Genesis 1 occur subsequently in Scripture: Psalm 33:9—"he spoke, and it came to be; he commanded, and it stood firm" (NIV); Psalm 148:5—"He commanded and they were created" (NIV); Hebrews

11:3—"the universe was formed at God's command" (NIV); 2 Peter 3:5—"by the word of God the heavens existed long ago and the earth was formed out of water." So we may conclude that by the living Word—the Son of God—the creative directives of the triune Godhead were carried out (Col. 1:16; Heb. 1:2); and by the living breath or Spirit of God the personal creative power of God was administered, "bringing to final form that which [had] been brought into existence by the Son"[8] (see also the comment on Romans 8:23–27). The close association of the divine breath and word—Spirit and Son—in creative acts may also be noted in other passages of the Bible: Genesis 2:7; John 20:22; 2 Timothy 3:16 (see the comments on these verses).

A passage in Isaiah specifically associates the Spirit of God with the wisdom of God as creator:

> Who has measured the waters in the
>     hollow of His hand,
> And marked off the heavens by the
>     span [of His hand] ...
> Who has directed the Spirit of the
>     LORD,
> Or as His counselor has informed
>     Him?
> With whom did He consult and who
>     gave Him understanding
> And who taught Him in the path of
>     justice and taught Him knowledge,
> And informed Him of the way of
>     understanding?
>
> —ISAIAH 40:12–14

What a beautiful description of the sovereign majesty of God, the Holy One (40:18, 25), thinking and planning in His Spirit the creation of the universe! The Hebrew verb in verse 13 for "directed" (*tkn*) is also used for "weighing" the heart (that is, its thoughts or motives—Prov. 16:2; 21:2; 24:12) in order to judge its moral condition. Also in the context of Isaiah 40:12–14 the series of words "informed," "consult," "understanding," "taught" and "knowledge" all support the sense of intellect, mind or will for *rûaḥ* in verse 13. That seems to be why the Septuagint translators (Jewish scholars in Egypt around 250–150 B.C.) of Isaiah used the Greek word *nous*, "mind," instead of *pneuma*. Paul quoted the Septuagint, rather than translating afresh from the Hebrew text, in Romans 11:34: "For who has known the mind of the Lord, or who became His counselor?"

Lloyd Neve has stated: "The spirit of Yahweh in 40:13 is the intelligent center of the very being of Yahweh himself, the purposeful power with which he planned and created the world."[9] Thus in Isaiah 40:13 it is proper to observe the rational and volitional aspect of God's Spirit. Truly, the *rûaḥ* that hovered over the lifeless deep, sovereignly blowing to bring purposeful design and life into the world, was God, the Holy Spirit.

## God's Creative Breath—Genesis 2:7

Genesis 1:1–2:4a concludes with humanity (Hebrew *'ādām*), both male and female (1:26–27), as the last in the series of the creative acts of God. Genesis 2:4b–25 describes in detail the creation of the first human couple by "the LORD God" (*Yahweh 'elōhîm*). His covenant name Yahweh, explained to Moses in a dramatic encounter (Exod. 3:1–15; 6:2–8), is here added to assure the Israelites that the same deity who redeemed and delivered them from Egypt is truly the creator of all humankind.

Genesis 2:7 may be paraphrased, "And Yahweh God as a potter molded the [first] human [*'ādām*] of clay dust from the ground [*'ādāmāh*], and He breathed strongly into his nostrils the breath of life [*nišmat ḥayyîm*], and the [first] human [*'ādām*] became a living being [*nepeš ḥayyîm*]."

Several important truths about humans may be noted in Genesis 1:26–27 and 2:7. First, humanity is a special creation of God. While animals, birds and creeping things are also called *nepeš ḥayyîm,* "living creature(s)" (1:20–21, 24; 2:19), only humans are said to have been made in God's image.

This radically new element in the series of God's creative acts is what immediately placed human beings on a higher plane of existence than the animals (compare Ps. 8:3–8). Humanity did not evolve gradually into its full nature; it was completed at once by the direct, personal act of God. The Hebrew verb for "created" in 1:27, *bārā',* is used in the Old Testament only of God's activity; never does any other being or power perform *bārā'*-work. (Author's note: When I have translated a single Hebrew word using more than one word in English, the resulting word cluster has been hyphenated; for example, "*bārā'*-work"; "glory-presence.")

Second, Genesis 1 and 2 explain how humans are constituted. The follow-ing in-depth study of the constituent parts of the human being is important in order to understand properly the work of the Holy Spirit with people. Because God formed the very first human being of dust from the ground, it is obvious that God purposely designed humans to be corporeal beings—that is, beings with bodies. Note the close relationship of the terms in Hebrew for human and the source of human material substance: the human (*'ādām*), the ruddy one, is formed from the reddish soil or ground (*'ādāmāh*).

This fact is repeated over and over again in the Old Testament: "Thou hast made me as clay; and wouldst Thou turn me into dust again?" (Job 10:9; see also 4:19; 33:6). "He Himself knows our frame; He is mindful that we are but dust" (Ps. 103:14; see also 104:29; 146:4). Isaiah 29:16 and Jeremiah 18:4, 6 picture God as the divine potter. In the New Testament, Paul contrasts the first Adam—and all his descendants, that is, the whole human race—with Jesus Christ, the last Adam: "The first man is from the earth, earthy [Greek *choïkos*, "made of dust"]; the second man is from heaven" (1 Cor. 15:47–49). Not until God breathed into the dust-made body, however, did He call His creation "very good" (Gen. 1:31).

Within their bodies humans contain the breath of life. As J. Rodman Williams has explained, until that living breath or life-principle was imparted, the molded body was "still nothing but dust—an inanimate, lifeless entity." Every living creature including the human being has the breath-spirit of life (*nišmat rûaḥ ḥayyîm*, Gen. 7:22–23; also called simply "the breath of life," *rûaḥ hayyim*, 6:17; 7:15). But the breath of life that animals have is not said to have been inbreathed by God personally, and no special relationship to God is predicated for animals. Williams concluded:

> Only man has his breath infused directly from the inbreathing of God. This means ... that man is created by God in a unique and intimate relationship to Him. Thus the breath that God breathes into man's nostrils is more than physical breath (though it is that too). It is also spiritual breath because God is spirit.... Thus man has in him the breath of life, which, though in one sense physical and thus the same as all the animal world, is also spiritual. God has breathed into man a spirit that totally transcends anything hitherto in all creation—a spirit that has a unique relationship with the living God.[10]

That the human spirit comes from God is confirmed by other Scripture passages: "Then the dust [of the body] will return to the earth as it was, and the spirit will return to God who gave it" (Eccles. 12:7); "the Lord, who . . .

founded the earth and formed the spirit of man within him" (Zech. 12:1, RSV).

The term "breath of life" in Genesis 2:7 is closely equivalent to the term *rûaḥ* ("breath" or "spirit"), as already noted in comparing Genesis 2:7 with 6:17, 7:15 and 7:22. Therefore the origin of the human spirit can be traced to God in still other passages where *nĕšāmāh*, "breath," is used.

In Hebrew, *nĕšāmāh* and *rûaḥ* are often paralleled in poetry for emphasis: "as long as my breath [*nĕšāmāh*] is in me, and the spirit [*rûaḥ*, "breath," NIV] of God is in my nostrils" (Job 27:3, RSV). "God . . . who gives breath [*nĕšāmāh*] to the people on it [the earth], and spirit [*rûaḥ*] to those who walk in it" (Isa. 42:5). "Then the spirit [*rûaḥ*] of man would grow faint before me— the breath [*nĕšāmāh*] of man that I have created" (Isa. 57:16, NIV).

It is the spirit that enlivens the body. James called faith without works dead "just as the body without the spirit is dead" (James 2:26). It is also the human spirit that provides the capacity to have communication and fellowship with God and to serve Him (Isa. 26:9; John 4:24; Rom. 1:9; 8:16). The spirit, therefore, is the very essence of human nature (Ps. 31:5; 1 Cor. 2:11; 5:5). "It is the quintessential self, the base and center of the various other functions of the living person."[11]

For instance, the spirit of a person can sustain him or her through an illness (Prov. 18:14). And the spirit (*nĕšāmāh*) of a human being ('*adām*) is the lamp or spotlight the Lord uses to search out all of that person's innermost being (Prov. 20:27). Here spirit is seen functioning with moral consciousness (that is, as the conscience).

In the Old Testament the figurative term "heart" (Hebrew *lēb*) is often used instead of "spirit" in the sense of the inner person. For example, Proverbs 25:3 says, "The heart of kings is unsearchable." The heart also represents the moral center (Jer. 17:10—"I, the LORD, search the heart"); the self (2 Chron. 25:19—"Your heart has become proud in boasting"); the whole person (Deut. 11:16—"Beware, lest your hearts be deceived and you turn away and serve other gods").

In Psalm 51:10 "a clean heart" is parallel to "a steadfast spirit." In the Bible, "heart" as well as "spirit" is sometimes used in the sense of conscience (1 Sam. 24:5; 25:31; 1 John 3:20–21). It is on the "heart," in the sense of our spirits, that God by His Spirit inscribes His law under the New Covenant (Jer. 31:33). And in the New Testament the "heart" (that is, spirit) is said to be the dwelling place of Christ by the Spirit (Eph. 3:17; 2 Cor. 1:22).

A human is both body and spirit. So fashioned by God, the human is a living being (*nepeš ḥayyîm*, Gen. 2:7). The Hebrew word *nepeš* (also spelled *nephesh*) is usually translated "soul" in the King James Version (428 times out of 750 occurrences). It stands for the appetite (Num. 11:6; Prov. 23:2; Eccles. 6:7) and is the seat of other desires and emotions as well (Exod. 23:9; Eccles. 6:3; Song of Sol. 1:7; Hos. 4:8). This term denotes the human as a person or individual (Exod. 16:16; Lev. 27:2, NIV; Num. 5:6); hence it is the "self" (Num. 30:12–13, RSV), one's very life (Lev. 24:17; Josh. 2:13). Similarities between the functions of the *nepeš*, "soul," and the *rûaḥ*, "spirit," in humanity are readily apparent.

Professor Williams has superbly articulated the connection between "soul" and "spirit":

> As we begin to reflect on man as a 'living being" or "soul," we are not to understand this as a third part of man but as the resulting expression of spirit functioning through body. It might be said that spirit is the principle of man as soul. Soul (or life) is grounded in spirit and so is inseparable from spirit, but it is not a third part. It is the *whole of life* through which the spirit of man expresses itself.... Man as living soul, by virtue of being grounded in spirit, is self-transcending in every area of his conscious life.
>
> The "soul," then, is the *kind of life* man has. Soul represents the human act of living in its various intellectual, emotional, and volitional dimensions. Soul is that which proceeds from the depths of the spirit as it animates the body [italics his].[12]

Vitally important is the fact that, as a living "soul" made in God's image, humanity was empowered with freedom to choose in relation to God's will. Before Adam and Eve's fall human free will included the *ability* to obey God, acting in harmony with His Spirit and unhindered by the dominion of sin.

Two New Testament passages seem to make a clear distinction between "soul" (Greek *psychē*) and "spirit" (*pneuma*). In 1 Thessalonians 5:23 Paul prays that "your spirit and soul and body be kept sound and blameless at the coming of our Lord Jesus Christ" (RSV). Hebrews 4:12 speaks of the word of God which "penetrates even to dividing soul and spirit, joints and marrow" and "judges the thoughts and attitudes of the heart" (NIV).

Instead of dividing "soul" and "spirit" in these verses into separate entities of the human being, it is better to understand them from the standpoint of poetic Hebraic thought, which parallels ideas. According to the Hebrew fondness for synthesizing, "soul" and "spirit" are close synonyms emphasizing the total person. Compare Luke 1:46–47 (RSV), "'My soul magnifies . . . and my spirit rejoices,'" and Mark 12:30, "Love the Lord your God with all your heart . . . soul . . . mind, and . . . strength."

The reference in Hebrews 4:12 to piercing or penetrating as far as the division of soul and spirit seems to mean that God's Word probes the innermost recesses of the total human personality. Therefore we may conclude that humanity, as an integrated living being, is essentially the combination of body (dust from the ground) and spirit (breath from God).

A third main teaching to be derived from Genesis 2:7 pertains to the involvement of God's Spirit in the creation of humanity. The strong breathing by God of the breath of life into the nostrils of the first human most certainly suggests the vitalizing breath of His Spirit. Several Old Testament passages support this deduction by referring to the ongoing, quickening function of the Spirit in the creating and sustaining of life. Job declared, "As long as I have life [*něšāmāh*] within me, the breath [*rûaḥ*] of God in my nostrils . . ." (27:3, NIV). His friend Elihu defended his right to speak up: "The Spirit [*rûaḥ*] of God has made me, and the breath [*něšāmāh*] of the Almighty gives me life" (Job 33:4). Speaking of God's sovereignty, Elihu observed:

If He should determine to do so,
If He should gather to Himself His spirit [*rûaḥ*] and His breath [*něšāmāh*],
All flesh would perish together,
And man would return to dust.

—Job 34:14–15

Describing God's providential care of His creatures the psalmist sang:

Thou dost hide Thy face, they are dismayed;
Thou dost take away their spirit [*rûaḥ*], they expire,
And return to their dust.
Thou dost send forth Thy Spirit [*rûaḥ*], they are created;
And Thou dost renew the face of the ground.

—Psalm 104:29–30

The creative and nurturing role of God's Spirit with respect to animate life is thus clear.

Because humanity was created by God's Spirit-breath, the human being originally was able to be responsive to the control of the Spirit who formed it.

Humankind died spiritually, however, upon the entrance of sin (Gen. 2:17; Rom. 6:23), and physical death followed in due course (Gen. 5:1–5).

Spiritual death does not imply nonexistence. It means separation from God, brought about by self-will, disobedience and rebellion against God's sovereign authority. The spirit of the unsaved person is dead to God, dead in trespasses and sins (Eph. 2:1–3). Therefore in order to have fellowship with God the spirit of every human being needs to be made alive (Eph. 2:5), regenerated and renewed by the Holy Spirit (Titus 3:5).

At the same time we must recognize, as the Wesleyan scholar Charles Carter has written, that "the re-creative work of the Spirit is both personal and racial, both individual and social." In salvation history God's Spirit functioned mainly through the chosen people Israel, divinely called to the service of God in order to make known to the nations His special revelation.[13]

To summarize, we have seen that when God breathes creatively, something new comes into being. When His mouth breathed forth the divine word, the heavenly bodies were made (Ps. 33:6). When His Holy Spirit-breath and power overshadowed the virgin Mary, the incarnation of the Son of God began (Luke 1:35). When His risen Son breathed on His disciples and imparted the Holy Spirit, the new creation began for them (see the comment on John 20:22). When He breathed His Word to His prophets and apostles and moved on them by the Holy Spirit, the holy Scriptures were produced (2 Tim. 3:15–16, NIV; 2 Peter 1:21). When His Spirit breathes on the returnees to Israel, new spiritual life (regeneration) will occur (Ezek. 37:9–14). Clearly it was God the Spirit who was the divine breath that fashioned the living man in Genesis 2:7.

### The Spirit of God As Judge and Advocate—Genesis 6:3

In each successive generation after Adam the wickedness of humanity accelerated. The more people alienated themselves from God, the more they opened themselves to demonic activity. Divine beings (literally, "sons of the gods," *běnei-hā'elōhîm;* compare Job 1:6) saw how beautiful were many of the human females (literally, "daughters of the human race," *běnôthhā'ādām),* and they sinned by taking for themselves any women they chose (Gen. 6:1–2). Apparently these beings, who may have been fallen angels or wicked spirits (known in medieval times as *incubi),* invaded and possessed human males and thereby generated the Nephilim (KJV, "giants").

Genesis 6:4 implies that this type of perverted reproduction occurred "whenever sons of the gods were going in to daughters of the human race, and they kept bearing children to them" (literal translation). The resultant offspring gained a reputation as infamous heroes before the deluge (v. 4). Peter and Jude refer to angels who sinned prior to Noah's flood, perhaps by immorality as gross as that at Sodom (2 Pet. 2:4–5; Jude 6–7).

The Nephilim undoubtedly aggravated the prevailing corruption in society, until the earth was filled with violence (vv. 11, 13). The Hebrew word *ḥāmās,* "violence," covers all kinds of lawlessness (Zeph. 3:4) and crimes—social oppression (Jer. 22:3), fraud (Mic. 6:11–12), idolatry (Ezek. 8:17), warlike brutality (Jer. 51:35) and murder (Judg. 9:24). In ancient thought the very land was considered to be polluted by innocent blood shed on it (Num. 35:31–34). No doubt all kinds of sexual perversion including bestiality were involved in the corruption and pollution that defiled the earth (compare Lev. 18:20–28).

Because of such universal abominations God pronounced judgment on the earth as well as on its inhabitants. Both human and beast came under the condemnation, for all were infected by such depravity. God found it necessary to wash the entire world clean of all its corruption (Gen. 6:13, 17).

This was the extremity of evil which provoked Yahweh to say, "My Spirit shall not plead [*yādôn*] with mankind forever; in their going astray they are flesh—mortal, frail and erring! Therefore their days shall be only 120 years more until judgment" (Gen. 6:3, author's paraphrase). Some English versions, depending on the Septuagint and other early translations, have "My spirit shall not abide in man for ever" (for example, RSV). It is better, however, to stay with the Hebrew text and render *yādôn* (from *dîn*) as "strive" (KJV, NAS), "contend" (NIV) or "plead."

The verb *dîn* is a judicial term and basically signifies "to judge." It does mean to bring judgment on someone (Gen. 15:14). But it also denotes governing and providing justice for one's people (Gen. 49:16, NIV). Sometimes it conveys the sense of disputing or conducting a lawsuit (Isa. 3:13). It can also mean to plead the cause, the legal case, of the needy and orphans (Jer. 5:28); in other words to defend, vindicate (Gen. 30:6) or act as advocate. E. A. Speiser argued for this sense of *yādôn* in Genesis 6:3: "shall not answer for man" or "shall not protect man."[14]

Therefore in Genesis 6:3 God was saying that after 120 years He by His Spirit would no longer plead with antediluvian sinners to repent. He would stop convicting and reasoning with them about their sins (compare Isaiah 1:18). He would stop interceding and going to their defense. He would cease acting as their advocate and helper. His Spirit would no longer undertake "to restrain the power of Satan and the display of sin of the human heart."[15]

Why? Because their wickedness had totally corrupted the earth. Judgment of Noah's world could not be averted.

The Bible warns repeatedly that God will not answer in the day of calamity when people have adamantly rejected Him and ignored His reproofs (Prov. 1:24–32; Ps. 2:2, 4; Isa. 1:15; 65:12; 66:4; Jer. 7:8–20; Zech. 7:11–14; Heb. 10:26–30). In the case of Israel, God in His marvelous compassion kept admonishing them for centuries by His Spirit through His prophets (Neh. 9:26–30; compare 2 Kings 17:7–23). Nevertheless, hardness of heart eventually brought on defeat and captivity. The restraining work of God's Spirit will cease on earth once again when people permit the "man of lawlessness" to deceive them (2 Thess. 2:3–7).

### *The Spirit of Wisdom and Discernment—Genesis 41:38*

Joseph is the first individual in the Bible who is called wise. Thus he is the pattern for many leaders who come after him, in whom the gifts of wisdom and discernment are also evident—Moses, Joshua, David, Solomon, Daniel, the Messiah.

Before interpreting Pharaoh's dreams, Joseph testified that God would give Pharaoh a favorable answer (Gen. 41:16). Joseph concluded by emphasizing that God, *hā'elōhîm*—the (one true) God—had predestined the ruinous famine and would soon carry it out (v. 32). He then recommended a plan to mitigate the severity of the seven-year famine (vv. 33–36).

Pharaoh and his courtiers immediately recognized that Joseph was the man to administrate this sensible program: "Can we find anyone like this man, one in whom is the spirit of God [*rûah 'elōhîm*]?" (v. 38, NIV). This mighty ruler, himself worshiped in Egypt as an incarnate god, admitted that God—Joseph's God—had revealed all this to Joseph; therefore no one was so discerning (*nābôn*, from *bîn*) and wise (*hākām*) as he (v. 39).

How should the expression *rûah 'elōhîm* in verse 38 be translated? As "a spirit of the gods" (NIV margin), "a divine spirit" (NAS), "the Spirit of God" (RSV, TLB), or "the spirit of God" (KJV, NIV, TAN)? The NIV Study Bible says the word "spirit" probably should not be capitalized "since reference to the Holy

Spirit would be out of character in statements by pagan rulers."[16]

This seems to be correct in the case of Daniel whom the Babylonians recognized to be a man "in whom is the spirit of the holy gods" because of his superior wisdom (Dan. 4:8–9, 18; 5:11, 14). Nevertheless in Joseph's case because of his testimony about God and because the Hebrew expression is identical with that for "Spirit of God" in Genesis 1:2, the author of Genesis no doubt intended the reader to see in 41:38 a reference to God's Spirit (see additional comments on Proverbs 1:20–23).

A later Scripture passage (Ps. 105:17–22) looked upon Joseph as one of the anointed patriarchs (v. 15) to whom the covenant word of Yahweh came (v. 8). He was depicted as one who taught wisdom to Pharaoh's elders (v. 22). Since the entire psalm extols God's providential works, the clear inference is that Joseph obtained his counseling ability from Yahweh.

Approximate contemporaries of Joseph were Job and his friends, who probably lived in the period 2000–1500 B.C. Younger than the others, Elihu said it was not mere age that makes people wise (Job 32:4–7, 9). Instead, he argued, "there is spirit [*rûaḥ*] in man, and the breath [*nĕšāmāh*, "inspiration," KJV] of the Almighty gives them understanding" (Job 32:8, author's translation).

The verb "give understanding" has the same root (*bîn*) as the word "discerning" in the description of Joseph (Gen. 41:39). Clearly, according to Elihu's statement, the ancients believed that God by His Spirit furnished wisdom and understanding to people through the avenue of the human spirit.

Elihu's insight is corroborated by biblical references to a spirit of wisdom, as in the cases of the skillful artisans for the tabernacle (Exod. 28:3), Joshua (Deut. 34:9) and the Ephesian church (Eph. 1:17). These passages speak of the human spirit imbued with the divine charisma of "spiritual wisdom and understanding" (Col. 1:9), supplied by the Spirit of wisdom (Exod. 31:3; Isa. 11:2).

# THREE

# The Era of Charismatic Leadership in Israel
## (1500–1000 B.C.)

**F**rom Moses to Malachi biblical revelation concerning the Spirit of God pertains largely to His dealings with the nation of Israel. Most often the Spirit makes His appearances in His equipping of individuals either for leadership or for delivering God's prophetic messages. Because of the thousand-year history of Israel as a nation in the Old Testament, we have ample opportunity to study the role of God's Spirit in the governing of His chosen people. To see how the Spirit used people in Old Testament times is instructive for us as New Testament believers.

Israel was constituted a theocratic nation—that is, her government was one in which God was the supreme ruler. Gideon clearly accepted this revealed order of society when he resisted an attempt to make him king: "I will not rule over you myself, nor shall my son rule over you; the LORD alone shall rule over you" (Judg. 8:23, TAN; compare 1 Samuel 8:7).

In order to carry out His divine rule Yahweh handpicked men and women to be His agents. Most of these were very ordinary people, often with two strikes against them socially. But endowed with God's Spirit they were enabled to carry out His holy purposes. Some became warriors and judges; some became kings; others became skilled craftsmen, wise teachers, poets or Levitical singers; still others became spokespersons for God. These charismatics—persons divinely gifted with unusual ability and spiritual power—were an absolutely essential component of Yahweh's reign over His covenant nation.

## *The Period of Moses and Joshua*

At the inception of Israel's national existence, the man Moses shines forth like a lighthouse. Perhaps the greatest leader in all Israel's history, Moses is remembered in later times as a man of the Spirit.

The psalmist rehearsed God's activity in connection with wayward Israel and stated, "They rebelled against the Spirit of God, and rash words came from Moses' lips" (Ps. 106:33, NIV). Here is an indication that as Israel's leader Moses was closely in tune with God's Spirit. In a long formal prayer recorded in Nehemiah 9, the Levites recount that God gave His "good Spirit" during the forty years of Israel's desert journey in order to instruct them (vv. 19–21). At that time the Spirit was given primarily to Moses, through whom Yahweh performed many miracles (Deut. 34:10–12) and sent forth His word to His covenant people (Num. 12:6–8).

The most striking incident in Moses' career revealing his anointing by God's Spirit occurred during Israel's march from Mount Sinai to Kadesh-barnea. The Lord "took of" His Spirit who was upon Moses and anointed seventy elders to assist Moses in carrying the burden of the complaining people (Num. 11:25; see the comment on Numbers 11:4–30).

Moses and those tribal leaders were not the only ones directed by God's Spirit in that period. Bezalel (of the tribe of Judah) was filled with the Spirit of God, "with skill, ability and knowledge in all kinds of crafts" (Exod. 31:3; 35:31, NIV). As instructors of the Israelite craftsmen engaged in constructing the tabernacle and its furniture, he and Oholiab (a Danite) were equipped by the Spirit for their task (Exod. 35:34–36:1), along with the tailors who made the high-priestly garments (Exod. 28:3). By pervading them with His creative presence God endowed the artisans with charismatic ability (defined as *ḥokmāh*, "wisdom," KJV) beyond any natural talents of their own.

In like manner Joshua, the son of Nun, is described as "a man in whom is the Spirit" (Num. 27:18). In this verse the Hebrew preposition *b*, "in," can also mean "with"—"with whom is the Spirit"—true also in the case of Joseph (see the comment on Genesis 41:38). The emphasis is not on the Spirit's *living in* these individuals but rather on the *result* of His presence.

A similar statement regarding Joshua clarifies the purpose of the Spirit's ministry to him: He was "full of the spirit of wisdom, for Moses had laid his hands upon him" (Deut. 34:9, RSV). Thus Joshua was provided with divine charisma to be the shepherd-leader of God's people, as Moses had requested

(Num. 27:16–17). In none of these cases, however, does the context suggest a continuous indwelling of the Spirit for the purpose of holiness and fellowship with God.

## Moses and the Seventy Spirit-Anointed Elders—Numbers 11:4–30

A passage in Numbers 11 clarifies how Moses could lead the fledgling nation of unruly Israelites for forty years. God had evidently been supplying His Spirit-empowerment constantly to Moses ever since the burning bush experience (Exod. 3). Moses, with Aaron's help, was commissioned by Yahweh to speak to the elders of Israel (Exod. 3:16–18) and, with Aaron's help, to confront the pharaoh of Egypt time and time again (Exod. 5:1ff.). Moses was enabled to perform many miracles, from throwing down his staff—which became a serpent (4:1–9; 7:8–12)—to dividing the Red Sea waters (14:16).

In time, however, the constant grumbling of the people for meat to supplement their monotonous manna diet disturbed Moses. He begged Yahweh to take his life immediately (Num. 11:4–15). Instead, Yahweh ordered him to gather seventy of Israel's elders to help him meet this crisis (v. 16). These were probably selected from the men Moses had previously chosen to help him judge the people (Exod. 18:17–26). They may even have been the same seventy elders who had stood in God's presence at the covenant ratification ceremony (Exod. 24:1–11).

Yahweh further explained His plan: "I will take of the Spirit who is upon you, and will put Him upon them; and they shall bear the burden of the people with you, so that you shall not bear it all alone" (Num. 11:17). This episode strikingly illustrates that God's purpose in every age for His charismatic empowerment is to enable the recipients to minister to others, "for the common good" (1 Cor. 12:7).

Did God's "taking of" the Spirit diminish Moses' ability to minister? No. As the medieval rabbi Rashi commented, there was no diminution of the anointing on Moses, just as the light of the golden lampstand in the tabernacle was not diminished when the other lamps of the sanctuary were lit from it. Another explanation is based on the seldom-used Hebrew verb 'āṣal, translated "take" in verses 17 and 25, which means to reserve or withhold, but not to remove. This verb does not indicate that Yahweh takes away from Moses part of the rûaḥ already equipping him, but that He "withholds some of that which is constantly being granted to Moses to bestow it on the elders."[1]

Sharing of the Spirit may be noted in other instances as well: The same Spirit that was on Elijah rested or settled (*nûaḥ*) upon Elisha (see the comment on 2 Kings 2:9, 15). The Spirit who descended and remained on Jesus (John 1:32–34) came to rest upon the 120 disciples at Pentecost (Acts 2:3) and is called the Spirit of Jesus (Christ) (Acts 16:7; Phil. 1:19; 1 Pet. 1:11).

When Yahweh fulfilled His promise by sending the Spirit to rest upon the elders, they prophesied (Num. 11:25). No message is recorded and no indication is given of the content of their prophesying. Some scholars believe it was unintelligible ecstatic utterance. Others hold that it may have been praise to God, similar to the prophesying of Samuel's young prophets (1 Sam. 10:5) and the practice of David's temple singers who prophesied in worshiping the Lord (see the comment on 1 Chronicles 25:1–3). Leon Wood has suggested that Eldad and Medad were singing with joy and exuberance as they ran through the camp.[2]

Whatever the exact nature of the utterance, the prophesying served as a charismatic sign of the Spirit's empowering. The Spirit no doubt kept on equipping the seventy for the duration of the emergency.

The charismatic manifestation that marked the elders' entrance into their new task of burden bearing was not ongoing. Scripture is careful to note that those who prophesied outside the camp "did not do so again" (Num. 11:25, NIV). (The King James Version translation "and did not cease" is not valid in this context.)

Herein lies one of the major differences between the Spirit's manifestation before and after Pentecost. Then it was occasional, sporadic, temporary; now, since Pentecost, it is continuously available. But in neither dispensation can the believer store up spiritual anointing. It is to be used at the very time of supply by God (see the comment on Galatians 3:2–5, 14). The Spirit's empowerment is not some *thing* we can possess; we need to be continually filled and refilled with the Spirit (see the comment on Ephesians 5:15–21).

The other difference in the Spirit's outpouring before and after Pentecost is clearly portrayed in Moses' reaction to Joshua's concern about two men prophesying apart from the larger group: "Would that all the LORD's people were prophets, that the LORD would put His Spirit upon them!" (Num. 11:29). Much later, Joel foretold the time when all classes of God's people would receive the outpoured Spirit (Joel 2:28–29), and all could prophesy to confirm

His presence with them (1 Cor. 14:1, 5, 31).[3] But until that day only the select few leaders and prophets in Israel experienced Spirit-anointing.

## Balaam, the Heathen Diviner—Numbers 24:2

The enigmatic Balaam was a heathen diviner (Josh. 13:22), not an Israelite or a prophet. Yet he uttered a number of prophetic oracles regarding Israel (Num. 23–24). His home was in Pethor in northwestern Mesopotamia (Num. 22:5; Deut. 23:4). Haran, where Abraham and Laban had lived (Gen. 11:31; 27:43) and Yahweh continued to be invoked (Gen. 29:33, 35; 30:24; 31:49), was about sixty-five miles to the east. This proximity may explain how Balaam knew about Yahweh (Num. 22:8, 18; 23:26; 24:13).

Balak, king of Moab, feared the vast hordes of Israelites camping in his country. Because he knew he could not withstand Israel militarily, he hired Balaam to call down evil on Israel by the ancient practice of pronouncing execrations. God forbade Balaam to curse the Israelites (Num. 22:12), but Balaam persisted in going with Balak's envoys.

Balaam tried sorcery to obtain omens (23:23; 24:1) in order to curse Israel. Like the *baru*-priests known in Babylonian cuneiform tablets, he probably examined the livers (compare Ezekiel 21:21) and entrails of the bulls and rams that Balak had sacrificed (Num. 22:40–41; 23:2, 14, 28–30). But Yahweh encountered Balaam with manifestations (23:4, 16, TAN) and put messages in his mouth that blessed instead of cursed Israel (23:5, 11–12, 16).

Finally the Spirit of God came upon Balaam (24:2; see the comment on Judges 3:10). The Spirit gripped an unwilling subject and used him contrary to his own ends. God by His Spirit now totally dominated Balaam. Unlike occult spirits God's Spirit could not be conjured or coerced.[4]

In Balaam's third and fourth oracles his eyes were opened (Num. 24:3–4, 15–16). He was given heightened revelations of Israel's invincibility and distant future. The terms "star out of Jacob" and "scepter out of Israel" (24:17) ultimately pointed to the messianic ruler (compare Revelation 22:16; Genesis 49:10; Hebrews 1:8).

It may seem strange that God would use a pagan fortune-teller immortalized for his consuming greed (2 Pet. 2:15; Jude 11; Rev. 2:14). "But," as Stanley Horton has explained, "God was protecting His people from an enemy they did not know about, and He purposed to use His Holy Spirit to do it."[5] In spite of his desire for personal gain through cursing the Israelites, Balaam under the power of God's Spirit was forced to pronounce blessing on them.

Later on, in reminding Israel of the incident, Yahweh spoke through Joshua, "But I was not willing to listen to Balaam. So he had to bless you, and I delivered you from his hand" (Josh. 24:10; compare Deuteronomy 23:5). Great may be the hostility of the powers of darkness against the children of God, but "greater is He who is in you than he who is in the world" (1 John 4:4).

## The Period of the Judges and the Early Monarchy

Charismatic leadership continued to characterize the style of government in Israel until well into the reign of King David. In its purest form God's theocratic rule of His covenant people requires a minimum number of human representatives. Ideally, they should be persons who are sensitive to hear and respond to His voice. Such was Samuel, the last of the judges (1 Sam. 7:15–17) and one of the earliest prophets in Israel. Of him it is recorded that Yahweh was with him from his early boyhood experience when Eli was the high priest (1 Sam. 3:19) and that Yahweh continued to appear at Shiloh and reveal Himself to Samuel through His word (3:21).

Samuel was a prophet or "seer" who was enlightened directly by the Lord (1 Sam. 9:17) and was gifted repeatedly with a "word of knowledge" or a prophetic directive or warning to the king (9:20; 10:2–6; 13:13–14; 15:1–3, 22–23). In his latter years Samuel schooled a band of younger prophets. They were known for their prophesying to the accompaniment of the musical instruments of that time (10:5; 19:20).

Those Israelites who preceded Samuel as leaders throughout this period invariably were persons of lesser spiritual stature than he. Nevertheless, the Spirit of Yahweh was actively present with them to incite and fill them with power to accomplish mighty deeds. We know them as the judges. The Hebrew term *šōphēt* in that day meant "magistrate," "governor," "leader."

In no instance did God pick someone to be a judge who had family prestige or personal reputation. Othniel was "little brother" to Caleb, Ehud was left-handed, Deborah a woman, Gideon the youngest in his obscure family, Jephthah the son of a harlot, and Samson an undisciplined loner. Yet when the Spirit stirred them, came upon them and invested them with charismatic ability, by faith they "conquered kingdoms" and "administered justice" (Heb. 11:32–33, NIV). How illustrative of what the Holy Spirit will do with believing Christians today!

Up to and including the reign of David, Israel's leaders were chosen directly by the Lord. There was no such thing as hereditary authority. Old Testament scholar John Bright explained: "It was a type of authority perfectly expressive of the faith and constitution of early Israel: the God-King's direct leadership of his people through his spirit-designated representative."[6] Each individual was recognized and followed by the people because of the evidence of Yahweh's Spirit upon him or her.

At the inception of the Israelite monarchy this rather immediate form of divine government was still God's pattern. The new ruler to be anointed by Samuel was at first designated by the Hebrew term *nāgîd* (1 Sam. 9:16; 10:1; variously translated as "prince," "captain," "leader," "ruler") rather than by *melek*, "king." David also was to be the appointed *nāgîd* over Yahweh's people (1 Sam. 13:14; 25:30; 2 Sam. 5:2; 6:21; 7:8). The Davidic Messiah is described prophetically as "a leader (*nāgîd*) and commander for the peoples" (Isa. 55:4). Daniel, too, under inspiration designated the One to appear at the end of the sixty-ninth "week" as "Messiah the Prince [*nāgîd* ]" (Dan. 9:25).

The term *nāgîd* denotes one who is prominent or conspicuous—perhaps with the underlying notion that he has been declared so or appointed to his position by the Lord, but certainly not one who is ruler only by heredity. Even when the term *melek* replaced *nāgîd* as the common designation for Israel's earthly ruler, the king was always considered to be subservient to Yahweh, the absolute monarch. The outward form of the theocracy had changed, but the ultimate authority was the same.

In his earlier years David showed himself as one certainly anointed by God's Spirit, a true charismatic. Following his amazing triumph over Goliath, he continued to fight the Lord's battles (1 Sam. 17:47; 18:17; 25:28). When the Philistines invaded the heartland of Judah to attack David's new capital at Jerusalem, he twice inquired of the Lord himself, apparently without the aid of a prophet.

On both occasions he heard directly from God, followed the divine directives and defeated the enemy decisively (2 Sam. 5:17–25). No doubt his testimony in song recorded in 2 Samuel 22 (repeated in Psalm 18) comes from the earlier part of his career: "Thou hast girded me with strength for battle; Thou hast subdued under me those who rose up against me" (22:40; see v. 1 for the historical setting). David ended his song by recognizing himself to be the Lord's anointed king (22:51; compare Psalm 20:6; 28:8).

David was considered to be a prophet by Jews in New Testament times. Referring to Psalm 16:8–11, Peter at Pentecost preached that because David was a prophet he looked ahead and spoke of the resurrection of Christ (Acts 2:29–31). Jesus also indicated the charismatic endowment of David: In debating the nature of the Messiah with the Pharisees, Jesus asked them, "Then how does David in the Spirit call Him 'Lord'?" (Matt. 22:43). He then quoted the first verse of Psalm 110, which was attributed to David by the Jews.

David's last piece of poetry gives credence to this Jewish belief; in introducing God's announcement to him of an everlasting covenant David described his inspiration by the Spirit in this way:

> The oracle of David, the son of Jesse,
> > the oracle of the man who was raised on high,
> the anointed of the God of Jacob,
> > the sweet psalmist of Israel:
> The Spirit of the Lord speaks by me,
> > his word is upon my tongue.
> The God of Israel has spoken,
> > the Rock of Israel has said to me....
>
> —2 SAMUEL 23:1–3A, RSV

Without equivocation David equated the Spirit of Yahweh with the God of Israel who spoke directly to him, resulting in his giving forth prophetic revelation (Hebrew *nĕ'um,* "oracle").

David not only wrote many of the psalms that are in the Old Testament canon, but he also saw in a vision the plan of the temple he longed to build for Yahweh. The chronicler records that David gave to Solomon the plans for the temple and all its rooms, "the plan of all that he had in mind"—literally, "the plan of all that was *by the Spirit* [Hebrew *bārûaḥ*]" (1 Chron. 28:12).

Verse 19 continues with David's words: " 'All this is in writing,' David said, 'because the hand of the LORD was upon me, and he gave me understanding in all the details of the plan' " (NIV). Just as Moses was shown on Mount Sinai a pattern of the things to be made for the earthly tabernacle (Exod. 25:9, 40; 26:30; Acts 7:44; Heb. 8:5), so David by the operation of the Spirit saw the divine blueprint for the temple that his son Solomon would build.

Demos Shakarian, founder of the Full Gospel Business Men's Fellowship, related a somewhat similar experience in modern times. An illiterate eleven-year-old Russian Pentecostal boy, Efim, received in 1853 a vision of charts and a message in beautiful handwriting. The map and the words he laboriously copied for seven days warned the Christians to flee Russian Armenia and cross the Atlantic Ocean to America. Those who heeded God's warning avoided the later terrible persecutions of the Armenians.[7]

In other areas of David's administration, however, he began to depend less and less on Spirit-anointing and more and more on human methods. His monarchy fast became institutionalized. As John Bright stated it so well:

> With dramatic suddenness David's conquests had transformed Israel into the fore-most power of Palestine and Syria . . . . The very nature of such a state betokened a sweeping change from the old order. Israel was no longer a tribal confederacy led by a charismatic *nāgîd* who had been acclaimed king, but a complex empire organ-ized under the crown . . . . The center of this new Israel was actually David himself.[8]

In the latter part of his reign the census that David ordered most likely had as its purpose extensive fiscal reorganization and conscription of labor as well as of troops (2 Sam. 24; 1 Chron. 21). The nation's trust was no longer in God alone. War was for *conquest* of additional territory; it was no longer "holy war" to fight along with Yahweh against *His* enemies.

With Solomon the changeover became set. Dynastic succession seemed to give irreversible permanence and stability to the government in Jerusalem. Only in the earliest year or so of his reign did the youthful king give any sign of charismatic leaning, and that was in his prayer at Gibeon for wisdom and discernment (1 Kings 3:6–9). Soon, however, Solomon patterned his court after the example of the pharaohs in Egypt. He sealed foreign alliances by marriage, bringing numerous foreign princesses into his harem and their idols with them (1 Kings 11:1–8). During his reign, as R. K. Harrison has written, Solomon "transformed the concept of kingship from the idea of charismatic or divinely inspired leadership current in the days of the early monarchy to that of typical Oriental despotism."[9]

Israel was no longer a simple theocracy with divinely appointed and empowered leaders. Much too quickly the nation had become like all the other nations, even as the majority of the people had wanted back in Samuel's day. They were the ones who had stubbornly refused to listen to his early warnings (1 Sam. 8:4–20). John Bright described the change:

Far more significant than any single measure taken by Solomon was the gradual but inexorable inner transformation that had overtaken Israel, which by Solomon's day was virtually complete. Little was left of the old order. The tribal confederacy with its sacral institutions and charismatic leadership had given way to the dynastic state, under which all aspects of the national life had progressively been organized. In the process the whole structure of Israelite society had been profoundly affected.[10]

But Yahweh was not dethroned. He had not abdicated His rule over Israel nor renounced His covenant promises. Yahweh would continue by His Spirit through His prophets to face the people with their responsibility to heed His *torah*—His instruction, His law.

Keeping in mind this summary of the developments in how Israel was governed, we can now examine each period more closely, beginning with the judges.

### Spirit-Empowered Judges—Judges 3:10; 6:34; 11:29; 14:6

The most recognized of the Old Testament charismatic leaders are the judges. While not judicial officials in the modern sense, they ruled as magistrates, keeping law and order in peacetime and achieving "justice" for the various tribes by vindicating their cause in battle against enemies. They were Spirit-empowered chieftains whom Yahweh raised up to deliver Israel "from the hands of those who plundered them" (Judg. 2:16).

Most of the people of this period were indulging in Canaanite idolatrous practices and acting selfishly—"everyone did what was right in his own eyes" (Judg. 17:6; 21:25). Few individuals designated as prophets were heard from in this period, but there were exceptions: the prophetess Deborah (4:4) and a nameless prophet (6:8–10). Prophetic visions were infrequent until the Lord revealed Himself to young Samuel (1 Sam. 3:1, 19–21). Some of the judges, however, did exercise a degree of prophetic authority whenever they spoke forth the Lord's rebuke to the nation for transgressing His covenant (Judg. 2:20).

Four of the judges are specifically mentioned as being empowered by the divine Spirit—Othniel, Gideon, Jephthah and Samson. (This is not to suggest that the other judges operated only in their natural wisdom and strength.) The Spirit's activity is described in several different ways in the original text.

Othniel, the first of the judges, sets a pattern for those who follow. Of him it is said: "The Spirit of the LORD came upon him, and he judged Israel. When he went out to war, the LORD gave Cushan-rishathaim . . . into his hand, so that he prevailed over [him]" (3:10).

The beginning Hebrew words here are *watĕhî 'ālâw rûaḥ YHWH*. The verb and preposition combination (*hāyāh* plus *'al*) means "be actively present upon." The same expression occurs in connection with Balaam (Num. 24:2), Jephthah (Judg. 11:29), Saul and his messengers (1 Sam. 19:20, 23), a prophet named Azariah (2 Chron. 15:1), and a Levite Jahaziel (2 Chron. 20:14). In every instance, whether providing ability or inspiring a message, the Spirit's sovereignty is apparent, and the unannounced suddenness of His coming is usually implicit.

Gideon is the next judge specified as having had the Spirit take possession of him: "So the Spirit of the LORD came upon [*lābĕšāh*, literally "clothed"] Gideon, and he blew a trumpet, and the Abiezerites were called together to follow him" (Judg. 6:34). The Hebrew verb *lābaš* (put on, wear, clothe, be clothed; see also 1 Chronicles 12:18; 2 Chronicles 24:20) suggests either that the Spirit clothed Gideon or that He clothed Himself with Gideon.

The figure of the Spirit clothing Gideon and being upon him is more in harmony with His coming upon Othniel and Jephthah (see above) and the usage of the verb in Job 29:14, "I put on righteousness, and it clothed me." In Judges 6:34 the Greek Septuagint translates *lābaš* by *enduō*, "to endue" or "to invest." This same Greek verb is used in Luke 24:49: "I am sending forth the promise of My Father upon you; but you are to stay in the city until you are clothed with power from on high."

Two expressions describe the Spirit's actions with Samson. Judges 13:25 says, "The Spirit of the LORD began to stir [*pā'am*] him in Mahaneh-dan." The verb means to trouble or agitate the human spirit (Gen. 41:8; Ps. 77:4; Dan. 2:1) and hence to impel or thrust a person into action.

The other expression occurs three times (Judg. 14:6, 19; 15:14): "The Spirit of the LORD came upon him mightily." The Hebrew verb and preposition here are *ṣālaḥ* plus *'al*, literally "rush upon." The verb is used for running or dashing to the Jordan in 2 Samuel 19:18 and for breaking forth or sweeping through like a fire in Amos 5:6.

The verb *ṣālaḥ* is used several times for God's Spirit coming on King Saul (1 Sam. 10:6, 10; 11:6) as well as for an evil spirit coming on him (1 Sam. 18:10). This verb is used once regarding David: "The Spirit of the LORD came mightily upon David from that day forward" (1 Sam. 16:13). Only in David's case is the Spirit's enabling said to be continuous (see the comment on 1 Samuel 16:13).

Michael Green has likened the action of God's Spirit upon the judges and Saul to the violent force of an uncontrollable desert wind. He added that throughout the Old Testament the writers continue to emphasize "God's violent invasion from outside our experience, disturbing and mysterious like the wind."[11] Jesus Himself compared the sovereign renewing work of the Spirit to the unpredictable wind (John 3:8). But the purpose of the Spirit in the judges was always to act redemptively, "sometimes to chastise, on other occasions to console, and to deliver when the time was ripe."[12] Their activity provides valuable insights into the work of the Holy Spirit in the modern renewal movement.

### King Saul and the Spirit of God—1 Samuel 10:6–10; 11:6; 16:14; 19:18–24

At God's command Samuel anointed Saul with oil to be the first king of Israel (1 Sam. 10:1). Then he foretold that Saul would meet a procession of prophets carrying musical instruments and prophesying—most likely giving inspired praise to God (see the comment on Numbers 11:4–30). The Spirit of Yahweh would come upon him mightily (literally, "rush upon him"; see the comment on Judges 14:6 in reference to Samson). Saul, too, would prophesy and be changed into another man (1 Sam. 10:6). As he turned to leave Samuel, God changed Saul's heart (10:9, literally "turned around for him another heart").

What does this change of heart signify? Some scholars believe these statements indicate that a real conversion took place which fitted Saul to rule as Yahweh's anointed. Chester Lehman wrote: "This operation of the Spirit worked a complete change in Saul comparable to the New Testament experience of the new birth."[13]

On the other hand, Leon Wood interpreted Saul's changed heart to connote merely "the idea of a new attitude, a new emotional outlook."[14] This must have included a new willingness to accept the claim of God in his life, as in the case of Saul's valiant followers "whose hearts God had touched" (1 Sam. 10:26). Saul's change of heart (10:9) occurred *before* the Spirit rushed upon him the first time (10:10). While this onrushing of the Spirit was vigorous and not superficial, it was external and only temporary.[15] It seems best to conclude that Saul's "change of heart" produced no lasting inner transformation or regeneration in Saul.

The purpose of the Spirit's coming on Saul initially and again in 1 Samuel 11:6 before battle seems to have been twofold. First, the charismatic demonstration of prophesying and the new boldness against Yahweh's enemies gave proof that God Himself had chosen this man and was controlling him by His Spirit. It was divine certification to Israel of the newly instituted kingship. As it was noted by Lloyd Neve, "It is necessary that Saul, the first of the monarchs, receive the confirmation of the charismatic spirit."[16]

The second purpose of the Spirit's coming on Saul was that this timid, shy man (9:21), who hid among the baggage (10:21–22) and who had seemed small in his own eyes (15:17), needed to be empowered and ignited with righteous anger to lift the Ammonite siege of Jabesh-gilead (11:1–11). So he received power to wage war and ability to lead Israel—quite similar to the experience of the judges before him. Today, the same Spirit who endued the rustic Gideon and the bashful Saul with power is able to dispel our timidity and give us power and love and self-discipline (2 Tim. 1:7) to engage in spiritual warfare (Eph. 6:10–18).

Saul, however, did not continue to walk steadfastly with the Lord. On more than one occasion he foolishly disobeyed the clear commands of God given him by the old prophet Samuel. Therefore Samuel announced to him that the Lord was seeking to replace Saul with a man after His own heart (1 Sam. 13:13–14) and, later, that God had irrevocably rejected Saul as king (15:26, 28).

As a result the Spirit of the Lord departed from King Saul (1 Sam. 16:14), no longer coming on him to empower him and guide him in battle. This permanent departure probably happened even before young David was anointed for future kingship in a private family ceremony (16:13). The text goes on to tell how a son of Jesse, a brave warrior and skillful musician—namely David—was selected to play in King Saul's court (16:16–22).

Most likely the events of chapter 17, which recounts David's victory over the giant Goliath, took place between 16:13 and 16:14. Thus chapter 17 is a literary flashback to explain how it was that David, who was still only a shepherd boy when he fought Goliath (17:33–34), had become known as a valiant fighting man (16:18).

How could Yahweh, the good and holy God, send an evil spirit to "trouble" (KJV) or "terrorize" (NAS) King Saul (1 Sam. 16:14)? The Hebrew word rāʿah for "evil" basically means "bad" and here could have the sense of producing misery or severe depression. Thus it may not have been a morally evil demon.

Yet even if it were, the omnipotent Sovereign of the universe is ultimately in charge of all spirits including Satan—demonstrated in the case of Job (Job 1:6–12; 2:1–7). Recall the vision of Micaiah, the prophet, in which he saw the Lord send a lying spirit to entice wicked King Ahab into a battle that would eventuate in his death (1 Kings 22:20–22). God was not deceptive; rather Micaiah was warning Ahab of the consequences of refusing to heed God's truth and following the false advice of his four hundred court prophets. God not only permitted the lie; but, as Walter Kaiser has explained, God ordered the king's ruin "by the very instrument Ahab had sought to prostitute for his own purposes, namely, prophecy."[17] God *does* further harden the hearts of willfully disobedient persons, even of pharaohs and kings (Exod. 10:20, 27; 11:10; 14:4; Rom. 9:17–18).

On one subsequent occasion Saul again came under the power of the Spirit of God. The jealous king was pursuing David, who had taken refuge with Samuel at Ramah "in Naioth" (1 Sam. 19:18). The *naioth* were dwellings, perhaps in a compound like an abbey or monastery within the town. Saul sent three teams of messengers (probably hardened soldiers), one after the other, to arrest David. But when each detachment saw the group of prophets and Samuel prophesying, the Spirit of God "came upon" them *(hāyāh* plus *'al;* compare Judges 3:10), and they too began to prophesy.

Finally Saul himself went to Ramah. God's Spirit came even upon him, and he walked along prophesying until he reached the dwellings. Then he too stripped off his clothes as his messengers apparently had done and prophesied in Samuel's presence, falling down and lying naked all that day and night. His conduct reinforced the people's earlier saying: "Is Saul also among the prophets?" (1 Sam. 19:24; 10:11–12). This expression of surprise "underscores how alien Saul's spirit was from that of these zealous servants of the Lord."[18]

Saul's strange behavior is the basis for the claim of some scholars that Old Testament prophesying was an ecstatic experience or trance like that of the heathen prophets of Baal (1 Kings 18:25–29). Leon Wood has argued, however, that the Spirit came on the angry king to change his attitude toward the fugitive David. It was not that Saul became a frenzied ecstatic; rather the supernatural power of the Spirit turned the frustrated ruler into a praising man.[19]

George Montague noted: "Here is surely a manifestation of the Lord's presence and power, particularly as an effective shield for David."[20] The result was somewhat akin to Balaam's experience (see the comment on Numbers 24:2) by which Yahweh protected Israel. But then "Saul was suddenly taken with a sense of extreme melancholy and despair,"[21] and he lay in a stupefied condition for many hours.

How should we interpret this last reaction of Saul? He seems to have been paralyzed by a tremendous conflict between his own inner hostility and his realization of the Lord's holy presence. Certainly this behavior was not typical of the manner in which Yahweh's true prophets received His revelations. Saul's experience is a warning to all who seek to be filled with the Holy Spirit. They should first renounce all anger and resentment toward others as well as any previous involvement with evil spirits or occult practices.

## David's Continuing Anointing—1 Samuel 16:13

When Samuel took the horn of oil and anointed David to be the next king, the Spirit of Yahweh "came mightily upon David from that day forward." Samuel's liturgical act in obedience to the Lord was the occasion for God's supernatural act of sending His Spirit to "come in power upon" David (ṣālaḥ plus 'el; see the comment on Judges 14:6).

Later David was recognized by his troops as the Lord's anointed (2 Sam. 19:21). In several of his psalms David, the king, referred to himself as God's "anointed one" (18:50; 20:6; 28:8). Once God spoke in a vision to His faithful people that He had found David His servant and anointed him with His sacred oil (Ps. 89:19–20, NIV). The coming of the Spirit in power upon David legitimated his kingship spiritually.[22]

While the Spirit's empowerment of David was similar to that of his predecessors (Moses, Joshua, the judges, Samuel, Saul), it was even more extensive in its scope, its continuance, and its significance as a type. In David's case spiritual anointing endowed him with unusual strength and skill for battle. Witness his outstanding victory as a military novice over the Philistine champion Goliath. David also received exceptional ability to lead and rule in righteousness, so much so that all later kings of Israel and Judah were measured by his example (Solomon, 1 Kings 9:4, 6; King Asa, 1 Kings 15:11).

His anointing included the gift of prophecy, described so clearly by him in 2 Samuel 23:1–2: "The anointed of the God of Jacob, and the sweet psalmist of Israel, the Spirit of the LORD spoke by me, and His word was on my tongue." Clearly his musical ability and his writing of half the psalms (according to the

Jewish captions added later) were directed by the Spirit. Furthermore, David displayed an organizational gift from God in his preparations for the temple that his son Solomon would build in Jerusalem and in his selection of the personnel to conduct worship in it (1 Chron. 22–29). The very plan of the building was given him by the Spirit (1 Chron. 28:12, NIV; see the earlier comment in this chapter under "The Period of the Judges and the Early Monarchy").

Because the Spirit came on David "from that day forward," his anointing differed from that of the judges and King Saul in that it did not cease. J. Rodman Williams explained that with David's predecessors the Spirit's endowment was only occasional and temporary: for an emergency, for a specific task or for an utterance; "it was not an abiding reality."[23] Even after David committed adultery with Bathsheba, God did not take His Holy Spirit from him, because he sincerely repented (see the comment on Psalm 51:11).

Not until the coming of the Messiah, *the* anointed One, would anyone again enjoy such continuous anointing. At Jesus' baptism in the River Jordan the Spirit descended on Him and remained upon Him (John 1:32–33). After His ascension, Christ sent the Spirit to anoint all His followers (Luke 24:49; Acts 2:33, 38–39).

With respect to such a broad work of God's Spirit, David was unique among the kings of Israel and Judah. From the time of Solomon, the Spirit is never again specifically mentioned in relation to a reigning monarch. King Jehoshaphat, however, does seem to have identified with and promoted the ministry of the prophets during much of his reign: "Trust firmly in the LORD your God and you will stand firm; trust firmly in His prophets and you will succeed" (2 Chron. 20:20, TAN; compare 2 Chronicles 17–20). Temporary revivals emerged again during the more godly reigns of Hezekiah and Josiah. But apostasy from the covenant faith and spiritual hardening made most of the kings of Judah impervious to the working of God's Spirit.

Because the monarchy could continue simply by hereditary descent of the dynastic line—without any divine infusion—the kingdom of Judah tended to become more and more institutionalized and programmed. As a result the free gift of the Spirit disappeared from the royal government in Jerusalem, to reappear only in the coming Prince (Acts 5:31) in the messianic age.[24]

David alone is the royal prototype of the coming Messiah. The significance of David's anointing as a type is especially obvious. With reference to the covenant promises made to David (2 Sam. 7:12–16), Yahweh says, "I will make a horn sprout for David, I have prepared a lamp for My anointed one" (Ps. 132:17, TAN).

The coronation of every Davidic ruler raised expectations that he might be the Lord's anointed one, the ideal king. By faith it was recognized that God in His foreknowledge had already installed His anointed One, His divine Son as king on Mount Zion (Ps. 2:2, 6–7). The godly element looked in faith for a king who would be God Himself, wielding a scepter of righteousness, anointed by God with the spiritual oil of joy (Ps. 45:6–7). They foresaw a king who would rule with justice and compassion from sea to sea and whom all nations would serve (72:1–15).

The people hoped to the very end that even Zedekiah (the last king of Judah) might have been the Lord's anointed (Lam. 4:20). But neither Solomon nor Hezekiah nor any other descendant of David fulfilled those inspired descriptions before the dynasty collapsed. Both Jehoiachin and Zedekiah were taken captive to Babylon (2 Kings 24:12–15; 25:6–7). The signet ring had been removed from Judah (Jer. 22:24–30).

Yet even while hope flickered and died, the prophets were foreseeing a future David (Hos. 3:5; Jer. 30:9; Ezek. 34:23–24; 37:24–27). In him God's covenant promises would be fulfilled: David's house (dynastic line), his kingdom and his throne were established forever (2 Sam. 7:16; compare Isaiah 55:3–4). He would be Immanuel (Isa. 7:14), the Son given to us to reign on David's throne (9:6–7), the shoot that would sprout from Jesse's stump (11:1).

On Him the Spirit of the Lord would rest and remain (Isa. 11:2). Without hesitancy we may identify Him with Isaiah's Servant of the Lord. He would be God's chosen One, upon whom He would put His Spirit (42:1). He is heard in prophecy testifying: "The Spirit of the Lord GOD is upon me, because the LORD has anointed me" (61:1). He is Messiah the Prince ("the anointed leader," TAN) in Daniel's vision of the seventy weeks (Dan. 9:25–26), the Son of Man to whom the Ancient of Days has given everlasting dominion (Dan. 7:13–14).

Only Jesus of Nazareth can rightfully claim that He is this Messiah: the Christ, the anointed of God (Luke 4:16–21; Matt. 16:16–17; John 4:25–26), the suffering Servant of the Lord (Matt. 12:15–21; 20:28), the Son of David (Matt. 20:30–32; 22:41–45), the King of Israel (John 1:49–51; 18:33–37), the Son of Man and the Son of God (Matt. 26:63–64; Mark 8:31, 38; 14:61–62).

## David's Relationship to the Holy Spirit—Psalm 51:11

In Psalm 51 David cried out to the Lord in an intensely personal prayer of confession after his sin with Bathsheba:

> A pure heart create for me, O God,
>     and a steadfast spirit renew within me.
> Do not cast me away from Thy presence,
>     and Thy holy Spirit do not take from me.
> Restore to me the joy of Thy salvation,
>     and may a willing spirit sustain me.
>     —VV. 10–12, AUTHOR'S TRANSLATION FOLLOWING
>       APPROXIMATE HEBREW WORD ORDER)

The literary structure of these three verses in the original language is striking because the second line of each verse begins in identical fashion with the conjunction "and" plus the noun for "spirit," *wěrûaḥ,* followed by the modifying adjective—hence, "and spirit, a steadfast one"; "and Spirit, Thy holy One"; "and spirit, a willing one." We may observe a very close association between David's own human spirit and heart, which needed renewal, and God's perfect "holy" Spirit. David evidently had a keen awareness of the near presence of God's Spirit (see also Psalm 139:7).

We New Testament believers in Jesus are apt to become curious about the spiritual state of David and the other Old Testament believers in Yahweh. Was it possible for them to be spiritually renewed—"born again"—before Jesus came and died for our sins and rose from the tomb? If so, were they indwelt by the Spirit of God as New Testament believers are now indwelt by the Holy Spirit (Rom. 8:9, 11)?

As we meditate on the psalms and scriptural accounts of Abraham, Moses, Elijah, Elisha, Isaiah, Jeremiah and Daniel, we are constrained to believe that those spiritual giants walked with the Lord in a closeness of fellowship that all too few Christians know today. God certainly intended for the Israelites to experience spiritual life under the Sinaitic covenant. At the end of his lifework Moses urged the people to renew their commitment to Yahweh:

> The LORD your God will circumcise your heart... [to enable you] to love the LORD your God with all your heart and with all your soul, in order that you may live .... I have set before you life and death, the blessing and the curse. So choose life in

order that you may live, you and your descendants, by loving the LORD your God, by obeying His voice, and by holding fast to Him; for this [or He] is your life and the length of your days, that you may live in the land which the LORD swore to your fathers, to Abraham, Isaac, and Jacob, to give them.

—DEUTERONOMY 30:6, 19–20

Surely Moses indicated more than mere physical existence when he exhorted Israel to choose life. He was reminding them of their continuing, living covenant relationship with Yahweh to be expressed through willing obedience to the word of God (Deut. 4:1–2; 32:46–47).

Abraham and David were both justified by faith according to the apostle Paul (Rom. 4:1–9). He referred his readers to Genesis 15:6 concerning Abraham's faith and to Psalm 32:1–2 concerning David's being forgiven. Abraham furthermore was called "the father of us all" (Rom. 4:11, 16), the spiritual "father" of all who believe in the Lord. Therefore we may conclude Abraham was a saved man, himself spiritually alive unto God. This conclusion is enhanced by the examples of all the other Old Testament heroes mentioned in Hebrews 11, the great faith chapter.

Salvation and redemption in the Old Testament went far beyond deliverance from danger and political oppression. It included God's forgiving the iniquities of His people (Ps. 85:2; 86:5; 103:3, 12; 130:3–4), spiritual security in God their refuge and strength (Ps. 46:1–3; 91; 125:1–2), and their joy in the Lord (Ps. 16:11; 21:6; Jer. 15:16). Yahweh declared He would bring back the Jewish exiles from Babylon and give them a heart to know Him; He further promised, "They will be My people, and I will be their God, for they will return to Me with their whole heart" (Jer. 24:7).

The Old Testament saints, then, did experience a genuine spiritual change of heart equivalent to regeneration. God had made provision for atonement for sins through blood sacrifices (Lev. 16:15–34; 17:11) and called on people to repent (Ezek. 18:30–32). Therefore genuine forgiveness was available even before the cross.

David's plea not to take the Holy Spirit from him (Ps. 51:11) raises the question, Did the Holy Spirit indwell David? While there is ample evidence, as we have just seen, that people in Old Testament times could be forgiven of their sins and brought to spiritual life and fellowship with God, there is little reason to believe that the Spirit of God lived *in* such people to maintain their walk with Yahweh (see earlier comments in this chapter under "The Era of

Charismatic Leadership").

Psalm 51 suggests that David was deeply concerned not only about his personal relationship with God but also his public ministry to the Lord and to His people (vv. 13, 18–19). As the chosen and anointed king, David was the servant of Yahweh (2 Sam. 3:18; 7:5, 8, 19–29; Ps. 78:70; 89:20). He was the Lord's representative, ruling as His regent or deputy over the theocratic kingdom.

In the ancient world, including Israel, kingship was considered to be sacral—a sacred, ritual office that was part of the official religion—as well as a political position. As Yahweh's anointed, the king's person was considered to have an imputed sacredness that must not be violated (1 Sam. 24:6; 26:9). Therefore David was praying that he might continue to be maintained in the divine presence by God's Holy Spirit, who alone enables us to enter and dwell in that holy nearness (Ps. 15; 20:1–5; 21:1–6; 27:1–6).

David could vividly remember the terrible example of King Saul, from whom the Spirit of the Lord had departed (1 Sam. 16:14). Realizing the official as well as the private nature of his sin, David prayed that God would not take His Spirit from him and remove his qualification for his kingly office. In contrast to Samson's occasional anointing, David recognized that he needed the Spirit's continual anointing for special empowerment in order to rule the nation.[25]

Furthermore, as king and leader, David knew he needed the provision of divine guidance by God's Spirit for himself and for the nation (compare Psalm 143:10).[26] Likewise Yahweh had led His people by His Holy Spirit in the days of Moses (Isa. 63:10–14—the only other Old Testament passage in which the term "Holy Spirit" occurs).

We may conclude that the question of the indwelling of the Holy Spirit in Old Testament times is not given a "yes" answer by David's plea in Psalm 51:11. Two prophets who speak of the empowering and prophetic ministry of the Spirit of the Lord in their own lives are Micah (3:8) and Ezekiel (2:2; 3:24; 11:5, 24). In neither one does the Spirit seem to abide permanently to sustain spiritual life and fellowship with God (see chapter 4, "The Era of Prophetic Announcements to Israel"). The indwelling of the Holy Spirit in believers is the wonderful provision of our risen Lord Jesus Christ as a fundamental feature of the new creation, the chief means of grace for spiritual life furnished in the New Covenant (see the comments on John 7:37–39; 14:15–18; 20:21–23).[27]

## *The Beginnings of Charismatic Worship—1 Chronicles 25:1-7*

One of David's greatest accomplishments as king was the preparation he made for the public worship of Israel in Jerusalem. In addition to providing the plans and building materials for the temple his son Solomon was to construct, he organized and instructed singers and musicians to lead the nation in praise and thanksgiving. This was a new element in public worship not previously included in the rituals instituted by Moses and Aaron.

The house of the Lord signified the presence of Yahweh at the very seat of Israel's government. Its location next to the royal palace, with its inner courtyard higher on Mount Moriah than the great courtyard of the palace buildings (1 Kings 7:12; 2 Chron. 3:1), demonstrated Yahweh's sovereignty over the Davidic kings. Here the Lord was considered to be enthroned between the cherubim (2 Kings 19:15, NIV).

The dedication of the temple was the greatest religious event in Israelite history after the exodus from Egypt and the giving of the Law at Mount Sinai. King Solomon led the procession of the entire assembly of Israel to bring the ark of the covenant up from David's temporary tent (2 Sam. 6:17) to the newly finished temple (1 Kings 8:3-6). As the glory cloud of God's presence had filled the tabernacle upon its completion (Exod. 40:34), so now the glory of Yahweh filled the temple to indicate He had come to take up His abode among His people: "The cloud filled the house of the LORD, so that the priests could not stand to minister because of the cloud, for the glory of the LORD filled the house of the LORD" (1 Kings 8:10-11). What cause for heartfelt praise and worship!

The formal worship ritual of the people of Israel was based on their already existing relationship with Yahweh established in the Abrahamic and Mosaic covenants. Their sacrifices and offerings were those prescribed in Leviticus 1-7 and were often brought with accompanying shouts of joy and singing (Ps. 27:6). Another essential aspect of spiritual worship was prayer. As so many of the psalms reveal, the people directed their prayers to the God whom they knew to be "supremely great and supremely good."[28]

David added a new feature to the prescribed worship of Yahweh—music. He organized Levites into singing groups (1 Chron. 15:16) and devised musical instruments for giving praise (23:5; compare Amos 6:5). He and his officers selected certain Levites to take charge of the ministry of prophesying to the accompaniment of the musical instruments (1 Chron. 25:1-7). Verse 3 makes it clear that such prophesying consisted in giving thanks and praising the Lord. While training and supervision were involved, no doubt both the content and the expression of such worshipful music were often extemporaneous, prompted by the Spirit as in the case of "spiritual songs" in the New Testament churches (see the comment on Ephesians 5:15–21).

The new emphasis on musical instruments and song in official worship began, without much precedent, as a spontaneous move of God's Spirit.[29] Of course, the people of Israel had been singing songs of praise to Yahweh ever since the days of Moses and Miriam (Exod. 15:1–22). Also, Samuel's young prophets came prophesying with instruments (1 Sam. 10:5). But inspired music and singing had never been part of legitimate tabernacle worship.

The highest times of praise came no doubt during the annual pilgrim festivals. Large numbers would stream to Jerusalem (Ps. 84:5–11; 2 Chron. 30:1). The throng would march in procession with shouts of joy and thanksgiving (Ps. 42:4; Isa. 30:29) and enter the temple gates with praise (Ps. 100:4). Sacred dance (in the style of folk dancing) was also a recognized part of the processions and public worship (2 Sam. 6:14; Ps. 30:11; 149:3; 150:4; Jer. 31:12–14).

Spiritual expressions of worship, together with the Mosaic law and prophecy, form Israel's greatest contribution to humankind—all because they are from the heart of God.

### The Spirit of God and Wisdom—Proverbs 1:20–23

Wisdom is personified as Lady Wisdom in Proverbs 1:20–23; 7:4; 8:1–36 and 9:1–6. The Hebrew word ḥokmāh, a feminine noun, denotes practical, moral intelligence based on the revealed will of a holy God. Lady Wisdom is contrasted with the woman Folly (9:13–18), who was depicted as an adulteress, "wayward wife" (NIV) or "forbidden woman" (TAN) in 7:5.

In 1:20, Wisdom is seen lifting her voice in the public square to warn the naive and the scoffer. She says to those who do turn to her reproof, "I will pour out my spirit (rûḥî) on you; I will make my words known to you" (1:23). Because most people foolishly ignore or reject her counsel and do not choose the fear of the Lord, they will eat the fruit of their own way and be destroyed by their complacency (1:24–32). But the one who listens to Wisdom receives her "spirit" (that is, an ability to understand and apply her words) and "will live in safety and be at ease, without fear of harm" (1:33, NIV).

While we should not make an exact equation between wisdom and God's

Spirit in the Bible, it is nevertheless clear that true wisdom comes ultimately from God. As Aladair Heron explained, God's wisdom can be spoken of as "a kind of extension of Himself, much as we might speak of the skill of an artist as being expressed (and giving him satisfaction) in what he makes."[30] In the light of Proverbs 8:22–36 this is surely a valid description.

When the ancients encountered superior wisdom, they often were willing to acknowledge it as having a supernatural origin. The pharaoh recognized that it was the Spirit of God who made Joseph so discerning and wise (see the comment on Genesis 41:38). And it was the inspiration of the Almighty that imparted clearer understanding to Elihu's spirit (Job 32:8). Job and his friends probably lived in patriarchal times before Moses, but the Book of Job most likely was written in the Solomonic period, the golden age of Hebrew wisdom literature.

Elihu's experience suggests the possibility of a type of charismatic anointing of individuals in the era prior to Solomon. In fact, the British scholar J. W. McKay has written an article titled "Elihu—A Proto-Charismatic?" He explained that the purpose of Elihu's speeches is "to lift the sufferer into a healing confrontation with the Almighty." He believes Elihu speaks under divine compulsion (Job 32:18–20; 33:3–4, 14–18) like a modern Pentecostal or charismatic Christian who is convinced that God is powerful to intervene, that "belief can be proved by experience, particularly in a healing and renewing experience of God in his spirit."[31]

Elihu's part is to lead Job into a renewing encounter with God by drawing Job's mind from his afflictions to God's righteousness (Job 33:8–36:21) and to God's majesty (36:22–37:24). In this way he prepares Job for the appearance of the Lord in the storm (chap. 38–41). The result is that Job's questions about divine injustice are finally forgotten. He is truly caught up in wonder and praise as he "sees" God and repents in dust and ashes (42:6). The charismatic believer today should likewise lead others to praise and magnify the Lord.

Much of the practical wisdom in the common lore of the ancient Near East is found restated in the Old Testament. But Israel excelled the other nations in that its wisdom and understanding were derived primarily from the statutes and judgments of Yahweh's Torah (from *yārāh*, "to instruct") or "law" (Deut. 4:5–8). And Solomon, the author of many of the proverbs in the Old Testament (Prov. 1:1; 10:1; 25:1; 1 Kings 4:32), had asked for and received from God a wise and discerning mind to be able to distinguish right from wrong and to govern his people with justice (1 Kings 3:5–12; 4:29–34; 10:4–9).

Not surprisingly, Jewish wisdom literature has as its theme "The fear of the LORD is the beginning of wisdom" (Prov. 9:10; 1:7; Job 28:28; Ps. 111:10; compare Ecclesiastes 12:13). Awe, respect and reverence for God as the sovereign creator and covenant Lord are the basic ingredients of true wisdom.

In the New Testament, James contrasts the wisdom from above with earthly, natural, demonic wisdom (James 3:13–18). The Holy Spirit is the Spirit of truth (John 14:17) who guides us into all the truth (John 16:13). Paul prayed that Christians would be given a spirit (or spiritual sensitivity) able to receive wisdom and revelation concerning God and His glorious plan of redemption (Eph. 1:17). Such comprehension of the wisdom of God can only be a work of the Spirit of God (1 Cor. 2:6–16).

Returning to the poetic words of Proverbs 1:23, we are given a beautiful picture of divine wisdom pouring out its spirit in words of advice and comfort to us. The verb *nābaʿ*, "pour out," implies that wisdom's spirit will gush forth and overflow in a mighty stream. The verb is used elsewhere of the mouth "spouting" or "gushing" folly and evil words (Prov. 15:2, 28). Proverbs 18:4 describes the words of a person's mouth in similar terms: "deep waters," that is, revealing profound plans (compare 20:5); a "bubbling brook" (*naḥal nōbēaʿ*), that is, an overflowing stream of refreshing ideas; a "fountain of wisdom," that is, communicating to others the life and wisdom of God (compare 10:11, 31; 13:14; Psalm 36:9; Jeremiah 2:13). The RSV translates *nābaʿ* as "pour forth" praise in Psalm 119:171 and "pour forth" the fame of God's abundant goodness in 145:7.

Thus the figurative description of wisdom in Proverbs 1:23 anticipates the prophecies concerning the outpouring of the Holy Spirit as well as the charismatic outpouring of words through which the Spirit expresses Himself.[32]

# FOUR

# The Era of Prophetic Announcements to Israel
## (1000–400 B.C.)

From the middle of David's reign onward the Israelite kings seldom seemed disposed to hear the voice of God directly. But God was not finished speaking to them or to His people. Instead, He selected special men and women to be prophets and anointed them with His Spirit to speak for Him to the rulers and their subjects.

In the Bible the prophet is one called by God to speak for God. The Hebrew word for "prophet" is *nābîʾ*. While the origin of the word is not certain, it may have been derived from an old Semitic word root known in Akkadian as *nabû*, "to call"; hence one who is called (by God). At any rate, the Old Testament usage of the word is clarified in a couple of passages concerning Moses.

The first such passage follows God's command to Moses to go speak to Pharaoh. Moses complained that his speech was impeded so that Pharaoh would not listen to him (Exod. 6:29–30). Yahweh replied, "See, I place you in the role of God to Pharaoh, with your brother Aaron as your prophet. You shall repeat all that I command you, and your brother Aaron shall speak to Pharaoh to let the Israelites depart from his land" (7:1–2, TAN; compare 4:15–16). A *nābîʾ* is clearly a person authorized to speak for another.

In the second passage (Deut. 18:9–22) Yahweh made a formal announcement of the office of *nābîʾ*, which was to continue after Moses. God prohibited any consultation by Israelites with the Canaanite sorcerers and their occult practices (18:9–14). Instead, He would raise up a series of prophets who, like Moses, would speak in Yahweh's name, and He would give them His revelation (18:15–22).

In 18:18 the essential nature of the work of a true prophet is clearly stated: "I will raise up a prophet from among their countrymen like you, and I will put My words in his mouth, and he shall speak to them all that I command him." While the description is of only one prophet, it is obviously a collective reference to all the genuine prophets of the Lord who will follow. As Edward J. Young, one of America's finest Old Testament scholars, explained, we should regard the prophet described in 18:15–19 as "an ideal person in whom are comprehended all true prophets. The prophetical order is thus an ideal unity, which is to find its focus point in the historic Christ. For the Spirit of Christ was [upon] all the true prophets."[1]

On the basis of Deuteronomy 18:15–18, many Jews by New Testament times were expecting "the Prophet" to appear at any moment (John 1:21; 6:14; 7:40). The Jews generally understood the Prophet to be the forerunner of the Messiah (John 1:21–25). The apostles, however, preached that Jesus Himself, the Messiah, was the Prophet (Acts 3:20–26).

During the Old Testament period the prophets of the Lord performed various duties. The prophets' chief function was not so much to foretell the future as to "tell forth" the warnings of God to His people regarding their covenant responsibilities. This Spirit-led activity was clearly recognized by Ezra in his national prayer of confession:

> In your compassion you delivered them time after time. You warned them to return to your law, but they became arrogant and disobeyed your commands . . . . For many years you were patient with them. By your Spirit you admonished them through your prophets. Yet they paid no attention, so you handed them over to the neighboring peoples.
>
> —NEHEMIAH 9:28–30, NIV

Many of those prophets suffered greatly from their own countrymen for their obedience to the Lord. Some, like Jeremiah, were threatened, beaten and imprisoned (Jer. 20:2; 26:8–15; 32:2–5; 37:14–16; 38:1–13; Heb. 11:36). Others were assassinated (Luke 11:47–51; Matt. 23:31, 37). For example, during the reign of King Joash in Judah, the people reverted to idolatry after the death of the godly old priest Jehoiada (about 800 B.C.). So Yahweh sent prophets to them to bring them back to Him. Though the prophets testified against them, the people would not listen (2 Chron. 24:15–19).

Then the Spirit of God "came on" *(lābĕšāh)* Zechariah, the son of Jehoiada the priest, as upon Gideon of old (Judg. 6:34). He stood above the people and declared, "This is what God says: 'Why do you disobey the LORD's commands? You will not prosper. Because you have forsaken the LORD, He has forsaken you'" (2 Chron. 24:20, NIV). But they conspired against Zechariah and by order of the king stoned him to death in the courtyard of the temple.

Throughout the prophetic era the primary activity of God's Spirit that is noted with regard to Israel was the inspiration, the breathing forth, of Yahweh's word through His servants the prophets (2 Kings 17:23; 21:10; 24:2; see also the Introduction [page 3] and the comment on 2 Peter 1:19–21). A passage in the Book of Zechariah states this very clearly: "But they refused to pay attention. . . . They made their hearts as hard as flint and would not listen to the law or to the words that the LORD Almighty had sent by his Spirit through the earlier prophets" (Zech. 7:11–12, NIV). The preposition "through" in the last phrase of verse 12 is *bĕyad,* "by the hand of," which covers the writing as well as the spoken ministry of the prophets.

Some of the prophets kept the royal annals and wrote the history of their country (2 Chron. 12:15; 26:22; 32:32). On occasion they acted as advisors, and even as critics, of the kings. Prophets also expounded the true meaning of the Law of Moses and exhorted the people to live by it as opposed to mere formal observance of it (for example, Isaiah 1:10–20; 58:1–7; Jeremiah 7:1–15, 21–26; Micah 6:6–8).

The prophets preached true patriotism, which actually meant covenant faithfulness. In times of crisis they sought to maintain the morals of the nation as a whole through the word of promise and hope. But when their message was slighted or rejected by the majority they did not stop; they appealed to the godly remnant of Israel (Amos 5:14–15; Mic. 2:12–13; 4:7; 5:7–8; 7:18). Truly there is much in the lives of these servants of Yahweh for us to emulate today as servants of Christ.

## Elijah, the Model Prophet

The next great prophet after Moses was Samuel. He was revered as such by later generations (2 Chron. 35:18; Ps. 99:6; Jer. 15:1; Acts 3:24; 13:20; Heb. 11:32; see also chapter 3 under "The Period of the Judges and the Early Monarchy"). Yet it was not Samuel but Elijah who was the representative of the prophetic movement in the Old Testament.

Apparently there was never an hereditary office of prophet. The only known instance of both father and son being a prophet or seer is that of Hanani (2 Chron. 16:7) and his son Jehu (1 Kings 16:1–7; 2 Chron. 19:2f.; 20:34). Neither of Samuel's sons, dishonest as they were, succeeded him as a prophet in Israel (1 Sam. 8:1–5). After Samuel died, the company of young prophets he directed (1 Sam. 10:5, 10; 19:20) seems to have dispersed. Not until the time of Elijah and Elisha do we read of similar training communities. The members of these "schools" were known as "sons" or disciples of the prophets (1 Kings 18:4; 20:35; 2 Kings 2:3, 5, 7; 4:1, 38; 6:1–7). During the intervening period from Samuel to Elijah, however, there were God-appointed individuals who performed the work of a prophet such as Gad, Nathan, Shemaiah and Ahijah.

God sovereignly raised up Elijah to be the spiritual leader in a time of extreme apostasy. Elijah became the model or pattern of all prophets after Moses. Proof of this role is the appearance together of Moses and Elijah, respectively representing the Law and the prophets of the Old (Sinaitic) Covenant, with Jesus on the Mount of Transfiguration.

Elijah and his protégé Elisha were truly charismatic individuals similar to the judges and Samuel. Yet Scripture seldom refers specifically to God's Spirit in connection with their ministries and never mentions that they "prophesied." There are, however, a number of indications of supernatural activity in their careers.

The many miracles they performed testify to this fact. Obadiah, a servant of King Ahab, believed that the Spirit of Yahweh would carry Elijah away, so that Ahab could not find him (1 Kings 18:12). The company of the prophets from Jericho likewise believed that the Spirit of Yahweh had supernaturally lifted Elijah to some remote mountain or valley (2 Kings 2:16). These two incidents suggest that the prophets were familiar with, and may have actually experienced, bodily transportation by the Spirit, as in the case of Philip the evangelist (Acts 8:39).

Presumably God's Spirit rested upon Elijah quite continuously, as He did upon Moses and David. Elisha had ample opportunity to see the Spirit move through his master. Therefore at the time of Elijah's translation to heaven the younger man asked, "Let a double portion of your spirit be upon me" (2 Kings 2:9; see the comment on 2 Kings 2:1–18). Elisha's subsequent ministry is testimony that there was indeed a transference of spiritual power and prophetic authority.

Elijah preceded the great writing prophets who later denounced the iniquity and idolatry of both Israel and Judah. He refused to identify himself with the apostate shrines at Dan and Bethel set up by Jeroboam I (1 Kings 12:26–33). At Mount Carmel he was Yahweh's agent to rebuke and judge the prophets of the Canaanite god Baal.

The twelve stones for his altar represented the twelve tribes of Israel (1 Kings 18:31; compare the twelve stone pillars Moses erected around the altar he built at the foot of Mount Sinai, Exodus 24:4). These stones indicate that Elijah hoped to reunite the monarchy by eradicating Baal worship. It was a crucial period for the kingdom of Judah as well as the kingdom of Israel. At that time the two neighboring kingdoms were allies, and the door was open for Baalism to overwhelm Jerusalem as well as Samaria (compare Elijah's letter written to King Jehoram of Judah, 2 Chronicles 21:11–15). Every miracle of Elijah was a polemical attack on the false worship of Baal.

In a number of other ways besides the altar and twelve stones the Bible depicts Elijah as a second Moses. For instance, he too met God at Horeb on Mount Sinai (1 Kings 19:8–18). There was the display of a great and powerful wind (*rûaḥ*), as well as an earthquake and fire (19:11–12a) as in Moses' day (Exod. 19:16–18).

In Elijah's case, however, God's voice (*qôl*) was not thunderous (Exod. 19:19) but was a soft murmuring sound (1 Kings 19:12b, TAN), a still small voice (KJV), a voice (*qôl*) of a gentle whisper (NIV). Yahweh was graciously recommissioning His servant with an exhibition of His *rûaḥ* in power as well as gentleness (19:11–18). Similarly He had shown His Spirit-glory-presence to Moses on the mount (Exod. 33:14–34:7; see chapter 1, "The Nature of God's Spirit") and later manifested His Spirit (*rûaḥ*) upon the seventy elders to encourage the despairing Moses (see the comment on Numbers 11:4–30).

Elijah, then, was the hinge figure or bridge in the prophetic line from Moses to Jesus. He was the one who kept the messianic hope alive during the period of deepest crisis in God's covenant relationship with Israel.

## The Canonical Prophets As "Men of the Spirit"

Oddly enough, the canonical or classical prophets of the Old Testament seldom claim the anointing of God's Spirit for themselves. These are the men, often called the major and minor prophets, whose books were inspired by God and have been accepted by Jews and Christians alike as holy Scripture.

The Roman Catholic scholar George Montague has noted that in the Book of Amos (about 760 B.C.), one of the first of the classical prophets, the concept of the Spirit is "singularly absent."[2] Yet Amos clearly recognized that prophetic revelation comes straight from God:

> Surely the LORD God does nothing
> Unless He reveals His secret counsel
> To His servants the prophets.
> A lion has roared! Who will not fear?
> The Lord GOD has spoken! Who can but prophesy?
>
> —AMOS 3:7–8

Lloyd Neve has observed that no genuine prophet (except Micah) claimed for himself inspiration by the Spirit of Yahweh.[3] The Spirit of God is not mentioned in the writings of Jeremiah, Nahum, Habakkuk and Zephaniah. This absence is especially remarkable in the long book of Jeremiah, who gives more insights into his personal life than does any other prophet. Yet the New Testament clearly states that the Holy Spirit testifies to us regarding the New Covenant as He speaks through the writing of Jeremiah (Heb. 10:15–17, quoting Jeremiah 31:33–34). Jonah and Obadiah also do not mention the Spirit.

This silence about God's Spirit by the pre-exilic prophets in Judah seems to have been a safeguard against their being wrongly identified with their false prophet contemporaries. It was, as Montague explained, a reaction on the part of God's true servants "to the non-rational seizures or trances with which the professional prophets had come to be identified."[4] Those ecstatic prophets often "raved" on (*hithnabbēʾ*) like the prophets of Baal (1 Kings 18:29; 22:10; Jer. 23:13; Ezek. 13:17). Neve termed them *rûaḥ* prophets, "windy" prophets, on the basis of Jeremiah 5:13: "The prophets are as wind (*rûaḥ*), and the word is not in them."[5]

The Lord subsequently explained to Jeremiah, "The prophets are prophesying falsehood in My name. I have neither sent them nor commanded them nor spoken to them; they are prophesying to you a false vision, divination, futility and the deception of their own minds" (14:14). God's most lengthy and scathing denunciation of these prophets is found in Jeremiah 23:9–40:

They are godless and adulterers; they strengthen the hands of evildoers rather than turning them from wickedness. Instead of standing in the council of Yahweh to hear His word, they say, "I had a dream!" and prophesy their lying dreams to make His people forget His name. No wonder, then, that Jeremiah emphasized the word of Yahweh (well over a hundred times; for example, 1:2, 4, 9; 15:16; 23:28–30) rather than the Spirit.

In spite of their reluctance to discuss their spiritual empowerment the prophets were by and large the only genuine charismatics during the divided monarchy period. They were the ones who could truly be called "men of the Spirit." This expression is suggested by a literal rendition of *'îš hārûaḥ,* "man of the Spirit," in Hosea 9:7 (NAS, marginal note). Apparently this was a popular description of a prophet in those days.

Hosea warned Israel that the time of their punishment was coming soon (9:7a). The proof of their rejection of Yahweh was heard in their contempt for His true prophet (which Hosea quotes):

> [You] the prophet [are] a fool,
> the man of the Spirit—insane,
> Because of your great iniquity
> and great hostility!
>
> —HOSEA 9:7B, AUTHOR'S TRANSLATION

Hosea countered their abusive language regarding himself:

> The prophet, along with my God,
> is the watchman over Ephraim,
> yet snares await him on all his paths,
> and hostility in the house of his God.
>
> —HOSEA 9:8, NIV

Thus Hosea was recording his own experience of hostile opposition by the Baal worshipers of the Northern Kingdom. Similarly when Micaiah, a prophet of Yahweh a century earlier, had opposed the joint military campaign of Ahab and Jehoshaphat, he was slapped on the cheek by Zedekiah, the leader of Ahab's four hundred prophets. Zedekiah said derisively, "How did the Spirit of the LORD pass from me to speak to you?" (1 Kings 22:24). This very mockery indicates a common belief that God's Spirit did speak to and through His prophets.

Micah and his fellow prophets faced much of the same heckling from the citizenry of Judah regarding their preaching:

> "Stop preaching!"—they preach on.
>     "You should not preach about such things;
> [If you do] disgrace will not leave [us]."
>
> —MICAH 2:6, AUTHOR'S TRANSLATION

Micah replied, referring to their further objection that it was not God's normal way of doing things to become peevish and for His Spirit to lose patience with His covenant people:

> Should this be said, O house of Jacob:
>     "Has the Spirit of Yahweh lost patience?
> Are these His doings?"
>
> —MICAH 2:7A, AUTHOR'S TRANSLATION

The Lord then intervened in defense of His prophet:

> Do not My words have good results
>     for him who walks uprightly?
>
> —MICAH 2:7B, AUTHOR'S TRANSLATION

Notice that while the populace as a whole did not enjoy being accused of wicked schemes (Mic. 2:1–5), it nevertheless recognized that the Spirit of Yahweh did work through His prophets. But the people expected Him to pronounce only kindness and never judgment on them, no matter what their conduct might have been. There is a similar tendency today in some charismatic circles to limit genuine New Testament prophesying to positive messages which only upbuild and comfort and never rebuke or warn.

In rebuking the leaders of his nation, Micah pronounced Yahweh's condemnation of the false prophets who were leading His people astray (3:5–7). Those deceiving prophets, who practiced divination and gave messages only when they were paid well, would get no answer from God and thus be put to shame. Micah then was provoked into contrasting his own experience as a prophet who did have the Lord's anointing:

> But as for me, I am full of power—
>     with-the-help-of ['et] the Spirit of Yahweh—

> and of judgment and courage,
> to declare to Jacob his rebellion
> even to Israel his sin.
>
> —MICAH 3:8, AUTHOR'S TRANSLATION

Micah claimed that he consistently received power (*kōăḥ*) from Yahweh. In the second line the Hebrew word *'et* is understood to be a preposition meaning "by" or "with the help of," as in Genesis 4:1 when Eve said, "I have gotten a manchild with the help of the LORD." The literal meaning indicates that Micah was not claiming to be filled with the Spirit in the New Testament sense. But he did testify of judgment (*mišpāt*) and courage (*gĕbûrāh*—valor, strength of resolve) to speak boldly in Yahweh's name, unpopular though his message might have been.[6]

In similar fashion Isaiah described Yahweh as being "a spirit of judgment for him who sits in judgment and of valor [*gĕbûrāh*] for those who repel attacks at the gate" (28:6, TAN). This same holy boldness or confidence is a mark of those anointed with the Holy Spirit from Pentecost onward in the early church (Acts 4:13, 29, 31; 14:3).[7]

Ezekiel was the only other prophet who described the operation of the Spirit in his life and ministry. Transplanted into a new environment, he could feel at liberty to speak freely of the Spirit of God.[8] It was his mission to explain the purposes and workings of the sovereign Yahweh to the disillusioned Jewish exiles in Babylon and to rally their hopes. He insisted that God had not forgotten His covenants nor abandoned His people. God was with them in their captivity.

In a remarkable vision, Ezekiel saw four living beings (1:5–11), which were cherubim (compare 10:9–15). They were directed by *the* Spirit [*hārûaḥ*; note the definite article in 1:12, 20]. Each of the beings controlled one of the four wheels of a vehicle that seemed to be supporting the heavenly throne of God. From the highly mobile throne His radiant glory-presence shone forth like a beautiful rainbow (1:26–28). The significance seems to be that Yahweh is free to move instantly by His Spirit anywhere in His universe for covenant dealings with His people.

Undoubtedly the reader was expected to identify the Spirit mentioned in chapter 1 with the Spirit who entered Ezekiel and set him on his feet (2:2; 3:24). The Spirit on certain occasions also lifted him up and carried him away in a vision (3:12, 14; 8:3; 11:1, 24; 43:5). That God's Spirit is meant is certain from 11:5: "Then the Spirit of the LORD fell upon me."[9]

The entrance of the Spirit into Ezekiel (2:2) did not result in continuous indwelling because the same act was repeated in 3:24. The permanent indwelling of the Spirit that Jesus promised is a feature only of the New Covenant. The purpose of the Spirit's activity with Ezekiel was to enable him to prophesy by receiving and speaking forth the word of Yahweh (3:24–27).

Ezekiel's statement in 11:5 that the Spirit of Yahweh "fell upon" (a form of *nāphal* plus *'al*) him and spoke to him is unique in the Old Testament. It describes an action like that of the Holy Spirit falling upon Cornelius and his household (see the comment on Acts 10:44–48). The use of the verb *nāphal* by Ezekiel may be compared with the hand of the Lord falling upon Ezekiel as he was sitting in his house (8:1). Also it is said in 1 Kings 18:38 that the fire of the Lord fell and consumed both Elijah's burnt offering and the altar he built. Both were one-time acts.

The falling of the Spirit on Ezekiel, then, does not seem to denote indwelling, as some scholars such as Leon Wood have claimed. Wood, however, did help us understand the incident by stating that the Spirit came on Ezekiel to tell him what to say.[10] It was an act of prophetic inspiration.

In an enlightening chapter on the prophetic experience, Wood generalized from the experiences of Ezekiel and others to explain how the true prophet received divine revelation. There is no indication of the prophet's working himself into an ecstatic frenzy; rather he was influenced from the outside by the Spirit of God. Wood described the process in detail:

> Reason was transcended, while it still retained its natural power. There was a contact with the divine, without any negation of the human. The human mind was enabled to move beyond its finite limitations and come away from the moment knowing more than it had before. The center of the experience was always the "word" of God. A message was communicated, and the prophet was convinced that God had spoken it. Afterwards, he would go forth and assert without hesitation, "Thus saith the LORD."[11]

Like the other prophets, Ezekiel was appointed by Yahweh to be a watchman to the house of Israel: "Whenever you hear a word from My mouth, warn them from Me" (3:17; compare 33:7). In spite of much backsliding or apostasy on Israel's part (Jer. 3:6–13), Yahweh would not forsake His covenant promises to Abraham. The Lord had said that through Abraham's seed He would bless all the families of the earth (Gen. 12:3).

But the nation of Israel kept on breaking the covenant God made with them at Sinai until finally He fulfilled the curses their disobedience evoked (Deut. 28:15–68). He had warned them again and again by His messenger-watchmen. But they kept mocking His prophets and despising His words until His anger was aroused and there was no remedy (2 Chron. 36:15–16).

Nevertheless, prior to, during and after the Babylonian exile, God made repeated announcements through His prophets that He would anoint a descendant of David to be His representative king. Through that individual, Yahweh would re-establish His rule over His chosen people, and He would send forth His renewing Spirit worldwide. Thereby Yahweh would consummate His government of all the earth.

### Elijah's Translation and Elisha's Anointing—2 Kings 2:1–18

"And it came about when the LORD was about to take up Elijah by a whirlwind to heaven, that Elijah went with Elisha from Gilgal" (2 Kings 2:1). Webster's first meaning of the verb *translate* is "to change from one place, position, or condition to another; transfer; specifically . . . to convey to heaven, originally without death."[12]

Elisha, chosen by God to be Elijah's successor (1 Kings 19:16), had often observed the remarkable power of his master's ministry. Now the time of Elijah's departure was at hand (for this expression see 2 Timothy 4:6b, KJV). Therefore Elisha requested, "Let a double portion in-the-form-of-your-spirit (*bĕrûḥăkā*) pass on to me" (2 Kings 2:9, literal translation).

That Elisha was indeed referring to the Spirit of God is indicated by the observation of the young prophets from Jericho later that day: "The spirit of Elijah rests on [*nāḥāh* plus *'al*] Elisha!" (2:15). Surely those disciples were talking about the divine Spirit who so frequently manifested Himself through their now-departed teacher (see the comment on Luke 1:13–17). The same Hebrew verb-and-preposition combination is used of the Spirit of the Lord in Numbers 11:25 and Isaiah 11:2 (see the comments on those passages).

Elisha was not asking for two times the amount of anointing by the Spirit that Elijah had, but for the double portion of the first-born principal heir (Deut. 21:17). He was asking for the right to be Elijah's chief successor in his ministry and in leadership of the schools of the prophets.[13] It was a noble task that he desired (compare 1 Timothy 3:1, RSV, NIV). Elisha also needed the assurance of the special empowerment of Yahweh's Spirit to be able to face the continuing challenge of Baalism.[14] Elisha was careful to follow Elijah's last instruction (2 Kings 2:10). He kept his eyes fixed on his master as the older prophet suddenly ascended to heaven. He exclaimed, "My father, my father! Israel's chariotry and horsemen!" (2:12, author's translation), as if to say, "You have been Israel's first line of defense!"

Elisha recognized the great value of his spiritual mentor to himself as well as to the nation as a whole. Because of Elisha's unswerving stand for the Lord, at the end of his career the king of Israel could say the very same thing of him (2 Kings 13:14). Godly ministers are always a nation's "secret weapon" as they lead God's faithful people in spiritual combat against the forces of darkness.

After his exclamation regarding Elijah's worth, Elisha grasped his own clothes and tore them in pieces. He was indicating that he would no longer put any confidence in himself, in his own abilities (compare Ephesians 4:22–24). Instead, he picked up the cloak that had fallen from Elijah. With that garment Elijah had struck the water of the Jordan so that the river divided to allow them to cross on dry ground (2 Kings 2:8), much as Moses had used his staff at the time of Israel's crossing the Red Sea (Exod. 14:16).

Elisha, too, struck the water, and it parted right and left so he could recross the Jordan. His use of this cloak symbolized to one and all that he had succeeded to Elijah's ministry and also demonstrated that the power of the Spirit was now clothing him (as the Spirit of the Lord had clothed Gideon in Judges 6:34). As a result of Pentecost all of Christ's followers may be clothed with this same supernatural power (see the comment on Luke 24:44–53).

## The Spirit of Judgment and Burning—Isaiah 4:4

Isaiah uses the Hebrew word *rûaḥ* fifty times in various ways. In at least a dozen passages it refers to God's Spirit. His first reference to the Spirit of God occurs in a messianic text, Isaiah 4:2–6.

Verse 2 is introduced by the frequently used eschatological term "in that day" (for example, Isaiah 2:11–12, 20; Jeremiah 30:7–8; Zephaniah 3:11, 16; Zechariah 12–14), which indicates the Day of the Lord (*yôm Yahweh*, Isa. 13:6, 9). The Day of the Lord is that future period when God will intervene in the world, first in catastrophic judgment and then in unparalleled blessing. Instead of working providentially as now, He will manifest His awesome presence so unmistakably that it can no longer be called the day of humankind.

"The proud look of man will be abased ... and the LORD alone will be exalted in that day" (Isa. 2:11; compare 2:6–22).

"In that day the Branch of the LORD will be beautiful and glorious" (Isa. 4:2). The Branch (*ṣemaḥ*) is a messianic title (Jer. 23:5; 33:15; Zech. 3:8; 6:12) related to the shoot (*ḥōter*) and branch [*nēṣer*] from the stump and roots of Jesse (Isa. 11:1). Thus the Branch is descended from David. Presumably by the blood of the Lamb, the Lord will wash "away the filth of the daughters of Zion" (4:4a), so that the survivors of Israel will be called holy, even all who are recorded for (eternal) life in Jerusalem (4:2–3).

In 4:4b the Lord says He will cleanse the bloodstains from Jerusalem by "a spirit of judgment and a spirit of fire" (NIV). The twofold use of "spirit" (*rûaḥ*) is most likely a double reference to God's Spirit. The same term "spirit of judgment" (*rûaḥ mišpāṭ*) in Isaiah 4:4 occurs again in 28:5–6, a passage very similar to 4:2–6: In that future day the Lord Himself will be a glorious crown to His remnant people and a spirit of justice and strength to the rulers who must exercise judgment and repel attacks on the city.

In Isaiah's day, as John Oswalt commented, "the kings frequently lacked the nerve to stand up to the vested interests of injustice or to inspire those who faced the enemy."[15] But in the messianic age, God's Spirit will impart wisdom and courage to rule justly to those who reign with Christ (Matt. 19:28; 1 Cor. 6:2). Therefore Isaiah 4:4b must mean that the Lord will purge the blood of all the crimes and warfare in Jerusalem "by His Spirit who administers judgment, yes, the Spirit who dispenses burning" (author's translation).

Fire and burning are terms used symbolically to represent the very character of the righteous, holy God. He manifested Himself in the continuously burning bush to Moses (Exod. 3:2–3) and in the burning fire on Mount Sinai (Deut. 4:11; 5:23; 9:15). He is said to be a consuming fire (Heb. 12:29).

Also note the description of Israel's God in His destruction of Assyria: "The Light of Israel will become a fire, their Holy One a flame" (Isa. 10:17, NIV). Yahweh will smelt away the dross of His people (Isa. 1:25), bringing "the third part" (the surviving remnant) into the fire (Zech. 13:8–9). When the Lord comes back He will be like a refiner's fire; He will purify the descendants of Levi and refine them like gold and silver, so that they may bring offerings in righteousness (Mal. 3:1–4).

The New Testament continues the picture of God coming by His Spirit to purge and purify His people. John the Baptist confessed that the one coming after him would baptize with the Holy Spirit and fire and burn up the useless chaff (see the comment on Matthew 3:11–12). Also the "tongues as of fire" at Pentecost (Acts 2:3) point to God's Spirit coming to purify and enlighten the church.

The closing verses of the Isaiah passage (4:5–6) depict Yahweh creating (Hebrew *bārā'*) a sheltering canopy over the cleansed and perfected remnant. They are assembled on Mount Zion to worship His glorious presence. John sees them as pure and blameless, standing with the Lamb on Mount Zion in the New Jerusalem before God's throne and singing the new song of redemption (Rev. 14:1–5, NIV; compare Isaiah 12:1–6).

The canopy will be a cloud of smoke by day and a glow of flaming fire by night, reminiscent of the pillar of cloud and fire that manifested God's Spirit-presence at the exodus (Exod. 13:21; 14:19–20) and over the tabernacle (Exod. 40:34, 38). Therefore as the Spirit of God was present at the original creation (Gen. 1:2) and at the start of the new creation (John 20:22; 2 Cor. 5:17), we can be certain that at the creation of the new heavens and the new earth (Isa. 65:17–18; compare 41:18–20) the Spirit will be actively present, represented by the glory cloud.

## The Spirit Who Rests on Immanuel—Isaiah 11:2

In studies of Isaiah, chapters 7–12 are often called the Book of Immanuel. The virgin-born son whose name means "God with us" (7:14) is the central figure in this section. His name recurs in 8:8 and in Hebrew in 8:10 as the divine person already existent and watching over His land.

He is the child born to us, the Son given to us, on whose shoulders the government will rest. His four throne names will be Wonderful Counselor, Mighty God, Father of Eternity, Prince of Peace. There will be no end of the extension of His government and peace. He will firmly establish the throne and kingdom of David (compare 2 Samuel 7:12–16) and uphold it with justice and righteousness forever (Isa. 9:6–7).

The ruler of the glorious future age (Isa. 11:1–12) is the Branch stemming from the roots of Jesse (v. 1). He is obviously the same as Immanuel. He will judge the poor with righteousness and decide with equity for the humble people, the meek of the earth (11:3–5). As a result, in that day the meek shall have increasing joy in the Lord, and the needy of humankind will rejoice in the Holy One of Israel (Isa. 29:19). But how can a ruler on earth exercise authority apart from the political intrigues that have bedeviled human governments down through history? His kingship must be more noble than the world has yet seen.

Yes, Immanuel the Messiah *will* govern with perfect justice, because, like David, He will be continuously endued with the Spirit of God:

> The Spirit of Yahweh will rest on Him—
>> the Spirit of wisdom and of understanding,
>> the Spirit of counsel and of might,
>> the Spirit of the knowledge and fear of Yahweh;
> and He will delight in the fear of Yahweh.
>> —ISAIAH 11:2–3A, AUTHOR'S TRANSLATION

The six descriptive terms are not attributes or qualities of the Spirit Himself but fruits or effects of the Spirit's work.[16] It is the fruit that the Messiah will bear (compare 11:1b). As the Servant of the Lord, He will prosper and be successful in His ministry (Isa. 52:13), because God will put His Spirit upon Him (42:1) and anoint Him (61:1).

The reference to the divine Spirit in Isaiah 11:2 is undoubtedly the source of the later expression "the seven Spirits of God" (Rev. 1:4; 3:1; 4:5; 5:6) and of the concept of the sevenfold gifts of the Holy Spirit in church tradition. In the Greek Septuagint and the Latin Vulgate translations, the word "piety" was substituted instead of "the fear of the LORD" in its first occurrence in the passage set forth above (at the end of 11:2), thus bringing the "gifts" to seven by including "the fear of the LORD" from 11:3a.[17]

The central shaft of the Jewish menorah, the seven-branched lampstand of the tabernacle (Exod. 25:31–32), has long been regarded as a symbol of the Spirit of the Lord. The other manifestations of the Spirit are the three pairs of branches: the first, relating to the mind and intellect; the second, relating to practical planning and strength; and the third, relating directly to a person's spiritual relationship with the Lord.

Enablements bestowed temporarily on charismatic leaders and other chosen individuals in earlier times are to be given in full measure to the messianic king. Wisdom and understanding were qualities imparted by God's Spirit to Joseph, Joshua and Elihu. The Spirit of counsel could be a reference to the Spirit resting on the seventy elders to enable them to assist Moses in judging the people. His might (*gĕbûrāh*—strength and courage) reminds us of the valorous deeds of the Spirit-empowered judges.[18] David, the anointed king, testified that he ruled in the fear of God (2 Sam. 23:1–3). The charisma of the Spirit largely disappeared from the line of kings after David; but it will be renewed in the messianic age, both on the Davidic shepherd-king (Ezek. 34:23–24; 37:24–25) and on His followers (Ezek 39:29; Isa. 32:15).

## The Spirit Poured Out From on High—Isaiah 32:15

Isaiah's prophetic announcement of the outpouring of God's Holy Spirit may be the earliest of its kind:

> Until the Spirit is poured out upon us
>     from on high,
> And the wilderness becomes a fertile field
> And the fertile field is considered as a forest.
>
> —ISAIAH 32:15

This verse appears in a section (Isa. 32–35) describing the coming era of renewal and restoration. A king at long last will reign in righteousness, and rulers will rule with justice (32:1, NIV). Therefore the messianic age is in view.

Each of the redeemed will be like the Lord Himself in the sense of providing refuge and shelter to others (32:2; compare 25:4). The redeemed will be like irrigation channels (from Hebrew *peleg*) in a desert (32:2; compare Proverbs 21:1), even as Jesus promised concerning those who would come to drink of Him (see the comment on John 7:37–39).

Before the renewal foretold in Isaiah 32:1–8 can come to Jerusalem and Judah, there must be severe chastening on citizenry (depicted as women) and palace alike (32:9–14). The scheming rulers described in Isaiah 28–31 will *not* bring peace and prosperity to the nation, let alone to the world. Because of their refusal to heed the Lord, He has poured out (*nāsak*) upon them a spirit (*rûaḥ*) of deep sleep (29:10). This spiritual dullness, a hardening in unbelief, has continued among Jewish people from Isaiah's time to Paul's day and until now (Rom. 11:7–8, 25).

Israel's spiritual blindness and complacency would not begin to disappear until another spirit comes, "until a Spirit from on high is emptied upon us" (literal translation). While the Hebrew word for Spirit (*rûaḥ*) has no definite article, it must refer to God's own Spirit because He comes from "on high" (*mārôm*) where God, the high and lofty One, dwells (Isa. 57:15; compare 24:21). God's

Spirit is clearly mentioned two chapters earlier when the leaders of Judah are rebuked for not having sought Yahweh's prophetic word to give direction before planning an alliance with Egypt: "'Woe to the rebellious children,' declares the LORD, 'who … make an alliance, but not of My Spirit'" (30:1).

The action of pouring out (yĕʿāreh) the Spirit is similar to that of Rebekah emptying her jar of water into the trough for the camels (Gen. 24:20). The verb ʿārāh is also used in Isaiah 53:12 of the Servant of the Lord, who poured out or emptied His soul, His very life, unto death, implying a complete giving of Himself (compare Philippians 2:7–8). Thus God has given Himself freely and totally in sending both His Son and His Spirit to us.

This Spirit is seen as the channel of all the eschatological blessings that follow.[19] His outpouring is a distinctive aspect of the new creation. Only God's power can turn the wilderness caused by human wickedness, the desert brought on by human depravity, into a fertile field. As Edward J. Young commented, "Only the Spirit will be able to restore what the sin of man had destroyed."[20]

Isaiah had announced in 29:17 that in a very short time Lebanon with its mighty cedars (depicting world rulers; compare Isaiah 2:13; 10:33–34) would be turned into mere farmland, and the farmland would seem like a scrub thicket (yaʿar, as in Isaiah 21:13; Hosea 2:12; Micah 3:12). In 32:15, Isaiah reversed the metaphor to describe a positive result: Through the Spirit's blessing the desert will become fertile farmland, and farmland will seem like a stately thick forest (yaʿar, as in Isaiah 44:14, 23; Zechariah 11:2; 2 Samuel 18:6–9).

In beautiful poetry the benefits of Immanuel's rule are portrayed. "Just as the Spirit comes upon the Messiah and endues Him so that He judges with righteousness (11:2–5), so also when the Spirit is poured out upon the land, judgment and righteousness dwell therein."[21] The effects of God's righteousness will be peace and lasting security (32:16–17). It is the Spirit who executes in our lives this peace that Christ achieved for us at Calvary (Rom. 5:1; 15:13; see the comment on Romans 14:17). As His flock, God's people will dwell in peaceful pastures and live in undisturbed places of rest (Isa. 32:18).

What God by His Spirit began at Pentecost He will bring to completion when His Spirit-anointed King returns. Then all those reigning with Him will likewise be Spirit-filled, and at last there will be enduring peace.

## The Spirit of Yahweh and the Word of Our God—Isaiah 40:6-8

All flesh is grass,
  and all the goodliness [*ḥesed*] thereof is as the flower
  of the field:
The grass withereth, the flower fadeth:
  because the spirit of the LORD bloweth upon it:
  surely the people is grass.
The grass withereth, the flower fadeth:
  but the word of our God shall stand for ever.

—ISAIAH 40:6–8, KJV

How are people made ready to receive the Lord's salvation? Chapter 40:1-11 is the prologue to the second half of the Book of Isaiah (40–66), often called the Book of Consolation. God's command goes forth to comfort His people and to prepare a way for the Lord in the wilderness (vv. 1–3). The proud mountains must be made low before the full glory of the Lord will be revealed, and all humankind together will see it (vv. 4–5).

In God's sight humans are only "flesh" (that is, frail, weak and mortal). But they boast of their goodness, their beauty, their strength—various ways *ḥesed* has been translated in verse 6. Yet humans seem to last only as long as grass and flowers.

Perhaps this is figurative language for the brief, ephemeral beauty of human accomplishments and rule (compare Isaiah 28:1, 4). Their professions of loyalty, faithfulness and covenant commitment—the more usual meanings of *ḥesed*—fade quickly in the heat of trouble and conflict. It is the Spirit-breath (*rûaḥ*) of Yahweh blowing upon them to destroy their pride and convict them of their sin.

Hosea likewise describes the *rûaḥ* of Yahweh coming to plunder the treasures of Ephraim (the Northern Kingdom):

Though he may flourish as the reed plant,
  the east wind, *the wind of the LORD*, shall come,
  rising from the wilderness;
and his fountain shall dry up,
  his spring shall be parched;
it [the wind] shall strip his treasury
  of every precious thing.

—HOSEA 13:15, RSV, ITALICS ADDED

In light of human frailty we may ask what can ever lead people in a better way, to a better life. How can weak humanity be comforted? God's answer is that our only hope lies in that which does not fail: the activity of the imperishable, enduring Word of God preached to us (1 Pet. 1:24–25, quoting Isaiah 40:6–8). It is the gospel word telling us that our iniquity is pardoned (Isa. 40:2). It is the good news that the Sovereign Lord ('*Adonai Yahweh*) will come to rule. He will come as a Messiah-shepherd, like David of old, to tend His flock, gather the lambs in His arms and gently lead the nursing ewes (40:10–11; compare Psalm 78:70–72).

By the creative word of the Lord acting in conjunction with the Spirit-breath (*rûaḥ*) of His mouth, the heavens were made (Ps. 33:6). From the same mouth of the Lord (Isa. 40:5) comes forth His purging Spirit-breath and His comforting word (Isa. 45:23; 55:11)—both divinely powerful to achieve salvation for sinners. This is the glorious message of hope proclaimed in Isaiah 40–66.

## God's Spirit-Endued Servant—Isaiah 42:1–4

Isaiah 42:1–4 opens the first of a series of what have been called Servant songs in the second half of Isaiah (42:1–9; 49:19a; 50:4–10; 52:13–53:12; some include 61:1–3). Who is the servant of whom God speaks in these passages?

Surely He is other than the nation whom God addresses as "Israel, My servant, Jacob whom I have chosen, descendant of Abraham My friend" (41:8). For the nation of Israel was a spiritually blind and deaf servant, a failure as God's messenger and witness to the other nations (42:18–19). Even though Yahweh will help a remnant (46:3) of His servant Jacob and pour out His Spirit on their descendants (44:1–3), they are still a sinful servant, whose transgressions He must wipe out (44:21–22; 43:24–25).

The Servant of 42:1–4, however, is an individual in whom the Lord delights (42:1). Nevertheless He is inextricably identified with His people Israel. In the second song He announces that God said to him, "You are My Servant, Israel, in whom I will show My glory" (49:3). He is the ideal Israel. He is all that God called His people Israel to be—and far more—embodied in one Person. A century ago the conservative German scholar Franz Delitzsch explained this relationship with remarkable clarity:

> The idea of "the servant of Jehovah" assumed, to speak figuratively, the form of a pyramid. The base was Israel as a whole; the central section was that Israel, which was not merely Israel according to the flesh, but according to the spirit also; the apex is the person of the Mediator of salvation springing out of Israel.[22]

God calls Him "My Servant … My chosen one." The Hebrew word for "servant," 'ebed, often means "slave" (for example, Deuteronomy 5:6, 15), someone totally subjugated to work for another. But 'ebed was also used in the royal terminology of the ancient Near East in the sense of a "trusted envoy" or "confidential representative."[23] Moses was that kind of servant of the Lord (Deut. 34:5; Num. 12:7); so were Joshua (Josh. 24:29), David (2 Sam. 7:5, 8) and the prophets (2 Kings 17:13; Jer. 7:25).

God says of His Servant, "I have put My Spirit upon Him." The verb and preposition combination nātan plus 'al is the terminology of anointing with oil used in some of the Levitical ceremonies (Lev. 14:17–18, 28–29). Moses employed this idiom in his wish for all of God's people to be prophets and "that the LORD would put His Spirit upon them!" (Num. 11:29). So even though the term "anointed one" or "messiah" is not attributed to the Servant of the Lord in Isaiah, His anointing or "messiahship" is definitely in view here. That is why we can assuredly identify Him with Immanuel on whom the Spirit rests in 11:2 and with the one who speaks in 61:1: "The Spirit of the Lord GOD is upon Me, because the LORD has anointed Me."

By announcing that He has endued the Servant with His Spirit, God declares that He has fully equipped His Servant for His mission.[24] He will bring forth justice (mišpāṭ) to the nations. In Hebrew mišpāṭ means far more than judicial sentence. It is the principle or standard of divine holiness and truth which the Lord teaches to His people in His torah, His instruction or law.

Righteousness and justice are the foundation of His throne, which symbolizes His eternal rule of the universe (Ps. 89:14; 97:2). They are the basis of the gospel and of the kingdom of God as proclaimed in the New Testament (Matt. 6:33; Rom. 1:17). To establish this just, right order in the world is too difficult a work for humanity alone. It requires the empowering of God Himself.

Through the Spirit the Servant receives the charismatic enablement to accomplish this task.[25] The task is prophetic—to proclaim salvation without inciting revolution (v. 2). It is pastoral—to care for the weak and helpless (v. 3). And it is magisterial—to establish justice (v. 4) in conjunction with a law (v. 4) and a covenant (v. 6).

The Servant's role appears to be modeled after that of Moses, who was also endued with God's Spirit (see the comment on Numbers 11:4–30). Moses led the Israelites out of Egypt in the first exodus. Moses was the type prophet (Deut. 18:15, 18) of *the* Prophet expected by the Jews (Matt. 21:11; Luke 24:19, 21; John 1:21, 25; 6:14; 7:40). Moses bore the burden of his people's needs (Num. 11:11–14). And Moses was the lawgiver and mediator of the Old Covenant.

In a parallel way the Servant will give His new commandment of love (John 13:34–35), the perfect law that leads to liberty instead of to bondage (James 1:25). The Servant will be mediator of a new and better covenant (Heb. 8:6; 9:15) to Jewish people and Gentile nations alike (Isa. 42:6; 49:6, 8; Jer. 31:31–34). And the Servant will lead people out of prisons of sin and dungeons of darkness (Isa. 42:7) in a new, worldwide exodus.

Israel of old could not accomplish deliverance for the earth (Isa. 26:18). But the church works together with Christ in the ministry of reconciliation in this day of salvation (2 Cor. 5:18–20; 6:1–2, quoting Isaiah 49:8 regarding the Servant). Paul and Barnabas said the Lord commanded *us* to be a light to the Gentiles and to bring salvation to the end of the earth (Acts 13:47). They were quoting Isaiah 49:6, which is Yahweh's commission to His Servant. Therefore as members of His body we are enabled to carry out His commission with Him when God puts the same Spirit upon us.

## The Outpouring on Israel's Descendants—Isaiah 44:1–5

Isaiah 44:3 is the second of the four great prophetic promises of the outpouring of God's Spirit (see the comments on Isaiah 32:15; Ezekiel 39:29; Joel 2:28–32). In this oracle God calms the fears of His servant-people Jacob by saying:

> For I will pour water on the thirsty one
>     and streams on dry ground;
> I will pour My Spirit on your offspring
>     and My blessing on your descendants.
>
> —ISAIAH 44:3, AUTHOR'S TRANSLATION

The fructifying Spirit (of Isa. 32:15) is here poured (*yaṣaq*) directly upon God's chosen people. Because of the frequent use of this verb for the pouring of anointing oil (Gen. 28:18; 35:14; Lev. 2:1; 8:12; 14:26; 21:10; 1 Sam. 10:1; 2 Kings 9:3, 6), the action foretold in Isaiah 44:3 may be understood as a supernatural anointing.

"My Spirit" is closely equivalent to "My blessing." Therefore the outpouring on Jacob's offspring (that is, on Israel) must be part of the fulfillment of God's promise to Abraham that in him all the families of the earth will be blessed (Gen. 12:3). In fact, God's continual outpouring of His Spirit is portrayed in prophecy as the clearest sign accompanying the advent of Messiah, *the* seed of Abraham (Gal. 3:5–16). It is Yahweh's refreshing answer to the spiritually dry and thirsty condition of His chosen nation, pictured by Ezekiel as a valley full of dry bones (37:1–4).

Later in Isaiah we hear the universal invitation to everyone who thirsts to come to the waters of salvation (55:1; compare 12:3; John 4:14). We are also reminded of Isaiah's figurative descriptions of the new exodus when Yahweh will give rivers in the desert (Isa. 43:19–20). The desert will blossom as the rose, and waters will burst forth in the wilderness and streams in the desert (35:1–7). God will open rivers on the bare heights and fountains in the midst of the valleys and make the wilderness a pool of water and the dry land springs of water (41:17–20).

Returning to Isaiah 44:1–5, the last verse may be translated:

> This one will say, "To Yahweh I belong";
>     another will call himself by the name "Jacob";
> another will write with his own hand, "Belonging to Yahweh,"
>     and surname himself by the name "Israel."
>
> —AUTHOR'S TRANSLATION

Lloyd Neve pointed out that the personal nature of the Spirit's work among the nations is evident in this verse. "Here is described the Spirit's regenerating work in non-Israelites, joined as proselytes to the covenant community.... If only Israelites are meant, there would be no purpose in their taking the name Jacob."[26] A marvelous result of the outpouring of the Spirit beginning on the Jews at Pentecost is that the heathen are attracted, one after another, to ally themselves with the Lord.

### The Servant and the Spirit Sent by God—Isaiah 48:16

Yahweh, the God of Israel, the first and the last, the Redeemer, the Holy One of Israel, is the speaker throughout nearly all of Isaiah 48. But who is the speaker in the last line of verse 16? "And now the Lord God ['*Adonai Yahweh*] has sent Me, and His Spirit."

The identification of the speaker in this statement depends upon a proper translation. The Hebrew wording clearly calls for a translation such as that of the RSV or NAS (as above), not that of the KJV which makes "His Spirit" part of the subject. Obviously the speaker cannot be Yahweh, because he makes a distinction between himself and the Lord. The speaker cannot be the prophet because the speaker and the Spirit, both sent by the LORD, seem to be persons of equal rank.

The expression "but now" (wě‘attāh), as in Isaiah 16:14; 43:1; 44:1, sets forth a significant contrast between what precedes and what follows. Sometimes in Isaiah "now" marks the turning point of salvation (29:22; 33:10; 43:19; 48:7; 49:19; 59:21). Here the contrast is between the task Yahweh has assigned to Cyrus, whom He loves in the sense of choosing him to carry out His purpose for Babylon (48:14–15), and the commission given to the speaker.

The speaker can only be the Servant of the Lord *par excellence,* already introduced in 42:1–9. The short statement here forms a prelude to His own words in 49:1–6 about His mission to restore Israel and be a light to the Gentiles. In 50:4–9 the Servant refers to God four times by the same compound name He uses in 48:16, "Adonai Yahweh."

As E. J. Young explained, "Here he declares that God had sent him, for he is the true instrument who will accomplish the great redemption that alone can bring well-being and peace. The work of Cyrus was but a preparation for his coming."[27]

The position in the sentence of the words "and His Spirit" (wěrûḥô) may indicate the sense of together "with his Spirit" (see the NIV). The Tanakh, following the ancient Aramaic targum translation, reads, "And now the Lord God has sent me, endowed with His spirit." It is clear that the Servant would not come alone, but that His entire ministry would be in the power of the Spirit.

Thus Isaiah 48:16 contains the clearest statement in the Old Testament of the Trinity, God in three Persons.

## The Spirit's Call to Battle—Isaiah 59:19

Isaiah 59:15b-21 describes the victorious march of Yahweh against the rebellious sinners among His people (56:9–59:15a) and against His adversaries and enemies abroad (59:18). People from every direction will revere the name of the Lord and His glory-presence (59:19a). He will come as redeemer to Zion, to those in Jacob who turn back from transgression (59:20). And He will make a New Covenant with this saved remnant (see the comment on Isaiah 59:21).

The overall interpretation of the passage is clear as it explains how Israel will be transformed from its wicked past to its glorious future (Isa. 60–62). The words of 59:19b within this larger context, however, have been misunderstood in nearly all of the modern translations and commentaries. Only the KJV translation (followed by NKJV) was correct in its rendering of *rûaḥ Yahweh*: "When the enemy shall come in like a flood, the spirit of the LORD shall lift up a standard against him." There is a better translation, however, of the statement as a whole.

By carefully following the Hebrew word order and by keeping in tune with the entire paragraph (59:15b–21), which focuses on the Lord's actions, verses 19–20 may be rendered:

> So they will fear from the west the name of Yahweh
> and from the rising of the sun, His glory;
> for He will come like the river as Adversary,
> the Spirit of Yahweh lifting up a standard with Him.
> But He will come to Zion as Redeemer,
> and to those who turn from transgression in Jacob
> —the prophetic declaration of Yahweh.
>
> —AUTHOR'S TRANSLATION

As Yahweh had sent the Assyrian king to be an enemy against Israel and Judah to punish them (Isa. 8:7–8; 28:2), so now He Himself would be the Adversary (*ṣār;* compare Lamentations 2:4) to repay all of His adversaries (from *ṣār*) and enemies with wrath and retribution (Isa. 59:18; compare 63:1–6). As the Assyrian armies of Tiglath-pileser and Sargon and Sennacherib overflowed Israel and Judah like the mighty flood waters of the Euphrates River (8:7–8), so Yahweh Himself would come like such a destructive flooding river.

But what about the *rûaḥ Yahweh* in the last line of Isaiah 59:19? Should it be translated "the wind of the LORD" (RSV, NAS, TAN); "the breath of the LORD" (JB, NIV); or "the spirit of the LORD" (KJV)? Isaiah elsewhere used *rûaḥ Yahweh* (11:2; 40:7, 13; 61:1; 63:14) only of the Spirit of the Lord. It is not likely that in 59:19 he meant a natural wind sent by God.

We may conclude that it is the Spirit of Yahweh who is being depicted as lifting-up-a-banner (*nōsĕsāh*) to rally the righteous sons of Zion. Then they will stand with Messiah against His foes in the day of His power (compare

Psalm 110:2–3). The verb *nōsĕsāh* seems to have been derived from the noun *nēs*, a battle standard or banner raised as a signal.[28] Psalm 60:4 uses both this noun and another form of this verb:

Thou hast given a banner [*nēs*] to those who fear Thee,
That it may be displayed [*hithnōsēs*] because of the truth.

The word *nēs* appears in the compound name "The LORD is my banner" (*Yahweh-nissî*, Exod. 17:15). It is one of Isaiah's favorite words. In Isaiah 11:10, the Messiah Himself will stand as a peaceful signal (*nēs*) to attract the Gentiles; and in 11:12, He will lift up a standard (*nāsā' nēs*) to summon the nations and to assemble the dispersed ones of Judah and Israel (see also 5:26; 13:2; 18:3; 30:17; 31:9; 49:22; 62:10).

Are we fixing our eyes on the Spirit's battle standard even now as we await Christ's return? Are we asking the Holy Spirit to empower us and clothe us in the full armor of God in order to stand against all the spiritual forces of wickedness today (Eph. 6:10–18)?

## Yahweh's Covenant and His Spirit—Isaiah 59:21

Isaiah 59:21 is the only verse in the Old Testament that mentions God's Spirit in connection with the New Covenant. One of the results of Yahweh's coming as redeemer to the penitent ones in Zion (see the comment on Isaiah 59:19) is to make a covenant with them. The feature of that covenant which is described here concerns Yahweh's Spirit:

"As for Me, this is My covenant with them," says the LORD: "My Spirit which is upon you, and My words which I have put in your mouth, shall not depart from your mouth, nor from the mouth of your offspring, nor from the mouth of your offspring's offspring," says the LORD, "from now and forever."

In no previous covenant did the Lord promise that He would put His Spirit upon each individual believer (the pronouns "you" and "your" are singular throughout v. 21). It was not until Pentecost that God began sending His Spirit upon His people worldwide. Therefore this covenant must be the New Covenant foretold by Jeremiah (31:31–34; quoted in Hebrews 8:8–12), the same as the "everlasting covenant" that God would make with His people (Isa. 55:3; 61:8; Jer. 32:40; Ezek. 16:60; 37:26). The Servant of the Lord, Jesus, the Messiah, is the very heart of that covenant, for Yahweh appointed Him to be a covenant for the people (Isa. 42:6; 49:8).

Isaiah had already announced the outpouring of the Spirit that is to occur in the messianic age (32:15; 44:3). Now the Lord declared through the prophet that His Spirit would be upon the redeemed person just as the Spirit of Yahweh would be upon the Servant-Messiah (11:2; 42:1; 61:1). Each one would have the charismatic potential to speak forth a message of God. The Spirit would act as the Spirit of prophecy, so that the words which the believer would speak would be anointed words. This is the same promise that Joel proclaimed: "I will pour out My Spirit on all mankind; and your sons and daughters will prophesy" (2:28; see the comment on Joel 2:28–32).

Isaiah emphasized that the gift of God's Spirit and His enablements under the New Covenant would be continuous: "My words shall not depart from your mouth." Joel emphasized that the gift of the Spirit would be all-inclusive. Then Moses' wish would be fulfilled: "Would that all the LORD's people were prophets, that the LORD would put His Spirit upon them!" (Num. 11:29). The fact that Spirit-guided words would continue to come from the mouths of God's redeemed people in generation after generation was a clear prophetic indication that the charismatic gifts of the Spirit were not to cease after the generation of the apostles.

## The Anointing of Yahweh's Servant—Isaiah 61:1–3

> The Spirit of Adonai Yahweh is upon Me,
>     because Yahweh has anointed Me
>     to bring-good-news to the helpless.
> He has sent Me
>     to bind-up the brokenhearted;
>     to proclaim liberty to the captives
>         and opening-of-eyes to those imprisoned [in darkness];
>     to proclaim the year of Yahweh's favor
>         and the day of vengeance of our God;
>     to comfort all who mourn—
>     to provide for those who mourn in Zion;
>     to give them a priestly-turban [pĕ'er]
>         instead of ashes ['ēper],
>         the oil of gladness
>             instead of mourning,
>         a garment of praise
>             instead of a spirit of despair.

So they will be called the oaks of righteousness
the planting of Yahweh, that He may be glorified.

—AUTHOR'S TRANSLATION

Who was the one proclaiming his ministry in this beautiful passage? Isaiah himself? But the prophet never spoke of himself or his prophetic office at such length as this.

In the context of Isaiah 60–62 the speaker was the one who would bring about the future glory of Zion. He could be none other than the Servant of Yahweh of whom and to whom Yahweh spoke in the first and fourth Servant songs (42:1–9; 52:13–53:12). He was the same one of whom Yahweh said, "I have put My Spirit upon Him" (42:1). He was the same individual who spoke for Himself in 48:16b (see the comment there) and in the second and third Servant songs (49:1–9; 50:4–9). Therefore we may call this passage a fifth Servant song.

While the title "Messiah" (māšîaḥ) is not used here, the fact that the speaker said, "The LORD has anointed [māšaḥ] Me," clearly indicates He is the Messiah. Our Lord Jesus confirmed this conclusion when He read from this passage in the synagogue in Nazareth. He rolled up the scroll and added His comment, "Today this Scripture has been fulfilled in your hearing" (Luke 4:14–21; see the comment there).

The initial task of the Servant's ministry is to evangelize, to bring good news to the helpless people of the world (Isa. 61:1a). That news is the comforting gospel of 40:9 and 52:7 that God has come in person to bring salvation and peace. The helpless ('anāwîm) are the poor, the afflicted, the oppressed, the humble, the meek.

Actually, all are helpless in their lost, sinful condition (Rom. 3:23), but only those who humbly admit their helplessness are willing to receive the good news. It takes the convicting work of the Spirit to prepare their hearts. Therefore, as E. J. Young pointed out, the abiding anointing of the Spirit is essential to the Servant so that His ministry described here may be carried out.[29]

In the power of the Spirit, the Servant will proclaim both liberty (děrôr) to the captives and the year of Yahweh's favor. These two expressions allude to the Year of Jubilee in Leviticus 25:8–55. The Israelites were to consecrate the fiftieth year and proclaim liberty (děrôr, "release," NAS) throughout the land to all its inhabitants (25:10). The Lord had graciously decreed that once every fifty years indentured servants were to be released, debts canceled and landed property returned to the original Israelite family.

Nevertheless, there is no historical evidence in the Old Testament or elsewhere that a jubilee year was ever properly observed. (Jeremiah 34:8–14 refers only to a *sabbatical* year release of servants.) The return of Jewish exiles to their land from Babylon could in a certain sense be considered a jubilee fulfillment, for the captives were absent fifty years, from the destruction of Jerusalem until Sheshbazzar led back the first contingent, 586–536 B.C.

In the fullest sense, however, the jubilee concept pointed forward to liberation from the bondage of sin and its terrible consequences. J. Barton Payne stated it well: "The Year of Jubilee foreshadows the restoration of all that has been perverted by mankind's sin, the establishment of the true liberty of the children of God, and the deliverance of creation from the bondage of corruption to which it has been subjected on account of human depravity."[30] Such jubilee deliverance would await the messianic age when the Spirit-anointed Servant would not only proclaim salvation but also die to pay redemption's price.

In carrying out the ministry of Isaiah 61:1–3, Jesus, the Servant-Messiah, not only "rescued the perishing" Himself but also demonstrated by His example what our ministry to others should be. Furthermore, we *can* continue this ministry of His to the helpless, because He has promised to pour out on every believer the same empowering Spirit who came upon Him.

## God's Promise of His Indwelling Spirit— Ezekiel 36:27; 37:14

On the night before news reached the Jewish exiles in Babylonia that Jerusalem had been destroyed (Ezek. 33:21–22; in 586 B.C.), the Lord gave Ezekiel a series of six prophetic messages regarding the restoration to Palestine and the long-range future of God's people. First, God explained that He had removed Israel from her land and laid it waste because of her idolatrous practices (33:23–33). Next, He would get rid of their selfish, arrogant rulers who fleeced the people, and He would take over leadership Himself to shepherd them and send His servant, the Davidic Messiah, to care for them (34:1–31).

The third message was about the land God had given to Israel. As Sovereign Lord He would devastate Edom (and all nations) who heartlessly took advantage of Jerusalem, and He would again make the mountains of Israel fruitful and repopulate the land (35:1–36:15). The fourth message pertained to the people themselves and their need of cleansing and spiritual renewal (36:16–37:14).

Fifth, Israel and Judah would be reunited into one nation in their land with one king, David's greater Son. The promises of the Abrahamic, Mosaic and Davidic covenants would be fulfilled in the establishment of the New Covenant of peace (37:15–28). In the sixth message God foretold how He would thwart the final attempt of enemy armies led by Gog to plunder His people Israel, who at last would be dwelling securely in their own land (38–39).

At the center of these oracles of hope is the good news of coming spiritual renewal (36:25–29). In two ways the Sovereign Lord would vindicate the holiness of His great name, which had been profaned among the nations by His people Israel. First, He would punish His people by exile because they had defiled His land with their idols (36:17–20). Then He would regather a remnant of His people to their land (vv. 22–24), cleanse them from all their iniquities (vv. 25–33a) and make the once desolate land like the garden of Eden as a testimony to the surrounding nations (vv. 33b–36).

God's work of saving Israel from their moral uncleanness (v. 29) consisted of three main aspects. Verse 25 says He would "sprinkle clean water" on them as a ritual act of cleansing (compare Numbers 19:17–19; Psalm 51:7) from all the filthiness of their idolatrous practices (compare Ezekiel 37:23; Jeremiah 33:8). Verse 26 says He would give them a new heart and a new spirit. Verse 27 says He would put (literally "give"; from *nātan*) His own Spirit within them (*bĕqirbĕkem*) and thereby cause them to walk in His laws. The Hebrew prepositional phrase for "within," *bĕ* plus *qereb* (literally "in the midst of," "inside of"), points to the inward part or "heart" as the seat of human thought and emotion (for example, Psalm 51:10; 64:6; 94:19; 103:1; Isaiah 26:9).

The "water" of verse 25 and the "new spirit" of verse 26 were brought together in Jesus' description of the new birth in John 3:5. On the basis of Ezekiel's writings, our Lord expected the prominent Jewish teacher Nicodemus to comprehend these concepts of radical inner cleansing and regeneration (see the comment on John 3:1–8). God's promise to impart His Spirit to indwell believers, however, was a new feature not previously provided in His covenants with Abraham, Moses and David.

Idolatry, which the Lord condemned in Ezekiel 36:18, was the chief sin of the Israelites in the Old Testament. Idolatry is loving anything or anyone else, including our own selves, more than the Lord. Loving the world is still the chief sin of Christians (1 John 2:15–17).

Idolatry expresses the rebellion of the human heart in refusing to submit to the Lord, obey His will and worship Him alone. Only on the basis of the blood of the sacrificed substitute, Jesus, can this sin or any other be truly pardoned and cleansed (1 John 1:7, 9). But in the ceremonial cleansing of water baptism we acknowledge our sins through repentance and renounce the defilement of our former lifestyle (compare Acts 22:16).

By the people's repentance and conversion the Lord would soften their hard, stony hearts and renew their spiritual attitude. As a result they would have a new sensitivity toward God and the resolve to follow Him. This much was promised (Jer. 24:5–7; Ezek. 11:17–20; 18:31–32) even to those who decided to return from Babylon with Sheshbazzar (Ezra 1:5, 8; 5:13–16) and later with Ezra (8:21–23). A changed, transformed personality is the result of salvation and regeneration, always and only the unique work of God's divine grace regardless of the period of human history (Titus 3:3–7; see the comment on Psalm 51:11).

God's gift of His indwelling Spirit belongs only to the time of the New Covenant. Although Ezekiel did not employ the term *New Covenant* as Jeremiah did (Jer. 31:31–34), the fourth message to Ezekiel was put into a covenant framework by the formula used in Ezekiel 36:28: "You will be My people, and I will be your God" (compare Leviticus 26:9, 12; Jeremiah 31:33; Ezekiel 34:25–31). Then in Ezekiel 37:26–28 God clearly specified that the entire renewal would be under an everlasting covenant of peace that He would make with the children of Israel. By putting His Spirit within His people the Lord would guarantee the effectiveness of the New Covenant.

The indwelling of the Spirit is a totally new dimension of the Spirit's work, as Roger Stronstad stated. He continued:

> By His Spirit God will cleanse and purify His people from their sins, create new life in them, and impart to them the ability to keep His covenantal demands.... With God pouring out His Spirit upon them, the future community of the Lord's anointed will receive both charismatic and moral or spiritual power.[31]

The giving of new life and inward renewal by the Spirit must precede the giving of charismatic power by the Spirit. It is the quickening, indwelling Spirit who impresses the Word of God (His *tôrāh*—law or teaching) on the believer's heart under the New Covenant (Jer. 31:33) and gives him or her the desire to obey the Lord.

In 37:1–14, Ezekiel described a vision he had that illustrates how God would put His Spirit within His people. He saw dry bones filling a broad valley plain (depicting Babylonia and all places where Jews were "buried" in exile). The bones represented the whole house of Israel, whose hope had perished (v. 11). Sovereign Yahweh would bring back the "bones" to their homeland (v. 12) and reunite them into a "body" with muscle and flesh and skin. But as a nation it would be spiritually lifeless. So the Lord said to him:

> Prophesy to the breath [*hārûaḥ*], prophesy, son of man, and say to the breath [*hārûaḥ*], "Thus says the Lord GOD, 'Come from the four winds [*rûḥôth*, plural of *rûaḥ*], O breath [*hārûaḥ*], and breathe [from *nāpaḥ*, as in Genesis 2:7] on these slain, that they come to life.'"
>
> —EZEKIEL 37:9

The Lord then explained to Ezekiel that He would cause His people to come out of their grave-like ghettos in foreign lands (v. 13). "I will put My breath [*rûḥî*, that is, My Spirit] into you and you shall live again, and I will set you on your own soil" (v. 14, TAN). The obvious play on the meanings of *rûaḥ* as breath, wind and spirit affords a vivid picture of God personally breathing His own Spirit-breath into His restored people. This act is in conjunction with the spiritual rebirth of Israel in fulfillment of Yahweh's covenant promises to His servants Jacob and David (Ezek. 37:21–26).

### The Outpoured Spirit As Covenant Sign—Ezekiel 39:29

Ezekiel 39:29 closes the six prophetic messages of restoration and hope for God's chosen people Israel that began with Ezekiel 33:23. Chapter 39:21–29 is the conclusion to the *entire series,* not merely to chapters 38–39 about Gog and Magog. Hence it is not necessary to consider the outpouring of God's Spirit spoken of in 39:29 as happening *after* the invasion of Gog and his hordes (38:2–6) and their destruction and burial (38:18–39:16).

The Lord declared to Ezekiel that He would begin His merciful work of restoring the fortunes of Jacob "now" (*'attāh,* 39:25). The work of spiritual renewal in God's people Israel had begun with His cleansing process of judgment by the Babylonians in Ezekiel's own day (vv. 21–24). It did not require another enemy invasion; it did not await that final End-Time attempt to destroy God's people. As a result of their return from dispersion in many lands (vv. 27–28) and their spiritual renewal (36:24–33), they would "dwell in their land secure and untroubled" (39:26b, TAN; compare 34:25–28; 38:8, 11; Jeremiah 23:5–6; 33:16; Zechariah 14:11).

Then, declared the Sovereign Lord, "I will never again hide My face from them, for I have poured out [*šāpaktî*] My Spirit upon [*'al*] the house of Israel" (Ezek. 39:29, author's translation). While we know that this outpouring of God's Spirit prophesied by Ezekiel did not occur in his time, it was nevertheless a completed action in God's mind.

The NAS translation indicates that the glorious effusion of the Spirit would come at a time future to Ezekiel: "For I shall have poured out My Spirit on the house of Israel." This interpretation is in keeping with Joel's prediction of the outpouring that it will come about "afterwards," in the indefinite future. Joel used the same verb *šāpak* (to pour out) but foresaw the *universal* extent of the outpouring on "all flesh" (see the comment on Joel 2:28–32).

This outpouring should not be equated with God's putting His Spirit *within* (*běqereb*) His redeemed remnant-people (see the comment on Ezekiel 36:27; 37:14). That act relates more directly to the spiritual rebirth of the nation, to their reception of new life. In 39:29, however, Yahweh's pouring out of His Spirit would serve as an ongoing witness to Israel as well as to the nations that He is their God (vv. 27–29).

His outpoured Spirit would thus be the seal of the everlasting covenant of peace (37:26), the "New" Covenant announced by Jeremiah (Jer. 31:31–34; see the comments on Isaiah 59:21; 2 Corinthians 1:21–22; Ephesians 1:13–14). The presence of the Spirit of Yahweh poured out on His people would ratify the covenant relationship and act as a continuing guarantee of new life, peace and prosperity. It would represent "the divine mark of ownership, which accounts for Yahweh's intervention against Gog on Israel's behalf before the latter is even touched."[32] God's Spirit-presence would ensure that He would never leave any of the house of Israel at the mercy of their enemies and that He would never again hide His face from them; for He had hid His face from them during Nebuchadnezzar's invasions and destruction of Jerusalem (Ezek. 39:23–24).

Beginning at Pentecost the Lord has been pouring out His Spirit on His church during all of this age. At the end of this age, when Christ returns, He will pour out (from *šāpak*) "a spirit of grace and supplication" (NIV) on the inhabitants of Jerusalem to enable them to recognize the one whom they have pierced as their crucified Messiah (Zech. 12:10; compare Revelation 1:7). The verse in Zechariah suggests that Yahweh will graciously extend Himself by His Spirit to influence the nation that had violently opposed His Servant, so that they might respond to that grace and implore His favor.[33] There are also indications that Yahweh will continue to send forth His Spirit even after His servant David—the Davidic Messiah, Jesus Christ—returns to be king over the reunited people of Israel (Ezek. 37:21–28).

As a sign of the covenant, God's Spirit-presence must be perceivable in a continuing way. The Lord will keep on extending Himself in His powerful Spirit to protect His people from all harm (Ezek. 39:29; see above). He will continuously spread Himself as a canopy to shield them from searing sun and scorching heat (Rev. 7:15–17; see the comment on Isaiah 4:4). As the Spirit who is the conveyer of true, eternal life in the New Covenant (2 Cor. 3:6), God will keep on pouring Himself out in a river of life.

God by His Spirit is the source of all future blessing to fructify the land and make the desert blossom as a rose. He will cause His life-giving river to flow from His sanctuary in Jerusalem and water the Dead Sea valley (Ezek. 47:1–12; Joel 3:18). This river, which flows from the south side of Ezekiel's temple (47:1), will replace the huge cast-metal laver or "sea" that stood on the south side of the courtyard in front of Solomon's temple (2 Chron. 4:2–10). Therefore we may assume that the river will continue the work of cleansing, sanctification and renewal provided through the Holy Spirit (Titus 3:5; compare Ephesians 5:26), foreshadowed in the rituals involving the bronze laver (Exod. 30:17–21) and the "sea."

Zechariah declares that a fountain will be open to the residents of Jerusalem for cleansing from sin and impurity in the eschatological day (Zech. 13:1). That fountain may be, according to Zechariah, the source of the living water flowing out from Jerusalem (14:8). Jewish rabbis taught that the water ceremonies of the Feast of Tabernacles (compare John 7:37) symbolized the pouring out of the Holy Spirit from the New Jerusalem to replenish the world when the Messiah would come.[34]

His Spirit is the river whose streams make glad the city of God (Ps. 46:4). His people, as those streams, will channel this flow to every high hill (Isa. 30:25) and burning sand (Isa. 35:6–7, NIV). Along the riverbanks will grow trees whose fruit and leaves symbolize sustenance and healing for all peoples (Ezek. 47:12; Rev. 22:2). The Sovereign Lord will send forth His Spirit in never-ending supply as long as the New Covenant remains in effect, as long as

He is our God and we are His people and He dwells among us (Rev. 21:3; 22:1–5)—forever!

## "By My Spirit"—Zechariah 4:6

A favorite Old Testament verse of charismatic believers is Zechariah 4:6: "'Not by might nor by power, but by My Spirit,' says the LORD of hosts."

God's purpose for His covenant community, the task He has assigned them, the function that believers are to perform during this life, is suggested by what Zechariah learned from his fifth night vision (4:1–14). Zechariah saw a golden lampstand with seven lamps on top of it. While the Hebrew word *měnôrāh* is used in verse 2, this lampstand apparently was not the same as the seven-branched lampstand made for the tabernacle (Exod. 25:31–40).

The one in Zechariah's vision seems to have been a pedestal lamp with a large reservoir bowl on the top. The pedestal itself was very likely a hollow cylindrical column, as suggested by various Old Testament archaeological discoveries. Affixed to the rim of the large bowl were seven saucer-like lamps. Each of these apparently had seven wick "spouts" (NAS) or lips. These spouts were not channels (NIV) but constricted folds in the rim of the lamp to hold the wicks in place.

This lampstand, therefore, could have seven times seven or forty-nine flames, suggestive of God's plan that His chosen people Israel were to give light to the entire world. They were to be God's witness to the peoples that sat in darkness. This metaphor continued into New Testament times. Jesus told His followers that they were the light of the world (Matt. 5:14–16; John 8:12), and Peter reiterated this truth when he wrote, "You are a chosen race, a royal priesthood . . . that you may proclaim the excellencies of Him who has called you out of darkness into His marvelous light" (1 Pet. 2:9). In the eschatological future, Zion is to arise and shine, for her light has come—"and nations will come to your light, and kings to the brightness of your rising" (Isa. 60:1, 3).

Zechariah saw his eight night visions in 519 B.C. (Zech. 1:7–8) prior to the completion of the new building that replaced Solomon's temple, which had been destroyed in 586 B.C. For the small Jewish community to have any testimony whatsoever to the world of their day, it was essential that they get on with the job and finish the temple. The responsibility for this task lay in the hands of the civil leader, the Jewish governor Zerubbabel.

Apparently Zerubbabel was being harassed by his own countrymen who bemoaned the miserably poor beginnings, the "day of small things" (4:10; compare Haggai 2:3). Also non-Jewish peoples of the land tried to frighten the Jews from building by hiring counselors to frustrate their plans (Ezra 4:1–5). The problems stacked up like an insurmountable mountain (Zech. 4:7).

In those circumstances God graciously sent this famous message about His Spirit to Zerubbabel to encourage him (4:6–10). Earlier God had promised: "I have returned to Jerusalem with compassion; My house will be rebuilt in it" (1:16, literal translation; compare 8:9). Enabled by the Spirit, Zerubbabel *did* overcome the obstacles and completed the temple in only four more years (515 B.C.; compare Ezra 6:15).

While it was important for the Jews who had returned from Babylonian exile to complete God's house, it was even more crucial for them to witness to God's presence among them by their lives. God's initial word to Zechariah, before the series of night visions, was to tell the people not to be like their forefathers but to turn from their evil ways and from their evil deeds (1:3–6). The Lord was concerned that they "dispense true justice, and practice kindness and compassion each to his brother; and . . . not oppress the widow or the orphan, the stranger or the poor; and . . . not devise evil in [their] hearts against one another" (7:9–10). Later the Lord repeated this instruction so that He might do good to Jerusalem (8:9–17).

It was essential in order for their light to go forth to the world that their walk, as well as their worship, be a witness to His holiness, that their praise in the temple and their practice in the marketplace and the law courts be consistent. But such a consistent witness cannot be carried on in the flesh; it must be energized from an outside source.

In 4:11–14, Zechariah received explanation of the significance of the two olive trees on either side of the lampstand. The two trees, or their branches, are interpreted to be (literally) the two "sons of fresh oil," that is, the two anointed ones, who were standing by to serve the Lord (Adonai), the Sovereign of the whole earth. They were seen as emptying their golden olive oil into two gold pipes or funnels, which continuously supplied the reservoir bowl on top of the lampstand. (For oil as a symbol of the Holy Spirit, see the Introduction.)

In that day those two persons were Joshua, the incumbent high priest (Zech. 3:1–8; 6:11), and Zerubbabel, the governor of Judah and descendant of David (Zech. 4:6–10; Hag. 1:1; 1 Chron. 3:19). They were God's appointed representatives, through whom He could cause His Spirit to flow to the congregation of returnees from exile. It is by their joint effort that the spiritual and material prosperity of the nation was to be achieved. God uses human instruments and seldom operates independently of them.

These two offices—the priestly and the civil—would ultimately be combined in the ministry of the "Branch," the coming Messiah, for He would be a priest on His throne (Zech. 6:12–13), according to the order or pattern of Melchizedek (Ps. 110:4). Therefore Joshua and Zerubbabel were only types of Him who would actually pour out and give us His Spirit.[35]

While Zechariah 4:6 speaks specifically of the anointing of Zerubbabel with unusual, more-than-human strength and ability to complete his tasks, it announces God's principle of empowerment for all His servants. In the church, which is God's present temple (Eph. 2:21–22; 1 Cor. 3:16–17), *every* believer is a royal priest (1 Pet. 2:5, 9; Rev. 1:6) with the provision of the anointing of the Spirit (1 John 2:20).

In Zechariah 4:6 God's promise to all believers is that His task for us will not be accomplished by mere human resources: "not by might" (*ḥayil*, wealth, as in Genesis 34:29; Deuteronomy 8:17–18; Ruth 2:1, or prominence and influence, as in 1 Kings 1:42, NKJV); "nor by power" (*kōăḥ*, strength, as in Genesis 31:6; 2 Chronicles 14:11; 20:12; or ability, as in 1 Chronicles 29:24; 2 Chronicles 2:6). Rather we shall accomplish the Lord's work by His Spirit, by the supernatural enabling of His grace and wisdom and strength.

### Rest for the Returnees—Zechariah 6:8

Zechariah was informed in the last of his night visions (6:1–8) that God's Spirit was also at work among the Jews still returning from their exile in Babylon. God's angelic spirits, depicted as four chariots, were sent forth to patrol the earth in all four directions (vv. 1–6). Evidently their duty was to judge enemy nations and to guard the returnees traveling along the northern Fertile Crescent route.

Even after the first group of Jews came back and laid the foundation of the new temple (536–535 B.C.; Ezra 3), additional contingents needed to be able to come to Jerusalem to take part in the rebuilding of the temple and the city (Zech. 6:10, 15; Ezra 7:6–8; Neh. 2:7–9). Therefore Zechariah was told, "Behold, those heavenly chariot forces [compare 2 Kings 2:11; 6:17] who go toward the region of the north have enabled My Spirit to give rest in the region of the north" (Zech. 6:8, author's translation; compare RSV, NIV). The

NAS translation, "have appeased My wrath," unnecessarily follows the Septuagint Greek *thumon*, "wrath, anger."

It seems that God's Spirit, working in conjunction with His angels, was in charge of restoring Israel and Judah to the Promised Land from their dispersion in the "north" (Zech. 2:6–7; Isa. 43:6; Jer. 3:18; 16:14–16; 23:8; 31:8). As the Spirit of Yahweh led the Israelites in the wilderness and gave them rest and encouragement (Isa. 63:11, 14), so He was now encouraging the exiles to return and become involved in the temple reconstruction project.[36]

## The Universal Outpouring of God's Spirit—Joel 2:28–32

Peter quoted Joel 2:28–32 when he was explaining the supernatural happenings on the Day of Pentecost (Acts 2:16–21). Therefore the prophecy of Joel holds utmost significance for modern Pentecostal and charismatic readers.

Just when Joel ministered and wrote this book is not certain, because no contemporary rulers or known historical events are mentioned. Many conservative scholars have held that the book may be dated about 830 B.C. At that time the godly high priest Jehoiada was governing the kingdom of Judah during the boyhood of King Joash (2 Chron. 24:1–16), and Assyria was not yet threatening Jerusalem. This may explain the absence of usual historical data.

More likely, however, is an early post-exilic date about 500 B.C., not long after the second temple was finished in 515 B.C. The major enemies of Israel in bygone generations had collapsed: Nineveh had been destroyed in 612 B.C.; Babylon was captured in 539 B.C.; and Egypt was conquered by Persia in 525 B.C. Cyrus, the Persian, and his successors treated the Jews kindly and thus were not considered foes. There is no mention of a king or of any idolatrous practices. On the other hand, there is opportunity to summon the entire community for a solemn assembly at the temple (Joel 1:13–14; 2:12–17).

These factors reflect conditions in the decades immediately following the construction of Zerubbabel's temple (see Ezra 3–6). Therefore Joel may be considered as a successor to Isaiah and Ezekiel and one of the last of the writing prophets.

Joel 2:28–32 is the culmination of the Old Testament prophecies of the outpouring of God's Spirit (see the comments on Isaiah 32:15; 44:1–5; Ezekiel 39:29). It is a key passage in the Book of Joel, the theme of which is the imminent coming of the Day of the Lord.

Beginning in 2:18, Yahweh responded to the people of Zion who had heeded His call to repentance (2:12–13). First, in verses 19–26, Yahweh promised to restore the *land* from the ravages of the recent locust plague and terrible drought (1:2–12), as well as from future droughts and enemy invasions in the coming Day of the Lord (1:15–2:11). Then, as the transitional verse 27 indicates, Yahweh promised to bless His covenant *people* with His presence and keep them from ever again being put to shame.

His dwelling in the midst of His people would be characteristic of the ultimate phase of the Day of Yahweh (compare 3:17, 21; Isa. 24:23; 60:19–20). To begin, He would pour out His Spirit upon all humankind in anticipation of the great and dreadful phase of the Day of the Lord (Joel 2:28–32). In that day He would judge all the surrounding nations (3:1–16), and then Judah and Jerusalem would enjoy spiritual and material prosperity forever (3:17–21).

Joel 2:28–32 describes the Day of the Lord with reference to all peoples. The term *kāl bāśār*, "all flesh" (KJV), has the sense of every frail, mortal person as contrasted to the almighty, eternal God (compare Genesis 6:12–13; Job 34:15; Psalm 145:21; Isaiah 40:5–6; 66:16, 23–24; Jeremiah 25:31; 32:27; Ezekiel 20:48).

While this outpouring will affect all *classes* of people (Joel 2:28–29), the promise does not mean that every individual will be filled with the Holy Spirit. When He comes, He will expose the guilt of the world (John 16:8, NIV text note). To those who resist this convicting work and reject God's gift of His Son, the Spirit will eventually bring the outpouring of divine wrath (compare Ezekiel 20:33–34; see the comment on Isaiah 4:4).

But to those who are receptive the Spirit will bring spiritual power and supernatural abilities to serve God and combat evil. Like the seventy elders in Moses' time (see the comment on Numbers 11:4–30), they will have prophetic manifestations of the Spirit to encourage them and to confirm God's presence with them. In that way they will be strengthened to face the terrible trials leading up to and including the Day of Yahweh. Spirit empowering will enable them to survive, to be among "those who escape" (Joel 2:32).

All believers worldwide will come within the extent of this divine outflow. There will no longer be a spiritual aristocracy of charismatic leaders as under the Mosaic covenant. All races and categories of society will be included—Jew and Gentile, male and female, old and young, slave and free (see the comments on Acts 2:14–21; Acts 2:38–40).

When will God pour out His Spirit? The text of Joel 2:28 says: "And it will come about afterward (*'aḥarê kēn*)." The meaning is not "after this" (NAS), as if it were an event occurring chronologically after the restoration and blessing of the land (2:19–27). It is an overall term for the future, for eschatological times in general (Isa. 1:26, RSV, NIV; Jer. 16:16; 49:6). The equivalent two words in the Aramaic of Daniel 2:45 have been translated "hereafter" (KJV, RSV) or "in the future" (NAS, NIV).

Peter interpreted *'aḥarê kēn* to mean "in the last days" (Acts 2:17), departing slightly from the Greek Septuagint translation of Joel 2:28. To us Peter's phrase suggests the entire period between the first and second comings of Jesus Christ (compare "in the last days," 2 Timothy 3:1; James 5:3 with vv. 7–8; for similar expressions see 1 Timothy 4:1; 1 Peter 1:5; 2 Peter 3:3; Jude 18). The use of this phrase does not declare, however, that the outpouring will necessarily terminate at Christ's return.

The effusion of God's Spirit is to occur "in those days" (Joel 2:29), not merely on one day. From the study of Joel and other Old Testament passages (Isa. 32:15–20; 44:1–5; Ezek. 39:29 with 37:14–27; Zech. 12:8–13:1) as well as the New Testament, we may conclude that there was an *initial* fulfillment of the outpouring promises on the Day of Pentecost (Acts 2); there has been a *continuing* fulfillment throughout this church age and day of salvation (Acts 3:19; 2 Cor. 6:2); and there will be an *ultimate* fulfillment in conjunction with Christ's second advent and glorious reign (Acts 3:20–21).

Some of the charismatic gifts may cease because they are no longer needed after Christ returns (1 Cor. 13:8–10). Other results of the Spirit's outpouring, however, such as fellowship, protection and sustenance of health, will continue forever (see the comment on Ezekiel 39:29).

In Joel 2:28–29 God promises that He will pour (from *šāpak*, the same verb as in Ezekiel 39:29; Zechariah 12:10) Himself out as freely as water. Just as in the past He poured out (*šāpak*) His wrath like fire (Lam. 2:4) and like water (Hos. 5:10), so in the future He will pour out His Spirit in prophetic power. The effusion may begin as rain; it will become a veritable river.

Joel 2:23 contains an enigmatic statement that may suggest the Spirit's coming as rain. "For he [God] has given you a teacher for righteousness [*hammôreh liṣĕdāqāh*]. He sends you abundant showers, both autumn [*môreh*] and spring rains, as before" (NIV). This verse is at the heart of Yahweh's promise to restore the land to the fruitfulness of Eden (2:19–26; compare Isaiah 51:3; Amos 9:13–15). The primary reference of Joel 2:23 must be to the seasonal rains of Palestine (as in Deuteronomy 11:14; Jeremiah 5:24; Ezekiel 34:26; Zechariah 10:1). The Hebrew word *môreh*, however, usually means "teacher" (Job 36:22; Prov. 5:13; Isa. 30:20; Hab. 2:18), whereas *yôreh* is the more common spelling for the early or "former" (October) rain.

In two passages Isaiah associates God, the teacher, with the idea of His sending rain. First, "He, your Teacher will no longer hide Himself, but your eyes will behold your Teacher. And your ears will hear a word behind you, 'This is the way, walk in it' . . . Then He will give you rain for the seed which you will sow" (Isa. 30:20–21, 23). In the other passage God likens His word going forth from His mouth to rain coming down from heaven (Isa. 55:10–11; compare Deuteronomy 32:2; Job 29:22–23).

The Bible also employs the figure of rain to illustrate God's righteousness. "Rain down, you heavens, from above, and let the skies pour down righteousness" (Isa. 45:8, NKJV). Hosea 10:12 is especially helpful in understanding Joel 2:23:

> Sow with-a-view-to-righteousness [*liṣĕdāqāh*]
> Break up your fallow ground,
> For it is time to seek the LORD
> Until He comes to rain [*weyōreh*] righteousness on you.

The last line may also be translated literally, "until He comes and teaches righteousness to you."

Because righteousness (*ṣĕdāqāh*) is always an ethical attribute elsewhere in the Old Testament, as in Isaiah 45:8 and Hosea 10:12, Joel 2:23 involves more than actual rain. A literal translation of the key phrase *hammôreh liṣĕdāqāh* is "the teacher for righteousness" (NAS margin; NIV text note). This expression may be a veiled reference to the outpoured Spirit specifically foretold a few verses later.

Jesus promised that the Holy Spirit would come as the Spirit of truth, teaching us all things, convicting the world regarding righteousness and guiding us into all the truth (John 14:26; 16:8, 13; compare 1 John 2:27).[37] The outpoured Spirit is also the Spirit of Christ, the Teacher (compare John 13:13), the one who taught a higher righteousness than that of the scribes and Pharisees (Matt. 5:20). So it is in harmony with Joel 2:28 to find an allusion in 2:23 to God's gift of His Spirit, the Spirit of His Son, Jesus Christ (Gal. 4:6; Phil. 1:19; 1 Pet. 1:11).

Beginning with the initial downpour on Pentecost, God has been giving His Spirit in copious measure ever since. In Joel 2:28 the form of the verb *'ešpôk,* "I will pour out," can indicate progressive duration. As the conservative Lutheran scholar Theodore Laetsch explained, it "denotes the ever-renewed outpouring on generation after generation."[38]

In the eschatological Day of the Lord, the Spirit of God will continue to flow forth. "A fountain shall flow from the house of the LORD and water the Valley of Acacias" (Joel 3:18, NKJV). Supernaturally the river of God's blessing will keep on increasing, even through desert lands, until it freshens the Arabah (the Jordan valley) and the Dead Sea itself (Ezek. 47:1–12).

Isaiah, too, sings of that glorious day of ultimate renewal:

The wilderness and the desert will be glad,
    And the Arabah will rejoice and blossom . . . .
Then the eyes of the blind will be opened,
    And the ears of the deaf will be unstopped.
Then the lame will leap like a deer,
    And the tongue of the dumb will shout for joy.
For waters will break forth in the wilderness
    And streams in the Arabah . . . .
And a highway will be there, a roadway,
    And it will be called the Highway of Holiness . . . .
And the ransomed of the LORD will return,
    And come with joyful shouting to Zion.

—ISAIAH 35:1, 5–6, 8, 10

# FIVE

# An Overview of the Age of the Holy Spirit

## (5 B.C.–Today)

The present church age is truly the time of the outpoured Spirit of God. The prophets had characterized the coming messianic age as the period when Yahweh would pour out His Spirit on His servant people Israel and His blessing upon their descendants (for example, Isaiah 44:3). It was to be the age of the New Covenant. For the purposes of this study we are including in that age the years of preparation before the giving of the Spirit.

Malachi, ministering in the fifth century B.C., is traditionally considered to have been the last of the true prophets before the coming of the messianic age. So several centuries of God's silence stretched out between the time of Malachi and the appearance of John the Baptist. In fact, the last lines of Malachi's book look forward to John's ministry in God's announcement that He would send a prophet like Elijah before the dreadful Day of the Lord comes, to reconcile parents and children, lest God "come and smite the land with a curse" (Mal. 4:6).

By the time of Jesus' birth the hearts of devout Jews cherished a holy expectancy. Like Simeon, some were looking for the "consolation" (Greek *paraklēsis*) of Israel and the redemption of Jerusalem (Luke 2:25, 38; 23:51; the fulfillment of Isaiah 40–66 which is introduced by the words "comfort My people" in 40:1). The Spirit began once again to prophesy about the coming of the Messiah through some of those godly people, such as Elizabeth (Luke 1:41–45), Zacharias (1:64–79), Simeon (2:25–35), and Anna the prophetess (2:36–38). The virgin

Mary, too, burst forth in prophetic praise to God her Savior (1:46–55).

But what was happening in the rest of the Jewish community during the intertestamental period between Malachi and Matthew, from about 400 to 5 B.C.?[1] What we know about the period has been gathered to a great extent from Jewish religious literature written then: the Apocrypha (books included in Roman Catholic Bibles but not in Protestant Bibles); the Pseudepigrapha (popular books included in neither Roman Catholic nor Protestant Bibles); the Dead Sea Scrolls from the Qumran area, written by members of the Jewish Essene sect; the writings of the Jewish philosopher Philo of Alexandria (about 20 B.C.–A.D. 50); and the works of Josephus, the Jewish historian (A.D. 37–100), included here because of his extensive discussions of the prior centuries.

From these and other sources we can glean in particular some insights into how Jews of the period understood the Holy Spirit. What we find, in fact, is that these intertestamental writings reveal no significant changes beyond the Old Testament concept of the Spirit. Generally, the Spirit of God was regarded as the prophetic Spirit that was active from Moses to Malachi but was now silent.

In her in-depth study of the Greek term *pneuma* in Hellenistic Judaism, Marie Isaacs found that Philo and Josephus believed prediction and interpretation of dreams continued after the time of Malachi. They did not, however, attribute such prophetic activity in their day to the work of the Spirit. In the book called the Wisdom of Solomon (about 50 B.C.) the role of the Spirit was intellectualized so that wisdom and God's "holy spirit" were practically synonymous terms.[2]

The beliefs of the Qumran community perhaps came the closest of any in Judaism to those of the early church as found in the New Testament. For the Essene sectarians, the "holy spirit" was both a present possession and a future gift.[3] For example, the writer of the Thanksgiving Hymns, a text found in the Qumran library, thanked God for shedding His "holy spirit" upon His servant; and he beseeched God to purify him by His "holy spirit."

The Qumran monks believed there were two spirits, one of good or truth and the other of evil or falsehood, to which all human beings are assigned. God had allotted time to these two spirits until the end; until then the spirits of truth and perversity would do battle in the hearts of human beings.[4] Thus, while they spoke much of the Spirit, the Essenes did not develop a doctrine of the Spirit of God as a person co-equal with the Father.

It is in the New Testament that we find the fullest revelation and teaching about the Holy Spirit. Here the distinct personhood of the Spirit of God came into full view. The scope of His ministry to God's people broadened, and for the first time He began to indwell believers.

But according to the New Testament His principal work was always to represent the Son of God and to glorify Him (John 16:14). His life-giving activity and His coming in power were connected integrally with the teaching and saving work of Jesus the Messiah. He was not released to His fullest potential ministry until Christ had died on the cross and had risen and ascended on high. He was truly the Spirit of Jesus, the Spirit of Christ.

For the purposes of our study of the Spirit in the New Testament we shall subdivide this fourth era in the history of the work of God's Spirit into four categories:

(1) The preparation for the age of the Spirit—the Gospel records (presenting the life and teachings of Jesus).

(2) The beginning of the age of the outpoured Spirit—the Book of the Acts of the Apostles.

(3) The work of the Holy Spirit in this present age explained—the Epistles.

(4) The consummation of the age of the Spirit—the Book of Revelation.

As in the Old Testament sections of this book, our concentration will be on the exposition of key New Testament passages dealing with the Holy Spirit and His ministry to us. Because the New Testament period is shorter (only a century, 5 B.C.–A.D. 95) and its history better known than the times of the Old Testament, we will not find it necessary to give here a general overview of the Spirit's work in each of the sections of the New Testament.

Instead, the meaning of the biblical text and practical applications for Christians today will be of paramount concern. Hence we will make no attempt to survey all the recent literature on the subject of the Holy Spirit or to provide in-depth discussions of critical and scholarly issues such as the differences in viewpoint or emphasis between Luke, John and Paul regarding the person and work of the Spirit. All of the New Testament writings are considered to be the Word of God and therefore to possess an underlying theological unity, as well as His authority.

# SIX

# The Preparation for the Age of the Spirit: The Gospel Records

### The Baptism of Jesus—Matthew 3:11–17

The first important passage in the English New Testament that mentions the Holy Spirit is the account of Jesus' baptism in Matthew 3:11–17. This event, which introduced our Lord to His public ministry, is also described in the other Gospels (Mark 1:7–11; Luke 3:15–17, 21–22; John 1:31–34).

John the Baptist was preaching that the people must repent and confess their sins in order to prepare the way for their long-awaited Messiah. The Lord was about to appear to set up His kingdom. It would be the kingdom of heaven (or the kingdom of God, Mark 1:15)—that is, a kingdom with heavenly authority and governed according to principles originating in heaven (see John 18:36–37).

Therefore, righteousness was to be the primary characteristic of the kingdom and the requirement of all those who would enter it and submit to its rule (Matt. 5:20). Such righteousness is defined in the Bible as a right relationship with God granted by Him to us through our faith (Gen. 15:6; Rom. 1:17; see the Introduction).

So John commanded the people to stop their evil acts and to begin doing honest work and showing kindness as the proof of their repentance (Matt. 3:7–10; Luke 3:7–14). Then he would baptize them in the Jordan River as the sign that their sins were forgiven and cleansed away in God's mercy. Many of the Pharisees refused to be baptized by John and thus rejected God's purpose for themselves, for they would not acknowledge their own self-righteousness and their need for God's righteous plan of salvation (Luke 7:29–30).

Mark and Luke wrote that John preached "a baptism of repentance for the forgiveness of sins" (Mark 1:4; Luke 3:3), meaning a baptism conditioned on prior repentance with reference to the forgiveness of sins. This baptism, then, was a ritual of purification that acted as a seal of the candidates' spiritual reformation begun when they confessed their sins. But how did John's baptism in water explain and prepare the way for Jesus' baptism in the Spirit?

John announced that one was coming after him who was far greater than he was—whose sandals he was not even fit to remove! That one would baptize people, not in or with water as John did, but in or with the Holy Spirit and fire (Matt. 3:11; Luke 3:16). They would be just as thoroughly immersed in (or covered with) the Spirit as John's candidates were with Jordan's waters.

Not two baptisms were indicated here, but a single baptism in Spirit and fire.[1] The significance of the accompanying fire is suggested in the next verse: a burning up of the chaff. Chaff symbolizes what becomes useless and unfruitful after the kernels of grain mature, as well as what is sinful and evil (Ps. 1:4). The Holy Spirit comes to take charge of the sanctifying and purifying process in the believer's life. Thus the fire stands for the sufferings and chastening which every true child of God must endure (Heb. 12:5–11; 1 Pet. 1:6–7; 4:12–14; for the work of the Holy Spirit in sanctification, see the comment on 1 Corinthians 6:11).

Later on in His ministry Jesus announced that He had come to cast fire upon the earth (Luke 12:49–53). This burning (see the comment on Isaiah 4:4) would produce judgment and inevitable divisions but would have the ultimate goal of purifying His people from all evil (Mal. 3:1–3; 4:1–3). The full kindling of that fire would have to await Jesus' "baptism" on the cross, His total immersion in suffering; this He would first have to undergo (Luke 12:50). Only after His death and resurrection and the pouring out of the Holy Spirit would that process of judgment burn and purify in full measure.

Jesus came from Galilee to be baptized in water by John. When the latter objected because he knew Jesus was not a sinner, our Lord replied, "Permit it at this time; for in this way it is fitting for us to fulfill all righteousness" (Matt. 3:15).

By His incarnation Jesus was Son of God by nature and therefore righteous.[2] Because He came to provide righteousness for sinful humanity, He publicly identified Himself with those whom He came to redeem. So while on earth, Jesus always performed the religious duties of a godly Jew, such as synagogue worship, payment of the temple tax and attendance at the main feasts in Jerusalem.

As Jesus came out of the water, the Holy Spirit descended upon Him in bodily form like a dove, and a voice from heaven said, "This is My beloved Son, in whom I am well-pleased" (vv. 16–17). God in this way anointed Him to be Messiah (Christ, the anointed One) and put His seal of approval (John 6:27) on His Son at the beginning of His ministry. The dove was the sign which assured John that Jesus was the one who would be the baptizer in the Holy Spirit (John 1:32–33; see the comment on John 1:29–34).

As the Spirit came on judges and prophets in the Old Testament to empower them to minister, so now He came upon Jesus—but without measure (see the comment on John 3:34)—to enable Him to do His messianic work. Because He voluntarily limited Himself to teach and preach and heal by the Spirit's power, Christ our Lord became a perfect example for us. (For further comments on baptism in the Spirit see Acts 1:4–8; 2:1–4; 10:44–48; 1 Corinthians 12:13.)

## The Ministry of Jesus As the Pattern for All Christians—Matthew 4:23–25

Basically, Christ's work consisted of teaching, proclaiming the gospel and healing every kind of disease and sickness (see also Matthew 9:35; 15:30–31). He never turned away any sick people who came to Him, no matter what their diseases or pains. The people brought to Him demon-possessed persons, epileptics and paralytics; He healed every one of them. In explaining the gospel to Cornelius, Peter summed up Jesus' ministry: "You know of Jesus of Nazareth, how God anointed Him with the Holy Spirit and with power, and how He went about doing good, and healing all who were oppressed by the devil; for God was with Him" (Acts 10:38).

The authority of Jesus' words astonished the Jews, for He did not rehash the old religious traditions, as their scribes and teachers of the Law of Moses were doing (Matt. 7:28–29; Luke 4:32). His authority and power also amazed the people whenever He commanded unclean spirits to come out of their victims and they obeyed (Luke 4:33–36). We must remember that Christ never spoke or acted on His own initiative, but spoke and did only what the Father told Him and showed Him (John 12:49–50; 14:10; 5:19, 30; 8:28). He was full of the Holy Spirit, led by the Spirit and ministered in the power of the Spirit (Luke 4:1, 14).

All of this divine enabling is available to every child of God as well.

Compassion also motivated our Lord as He saw the crowds, "because they were harassed and helpless, like sheep without a shepherd" (Matt. 9:36, RSV; see also Matthew 14:14; Mark 6:34). His miracles served as more than the credentials of His messiahship and deity. They were not simply signs; they were also an essential part of His work of saving and helping the whole person.

Christ gave to His twelve apostles authority to conduct a similar ministry of preaching, teaching and deliverance (Matt. 9:35–38; 10:1, 5–8; Luke 9:1–6), and to seventy other disciples as well (Luke 10:1–9). After His resurrection the Lord Jesus commissioned His followers on several occasions to go into all the world to preach the gospel and promised that miraculous signs would be associated with those who believe (see the comments on Matthew 28:18–20; Mark 16:9–20). Christ planned for the Spirit-anointed believer to continue His ministry.

Later on He said, "He that believeth on me, the works that I do shall he do also; and greater works than these shall he do . . . And I will pray the Father, and he shall give you another Comforter . . . even the Spirit of truth" (John 14:12, 16–17, KJV). The record of the Book of Acts continues "all that Jesus began to do and teach" (Acts 1:1), so that the Holy Spirit may be said to be carrying on the ministry of Christ even today. (See also the comments on Luke 4:14–21; 10:17–20.)

We are warned, however, that even if a person has prophesied in the name of Jesus, exorcised demons in His name and worked many miracles, this is no sure evidence he or she is a born-again Christian. The fruit of the person's life is the proof (Matt. 7:20–23). Doing the will of God is the true test (see the comments on Galatians 5:22–23; Hebrews 6:4–6).

A case in point is that of some Jewish exorcists in Ephesus, including the seven sons of a priest named Sceva. These fellows invoked the name of Jesus over a demon-possessed man, who suddenly leaped on them and badly wounded them (Acts 19:13–16). So it is extremely important that we be wholly committed to Jesus Christ as Lord before we attempt to manifest any of the gifts of the Spirit.

The devil deceives people in order to turn them away from Christ. He is even able to give supernatural abilities to his followers so they can counterfeit the gifts and do great wonders (2 Thess. 2:9–10). On the other hand, Spirit-filled believers must be charitable enough to recognize that sincere

Christians in groups or denominations other than their own may have genuine power to cast out demons or perform miracles in Jesus' name (Mark 9:38–40; Luke 9:49–50).

## Jesus Christ, Our Healer—Matthew 8:14-17

The Lord Jesus Christ as a person of the Trinity may be compared to Yahweh, the God of the Old Testament. God clearly announced to Israel, "I am the LORD that healeth thee" (Exod. 15:26, KJV; "I, Yahweh, am your Healer," author's translation).

In this passage Matthew relates a prophecy of Isaiah to the healing ministry of Jesus: "He Himself took our infirmities, and carried away our diseases" (v. 17). The KJV reads: "Surely he hath borne our griefs, and carried our sorrows" (Isa. 53:4). However, the Hebrew word *holî* translated here "griefs," usually means "sickness" (for example, Deuteronomy 7:15; 2 Chronicles 21:15–19; Psalm 41:3; Isaiah 38:9); and the word for *sorrows* (*mak'ôb*) can refer to physical pain and disease as well as mental and emotional suffering (Job 33:19; Exod. 3:7; 2 Chron. 6:29).

Note that Jesus healed people by divine power before His suffering and death and that Matthew applies verse 4 of Isaiah 53 to Christ's ministry before Calvary. It is also evident from Isaiah 53:5 that the benefits of His bodily suffering as our substitute extend to our physical as well as our spiritual needs: "With His stripes we are healed" (see the comment on Matthew 12:15–21). The psalmist sang praise to the Lord, "Who forgiveth all thine iniquities; who healeth all thy diseases" (Ps. 103:3, KJV), revealing that God cares equally about our souls and our bodies.

The ultimate healing of the body of each believer is certainly included in Christ's atonement, for He will change our weak mortal bodies to be like His glorious body (Rom. 8:18–23; Phil. 3:21) at the resurrection. Even now we may enjoy some initial or "first fruit" benefits in the healing of our mortal bodies by the power of the indwelling Holy Spirit (Rom. 8:11).

Why are not all healed? Spiritual or divine healing is no more automatic than is salvation. Not everyone who makes a profession of faith is assuredly saved. Believing in Jesus Christ means understanding and believing who He really is, receiving Him personally and sincerely, and committing oneself unreservedly to Him as Sovereign Lord for time and eternity.

In like manner, while God is wonderfully gracious, He knows the motives of our hearts, the sincerity of the confession of our sins (1 Cor. 11:28–30) and the genuineness of our faith when we come to Him for healing. Therefore, in effect, Jesus asks the same crucial question that He asked the sick man at the pool of Bethesda, "Do you want to get well?" (John 5:6, NIV). In healing two blind men He touched their eyes, saying, "Be it done to you according to your faith" (Matt. 9:29).

Finally, we must humbly recognize the sovereignty of God in the timing and the method of His healing work, whether it be instantaneous, rapid, gradual or delayed, and whether it be miraculous or with medical help (see the comment on James 5:13–20).

### A Charismatic Word of Wisdom for the Persecuted Believer— Matthew 10:16–20

Spirit-filled Christians need not fear what they will answer during times of trial and danger. Christ promises that "it shall be given you in that hour what you are to speak. For it is not you who speak, but it is the Spirit of your Father who speaks in you" (Matt. 10:19–20).

This is an example of the charismatic manifestation of a word of wisdom (1 Cor. 12:8), the Spirit of God speaking in you. The parallel passage in Luke's Gospel (12:12) reads, "For the Holy Spirit will teach you in that very hour what you ought to say." Jesus also promised that when we are persecuted and brought before rulers for His name's sake, it will lead to an opportunity for a testimony. We should not prepare beforehand how to defend ourselves, because He will give us "power of utterance and a wisdom which no opponent will be able to resist or refute" (Luke 21:15, NEB).

Peter experienced this manifestation when he and John were on trial before the Jewish Sanhedrin (Acts 4:5–8). Overflowing with the Spirit, he preached Christ and salvation to the leaders and priests; they could only marvel and let Peter and John go (Acts 4:8–14, 21). On another occasion Jews were aroused by the miracles Stephen was performing among the people and began arguing with him. But he was full of faith and of the Holy Spirit, and "they were unable to cope with the wisdom and the Spirit with which he was speaking" (Acts 6:10).

### Isaiah's Prophecy of God's Spirit-Anointed Servant— Matthew 12:15–21

In Matthew's Gospel the prophecies of Isaiah were quoted or referred to at least fifteen times. In this passage Matthew showed that Jesus was the fulfillment of the wonderful prophecies about the Servant of the Lord in Isaiah (42:1–9; 49:1–7; 50:4–11; 52:13–53:12). God had put His Spirit upon Him, and He would bring forth justice to the Gentile nations as well as to the Jews (see the comment on Isaiah 42:1–4). He would be exalted and extolled, for He had been wounded ("pierced," NAS) for our transgressions and bruised ("crushed," NAS) for our iniquities; the punishment that procured peace for us had been upon Him, and by His stripes (His scourging with whiplashes, compare Luke 23:16, 22; Matthew 27:26) we were healed.

At this point in His ministry Jesus did not want those whom He healed to advertise the fact and thereby reveal His identity as the Messiah. This could have easily led to an abortive uprising against Rome. According to Isaiah's prophecy, the Servant of the Lord was not to be a rabble-rouser or a fanatical, demagogic preacher (Isa. 42:2; Matt. 12:19). His purpose was not to lead a military revolution but to achieve victory by tenderly caring for the unfortunate ("a bruised reed," "a dimly burning wick," RSV). His "hour"—the time for His redemptive sacrifice, His supreme work on earth—had not yet come (John 2:4; 7:6, 8; 8:20; 12:23, 27; 13:1; 17:1).

But now that He has been crucified and resurrected, His command no longer applies, and all Christians are to bear witness concerning Him openly and fearlessly.

### *The Unpardonable Sin: Blasphemy Against the Holy Spirit— Matthew 12:22–37*

The context of Jesus' teaching about this subject was the critical, defiant attitude of the Pharisees regarding His work of exorcizing evil spirits. They kept accusing Christ of casting out demons by the power and authority of Beelzebub ("Lord of flies," KJV, NIV; derived from "Beelzebul," RSV, NAS), the ruler of the demons. The name "Beelzebub" was a parody by true worshipers of Yahweh on the title and name of a Canaanite god adopted by the Philistines at Ekron (2 Kings 1:16). In Jesus' time the Jews applied this mocking name to Satan.

Specifically, therefore, the Pharisees were blaspheming or slandering the Holy Spirit by giving the devil credit for Jesus' miracles of exorcism, when in reality these were wrought by the Spirit of God (v. 28). But this false accusation was merely symptomatic of the underlying sin for which there is no forgiveness. In the parallel passage in Mark (3:29), Jesus said such a person was guilty of an eternal sin. In Matthew 12:33–37 the reason is clear—their evil, wrong ideas came from their corrupt hearts. Their words would condemn them, for these evidenced a fixed, unrepentant attitude of mind that persistently rejected the wooing and conviction of the Spirit.

The Holy Spirit is God's messenger to humankind, to convict us of sin and to convince us of divine truth (John 16:8–11). When people deliberately resist the Spirit's messages to their consciences—whether through their seeing a miracle, hearing a sermon, or reading the Scriptures or a Christian book or tract—they are shutting out the only force that can lead them to repentance. They are making their hearts callous to the Son's offer of forgiveness (John 3:36).

Only God knows when that hardening process has become permanent. None of those who are sorry that they have offended the holy God by their sin and who long to be forgiven by Jesus the Savior need fear that they have committed the unpardonable sin. On the other hand, it is dangerous to begin a course of spiritual insensitivity by attributing to Satan true manifestations of the Spirit such as the charismatic gifts of 1 Corinthians (see the comment on 1 Corinthians 12:4–11).

As Stanley Horton has warned, only God knows whether in any particular case a person's denial of the work of the Spirit comes from willfulness or from ignorance. He has known of some who attributed the Pentecostal experience to the devil but who later repented and were baptized in the Spirit and found the gift of tongues edifying.[3] (On the dangers of falling away and openly rejecting Christ, see the comment on Hebrews 6:4–6.)

### The Great Commission—Matthew 28:18–20

Each of the four Gospels (Matt. 28:18–20; Mark 16:15–18; Luke 24:46–49; John 20:21) and the Book of Acts (1:8) contain a missionary charge by the Lord Jesus, spoken to His disciples after His resurrection. Every Christian has thus been given the responsibility to be a witness of Christ.

Note the four "alls" in this passage: Jesus had received *all* power or authority to make this command, based on His personal triumph over Satan in the wilderness and His defeat of the forces of darkness at the cross. We are to go and make disciples of *all* nations, sealing them in their new faith by baptizing them in (Greek *eis,* unto, with reference to) the name (singular) of the triune God—of the Father, of the Son and of the Holy Spirit. Water baptism, therefore, is not optional but is clearly commanded by the risen Christ, and this is His "formula" (see the comment on Acts 2:38–40).

We are to teach the converts to observe, to be continually practicing, *all* things that Jesus taught and commanded us. And He has promised to be with us by His Spirit always (literally, *all* the days) even to the end of the world—that is, the end of this age, when He will return in person (compare the comments on Mark 16:9–20; Luke 24:44–53; John 20:21–23; Acts 1:4–8).

## Touching Jesus—Mark 5:25–34

The story in Mark 5:25–34 vividly illustrates the value of the human touch as a point of contact for faith—that is, as an aid to believing. The experience of the woman who was afflicted with a chronic hemorrhage also provides several other keys for the one who seeks healing.

First, she heard about Jesus and thought of Him as the one to help her in her desperate need. Second, she actually came to Him, overcoming her embarrassment and fear of the crowd. Third, she kept affirming her faith by saying to herself (the tense of the verb "said" in v. 28, KJV, implies repeated action), "If I just touch His garments, I shall get well" (v. 28). Finally, she reached out and touched the Lord's garment, thereby releasing her faith (exercising full-fledged trust without any doubt), and she was miraculously healed!

Other passages mention this normal reaction of wanting to touch the one who could give healing (Mark 3:10 and Luke 6:19; Mark 6:56 and Matt. 14:36). After Christ ascended and was no longer physically present, people naturally sought to come in contact with the apostles, through whom the healing power of God was channeled (Acts 5:15; 19:12).

There is no essential difference, as far as the flow of Christ's healing virtue or power (Greek *dunamis*, Mark 5:30) is concerned, between individuals' touching Him and His touching them (Luke 4:40). In one case, Jesus saw a woman who had been sick for eighteen years and was bent double. When our Lord laid His hands upon her, immediately she was made erect and began glorifying God (Luke 13:11–13).

In like manner Christians may lay hands on the sick in the name of Jesus to enable them to believe more easily (Mark 16:18; Acts 28:8). Peter took the hand of the cripple at the temple gate and lifted him up, and the man was healed (Acts 3:7). Physical contact also seems to aid the faith of the Lord's ministering servant as well as the faith of the person in need.

Just as Elijah and Elisha had raised people from the dead centuries earlier (1 Kings 17:21; 2 Kings 4:34), Paul lay upon Eutychus and embraced him, and the young fellow was restored to life (Acts 20:9–10; for the several aspects of the ministry of the laying on of hands, see the comment on Acts 6:6).

### Confirming the Word With Signs Following—Mark 16:9–20

Mark 16:9–20 is one of the few passages in the New Testament about which scholars still have a doubt regarding the original Greek text. In the two most trustworthy Greek manuscripts of the New Testament (Codex Vaticanus and Codex Sinaiticus, both copied around A.D. 350) the Gospel of Mark ends with 16:8. Yet other important early codices (known by the letter labels A, C, D and W) all contain this ending, as well as by far the greater number of later manuscripts. All the ancient versions (Old Latin, Syriac and the various Egyptian translations) have these verses, with the exception of some copies of these versions. Several Greek manuscripts and copies of versions do offer shorter substitutes in the place of verses 9–20.

Doubts also have arisen because the style of this passage seems to differ from the usually concrete and pictorial style of Mark. The church historian Eusebius and the Bible scholar Jerome in the fourth century were the chief authorities who doubted the passage. The present ending, however, was quoted by the Christian writers Tatian and Irenaeus in the second century, so it must have been written very early and accepted as canonical.

If Mark wrote his Gospel in codex form (a book with pages) instead of on a scroll, the last page of his original work may have been torn off and lost before additional copies could be made. In such a case, apparently some other recognized Christian prophet who was acquainted with the post-resurrection ministry of Jesus was inspired by the Spirit to supply this substitute ending. The New Testament scholar Henry B. Swete called it "an authentic relic of the first Christian generation." As Morton T. Kelsey explained: "This passage certainly represents the experience and expectation of the early church. . . .[It] becomes a primary indication that the practice of tongues (and other charismatic gifts) was not confined to the first days of the church."[4]

This is the only passage in the four Gospels where Jesus mentioned speaking in tongues ("they will speak with new tongues," Mark 16:17). In verses 17–18 the risen Lord clearly promised that signs would accompany those who believed as a result of Christians' going into *all* the world down through the centuries and preaching the gospel to *all* creation (v. 15). Therefore, these attesting miracles cannot be limited to the apostolic age but were meant to confirm the ministries of the servants of Christ in every generation. These "signs following" were to be the credentials of the ambassador of Christ and characteristic marks of God's people under the New Covenant. Jesus had already delegated to His disciples the authority to cast out demons and to heal the sick (Mark 6:12–13; Luke 9:1; 10:17, 19), and in Acts we read that this ministry of exorcism continued (5:16; 8:7; 16:18; 19:12). The "new tongues," new to the speakers because they had never learned them previously, were also the one new sign peculiar to this church age. They were first manifested on the Day of Pentecost (see the comment on Acts 2:1–4).

"They shall take up serpents" did not refer to religious ceremonies but to the act of getting rid of serpents without being harmed in the process (compare Paul's experience on Malta, Acts 28:3–6). The verb *take up* (Greek *airō*) can also mean "remove," "take away," "cast away" (Matt. 14:12; Luke 11:52; 1 Cor. 5:2; Eph. 4:31). Missionaries entering heathen territory have reported experiencing the fulfillment of the promise about miraculous protection against poison when they survived with no ill effects after being served poisoned food or drink. And many wonderful healings have been recorded in Acts and in the writings of Christian leaders during the early centuries of the church. All of these signs have occurred repeatedly in this century as well. (See the comments on Matthew 4:23–25; 28:18–20.)

## The Prophecy of the Spiritual Empowering of John the Baptist—Luke 1:13–17

Luke gave considerable prominence to the work of the Holy Spirit. In 1:13–17, his first passage mentioning the Spirit, Luke narrated how the angel had announced to the childless old priest Zacharias that his wife, Elizabeth, would bear him a son even though she was getting on in years. The boy was to be named John, and he would be filled with the Holy Spirit while yet in his mother's womb (v. 15), perhaps to enable the fetus to testify to the newly conceived Jesus (Luke 1:41).

Zacharias would understand by this, as in the cases of Samson and Jeremiah (Judg. 13:3–7; Jer. 1:5), that God was sanctifying or setting John apart to His special service from the moment of conception. The angel concluded by saying that John would go as a forerunner before the Lord "in the spirit and power of Elijah" (v. 17).

John the Baptist belonged to the dispensation of the Law and the prophets, to the period of the Old Covenant given at Mount Sinai through Moses. John was a prophet (Luke 1:76; 20:6), but even more than a prophet, for he was the predicted special messenger to prepare Messiah's way before Him (Mal. 3:1; Matt. 11:7–10; Luke 7:24–27). So there was no greater prophet than he in the Old Testament period (Matt. 11:11).

John was like the outstanding prophet Elijah in many ways. He was a stern preacher of moral righteousness who lived apart from society and wore a garment of camel's hair with a leather belt instead of a cloth sash (Matt. 3:4; 2 Kings 1:8). Most important, both John and Elijah were empowered by the Spirit of God.

In the Old Testament the Spirit had not been poured out on all of God's people. That empowering would not become available for all until Joel's prophecy began to be fulfilled at Pentecost (see the comment on Acts 2:14–21). Therefore, the younger prophet Elisha specifically requested that he might become heir to Elijah's spirit: "Let a double portion of your spirit be upon me" (2 Kings 2:9; compare v. 15). The "double portion" signified the rights of the firstborn son or chief heir (Deut. 21:17); thus Elisha was asking for the right to be Elijah's main successor, not to do twice as many miracles as his master.

More than the prophet's own human spirit is in view here, for in those days people expected the Spirit of the Lord to enable men and women to prophesy (1 Kings 22:24) and even to transport a prophet or a "man of God" miraculously to another place (see the comment on 2 Kings 2:1–18). Certainly Elijah's and Elisha's many miracles of healing, raising the dead, providing food and more demonstrated that they were empowered by the Holy Spirit. John the Baptist, however, manifested the power of the Spirit not as a worker of miracles but as a preacher of righteousness.

## The Conception of Jesus by the Holy Spirit—Luke 1:35

The virgin birth of Jesus Christ, the unique God-Man, is clearly taught in the Scriptures, especially in Luke 1:26–38 and in Matthew 1:18–25. From John 1:14, "And the Word became flesh, and dwelt among us," theologians have derived the term *incarnation* (from Latin *incarnare*, to make flesh). By this is meant that God took on human form in Jesus. Christ had no earthly father— Joseph served only as a foster father to give Him legal parentage and His royal ancestry in the house of David.

Jesus' conception cannot be explained scientifically. It was a creative miracle wrought by the Holy Spirit in the virgin womb of Mary. There is no suggestion of the Spirit's personally assuming human form and having physical intercourse with Mary, as in the ancient pagan legends concerning the reputed offspring of gods and humans. The angel said the power (*dunamis*) of the Most High would overshadow her, using familiar terminology from the Old Testament with reference to the pillar of cloud over the camp of Israel that symbolized the immediate presence of God (Exod. 13:21; Num. 9:15–23; 10:34).

In His birth, as in His entire life, Christ is the pattern and example for believers (1 Pet. 2:21). True Christians have experienced a supernatural rebirth or regeneration by the Holy Spirit (Titus 3:5). They have been born again spiritually (see the comments on John 3:1–8). Even as Jesus was baptized later on and empowered for His ministry when the Spirit came upon Him, so believers in Christ should experience the baptism in the Holy Spirit after this new birth (see the comment on Matt. 3:11–17).

## Jesus and the Prophecy of Isaiah—Luke 4:14–21

Some scholars claim that Jesus grew in His "messianic self-consciousness"—that is, in His awareness that He was actually the predicted Messiah of Israel. But this passage reveals rather clearly that from the start of His ministry Jesus knew His identity. When handed the book of Isaiah to read in the synagogue of His hometown of Nazareth, Jesus deliberately unrolled the long scroll almost to the inner end and found the place where it was written:

> The Spirit of the Lord is upon Me,
> Because He anointed Me to preach the gospel to the poor.
> He has sent Me to proclaim release to the captives,
> And recovery of sight to the blind,
> To set free those who are downtrodden,
> To proclaim the favorable year of the Lord.
>
> —LUKE 4:18–19

By comparing these words with the original passage in Isaiah 61:1–3 (see the comment on that passage), we can notice several differences. Some of these may result from Luke's having quoted the passage from the Septuagint version, the Greek translation made by Jewish scholars in Egypt two hundred years before Christ. But the fifth line of Luke's quotation seems to be an original comment on Isaiah's text added by Jesus Himself.

Our Lord obviously knew the passage well and had meditated much on it. But even though Isaiah's oracle continued for several lines more, Jesus suddenly stopped reading after the first line of Isaiah 61:2, rolled up the scroll, gave it back to the attendant and announced, "Today this scripture has been fulfilled in your hearing" (v. 21).

Which words in Isaiah's prophecy did Jesus refrain from reading? The next phrase in Isaiah reads, "to proclaim . . . the day of vengeance of our God." Undoubtedly Jesus stopped purposely because the "day of vengeance" still awaits His second coming. But the "favorable year of the Lord"—that is, the era of the Lord's favor and grace, describes His first coming and this present age.

From His baptism on, Jesus was full of the Holy Spirit and was led by the Spirit (Luke 4:1). After His temptation in the wilderness He returned in the power of the Spirit into Galilee (v. 14). He knew that He cast out demons by the Spirit of God (Matt. 12:28).

Although He had always existed as the Son of God with all the powers and privileges of deity, Jesus Christ did not regard His equality with God a thing to be selfishly exploited. He emptied Himself ("made himself of no reputation," KJV) by voluntarily depriving Himself of the use of His divine attributes and powers and took the form of a servant (Phil. 2:5–7). In this position of humility He depended completely upon the Father and the Spirit (John 5:19, 30).

As a Spirit-anointed man, Jesus is a perfect example for the Christian. All believers should know they are sons and daughters of God (1 John 2:3, 5; 3:24) and that they have the Spirit of Christ (Rom. 8:9). After their baptism in the Spirit, they should know that they can count on the Spirit to work supernaturally in and through them. Anointed with the same Spirit that descended upon the Lord Jesus, Christians should expect to do the works of healing and deliverance that Isaiah prophesied for the Messiah to perform (see the comments on Matthew 4:23–25; John 14:12–14).

## The Subjection of Demons to Christian Disciples—Luke 10:17–20

Luke 9 relates how Jesus called the twelve apostles together and sent them out preaching the kingdom of God, giving them power and authority to drive out all demons and to heal diseases (9:1–5). They returned after conducting successful healing and preaching missions and reported to Jesus (9:6, 10). Subsequently, in order to warn them against spiritual pride and personal kingdom-building, He taught them the importance of self-denial and cross-bearing (9:23–26). "If anyone wishes to come after Me, let him deny himself, and take up his cross daily, and follow Me" (v. 23).

In the same way, Spirit-baptized Christians who have had various charismatic gifts manifested through them should give ear to Jesus' exhortation. They too, as much as any other follower of Christ, must deny themselves and take up their cross every day (v. 23). They must be willing to suffer persecution and to lose their possessions, their position and power, and even their personal rights.

They must in fact accept these deathblows to their pride in a spirit of meekness without becoming angry at others or God. The crucified life means yielding their wills moment by moment to the control of the Spirit and staying fully surrendered to Christ the Son and God the Father. Each new day they should consider themselves dead to their old sinful tendencies and alive to God in Christ Jesus (Rom. 6:4–11).

The Lord Jesus appointed seventy other disciples in addition to the twelve apostles and sent them on ahead of Him, two by two, to prepare hearts where He Himself was going to come (Luke 10:1). Christ's principle of His laborers in the harvest working two or three together is basic and extremely important to follow, to strengthen their witness and to give each other the wisdom and encouragement that any one of them might lack from time to time. When two are agreed on earth about anything that they may ask of the Lord, He has said that it will be done for them by His Father in heaven; this promise includes binding evil powers and loosing people from their grip (Matt. 18:18–19).

Ecclesiastes tells us that two persons teamed together are better than one, for if one falls down the other can lift him or her up; though one of them may be overpowered, two can resist an adversary (Eccles. 4:9–12). Note other passages dealing with the two-by-two principle: Mark 6:7; 14:13; Luke 7:19; John 1:35–41; Acts 9:38; 10:7; 13:2–7; 15:36–41; 17:4, 14–16; 18:5; 19:22. Paul suffered severe discouragement when he remained alone in Ephesus and in the Roman province of Asia (Acts 19:22), until at last Titus rejoined him in Macedonia (2 Cor. 1:8–11; 2:12f.; 7:5–7).

The seventy returned with joy because they found that even the demons were subject to them when they used Jesus' name (Luke 10:17). Their use of His name was significant, because a person's name signifies all that the person represents—his or her character and reputation, authority and titles, power and influence.

The Lord explained to them why they had such success over Satan's forces. A fresh translation brings out the meaning of His words in verse 18: "I was watching Satan in the act of falling from heaven like lightning." Jesus saw in His own exorcisms (Matt. 12:25–29) and in the success of His disciples the beginning of the downfall of Satan's kingdom. "Like lightning" suggests that the devil's power would be broken worldwide, "as the lightning comes from the east, and flashes even to the west" (Matt. 24:27). The great dragon Satan would ultimately be cast down from heaven. Then he would no longer be able to accuse our Christian brothers and sisters before God (Rev. 12:7–10; compare Job 1:11; 2:5; Zechariah 3:1; Luke 22:31).

The actual reason for Christians having dominion at present over evil spirits is that Jesus Christ has delegated to us His divine authority "to tread upon serpents and scorpions, and over all the power (*dunamis*) of the enemy" (v. 19). "Serpents and scorpions" were symbolic terms for crafty and dangerous enemies and cruel oppressions (compare for serpents, Psalm 58:4; 140:3; Jeremiah 8:14–17; Revelation 12:9; 20:2; for scorpions, 1 Kings 12:11).

The apostle Paul promised that the God of peace would soon crush Satan under our feet (Rom. 16:20). This figurative language harked back to Psalm 91:13 and to Genesis 3:15. In the Genesis verse the serpent who deceived Eve was told that the "seed" of the woman (the virgin-born Messiah) would "bruise" (KJV, NAS) or "crush" (NIV) his head. Of course, this crushing will be completed by our Lord Jesus Christ at His return (Rev. 20:2–3, 10); but Paul's words "under your feet" suggested that even now we may experience signal victories over the devil. We now are seated or enthroned with Christ in the heavenlies, in the supernatural sphere where spiritual warfare is constantly being waged, and thus we fight from His position of supreme authority (Eph. 2:6–7).

Jesus was thrilled—"He rejoiced greatly in the Holy Spirit"—that God the Father had revealed "these things," about how to achieve victory over demons, to "babes," to His disciples who were uneducated in the wisdom and knowledge of this world (Luke 10:21–24). Yet He told them to rejoice, not in their momentary triumph over evil spirits, but in the knowledge that their names are recorded in heaven for eternity (v. 20). He warned them not to become so delighted in His delegated authority that their egos would become puffed up. Lucifer had in fact lost his place in heaven because of pride in himself and in the authority given him (as Isaiah 14:12–15 suggests).

## Persistent Asking for the Holy Spirit—Luke 11:5–13

In the Sermon on the Mount, Jesus had given almost identical instruction on the certainty of answer to prayer (Matt. 7:7–11). On this separate occasion, the Lord adds an interesting parable that places prayer on the basis of personal friendship with God (vv. 5–8). He climaxes His teaching by encouraging the child of God to keep on asking for the Holy Spirit, whereas in Matthew 7:11 the corresponding object of prayer was "good gifts."

In the Greek text in verses 9 and 10, the verbs "ask," "seek" and "knock," as well as the verb "ask" in verse 13, are in the present tense; this suggests that we are to keep on asking, to be as persistent as the man who went to his friend's home at midnight to get bread. We may also conclude that just as we ask in the Lord's prayer for God to give us each day our daily bread (v. 3), so our heavenly Father will keep on giving us the Holy Spirit day by day. Therefore, this passage is helpful instruction not only for the Christian seeking the baptism in the Holy Spirit, but also for the Spirit-baptized child of God to keep on walking in the fullness of the Spirit each day (see the comment on Ephesians 5:15–21).

## The Promise of the Father—Luke 24:44–53

The appearance of the risen Lord Jesus, described in Luke 24:44–49, came shortly before His ascension back to heaven. It must have occurred after He had met His disciples in Galilee (Matt. 28:7, 10, 16–20; John 21:1–23), because He commanded them to stay in the city of Jerusalem until they were endued with power from on high (v. 49). This is one of the occasions when Jesus commissioned His followers to be witnesses (see the comment on Matthew 28:18–20). Here Jesus stressed that they should preach in His name the doctrine of repentance leading to the forgiveness of sins (v. 47). The phrase translated "in his name" literally means "upon his name," on the basis of His name, which stands for His deity and authority and the finished work of redemption through His death and resurrection.

In verse 49 Jesus says literally, "And behold, I Myself am going to send forth the promise of My Father upon you." As a result, they would be clothed with power (*dunamis*) from on high, that is, with supernatural power. (For the figurative language of being clothed with a virtue or power, see Job 29:14; Psalm 93:1; in Judges 6:34—see the comment—the Hebrew literally says, "The Spirit of the Lord clothed Gideon.")

The promise of the Father refers to God's promised gift of the Holy Spirit. The outpouring of the Spirit was first promised through the prophets (Isa. 32:15; 44:3; Ezek. 39:29; Joel 2:28). In the upper room Christ had told His disciples that His Father would send the Holy Spirit in His name (John 14:26; compare 14:16; 15:26; 16:7). Just before He ascended to heaven, He specifically related the promise to the baptism in the Holy Spirit (see the comment on Acts 1:4–8).

On the Day of Pentecost, Peter explained the startling words of praise to God in other languages, which the crowds in the temple area had just heard, by saying about Jesus: "Therefore having been exalted to the right hand of God, and having received from the Father the promise of the Holy Spirit, He has poured forth this which you both see and hear" (Acts 2:33). When many Jews were convicted, Peter told them to repent and be baptized and that they too could receive the gift of the Holy Spirit, "for the promise is for you and your children . . ." (Acts 2:39).

Paul insisted that all of the Christian life should be lived in faith, because we receive the promise of the Spirit through faith (Gal. 3:14). And he taught as well that we are sealed with the promised Holy Spirit (literally, "the Holy Spirit of the promise," Ephesians 1:13).

According to verses 50–53, after the Ascension the disciples awaited the fulfillment of this promise with great joy. They were continually in the temple praising God, as well as devoting themselves to prayer (Acts 1:14). The earnest child of God today seeking the baptism in the Spirit may well imitate their attitude of expectancy, joyous praise, and prayerfulness.

## *Jesus, Lamb of God and Baptizer in the Holy Spirit— John 1:29–34*

John the Baptist was divinely commissioned to bear witness to the light, Jesus Christ. His two greatest statements about Jesus and His work are recorded in the first chapter of John. John points Jesus out as "the Lamb of God who takes away the sin of the world" (v. 29) and "the one who baptizes in the Holy Spirit" (v. 33).

First of all, Jesus is the perfect, infinite sacrifice who, like a sheep brought as a sin offering to the tabernacle, dies in the place of the sinner (Lev. 4–5). As the blood of the Passover lamb was put on the Israelite's doorway (Exod. 12:6–7, 13), so Jesus' blood was shed for the remission or forgiveness of our sins (Heb. 9:12–14, 22, 26) and to save us from eternal death (compare 1 Corinthians 5:7). As the scapegoat carried away the sins of the people into oblivion in the wilderness on the annual Day of Atonement (Lev. 16:20–22), so Jesus our Savior removes completely and permanently the sins of people all over the world who trust in Him.

Second, equally important to Jesus' atoning work through pouring out His lifeblood is His work of pouring out the Spirit. God's words to John in verse 33 may be translated literally, "This is the baptizer in the Holy Spirit." Just as surely as Jesus came to earth to seek and to save the lost (Luke 19:10), He returned to heaven to send the promised gift of the Holy Spirit to the church (see the comment on Luke 24:44–53).

John 1:33 clearly teaches that Jesus Christ, upon whom the Spirit remains, is the baptizer in the Spirit. It is not a minister of the gospel or some other Christian who does the baptizing, which distinguishes Spirit baptism from water baptism. So the one seeking the baptism in the Holy Spirit should ask the Father with confidence (see the comment on Luke 11:5–13) and expect to receive the gift from Christ Himself (see the comment on Matthew 3:11–17).

## Born of the Spirit—John 3:1–8

In talking to the Jewish teacher Nicodemus, our Lord Jesus spoke of salvation as a new birth: "Ye must be born again" (3:7, KJV). When Nicodemus questioned how an adult could be born a second time, Jesus explained, "Unless one is born of water and the Spirit, he cannot enter into the kingdom of God. That which is born of the flesh is flesh; and that which is born of the Spirit is spirit" (vv. 5–6).

The theme of the Gospel of John is life—eternal life (compare John 20:30–31). Because the aim of Christ's conversation was to tell Nicodemus how to have eternal life (John 3:15–16), He meant that to be born again was the only way to have this new kind of life. Jesus was not talking about another physical birth, about being "born of the flesh." The natural human birth produces only another weak, sinful human being with a mortal body controlled by a selfish inner nature or soul. "No," Jesus said in effect, "you have to be born of the Spirit. Only the one who is born of the Spirit has a true spiritual nature."

In the beginning God created humankind in His image (Gen. 1:27) and pronounced what He had made to be "very good" (1:31). Humanity's character reflects the rational and moral qualities of the nature of God, who is spirit (John 4:24; see the comment on Genesis 2:7). As a separate individual Adam was a free moral agent. That is, his will was free to choose anything he wanted, even to obey God or to rebel against His commandments and suffer the consequences.

Why then do human beings need a new birth? Very soon after their creation, Adam and Eve disobeyed God and thus broke their fellowship with Him. When they did, they died spiritually—what we call the fall of humankind. Through human reproduction they passed on that spiritual death to all their descendants. Therefore, the Bible says, human beings are "dead in. . . trespasses and sins" (Eph. 2:1), spiritually excluded from the life of God (Eph. 4:18). Without the control and guidance of God's Spirit, they live selfishly, operating only from their sinful nature. That is why Paul wrote, "We all once lived in the passions of our flesh, following the desires of body and mind, and so we were by nature children of wrath, like the rest of mankind" (Eph. 2:3, RSV).

The human spirit of the lost sinner is guilty, defiled and unresponsive to God, "dead" or asleep as far as God is concerned. But it is not nonexistent. The spirit of a medium, for instance, can make contact with evil spirits from the demonic realm.

Nevertheless, because of its wretched condition, the human spirit must be forgiven, cleansed and made alive to God—in a word, regenerated. This is essentially what happens when we repent of our sins, receive Christ and are converted or saved. On the basis of Christ's dying in our stead, God forgives us and reckons His perfect righteousness to our account; this is what Paul means by justification (Rom. 3:21–5:21).

God also sets us apart to Himself, counts us holy as He sees us in His dear Son and works to purify us; this is sanctification (1 Cor. 1:30; Eph. 5:26; Heb. 9:13–14; 10:22). Thus the image of God, which was terribly marred by the fall of Adam as well as by our own sins, is restored through the redemption which is in Christ Jesus.

In John 3:5 our need of cleansing and new life is primarily in view. In saying we must be "born of water," Jesus signified the *cleansing* aspect of regeneration, and by His expression "born of the Spirit," He referred to the *renewing* aspect of the Holy Spirit's work in regeneration (see the comment on Titus 3:4–7).

Jesus expected Nicodemus, an important Bible teacher in Israel at that time, to understand these things (John 3:10). He was not advancing some novel idea, for Ezekiel had long before prophesied about the new birth (36:25–27):

> Then I will sprinkle clean water on you, and you will be clean; I will cleanse you from all your filthiness....Moreover, I will give you a new heart and put a new spirit within you; and I will remove the heart of stone from your flesh and give you a heart of flesh [that is, a soft, spiritually responsive heart]. And I will put My Spirit within you and cause you to walk in My statutes.

These promises were to be part of the New Covenant (Jer. 31:31–34; 32:40; Ezek. 37:24–26), and now Messiah had come to initiate that covenant (see the comment on Ezekiel 36:27; 37:14).

But what is the water that cleanses? Nicodemus was well aware of the signification of Judaism's ritual washings (compare Jeremiah 33:8) and of what John the Baptist was preaching—the necessity of repentance. As Gary Burge points out in his masterful work on the Holy Spirit in John, the reference to water in John 3:5 is clarified by the mention of baptizing by John the Baptist and by Jesus' disciples in 3:22–30 and 4:1–3.[5]

Water thus symbolizes the cleansing action of God's Word when we respond to God by turning away from our sins. Paul wrote that Christ died to sanctify the church, having cleansed her by "the washing of water with the word" (Eph. 5:26). In the upper room, Jesus said to His disciples that they were already clean because of the word which He had spoken to them (John 15:3). The inner cleansing that results when we are convicted by hearing God's Word and we then confess our sins should be sealed as soon as possible by our submission to water baptism (Acts 2:38; 22:16).

Forgiveness and cleansing are not all that sinners need, however. They must also be "quickened" or made alive to God in their spirits. They must be tuned in to the frequency of heaven in order to hear and understand God's further teaching.

Only the Holy Spirit can produce this regeneration or new birth. "It is the Spirit who gives life" (John 6:63; compare 2 Corinthians 3:6). He is the one who plants the incorruptible seed of God's Word in the human heart (1 Pet. 1:23).

The Holy Spirit enters the human spirit and brings it from spiritual death to eternal life. Those who identify themselves unreservedly with Christ become spiritually one with the Lord (1 Cor. 6:17) and participate in God's divine nature (2 Pet. 1:4). By being born "again" (the Greek word *anōthen* can also mean "from above," John 3:31; 19:11; James 1:17; 3:15, 17), the individual becomes a new creature (2 Cor. 5:17, compare Ephesians 2:10). This means he or she is now a member of the new creation which is based on the resurrection of Christ and His defeat of sin, death and Satan.

The new factor in the new creation not previously available to believers in Yahweh is their abiding in God—in the Father and the Son—and God's abiding in them (John 14:20; 15:4–10; 1 John 2:24). It is Christ's indwelling them, "Christ in you, the hope of glory" (Col. 1:27). Because Jesus in His glorified resurrection body is now in heaven at the Father's right hand, it must be His Spirit that is in us (1 John 3:24).

Therefore, Paul clearly stated that if anyone does not have the Spirit of Christ, he or she does not belong to Him at all (Rom. 8:9). Lost sinners were described as "having not the Spirit" (Jude 19, KJV). So we may confidently say that all truly born-again believers have the Holy Spirit indwelling them (see the comment on John 20:21–23).

How can a person be born again? In the prologue of this Gospel, John declared that to as many as received Jesus Christ, the living Word of God, to those who believed in His name, He gave the right to become children of God. Such people experience a birth that is not one of "blood" (that is, physical descent), nor of the "will of the flesh" (sexual impulse), nor of the "will of man" (the desire of a husband for descendants), but of God alone (John 1:12–13).

Thus we must believe with biblical faith in Jesus Christ as God's dear Son who gave Himself to die in the sinner's place and who rose again bodily in proof that He had accomplished our redemption (John 3:16; Rom. 10:9–10; 1 Cor. 15:1–4). According to the Bible, believing in Christ includes three aspects: mentally assenting to the facts about Christ and the gospel message (John 12:11, 42); personally accepting Jesus as our Savior (John 9:35–38); and daily trusting and depending on Him, confessing Him (Rom. 10:9–10) and committing our entire life and destiny to His care and guidance (2 Tim. 1:12).

## The Spirit Without Measure—John 3:34

In times of the mighty outpouring of the Holy Spirit, we do well to remember that only to His Son, Jesus Christ, has God given the Spirit without limit. In John 3:34, "he whom God has sent" (RSV) refers to the Son of God—not, as some have suggested, to Jesus' followers. While John the Baptist and others were God's messengers and prophets, Jesus was uniquely both the message of eternal life and the predicted messenger of the New Covenant (Mal. 3:1b). He spoke the words of truth because He was and is the truth. Christ is God's ultimate and perfect spokesman because God did not give the Spirit to Him by measure (see the comments on Matthew 3:11–17; 4:23–25; Luke 4:14–21).

In this passage the evangelist was explaining (3:31–36) that Jesus was greater than John the Baptist, the last of the Old Testament line of prophets, because God gave Him the Spirit "not by measure" (*ou gar ek metrou didōsin to pneuma*). John had already stated that at Jesus' own baptism the Spirit had descended and remained upon Him (John 1:32–33). Later, Jesus would assert to the assembled crowd at Capernaum that on Him, the Son of Man, God the Father had set His seal (John 6:27, RSV). This divine certification and approval referred to the Holy Spirit who had descended upon Jesus at His baptism and to the accompanying voice from heaven, "This is My beloved Son, in whom I am well-pleased" (Matt. 3:16–17).

As Burge has said, Jesus' "endowment with the Spirit is permanent, full, and eschatological."[6] Thus the interpretation of 3:34 that views Jesus as the one to whom God has given the Spirit without measure is preferable to holding that Jesus is the one who gives the Spirit without limit to His disciples.

As Christ's follower, the Spirit-baptized Christian should humbly recognize that in Jesus alone is the work of the Spirit seen in fullest measure. In Him alone all the fullness of deity dwells in bodily form (Col. 2:9). Jesus did promise believers that they could perform the same works He did and even greater works (see the comment on John 14:12–14). But we must remember that God has allotted to each Christian a *measure* of faith (Rom. 12:3). Therefore those through whom the Spirit operates in an unusual way should recognize that their charismatic ministry is from God and should not think of themselves more highly than they ought to think (Rom. 12:3).

Jesus Christ is God's perfect revelation to humankind (Heb. 1:1–3). He is the head of the body; we are but members. No Christian will surpass Jesus in beauty of character and fruits of the Spirit, and no miracle, vision or utterance given through one of us by the Spirit will ever transcend the glory and perfection of Jesus' works.

## *True Worship—John 4:21–24*

In this hour, under the New Covenant, God is no longer requiring His worshipers to go to Jerusalem to worship. Jesus came to usher in a new era of worship as our high priest. At the moment of His death on the cross, the veil of the temple was torn in two from top to bottom, and the necessity of worship at the one temple ceased to exist. Christ stated simply but profoundly, "God is spirit; and those who worship Him must worship in spirit and truth" *(en pneumati kai alētheia,* 4:24).

God is spirit, that is, completely spiritual in His essence. At the same time, God's Spirit is the "medium" of His relationship with human beings. Therefore, if worship is to be effective, it must be spiritual in nature, and we must personally experience this medium through which God chooses to join Himself to humanity.[7]

Worship is thus a matter of inner devotion and wholehearted sincerity, not of outward ritual and ceremony. This is not to say that the latter have no proper function, for even spiritual worship may have certain liturgical forms to express its meaning. But it is true that the empowering of the Holy Spirit is needed to make worship genuine. Paul said that Christians worship by the Spirit of God (Phil. 3:3, NIV). The Spirit gives us a sense of the reality and presence of the triune God as He takes the things of Christ and the Father and shows them to us (John 16:14–15; compare Matthew 11:27).

Genuine worship that pleases God operates in the realm of truth—the true knowledge of God. The Lord Jesus has made possible a more intelligent worship of God by revealing in His teaching and through His perfect life and deeds on earth what God is really like. Even the Pharisees admitted that Jesus taught the way of God in truth (Matt. 22:16). The Spirit of truth (John 14:17; 15:26; 16:13) is the one who directs the heart to prayer and praise that is in full harmony with the truth about God as revealed in His Word.

God is holy; we should worship Him in the beauty of holiness (Ps. 29:2; 96:9). God is righteous and just; thus obedience is better than sacrifice (1 Sam. 15:22), and the practice of righteousness should characterize our lives (Matt. 5:20; 6:33; 1 John 2:29; 3:7, 10). God is love; therefore we are to love Him with all our hearts and souls and minds and strength, and our neighbor as ourselves (Luke 10:27).

The Lord is near to all who call upon Him in truth (Ps. 145:18). In the Old Testament, the Hebrew word often translated "truth" *('emet)* may also mean "faithfulness." True worship and service entail turning from every other god (any person, thing or ambition that is granted first place in our hearts) and yielding absolute loyalty to the one true and living God. Thus Joshua exhorted Israel to fear the Lord and serve Him in sincerity and in truth and to put away the idols which their ancestors had worshiped in Mesopotamia and in Egypt (Josh. 24:14; compare Jeremiah 4:1–2).

Worship in Spirit and truth is worship that is focused on the risen, exalted Christ and empowered by His Spirit.[8] As the incarnate Son of God and Lamb that was slain, Jesus Himself is worthy to receive the same adoration and loyalty that belongs to the Father (Rev. 5:8–14; 4:8–11).

## Rivers of Living Water—John 7:37–39

Tradition says that on the last day of the week-long Feast of Tabernacles celebrated in ancient Judaism, a procession of priests would draw water from the pool of Siloam and pour it out in the temple court. By that ceremony the people were reminded how God had provided water for their thirsty ancestors in the wilderness. This was the day described in John 7:37–39. During the feast that was held six months before Jesus' death, He stood—which was the posture of a prophet as opposed to the seated posture of a teacher—and publicly promised to quench the spiritual thirst of everyone who would come to Him and drink (v. 37).

Previously Jesus had offered "living water" to the woman of Samaria instead of the physical water from the deep well outside her village (John 4:10). On that occasion He had said, "Whoever drinks the water that I shall give him will never suffer thirst any more. The water that I shall give him will be an inner spring always welling up for eternal life" (John 4:14, NEB).

The Greek word *hallomenou* for "welling up" literally means "leaping." It describes the rapid movements of the beggar at the Gate Beautiful after he was healed (Acts 3:8) as well as of the cripple at Lystra (Acts 14:10), fulfilling the prophecy of Isaiah 35:6, "Then the lame will leap like a deer." The Greek Septuagint also uses the verb *hallomai* to speak of the Spirit of God leaping or coming mightily upon Samson (Judg. 14:6, 19; 15:14) and upon Saul (1 Sam. 10:10). Therefore Jesus' promise in John 4:14 may imply the energizing of the indwelling Spirit that will become available after His resurrection.

Undoubtedly on that festival day in Jerusalem our Lord had in mind such passages as Isaiah 12:3, "With joy you will draw water from the wells of salvation" (RSV, NIV) and Jeremiah 2:13, "They have forsaken Me, the fountain of living waters." In these verses, water symbolizes salvation and everlasting life, which alone can satisfy the universal desire for rest, peace and security both now and in the life to come. So to the crowd of worshipers in the temple Jesus promised that the person who continually comes to Him would have a constant supply of life and the indwelling Spirit.

Our Lord, moreover, added another great promise: "He who believes in Me, as the Scripture said, 'From his innermost being shall flow rivers of living water'" (v. 38). Punctuated differently, verses 37–38 could be rendered (as they appear in the NIV footnote):

> If a man is thirsty, let him come to me.
> And let him drink, who believes in me.
> As the Scripture has said. . . .

The effect of the latter rendition is to allow the next statement, "As the Scripture has said, streams of living water will flow from within him," to be the evangelist's explanation referring to Jesus, not Jesus' words for the believer. In this case, the "rivers" of the Spirit would flow from Jesus Himself. Similarly, Paul pictured spiritual drink flowing from the spiritual rock that accompanied the Israelites in the wilderness, "and the rock was Christ" (1 Cor. 10:4).

Some who accept this interpretation see in the water coming from Jesus' side on the cross (John 19:34) a fulfillment of the prophecy of 7:37–39. As Moses struck the rock in the desert and water came out of it (Exod. 17:6; Num. 20:11), so Jesus' side was pierced and from it flowed blood and water, symbolic of the Spirit released by Christ's death. Taken in this way, John understood the living Spirit to be none other than the life of the crucified and glorified Lord Jesus.[9]

Following the traditional punctuation, John 7:38 describes something more than receiving salvation as in the previous verse. Here the believer becomes a source of living water to supply others. Guided by the Holy Spirit, the apostle John explained what Jesus meant: "He was speaking of the Spirit which believers in him would receive later; for the Spirit had not yet been given, because Jesus had not yet been glorified" (v. 39, NEB). This passage is the clearest reference in the Gospel of John to the promise of the Holy Spirit fulfilled in the Spirit baptism beginning on the Day of Pentecost.

No particular passage of Old Testament Scripture is quoted word for word in verse 38, but similar language occurs in several places in Scripture. Isaiah 58:11, for example, describes a godly believer this way: "You will be like a watered garden, and like a spring of water whose waters do not fail." Jeremiah 31:12 employs this same expression.

Isaiah 32:2 says, "And each will be . . . like streams of water in a dry country" (see the comment on Isaiah 32:15). Consider furthermore the bridegroom's description of his bride, "a garden fountain, a well of living water, and flowing streams from Lebanon" (Song of Sol. 4:15, RSV). In addition, the child of God is exhorted in Proverbs to watch over his or her heart, "for from it flow the springs of life" (Prov. 4:23).

Jesus' figure of speech may also have been suggested by Ezekiel's vision of the life-giving river flowing from the eschatological temple in Jerusalem (Ezek. 47:1–12; compare Psalm 46:4; Joel 3:18; Zechariah 14:8). In this present age, however, each individual Christian is a temple of the Holy Spirit (1 Cor. 3:16; 6:19), out of which the Spirit may flow in blessing and healing power. The Old Testament in fact connects the coming of the Spirit with the pouring forth of refreshing streams (see the comments on Isaiah 32:15; 44:1–5).

Taking all these passages together, the clause "as the Scripture said" in verse 38 is entirely justified.

This beautiful word picture teaches us much about the overflowing life of truly Spirit-filled Christians. First of all, their own needs are met. Their own deep spiritual thirst is already being quenched through the regenerating and indwelling ministry of the Spirit of God living in their spirits (John 3:5; 7:37; 20:22). Then when Jesus baptizes them in the Holy Spirit, the Lord causes the Spirit to rise and overflow from where He is dwelling inside them, to inundate their entire being.

In many cases this experience brings about a needed release of the whole person, as if a dam were opened and the pent-up waters rushed forth. To use Dennis Bennett's illustration of an irrigation ditch, we might say that before the canal is filled, it is dry and so are the fields around. Then the gate of the reservoir is opened. First, the canal itself is washed clean of dust and debris, and grass and flowers spring up along its banks. But the water doesn't stop there; all along the way farmers open sluices, and the life-giving water streams out into the fields to make "the desert . . . rejoice, and blossom as the rose" (Isa. 35:1, KJV).

So [it is] with you and me. The reservoir, the well, is in us when we become Christians. Then, when we allow the indwelling living water of the Spirit to flow out into our souls and bodies, we are refreshed first. Our minds come alive in a new way to God's reality. We think of Him, even dream of Him, with a new frequency and joy. Our emotions respond, and we become happy in Him. Our wills respond, and we do what He wants. Our bodies respond, not only by feelings of well-being, but by actual renewed strength, health and youth. Then the living water pours out on others. They see the power and love of Jesus in His people. He is now able to use us to refresh the world around us.[10]

A second point to notice in Jesus' word picture is that the waters flow out from the belly and not the brain. The Greek word for "belly" or innermost being is *koilia*, the abdomen or body cavity containing the entire digestive tract, including the stomach (Matt. 15:17; Luke 15:16; 1 Cor. 6:13; Rev. 10:9–10). It also means the womb (Luke 1:15, 41–42; John 3:4).

Here, following the usage of the corresponding Hebrew word *beṭen* for "belly," the term denotes the hidden, innermost recesses of a person's being (Job 15:35; Ps. 31:9; Prov. 18:8; 20:27, 30; Hab. 3:16, all KJV). The Old Testament does not associate the human spirit with the head or brain or mental capacity but with the heart (Ps. 51:10, 17; Prov. 15:13; 17:22; Isa. 57:15; Ezek. 11:19; 18:31; 36:26). Paul also distinguished his spirit from his mind, for by means of tongues he could pray with the spirit, and he could pray with the understanding also (1 Cor. 14:14–15).

God's intention is for the Holy Spirit to "flow forth" from the innermost being of Christians and to control their entire person. Actually this is a great blessing to believers. As "Mr. Pentecost," David du Plessis, used to say, we no longer have to pump up the water and pour it forth ourselves; the rivers *flow* out of us. God does not expect Spirit-filled Christians to reach out to others by means of ingenuity or superior intelligence. Rather, believers are to wait for the Spirit to direct and empower them.

Third, Jesus made His promise to those who *continually* believe in and rely on Him. This is the force of the Greek present tense in the word "believes" in verse 38. An uninterrupted flow—continuous fruit bearing, regular witness and faithful service—results from depending on the Lord moment by moment and being continually filled with the Spirit (see the comment on Ephesians 5:15–21). In the new Jerusalem, the river of the water of life will enable the tree of life to bear twelve kinds of fruit, yielding its fruit every month (Rev. 22:1–2). Every believer should be such a tree now (compare

Psalm 1:3; Jeremiah 17:8).

Fourth, the word *rivers* in verse 38 suggests a copious flow of blessing. Those who abide in Christ bear "much fruit" (John 15:5). Believers are empowered to do the works of Christ, yes, even greater works (John 14:12). They experience the abundant life (John 10:10), always abounding in the work of the Lord (1 Cor. 15:58). The virtues of the Christian life abound in them so that they are assured of a glorious entrance into the eternal kingdom of our Lord and Savior Jesus Christ (2 Pet. 1:5–11). They please the Lord in all respects and are always increasing in the knowledge of God, strengthened with all might according to His glorious power (Col. 1:10–11). God enables them to fulfill "every good resolve and work of faith by his power" (2 Thess. 1:11, RSV).

A verse in Proverbs suggests one of the main channels through which the "rivers of living water" may flow out of the believer's life to others. "The words of a man's mouth are as deep waters, a flowing brook, a fountain of wisdom" (Prov. 18:4, JPS). Similar is Proverbs 10:11, "The mouth of the righteous is a fountain of life."

In the New Testament, James compared the mouth from which blessing comes with a fountain that sends forth "sweet" (fresh, pure) water (3:10–11, KJV; see the comment on James 3:1–12). The Holy Spirit brings forth prophecies that edify, exhort and comfort (1 Cor. 14:3). Spirit-overflowing Christians are those who talk with each other much about the Lord (compare Malachi 3:16), who love to sing psalms and hymns and charismatic songs, and who are always giving thanks for everything to God (Eph. 5:18–20).

## Greater Works Than These—John 14:12–14

The promise that the Lord Jesus made regarding prayer in John 14:12–14 is almost breathtaking. Preparing to place His ministry in the hands of His disciples, He said to them in the upper room and to us today, "He who believes in Me, the works that I do shall he do also; and greater works than these shall he do; because I go to the Father" (v. 12). There will be greater works through the church, His new body.

Most Bible commentators believe that the "greater works" are greater in quantity or are miracles of conversion in the spiritual realm. Jesus had scores of converts; the apostles numbered theirs in the thousands. Jesus ministered only to the Jews in Palestine; Peter opened the door for Gentiles to be saved at Cornelius's house, and the early Christians soon reached the known world.

Finis J. Dake, however, pointed out in his annotated Bible that by the term *works,* Jesus was referring to His miracles, healings, signs and mighty acts of power (Matt. 11:2; compare 11:5; John 5:20, 36; 9:3–4; 10:25, 32; 14:10–12; 15:24). His works included healing every kind of disease, casting out demons and raising the dead. He controlled the wind and the waves, walked on water, multiplied food and turned water into wine. The promise here is that each believer can receive the Holy Spirit and be endued with power so that potentially he or she can do all the works of Christ.

Dake continued:

> To make this a promise of spiritual works only, when He did (both) material and spiritual works, is a poor excuse for unbelief.... The greater works are not those of reaching more people by means of radio, television, and the printed page, for these are natural means and can be used by unsaved men who do not have the Holy Spirit power to do the works of Christ. No man can receive greater power than Christ, for He received the Spirit without measure (John 3:34; Isa. 11:2; 61:1–2). Therefore, the greater works could not consist of doing greater things than Christ could have done had He had the occasion to do them. The thought is that each believer can have equal power with Christ to do what He did as well as greater things if and when the occasion requires it.[11]

## Another Comforter—John 14:16–18, 26; 15:26; 16:7

Some of the most important passages in the Bible about the Holy Spirit occur in the upper room teachings of Christ (John 13–16). Only on that night before He was betrayed did Jesus ever refer to the Spirit as "Comforter." In response to the love and obedience of His disciples, He promised to ask the Father to give them "another Comforter" (14:16, KJV).

Much can be learned about the Holy Spirit from this expression. The Greek term for comforter, *paraklētos,* is difficult to translate by a single English word. Thus newer English versions have "Helper" (NAS), "Counselor" (RSV, NIV) or "Advocate" (NEB). In 1 John 2:1, the same Greek word is used of Christ and is translated in nearly all English versions as "Advocate." In John 14:16, the Amplified Bible also suggests "Intercessor," "Strengthener" and "Standby."

To cover all these meanings, an English word, *paraclete,* has been coined from the Greek term. Basically it means "one who is called alongside to help, to counsel or to intercede in behalf of someone else." A paraclete is like an intimate friend who acts as a personal adviser, such as an aide-de-camp, special consultant or private assistant to an emperor or a president.

The Holy Spirit is our Comforter, because He pleads, convinces and convicts when necessary; because He both strengthens and defends us in time of formidable attacks. Now we have two divine paracletes. Christ has gone to heaven to be the advocate who pleads the believer's case with the Father against the accuser, Satan. The Holy Spirit has come to earth to be the advocate who helps the believer take a stand against the world (John 15:18–27; 16:8–11). He also "comforts" churches by the exhortation and encouragement which He supplies through His gifts (Acts 9:31; 1 Cor. 14:3–5).

The phrase, "another Comforter," distinctly marks the personality of the Holy Spirit and His true deity. The Greek word *allos* for "another" indicates simply a distinction of individuals, not a difference in kind. Therefore the Spirit is another Paraclete of the same kind as Jesus, and our Lord is both a Person and God. The Holy Spirit is of the same divine essence or nature as God the Son. Thus He is also called the Spirit of Christ (Rom. 8:9; Phil. 1:19; 1 Pet. 1:11), the Spirit of Jesus (Acts 16:7; compare 16:6) and the Spirit of God's Son (Gal. 4:6).

Christ promised not to leave His disciples "comfortless" (v. 18, KJV). The Greek word is *orphanous*, "orphans." Disciples of a teacher were often called his children (Gal. 4:19; 1 John 2:1; 3:18); and when he died they considered themselves as orphans, as in the case of Socrates' friends. Jesus had just called His disciples "children" (John 13:33), and now He assured them that they would not be orphans, because He would come back to them in the sending forth of the Spirit at Pentecost. The coming of the Holy Spirit does not exclude Christ but instead makes real to us His continual presence and fellowship (John 14:21–23).

Jesus identified this other Comforter as the Spirit of truth in John 14:17; 16:13. John also used this description of the Spirit in his epistle (1 John 4:6; 5:7). Literally, the expression is "the Spirit of the truth," the truth about God, Christ and salvation. He is the Spirit of the truth because He guides us to the very fullness of the truth ("into all the truth," John 16:13). As the Jerusalem Bible points out, He teaches us to understand the mystery of Christ (Eph. 3:4; Col. 4:3), such as Jesus' fulfillment of the Scripture passages that bear witness of Him (John 5:39; 12:14–16) and the meaning of His enigmatic words (John 2:19–22), actions (John 13:6–7, 12–17) and signs (Matt. 12:38–40; 16:1–4).[12]

In John 14:26 Jesus gave the Comforter His full title, "the Holy Spirit." We need always to be reminded as He guides our lives that the moral character of the Spirit of God is holy. While He has come to glorify Christ and not Himself (John 16:14), we should always speak reverently of the Holy Spirit and honor Him as we honor the Father and the Son. It is possible to grieve the Holy Spirit of God by unwholesome words, bitterness and malice (see the comment on Ephesians 4:30).

Jesus' upper room discourses reveal several specific reasons for sending the Comforter. First, the Holy Spirit would come to teach Christians "all things" (14:26a), everything that is necessary for their salvation and fellowship with God and for the work of witnessing (compare Matthew 10:20; 1 John 2:27). Included are various truths which Jesus had not specifically taught during His time on earth (John 16:12–13, 25).

Part of this promise included bringing to remembrance the very words Christ spoke (John 14:26b), thus explaining how Matthew, Mark, Luke and John could write down the actual teachings of Jesus years after His ascension (see the comment on 2 Peter 1:19–21). The Spirit of truth, Jesus said, would also disclose to us what is to come (John 16:13), that is, announce future events. Often this revelation would be given by a prophecy, such as Agabus's warning of a coming famine (Acts 11:28).

Second, the Spirit would come to bear witness concerning Christ (John 15:26). He interprets and applies the message of redemption to the church and through the church to the world. By effecting miracles, the Holy Spirit, together with Christians, produces an irrefutable testimony to the fact that Jesus Christ has risen and is Lord (1 Cor. 12:3). As a result of the Pentecostal empowering (Acts 1:8), the Holy Spirit and believers in Christ bear a joint witness (Acts 15:28—"It seemed good to the Holy Spirit and to us"; Rev. 22:17—"The Spirit and the bride say, 'Come'").

Third, the Paraclete serves as the defense attorney for Christians when they are persecuted by the world. He not only instructs believers what they ought to say (see the comment on Matthew 10:16–20), but also takes the position of prosecutor against the hostile world by convicting it of the sin of unbelief and warning it of future judgment (John 16:7–11).

He reproves the world of sin, which is defined basically as the refusal to accept Jesus and His message (John 16:9). He convinces the world of righteousness, which was supremely demonstrated in Jesus Christ and vindicated when He rose victorious over sin and death and ascended to the Father. Now the Holy Spirit convicts sinners of their need of righteousness as they hear the Word of righteousness or as they see it exemplified in the life of a godly Christian. The Spirit convicts the world of judgment. The same ministry, death and resurrection of Jesus, whereby God condemned Satan, the present evil ruler of this world system, will be God's basis for judging the unrepentant sinner (compare Acts 17:30–31).

After studying the verses about the Comforter, we may ask, Who sent the Holy Spirit as Paraclete, and when did He come? Verses 16 and 26 of John 14 teach that the Father gives or sends the Spirit, whereas in John 15:26 Jesus said, "the Helper . . . whom I will send to you," and in John 16:7, "I will send Him to you." But there is no contradiction, for the Father and the Son always exist in closest intimacy.

John 15:26 is the most important of these verses, in which Christ says that He will send the Comforter to His disciples from (Greek *para*, from alongside) the Father, "the Spirit of truth, who proceeds from [*para*] the Father." The verb *proceeds* is in the present tense, suggesting that the Spirit as a person continuously comes forth from the presence of the Father.

On the basis of this verse, the Eastern Orthodox churches have always claimed that the Spirit eternally proceeds from the Father through the Son. They eventually split with the Roman Catholic churches, which believed that the Spirit proceeds from the Father and the Son. In keeping both with His being called the Spirit of Christ and with the equality of the Father, the Son and the Holy Spirit, the Western position seems to be more scriptural (see also Acts 2:33).

By these promises about the Comforter, did Christ intend to signify the giving of the Spirit to indwell believers after His resurrection (see the comment on John 20:21–23) or the Pentecostal outpouring of the Spirit on the church? In John 14:16 Jesus said, "I will ask the Father . . . ," indicating a future time when He would make a formal request of the Father to give the Spirit. In John 16:7 He stated that His ascension was a necessary precondition of the coming of the Spirit: "It is to your advantage that I go away; for if I do not go away, the Helper shall not come to you; but if I go, I will send Him to you." It is in His *absence* that the Lord Jesus would *send* the Comforter to them.

So Jesus clearly pointed to the Day of Pentecost and not to the night of His resurrection when He personally imparted the Spirit of life to indwell His followers. Peter's testimony in Acts 2:33 confirms this view: "Therefore having been exalted to the right hand of God, and having received from the Father the promise of the Holy Spirit, He has poured forth this which you both see and hear."

Our Lord further promised that when the Father gave another Comforter, the Spirit would be with us forever (14:16). In this age, since Pentecost, the Holy Spirit does not come on people temporarily merely to perform some task, as He did in Old Testament times. The pattern for the life and ministry of each believer in this age is to be found in Jesus Christ, and it is to be noted that at His baptism the Spirit descended *and remained* upon Him (John 1:33).

The continual anointing of the Spirit is an integral promise of the New Covenant: "'This is My covenant with them,' says the LORD: 'My Spirit which is upon you, and My words which I have put in your mouth, shall not depart from your mouth, nor from the mouth of your offspring. . . ,' says the LORD, 'from now and forever'" (Isa. 59:21; see the comment there). The Holy Spirit is not to be taken away from His work on earth but will be present during the Tribulation to aid believers (Mark 13:11; see the comments on Ezekiel 39:29; Joel 2:28–32; Acts 2:14–21) until the Antichrist will be revealed (Mark 13:14; see the comment on 2 Thessalonians 2:6–8).

Jesus revealed an additional aspect of the Spirit's coming ministry in the latter part of John 14:17: "But you know Him because He abides with you [*par' humin menei*], and will be in you [*kai en humin estai*]." The future tense of the last Greek word, *estai* ("will be"), is adequately supported by numerous ancient Greek manuscript copies and versions, although some important Greek manuscripts have *en humin estin* ("is in you").

Bruce Metzger, one of America's foremost Greek textual scholars, stated that a majority of the United Bible Societies committee in the third edition of its Greek New Testament interpreted the sense of the passage as requiring the future tense.[13] Gary Burge explained: "Just as Christ will be 'in you' (*en humin*, 14:20), so too the Paraclete dwells with you and will be 'in you' (*en humin*, 14:17)."[14]

The fact that up to the time of the Last Supper the Spirit was *with* the disciples but would be *in* them indicated a coming change in the relationship of the Spirit to Jesus' followers. Until then the Spirit of God had been present with them in the same way He had been with Old Testament believers (see the comment on Psalm 51:11). After Christ's resurrection (implied in Jesus' words, "I will come to you. After a little while the world will behold Me no more; but you will behold Me; because I live, you shall live also," 14:18–19) the Spirit would *live in* them.

When the apostles met the resurrected Jesus He imparted the Holy Spirit—His Spirit—to abide in them (see the comment on John 20:21–23). In this way Jesus' promise in 14:23 came to pass: "If anyone loves Me, he will keep My word; and My Father will love him, and We will come to him, and make Our abode with him."

To summarize, the ascended Christ would send the Spirit as paraclete at Pentecost to empower His followers, but He would personally infuse them with His Spirit after His resurrection to share His new life and enhance His fellowship with them.

## Receive the Holy Spirit—John 20:21–23

The setting of Jesus' command in John 20:21–23 was the upper room on the evening of the first day of the week, several nights after the crucifixion. The disciples had locked the doors for fear of the Jewish leaders. Suddenly Jesus was standing there among them. The reports were true; He had risen from the dead! He showed them the wounds in His hands and His side, and they were convinced. "How wonderful was their joy as they saw their Lord!" (John 20:20, TLB).

After greeting them again Jesus said, "As the Father commissioned [*apestalken*] Me, I am sending [*pempō*] you" (20:21, author's literal translation). Then He breathed on them and said to them, "Receive the Holy Spirit" (*labete pneuma hagion*, v. 22). This is obviously a pivotal statement and a determinative event in John's Gospel, as James Dunn insists.[15] But how should we relate this giving of the Holy Spirit to the outpouring of the Spirit at Pentecost?

Luke described an appearance of Christ after His resurrection (24:33–49), which may be the same event John reported in 20:19–23. At that time Jesus ordered His disciples to wait in Jerusalem until they would be endued with power from on high (Luke 24:49). So it does not seem possible that they could have received the supernatural empowering when Jesus breathed on them. Moreover, John could hardly have been describing the ultimate promised outpouring of the Spirit in such very different terms as a "Johannine Pentecost," as some have called it, considering that he himself had been present at Pentecost in the temple area.

Two other explanations have been presented by various scholars. First, some suggest that Jesus' act of breathing was merely symbolic, anticipating the sending of the Spirit at Pentecost. But the verb *receive* in 20:22 is *labete,* a Greek aorist imperative which, as the Lutheran scholar R. C. H. Lenski said, denotes reception then and there, and not a process of reception or a future reception. The breathing of Jesus was the actual means of bestowal, indicating that the Spirit came directly from Him.[16] An immediate reception best fits the climactic position of this passage in John's Gospel.

A second view is that the disciples received the new birth when Jesus breathed on them. They became spiritually alive for the first time. But it seems quite clear that they were already regenerate.

Their names had already been recorded in heaven (Luke 10:20). Peter had already been called "blessed" because he had openly testified that he believed Jesus was the Messiah, the Son of the living God (Matt. 16:16–17). The others also had already said they believed that Jesus came from God (John 16:30; compare 16:27; 17:8), and He had already pronounced the eleven apostles to be "clean" (John 13:10; 15:3). Jesus had prayed for them as individuals already belonging to the Father (17:9; compare 17:6–19). They already had genuine spiritual life in the same sense that Abraham, David and John the Baptist had had it.[17] (See the comment on Psalm 51:11.)

If neither regeneration nor future Pentecostal empowering can be in view in John 20:22, what did happen to the disciples? They lived under both the old and the new dispensations of God and experienced the transition from the Old to the New Covenant. At that moment they became partakers of the resurrection life of Christ, who had just risen from the dead.

Christ Himself is the first fruits of the resurrection (1 Cor. 15:20; Acts 26:23). He is the beginning of the new creation and the firstborn from among the dead (Col. 1:18). Therefore this appearance (John 20:19–23) was the first occasion when He could actually impart to them the life of the new creation, the abundant life that He came to give (John 10:10), eternal life in its fullest sense.

This event is the climax of the Gospel of John, the gospel of life in the Son of God (compare John 20:30–31). And this life is vitally, even inseparably, linked with the Holy Spirit. Since that night, those who put their trust in Christ receive His new life at the time of their regeneration.

As Jesus commanded His disciples to receive the Holy Spirit, He fulfilled His promise of a few nights earlier that the Spirit of truth would be in them (14:17; see the comment on John 14:16–18). The risen Christ was for the first time imparting the Holy Spirit (who is His Spirit, the Spirit of Jesus) to dwell *in* His followers. He communicated to them the Spirit of sonship (or, of adoption, KJV), the Holy Spirit, as the one who inwardly "testifies with our spirit that we are God's children" (Rom. 8:15–16, NIV).

For the very first time in history God by His Spirit took up residence in redeemed sinners. Heretofore, from Genesis until Jesus, God's Spirit had been present with His people to guide and protect them, abiding in their midst (Isa. 63:11; Hag. 2:5), and had come upon certain individuals to equip them to serve the Lord. Now, however, He came to indwell His children and conform them to the likeness of His dear Son (Rom. 8:29). For them and for us it means the beginning of fellowship in the life eternal with the Father and with His Son, Jesus Christ (1 John 1:2f; compare John 17:3, 21–26). As John explained it in his epistle, we know that we live in God and He in us because He has given us of His own Spirit (1 John 4:13, RSV; compare 3:24).

The Greek verb *emphusaō* for "breathe" occurs in the New Testament only in John 20:22. But it is used in the Greek Septuagint translation of Genesis 2:7 in the account of humanity's original creation: "The LORD God formed man of dust from the ground, and breathed into his nostrils the breath of life." This verb is also found in the Septuagint translation of Ezekiel's vision of the dry bones, depicting the rebirth of Israel to be God's covenant people: "Thus says the Lord GOD, 'Come from the four winds, O breath, and breathe on these slain, that they come to life'" (Ezek. 37:9). Spiritual as well as national resurrection is pictured here, because the Lord says in 37:14, "I will put My Spirit within you, and you will come to life."

The Hebrew word *rûaḥ* in these verses, like the Greek word *pneuma,* means either wind, breath or spirit, according to the context (see the comment on Ezek. 36:27; 37:14). Thus wind and breath are especially fitting symbols of God's Spirit in His invisible operation (John 3:8).

When God breathes, a creative act takes place. This was true of Adam's creation in the garden of Eden (Gen. 2:7). Job's friend Elihu recognized that the breath of the Almighty gave him life (Job 33:4). The psalmist said that all the hosts of heaven were made by the breath of God's mouth (Ps. 33:6).

Again we read that "all scripture is given by inspiration of God" (2 Tim. 3:16, KJV; literally, as in NIV, "all Scripture is God-breathed," Greek *theopneustos*). The Holy Spirit has inspired every word of the original manuscripts of the Bible so that it is truly the created product of God (see the comment on

2 Peter 1:19–21). Therefore we may conclude that when Jesus breathed upon His disciples His act had creative significance. It closely followed His death on the cross, which ended the Old Covenant and instituted the New Covenant by His blood.[18]

John 20:22 indicates the beginning of the new creation (Gal. 6:15) for believers and of their membership in the New Covenant. If anyone is in Christ (and Christ in him or her), that person is a new creation; the old order and old ways have passed away, new things have begun (2 Cor. 5:17). Christ abiding in His followers (John 15:1–5) by His Spirit is the new element, the key feature, the foundation stone of the new creation.

Because Christ lives in us by faith (Gal. 2:20), He is our life (Col. 3:4). Paul could write that Christ, the last Adam, became a life-giving Spirit (1 Cor. 15:45). Paul thereby directly associated the risen, exalted Christ (who is the resurrection and the life, John 11:25) with the Spirit (who gives life, John 6:63; 2 Cor. 3:6) in the establishing and maintaining of the new creation.

When the risen Lord Jesus breathed forth the Holy Spirit that first night after His resurrection, His creative work began transforming individual believers into a spiritual community. They became at that moment a new body, His body the church (not at Pentecost).[19] We are members of that body now, for we were created anew in Christ Jesus (Eph. 2:10).

As members we benefit greatly. Our new selves have been "created to be like God in true righteousness and holiness" (Eph. 4:24, NIV). By the power of His indwelling Spirit our new selves are being renewed to true knowledge (*eis epignōsin*) of God and His will, according to the image of its creator (Col. 3:10). In addition, God sent forth the Spirit of His Son into our hearts (Gal. 4:6) so that we might know we are children of God and coheirs with Christ (Rom. 8:16–17).

Along with the resurrection life of Jesus which the disciples received were the responsibility and authority to minister that resurrection life to others. For lost sinners to be born again, their sins must be forgiven. Therefore Jesus commissioned His disciples to act prophetically in pronouncing either God's grace or His judgment: "If you forgive the sins of any, their sins have [already] been forgiven them; if you retain the sins of any, they have [already] been retained" (John 20:23).

As the NIV Study Bible note explains, "God does not forgive people's sins because we do so, nor does He withhold forgiveness because we do. Rather, those who proclaim the gospel are in effect forgiving or not forgiving sins, depending on whether the hearers accept or reject Jesus Christ."[20] It is God alone who can forgive sins (Mark 2:7); the Christian worker can only declare what God has already done. What the Lord commits to us is the privilege of giving assurance of the remission of sins by God as we faithfully announce the terms of forgiveness to be found in the Word of God.

# SEVEN

# The Beginning of the Age of the Outpoured Spirit: The Book of Acts

### You Shall Receive Power—Acts 1:4–8

The Holy Spirit is a favorite theme of Luke's, who wrote both the third Gospel and the Book of Acts. Luke was inspired by God to select the source material (compare Luke 1:1–4) and to narrate the incidents that emphasize the charismatic activity and power of the Spirit (for example, Luke 1:35; 4:14; 10:19–21; 24:49; Acts 4:31, 33; 10:38). Therefore this book has appropriately been called "The Acts of the Holy Spirit."

The words of the risen Lord Jesus prove beyond the shadow of a doubt that the baptism in the Holy Spirit, and not the new birth, is the fulfillment of God the Father's "promise." He told them to wait in Jerusalem for what the Father had promised, "for John baptized with water, but you shall be baptized with [or "in"; Greek *en*] the Holy Spirit not many days from now" (Acts 1:5; see the comment on Luke 24:44–53).

Taken in connection with Acts 1:8 and 2:1–4, these words also show that the outpouring of the Spirit on the Day of Pentecost was the first historical occurrence of the baptism in the Spirit. This was to be the baptism that Christ Himself performs, as John the Baptist had originally announced (see the comment on Matthew 3:11–17). After Pentecost the Holy Spirit fell upon Cornelius and his household so that they spoke in tongues just as the first Christians did. That reminded the apostle Peter of these very words of Jesus in Acts 1:5: "And I remembered the word of the Lord, how He used to say, 'John baptized with water, but you shall be baptized with the Holy Spirit'" (Acts 11:16).

While giving His final instructions to the apostles concerning the kingdom of God, Jesus warned them about going forth excitedly but unprepared. He commanded them to wait in Jerusalem for the coming of the Holy Spirit before they began their service for Him. But they seemed more interested to find out when He, as Messiah, would restore political freedom to Israel. He did not correct the disciples regarding their expectation of a future literal kingdom but said it was not for them to know those dates. Much more relevant was the immediate task ahead of them.

"But you shall receive power when the Holy Spirit has come upon you; and you shall be My witnesses ... even to the remotest part of the earth" (Acts 1:8; see the comments on Matthew 28:18–20; Mark 16:9–20; Luke 24:44–53; and John 20:21–23). Here He clearly stated the effect and purpose of the baptism in the Spirit. It is power—power to be His witnesses.

The Greek word for "power" in Acts 1:8 is *dunamis*. It is not *exousia*, the power or right to become a child of God as in John 1:12, which speaks about the new birth. *Dunamis* means inherent strength (2 Cor. 1:8) or ability to perform effectively (Matt. 25:15; 2 Cor. 8:3). The power of the Holy Spirit is not an external possession that can be purchased or sold (compare Acts 8:18–20), but a living and abiding presence with the Christian. Those who have received the Spirit-baptism have a new potential. The more the Spirit overflows and uses them, the more powerful and skillful are their words and deeds.

The power to be Christ's witness (Acts 4:33) can be both miraculous (Acts 6:8) and moral (2 Cor. 6:6–7; Eph. 3:16; Col. 1:11). Christians are empowered to perform signs and wonders in order to bring others into obedience to Christ (Rom. 15:18–19) and give them full assurance of the gospel message (1 Thess. 1:5; Heb. 2:3–4; 1 Cor. 2:4–5). In the New Testament, believers were given power to heal and to cast out demons (Acts 8:6–7, 13; 19:11–12). But also the power of Christ enables them to endure and be strong in times of weakness and suffering (2 Cor. 12:9–10). This too is a witness.

Witnesses (*martyres*) are those who "testify" (from the verb *martyreō*) by act or word, their "testimony" (*martyrion*) to the truth. A distinctly legal term, as it still is, "testimony" in Christian usage came to mean the witness given to Christ and His saving and delivering power. Such witnessing often meant arrest and scourging (Matt. 10:17–18; Acts 16:16–24), exile (Rev. 1:9) or even death (Acts 22:20; Rev. 2:13; 17:6); hence the English word "martyr" came to mean someone who dies rather than give up the faith.

Witnessing is at the heart of all evangelistic and missionary activity. Several principles emerge from a study of the New Testament idea of "witness":[2]

(1) Witnessing is the universal obligation of every Christian (Luke 24:48; Acts 1:8). We are to entrust the message to others who will continue the witness (2 Tim. 2:2).

(2) Our testimony is to concentrate on the facts and meaning of Christ's earthly ministry, death and bodily resurrection (Acts 4:33; 10:38–41) and on the salvation from sin He offers (Acts 10:42–43; 1 Cor. 15:1–4).

(3) Christians are to confess Jesus Christ before others regardless of the opposition and their own personal safety or comfort (Matt. 10:32–42).

(4) Christian witnessing will be attended by the ministry of the Holy Spirit and the manifestation of His power (Mark 16:15–20; Rom. 15:18–19; Heb. 2:4).

## Pentecost!—Acts 2:1–4

The long-anticipated day had finally come! A new era in God's gracious dealings with humankind was dawning. God the Father would keep His promise; Jesus Christ the Son would pour forth the Spirit. Joel's prophecy was about to be fulfilled, and the messianic age would be inaugurated.

Unaware of the momentous significance of this day, multiplied thousands of Jews had congregated in Jerusalem for the Feast of Weeks. At the great Jewish feasts as many as 180,000 came to worship, and 120,000 to 150,000 of these might be pilgrims from other countries speaking other languages as their native tongue.[3]

The Feast of Weeks was the second of the three principal harvest festivals requiring the attendance of the godly Jew at the temple (Exod. 23:14–17; 34:18–23). The first was the Feast of Unleavened Bread, and the third the Feast of Booths or Tabernacles (Deut. 16:16). The middle feast was called the Feast of Weeks, because it came a week of weeks (seven weeks) after the Feast of Firstfruits, when a sheaf of newly cut barley was waved before the Lord (Lev. 23:10–16; Deut. 16:9–10).

Firstfruits closely followed the Passover. The Passover sacrifice began the week-long Feast of Unleavened Bread, and Firstfruits was the second day of that feast, the first day being observed as a Sabbath. On the fiftieth day after Firstfruits, every Hebrew male was to return to the Lord's house to present a new grain offering, the first fruits from his wheat harvest (Exod. 34:22; Lev. 23:15–21; Num. 28:26; Deut. 16:9–12). According to early Jewish writings (Tobias 2:1; 2 Maccabbees 12:31–32 in the Apocrypha), the feast was already called Pentecost before the birth of Christ. The term simply means "fiftieth" in Greek.

The average Jew in Old Testament times had no conception that the Day of Pentecost had any significance as a type. Much later, according to the Talmud, they began to observe it as the day commemorating the giving of the Law on Mount Sinai. This understanding was without scriptural warrant; the rabbis, however, calculated that God had appeared to Moses on the mountain top on the fiftieth day after Passover. The meaning of Pentecost to the Christian, however, is far richer.

Passover, of course, is a type of Christ, our Passover (lamb), sacrificed for us at Calvary (1 Cor. 5:7), and so it illustrates our redemption from death. The Feast of Unleavened Bread, which lasted for seven days, typifies the lifelong walk of the child of God separated from the leaven of sin and evil. The Feast of Firstfruits perhaps can be said to be a type of the resurrection of Christ, "the first fruits of those who are asleep" (1 Cor. 15:20, 23; compare John 12:24; Revelation 1:5). The crossing of the Red Sea a few days after the first Passover historically set Israel free from Egyptian slavery. Therefore its account often is used to depict our liberation from bondage—the bondage of sin—through our resurrection with Christ.

Alongside the significance of these feasts as types, Pentecost, coming as it does in connection with the grain harvest, pictures for us the great harvest of souls in this age that began that very day and resulted in the first Christian church. As the followers of Moses were united at Mount Sinai under the Old Covenant and were given the Law to prepare them to go forth to possess the Promised Land, so at Pentecost the disciples of Jesus were empowered by the Spirit under the New Covenant with God's law written on their hearts (Jer. 31:33) to go forth to give the gospel to the farthest corners of the earth.

Luke recorded that when the Day of Pentecost had come, or "was in process of being fulfilled" (Acts 2:1, Wuest's translation), the 120 disciples (Acts 1:15) were all together in one place (2:1). While many have supposed this place was the upper room because Luke used the word "house" (*oikos*, building, structure) in 2:2, several clues point to their being at the temple.

First, no roof-top room (Acts 1:13) of an ordinary Jewish home in crowded Jerusalem was large enough to handle 120 persons. Second, Luke specifically said that after Jesus' ascension His followers "were continually in the temple, praising God" (Luke 24:53). Third, the disciples were devout Jews and were expected to be present in the temple area for the ceremonies of the Feast of Weeks. Fourth, on several other occasions Luke referred to the temple by the term "house" (Greek *oikos*; see Luke 11:51; 19:46; Acts 7:47, 49; compare also Matthew 21:13; Mark 11:17; John 2:16; and often in the Old Testament it is called the house of God or the Lord's house).

Finally, the multitude gathered around the disciples right away upon hearing the sound of their voices praising God in many new tongues (Acts 2:6). Note that Luke indicated the crowd came to the Christians, not that the latter left their house to come to the temple. From a practical standpoint, this could happen only if the Christians were already in the broad open area of the temple court, for the streets of the city were like narrow, winding alleys. In addition, the traditional house of the upper room (compare Acts 1:13) is far removed from the site of the temple, on the opposite side of the city.

All the more wonderful that the Holy Spirit should fall (compare Acts 11:15) on the disciples of Jesus in plain view of the vast crowd of Jews present at the temple that morning. God sovereignly displayed His power on that occasion, just as His glory had filled the tabernacle (Exod. 40:34) and later the temple when Solomon dedicated it (1 Kings 8:10–11). Unique signs occurred for the initial outpouring of God's Spirit that seldom, if ever, have combined on subsequent occasions when people have received the Holy Spirit. First, symbolizing the Spirit as wind or breath, "suddenly there came an echoing sound out of heaven as of a wind borne along violently" (Acts 2:2, Wuest's translation), and it filled the whole temple where the disciples were sitting quietly. At the same time, symbolizing the consecrating work of the Holy Spirit coming to indwell God's people as His new temple (1 Cor. 3:16–17; 6:19), there appeared to them—therefore evidently not to any onlookers— tongues as of fire. These distributed themselves so that a flame rested on each one of the believers.[4]

John the Baptist had foretold this phenomenon when he announced that the one coming after him would baptize with the Holy Spirit and fire (see the comment on Matthew 3:11–17). Maynard James called the "cloven tongues like as of fire" the emblem of dynamic purification. He pointed out that Jesus had no need of purification from sin, for He had no taint of depravity. Hence the Holy Spirit who came "without measure" to the spotless Son of God appeared as a dove rather than fire.[5]

Another sign was given for the first time that day and has continued. In the early church it became the usual accompaniment of receiving the baptism in the Holy Spirit. According to the long ending of Mark's Gospel, Jesus had told His disciples that certain signs would accompany those who believe, and speaking with new tongues was one of those signs (Mark 16:17). When the disciples were inundated with the Holy Spirit, they "began to speak with other tongues, as the Spirit was giving them utterance" (Acts 2:4). This is the phenomenon often called glossolalia, coined from the two Greek words *glossa,* meaning "tongue," and *laleō,* meaning "to speak."

Without involving ourselves in a long proof, we can be certain that the "tongues" which the Christians spoke were not gibberish, but real languages.[6] However, these were "other" than their native language or any other language which they had ever learned. The non-Pentecostal scholar Charles Ryrie recognized that "the miracle was in the giving of the ability to speak these languages, not in sensitizing in some way the ears of the hearers."[7]

This sign was meant especially for the unconverted Jews present at the festival, just as Paul later wrote that tongues are for a sign, not to those who believe, but to unbelievers (1 Cor. 14:22). Certainly the result on the Day of Pentecost agrees with this stated purpose, because the Jews were amazed and marveled when each one heard his or her own particular language or dialect spoken by one of the Christians.

What they heard was not incoherent, unintelligible utterance, but men and women praising the Lord in languages which communicated "the wonderful works of God" (Acts 2:11, KJV). Most of them could account for it only by recognizing it as something miraculous and supernatural, although a few mockingly said the disciples must be drunk. It is evident from the experience of the Day of Pentecost that speaking in tongues is not only rational discourse in an unknown language but on occasion may be accompanied by a holy joy, a kind of divine inebriation.

The tongues of Pentecost, then, were a sign of the universal extent of the New Covenant. As such, were they meant to be a harbinger that in Christ God will one day reverse the confusion of languages and division of peoples stemming from His judgment at the tower of Babel (Gen. 11:1–9)?

Luke stated that the 120 brethren were "all filled with the Holy Spirit" (v. 4).

This was the baptism in the Holy Spirit for which Jesus had prepared the apostles just before His ascension (Acts 1:5). This was their reception of the gift of the Holy Spirit promised by the Father (see the comment on Luke 24:44–53).

We must remember that the Holy Spirit was already dwelling in the apostles, for the Lord Jesus had breathed into them His Spirit to make them members of the new creation on the night after His resurrection (see the comment on John 20:21–23). That new, deeper relationship consisted in the Holy Spirit's being joined to their spirits. From that moment on, they were spiritually united to the resurrected Christ (1 Cor. 6:17; Rom. 8:9).

Now, however, on the Feast of Pentecost, the Father and Son sovereignly poured out the Holy Spirit upon (*epi,* Acts 2:3) the waiting disciples (Acts 2:33; compare John 14:16; 15:26; 16:7). The Episcopalian leader Dennis Bennett has provided an interesting interpretation of this event:

> [The Spirit of God] overwhelmed them—this is what the Scripture means when it says He "fell upon them," or "came upon them"—baptizing their souls and bodies in the power and the glory that was already dwelling in their spirits. . . . He overflowed from them out into the world around, inspiring them to praise and glorify God, not only in their own tongues, but in new languages, and in so doing, tamed their tongues to His use, freed their spirits, renewed their minds, refreshed their bodies, and brought power to witness.[8]

(For additional discussion on being filled with the Spirit, see the comment on Acts 4:8; on other instances of speaking in tongues, see the comments on Acts 8:5–25; 9:1–22; 10:44–48; 19:1–7; 1 Corinthians 14.)

## Joel's Prophecy—Acts 2:14–21

A. J. Gordon of Boston once called Joel's prophecy of the outpouring of the Spirit the Magna Charta of the Christian church. Truly it is God's great charter of spiritual power and liberty for every true believer in Jesus Christ. Joel 2:28–32 (see the comment) was the passage which the apostle Peter used in order to explain the amazing events of the Day of Pentecost.

We may well ask, What was new or different about the coming of the Spirit on that day? Wasn't the Holy Spirit active throughout the Old Testament and during the life and ministry of Christ? Yes, certainly. But Pentecost marked a new beginning of the work of the Spirit in two ways: His coming was universal, and it was permanent.

First, the miracle of Pentecost was that the Holy Spirit was poured out upon *all* believers (Acts 2:1, 4, 17–18, 38–39). In Old Testament times, the Spirit of God came only to the few—chiefly to priests, kings, judges and prophets—whereas now He could be received by every child of God. Joel foretold the Spirit's being poured out "upon all flesh" (KJV), upon every significant division of humankind. Thus the Spirit's coming at Pentecost was universal in the four basic categories of human beings.

As to race, He was poured out upon both Jew and Gentile, "upon all mankind" (compare 1 Corinthians 12:13). As to sex, He came upon both male and female, "your sons and your daughters" (compare Galatians 3:28). As to age, He was given to both young and old, "your young men . . . and your old men." And as to social rank, He was poured out upon both slave and free, "even upon My bondslaves, both men and women."

This universal aspect was new and unique to this age. Moses had lamented in his day, "Would that all the LORD's people were prophets, that the LORD would put His spirit upon them!" (Num. 11:29; see the comment on Numbers 11:4–30). Joel's prophecy concerning the Spirit was as extensive as the promise that everyone who calls on the name of the Lord would be saved (Joel 2:32; Acts 2:21). Therefore Peter boldly declared that the promised gift of the Holy Spirit was for the Jews and their descendants and for all who are "far off"— that is, Gentiles (compare Ephesians 2:13, 17)—even as many as the Lord would call to Himself (Acts 2:39).

The second unprecedented feature of the outpouring of the Spirit at Pentecost is that He came to remain with those who receive Him. His power was now available to each and every believer constantly, for the needs and emergencies of every day. He no longer came upon a certain man or woman only occasionally and fleetingly, as He did on the judges.

As the Spirit descended upon Jesus at His baptism to remain upon Him (John 1:33), so the Lord promised that the Paraclete would remain with His followers forever (John 14:16). In this factor lies the import of God's prophecy to Isaiah in 59:21: "'And as for Me, this is My covenant with them,' says the LORD: 'My Spirit which is upon you, and My words which I have put in your mouth, shall not depart from your mouth, nor from the mouth of your offspring. . .;' says the LORD, 'from now and forever'" (see the comment there). Likewise John the Apostle wrote that the anointing which Christians receive from the Lord abides permanently in them (see the comment on 1 John 2:20, 27).

It is this constant supply of divine power which distinguishes the Pentecostal ministry of the apostles from their evangelistic tours during the lifetime of Jesus. Then He had had to delegate His power and authority for each mission (Luke 9:1–2), and sometimes they were unable to minister deliverance in particularly difficult cases (Mark 9:14–18, 28–29).

Joel's prophecy also clearly states that the outpouring of the Holy Spirit was not to be fulfilled all in one day. Thus the Bible scholar should not limit the supernatural signs of Pentecost to that day alone. Verse 17 says, "And it shall be in the last days"—plural—"God says, that I will pour forth of My Spirit upon all mankind"; and verse 18 repeats the idea by saying "in those days."

The power of Pentecost was meant for the entire church age. Prominent leaders of the early church such as Irenaeus, Justin and Origen testified that the miracles and gifts of the Spirit continued to be much in evidence well on into the second and third centuries, long after the close of the apostolic period. The power described in Acts began to wane, not according to God's directive will, but because apathy and worldliness crept in to quench the fire of the Spirit.

Now in the twentieth century God has been sending a revival of Pentecostal power to prepare the church for the coming of her Bridegroom. The outpouring is to continue to the very time that the wonders in the heavens above and the terrible signs on the earth beneath that Joel speaks of occur (vv. 19–20), just before the great and awesome Day of the Lord comes.

Someone may ask what connection Peter saw between the speaking in tongues that he and his associates experienced and the prophesying that Joel predicted (vv. 17–18). Since this is the part of Joel's prophecy that deals with speech, Peter quite obviously was implying that the telling of the mighty works of God in the various native languages of the Jewish pilgrims at the Pentecost festival was a fulfillment of Joel's words.

The term for "utterance" in Acts 2:4 also suggests that the newly empowered Christians were speaking forth the praises of God with a prophetic ring in their voices. The Greek word Luke used here, *apophthengesthai*, means to speak forth boldly as a prophet or other inspired person;[9] it occurs several times in the Septuagint in a prophetic context (Ezek. 13:9; Mic. 5:12; Zech. 10:2; and 1 Chron. 25:1, the clearest Old Testament example). The word appears again in Acts 2:14, where Luke wrote that Peter raised his voice and "declared" to the great crowd the message that follows. Later, in Acts 26:25, Paul was quoted as using the word to describe his speech when he said to

Festus, "I am not out of my mind . . . but I utter the words of sober truth."

In these last two instances, both Peter and Paul were speaking under an anointing as prophets. So we may conclude that the Holy Spirit gave the 120 the ability to speak as boldly and clearly as prophets, in this case in foreign languages that were readily understood by people from those countries. They did not, however, preach the gospel in the "other tongues." This was done by the apostle Peter in Greek or Aramaic, in a language known by every Jew who would come to Jerusalem in that period. The speaking with tongues served the purpose of gathering a large crowd around the disciples.

It is worthwhile to note that the disciples opened their mouths to speak and used their own lips, tongues and vocal cords to form the sounds. The Holy Spirit did not have to overcome their reluctance, but in the joy of the moment they voluntarily began to speak. Yet it was the Spirit who formed the words, so that each one uttered a language that was intelligible to someone who knew it. In like manner today, many when they are baptized in the Holy Spirit speak in a language which they themselves do not know (see the comment on 1 Corinthians 14).

## Receiving the Gift of the Holy Spirit—Acts 2:38–40

On the Day of Pentecost the Jewish worshipers asked two questions. When they heard the 120 Christians speaking in tongues, they asked, "What does this mean?" (Acts 2:12). Peter took his stand with the other apostles to explain the phenomenon and delivered his great sermon (2:14–36). This wrought conviction in their hearts and evoked their second question, "Brethren, what shall we do?" (Acts 2:37).

In his message Peter had explained that this was the beginning of a new era—the days foretold by the prophets—to be lived by the power of the Spirit. Thus their second question was really two in one: What shall we do to escape our share of guilt in the crucifixion of Jesus the Messiah, and what shall we do to experience the outpouring of the Holy Spirit which was promised us in Joel's prophecy? In his reply, Peter answered both questions at the same time:

> Repent and let each one of you be baptized upon the authority of Jesus the Messiah with respect to the forgiveness of your sins, and you shall then take the step of receiving the gift of the Holy Spirit. For the promise is for you and your children and for all who are afar off, as many as the Lord our God shall call unto Himself.
>
> —ACTS 2:38–39, AUTHOR'S TRANSLATION

With many other words he warned them and pleaded with them, "Save yourselves from this corrupt generation" (v. 40, NIV).

First, we should consider who may receive the promised Spirit, and then we shall discuss how to receive the gift.

Peter interpreted Joel's prophecy to refer to this whole gospel era by changing the prophet's word "afterward" (Joel 2:28, KJV) to "in the last days" (Acts 2:17), a recognized term for the present church age. Thus it is certain that the power of the Holy Spirit is meant for every born-again Christian, for every one who is saved throughout the entire period between the first and second comings of Christ (Acts 2:39).

Michael Harper has made this clear:

> The whole of the New Testament substantiates these two facts: first, that the only entry into the benefits of the New Covenant is by repentance and baptism. And secondly, that the benefits of the New Covenant include the gift of the Holy Spirit as well as the forgiveness of sins. From Pentecost onwards the Church faithfully proclaimed that Christ forgives *and* baptizes in the Holy Spirit. They taught that all who repent and believe are justified by faith, and that all who are justified by faith may receive the Holy Spirit by faith. The one should normally lead to the other.[10]

The offer of the gift of the Spirit, then, is just as extensive as the offer of salvation itself. The Greek word for "gift" in verse 38 is *dōrea,* not *charisma* (the term Paul and Peter used for a charismatic or spiritual gift; see the comments on Romans 12:3–8; 1 Corinthians 12:13; 1 Peter 4:10–11). *Dōrea* refers to the gift of salvation for all people in John 4:10, Hebrews 6:4, and Ephesians 2:8; to the gift of righteousness in Romans 5:15, 17; and to the gift of God's Son in 2 Corinthians 9:15. *Dōrea is* also the word that is used for God's gift of His Spirit in Acts 8:20; 10:45; and 11:17.

Peter said in verse 39 (KJV) that the promise is "unto you"—to the Jews present on that first Day of Pentecost; "and to your children"—to their descendants, that is, to all Jews since then; "and to all that are afar off"—to all Gentiles, who were considered by Jews as being "far off" from God and from the covenant promises made to Israel (Eph. 2:11–13, 17). He emphasized how broad this promise is by adding, "even as many as the Lord our God shall call." And every true Christian has been called or invited by God to come to His kingdom and glory (1 Thess. 2:12; 5:24; 2 Thess. 2:14; Rom. 8:28, 30; Eph. 4:1; 1 Pet. 2:9; 5:10).

Before going further, we must recognize that it is impossible to construct an exact biblical formula for receiving the Spirit. The instances of those who did receive, as described in the Book of Acts, are characterized by their variety.

According to Peter's words, God has set only two prior conditions for being baptized in the Spirit. The first is repentance, which denotes a change of mind according to the Greek word *metanoia*. The Amplified Bible enlarges upon the meaning of "repent" in verse 38 this way: "Change your views, and purpose to accept the will of God in your inner selves instead of rejecting it."

Repentance implies the previous work of the Holy Spirit to convict "concerning sin, and righteousness, and judgment" (John 16:8–11). Those who have no belief in God or have wrong beliefs concerning Christ as the eternal Son of God and redeemer by His sacrificial death must change their minds. Those who are harboring sin must renounce it completely. This often may produce and be accompanied by a deep sorrow for their past attitudes and deeds (compare 2 Corinthians 7:9–10).

The Holy Spirit also awakens a longing for truth and goodness, a desire for God; in short, He creates a hunger and thirst for righteousness and spiritual life and power. This deep inner longing for reality and power can be satisfied only by repenting and turning to Jesus Christ with all of our hearts. Repentance and saving faith or trust in Christ are thus the two sides of the coin called conversion.

The other condition is baptism in water. The obedience of the new believer in Christ as a responsible person is indicated by Peter's command that narrows down this detail to the individual, "Be baptized every one of you" (v. 38, KJV).

The author's translation given above of verses 38–39 brings out the meaning of the Greek prepositions here. Each convert is to be baptized "in the name of Jesus Christ" (*epi to onomati Iesou Christou*). In the Bible the name of a person often stands for his or her character or position and thus symbolizes the person's authority. Therefore we have paraphrased the words as "upon the authority of Jesus the Messiah."

The new Christian is to submit to baptism on the authority of the One who gave the threefold baptismal formula in Matthew 28:19 (KJV): "baptizing them in (Greek *eis*) the name of the Father, and of the Son, and of the Holy Ghost" (KJV). Peter's command, then, does not supersede trinitarian baptism but refers to it.

The Book of Acts does not establish a new baptism formula in the name of Jesus only. In fact, Luke uses three different Greek prepositions before the term "name." Here it is in "(*epi*, upon) the name of Jesus Christ"; in Acts 10:48 it is "in (*en*) the name of Jesus Christ"; and in Acts 8:16 and 19:5 it is "in (*eis*, into) the name of the Lord Jesus."

New Testament scholar F. F. Bruce has explained that the Greeks used the last of these three expressions to indicate that some property was transferred "into the name" of someone. Therefore those who were baptized bore public witness that they had become the property of Jesus and that Christ was their new Lord and owner. Bruce further commented that the longer expression in Matthew 28:19 was appropriate for Gentile disciples from all the nations who must turn from paganism to serve the living God, "whereas Jews and Samaritans, who already acknowledge the one true God, were required only to confess Jesus as Lord and Messiah."[11]

The author's paraphrase of verse 38 also guards against the notion of the doctrine of baptismal regeneration. This doctrinal error supposes that people are baptized "for the remission of sins" in the sense of "in order to obtain forgiveness of their sins." But the Greek preposition *eis*, usually translated "for" in this context, more exactly means "concerning," "with respect to" or "in reference to." This meaning of *eis* is evident in Acts 2:25; Romans 4:20; Ephesians 5:32; and 1 Thessalonians 5:18.

That this is the proper meaning of *eis* when used in the context of baptism for the remission of sins is quite clear in Mark 1:4 and Luke 3:3. These verses tell of John the Baptist, who preached a baptism of repentance for the forgiveness of sins. John's stern message demanding fruits in keeping with their repentance before he would baptize them (Luke 3:7–14) shows that baptism was never performed to effect repentance and forgiveness but only to bear witness to their repentance (see the comment on Matthew 3:11–17).

Acts 22:16, "Be baptized, and wash away your sins," does not actually teach baptismal regeneration. Paul's sins were forgiven instantly by God when he was converted on the road outside of Damascus, when he had called on the name of Jesus as Lord (22:10) three days before Ananias baptized him. But water baptism may be considered to wash off the stain or stigma of a person's past sins that still sullies the person's reputation. By the public confession of baptism, a new believer definitely renounces his or her past life, burying it once and for all, reckoning the old self to be dead and buried.

Having repented of sin and acknowledged faith in their new-found Savior Jesus Christ by water baptism, how may converts receive the gift of the Holy Spirit? Returning again to the author's expanded translation above, note that Peter exhorted his hearers to take an active part in receiving the outpoured Spirit. It is true that the KJV, RSV, NAS and NIV translations accurately render the Greek verb here for "receive" in its future tense: "and you shall receive the gift of the Holy Spirit" (v. 38). But the future indicative tense in Greek may have an imperative sense of command, [12] as it does in Mark 9:35, "If any one wants to be first, he shall be last of all, and servant of all"; Luke 1:13 (RSV), "You shall call his name John." Therefore Peter was saying that receiving the Holy Spirit is not a passive acquisition, but demands active appropriation.

This interpretation of Peter's words at the end of verse 38 is in keeping with Paul's insistence when he wrote to the Galatians that they had received the promise of the Spirit through faith (Gal. 3:14; see the comment on Galatians 3:2–5, 14). The miracle-working power of the Spirit is not an asset automatically provided to the believer in Christ, but must be claimed individually. The promise of the Spirit, like all other biblical promises (Heb. 6:12), must be received and inherited by faith. We do not gain the benefits of God's promises without consciously claiming them, any more than the Israelite invading Canaan under Joshua's leadership could possess his share of the promised land without actually treading upon it (Josh. 1:3).

Just as we receive new life in the Son of God by a definite act of personal faith, even so we receive supernatural power in the Spirit of God by an act of conscious faith. Sometimes, as in the case of Cornelius (see the comment on Acts 10:44–48), the two may be received simultaneously. However, the New Testament—as well as present-day experience—indicates that there are usually two moments of faith, on separate occasions.

The simple acrostic "READY" can provide an aid in remembering various important steps in receiving the baptism in the Holy Spirit:

R—*Repent.* Those who seek to be baptized in the Spirit should first of all repent of any and all sin and accept Jesus Christ as their Savior and Lord. As Christians desiring the gift of the Spirit, they will not knowingly be disobedient to the Lord, for the Holy Spirit is given to those who obey God (see the comment on Acts 5:32). They will gladly acknowledge Jesus as their Lord by submitting to water baptism.

The tremendous increase in recent years in cultic and occultic activity makes it necessary to sound a warning to those seeking the baptism in the Spirit. If in the past they have been involved in a false cult or have had any contact with the occult—fortune-telling, spiritist seances, magic (Acts 19:18–19), Ouija boards, horoscopes, reincarnation, ESP, hypnotism or witchcraft—then they must renounce all connection with these satanic practices. In some cases they may need to be set free from the grip of evil spirits before they are ready to receive the Holy Spirit. Attempting to be filled with the Spirit before they are delivered will only produce confusion or terrible conflict and cause other people to doubt the validity of the baptism in the Spirit.[13]

*E—Expect.* Because the Holy Spirit is appropriated by faith (Gal. 3:2, 14), those seeking the baptism in the Spirit must have an expectant attitude, believing that God will fulfill His promise to them. Knowing that the Holy Spirit has already been sent from heaven at Pentecost for all members of the church throughout this age, Christians may confidently anticipate the blessing of the Holy Spirit in their own lives and ministry.

*A—Ask.* Jesus Christ is the baptizer in the Holy Spirit (see the comment on John 1:29–34). Therefore candidates for this baptism should come to Jesus in prayer asking Him and expecting Him to pour out the Spirit upon them. Jesus encouraged His disciples to ask their heavenly Father to give them the Holy Spirit and to ask Him persistently (see the comment on Luke 11:5–13). We pray this way when we sense our deep need for more of God and become desperately thirsty.

*D—Drink.* Jesus gave His great invitation, "If any man is thirsty, let him come to Me and drink" (John 7:37). As Michael Harper has said, "If thirst is Jesus' condition for our coming to Him for power, then it follows that drinking will be the means of appropriation."[14] A person is filled with wine (Eph. 5:18) by the act of drinking; in a similar way a person is filled with the Spirit by "drinking," that is, by actively receiving the Holy Spirit through the prayer of faith (Gal. 3:2, 14; see the comment on John 7:37–39).

Drinking a liquid is in some ways comparable to breathing in air. So some have found it to be an aid to their faith to take several deep breaths as symbolic of breathing in the Holy Spirit when they ask to receive the baptism of the Spirit.

*Y—Yield.* The last step in becoming ready to receive the gift of the Spirit is the matter of yielding to God. Those seeking to be baptized and filled with the Spirit must be willing to yield control of every part of their being to the

Holy Spirit. To be filled with the Spirit means to be controlled by Him, for the Holy Spirit is a person, not a substance, an influence or a mere power (see the comment on Ephesians 5:15–21).

If you are a candidate for Spirit-baptism, yield yourself completely to Jesus as one who is alive from the dead, and also every member and faculty of your body as an instrument of righteousness to God (Rom. 6:13, 19; 12:1). Yield your will so that your motives are pure in seeking the baptism. Yield your members, especially your tongue as the organ of expression of the Holy Spirit through you (Acts 2:4). Because Satan can use the tongue, as he did Hitler's, to set a whole continent or world on fire (James 3:2–10), it is essential that you let the Spirit of God control your center of speech to glorify the Lord.

Because of the great stress in our Western culture on the intellectual training of the mind and its expression in rational speech, many find that the ability to talk with understanding is the last stronghold they are willing to surrender to the Lord. So your being willing to speak in tongues involves total sacrifice of yourself as a whole burnt offering to God (Lev. 6:9–13). Then the glory of His presence can fall upon you and be seen in your life! (Compare Leviticus 9:22–24.)

Remember that until you turn on the faucet there is no flow of water from the pipe. And until you open your mouth to speak, there is no free flowing of the Holy Spirit from your innermost being in worship to God and in ministry to others. So when the indwelling Spirit of Christ wells up within your human spirit, yield to Him and allow Him to manifest Himself as He overflows into your soul and body.

Do not resist the desire to praise and magnify God with whatever strange-sounding words He may form on your lips and tongue. The New Testament shows that the usual result of being filled with the Spirit is to speak, whether in tongues, in prophesying or in praise and thanksgiving (see the comment on Ephesians 5:15–21).

We cannot prove that those who were baptized in the Spirit in the apostolic period immediately spoke in tongues on every occasion. So it is better not to insist dogmatically that speaking in tongues is the invariable initial evidence of baptism in the Spirit. But we can say that the frequent pattern in the New Testament was for this sign to be manifested when people received the gift of the Holy Spirit (see the comments on Acts 8:5–25; 8:26–39; 10:44–48; 19:1–7). Many have experienced an overflow of the Spirit through singing or worshiping in tongues at a subsequent time. Perhaps Paul was one of these (see the comment on Acts 9:1–22).

The important thing is not to refuse to speak words you do not understand. For as Michael Harper described it, speaking in tongues is like a sacrament, an outward and visible sign of inward and spiritual grace.[15] It is a rich blessing, not something to avoid. Because of the several wonderful purposes of tongues, Paul wanted all the believers in Corinth to speak in tongues as a continuing manifestation of the power of the Holy Spirit (see the comment on 1 Corinthians 14).

A final word to Christians who are earnestly desiring to receive the gift of the Holy Spirit, yet feel hindered in one way or another. Many ask if it is possible to receive the baptism in the Spirit without speaking in tongues. Michael Harper's reply to this question is helpful:

> The honest answer is that it is possible to receive this blessing and not at the same time speak in tongues. In the early Church it seems to have been the normal accompaniment of the receiving of the Holy Spirit. But there are factors in our day that were not present then and which obscure the matter for us. I refer particularly to ignorance, fear and prejudice.[16]

He went on to explain that speaking in tongues was a well-known gift to the early Christians, and there was none of the prejudice and fear of this phenomenon that seems to cripple so many in our churches today when they think about this subject.

Other hindrances may be self-consciousness or unbelief. The shy or inhibited person may be prayed for with the laying on of hands to receive the Holy Spirit at a public meeting and later praise God in a new language when alone in the privacy of his or her home or while driving in the car. Remember that Jesus Himself said, "These signs shall follow them that believe . . . they shall speak with new tongues" (Mark 16:17, KJV).

## Peter, Filled With the Holy Spirit—Acts 4:8

"Filled with the Holy Spirit" and its companion expression "full of the Holy Spirit" are key phrases in the book of Acts. In Acts 4:8, the Greek aorist participle *plēstheis* implies that the Spirit at that moment took full control of Peter. The apostle sensed "an immediate sudden inspiration, giving the wisdom and courage and words which were needed at the time."[17] It was the Holy Spirit who acted to put the telling words of defense into Peter's mouth, providing the first fulfillment of Jesus' promise for His disciples when on trial (see the comment on Matthew 10:16–20).

Luke used the verb *filled* (*pimplēmi*) thirteen times in his Gospel and nine times in Acts. It occurs only twice elsewhere in the New Testament (Matt. 22:10; 27:48). Thayer, in his New Testament lexicon, noted that "what wholly takes possession of the mind is said to fill it."[18] In the aorist tense, the verb stresses the act of being filled, usually on that specific occasion, and by usage implies a temporary or sudden act or state. In Luke's descriptions, people were filled with fear (Luke 5:26), rage (4:28; 6:11), wonder and amazement (Acts 3:10), jealousy (5:17; 13:45) and confusion (19:29). In no case could this filling be said to initiate a permanent state of mind.

On the Day of Pentecost, the 120 Christians were all filled with the Holy Spirit (Acts 2:4). Again, a whole group of believers gathered with the apostles were filled with the Spirit after they united in prayer asking for boldness to witness (see the comment on Acts 4:29–33). In each case they were fully possessed or completely controlled by the Spirit to manifest the power of the Lord in a situation and in a way completely beyond their own human abilities.

Likewise, Paul was filled with the Spirit when Elymas the sorcerer opposed him and Barnabas. Paul received sudden spiritual power to know the man's very character and then to pronounce the verdict of divine punishment on him (Acts 13:9–11). Similarly, Peter had exposed the hypocrisy of Ananias and Sapphira by the Spirit's revelation and not by any power of his own (Acts 5:1–11). These are clear instances of the charismatic gift of a word of knowledge.

The cases of Elizabeth and Zacharias bear out the normal use of the verb *filled* in the aorist tense to describe a certain incident and not a permanent condition. Luke wrote that each was filled with the Holy Spirit (Luke 1:41, 67) and went on to record the prophecy that each one spoke forth. The only occurrence where the aorist of this verb may imply the beginning of a continuing state of fullness of the Spirit is in the statement of Ananias in Damascus to the newly converted Paul: "The Lord Jesus ... has sent me so that you may regain your sight, and be filled with the Holy Spirit" (Acts 9:17). More likely, however, this is Ananias's way of referring to the act of being baptized in the Holy Spirit.

The other prominent expression in Luke's writings, "full of the Holy Spirit," does seem to describe the normal spiritual state of the person. The adjective *full* (*plērēs*) used in this sense suggests the person is characterized by or thoroughly saturated with the Spirit or with spiritual attributes such as grace and truth (John 1:14), wisdom (Acts 6:3), faith (6:5), grace and power (6:8). Dorcas, for example, was "full of good works and almsdeeds" that she continually did (Acts 9:36, KJV). Luke characterized the following as full of the Holy Spirit: Jesus (Luke 4:1); the seven to be chosen as deacons (Acts 6:3)—Stephen in particular (6:5; 7:55)—and Barnabas (11:24).

The Greek verb *plēroō*, which corresponds to the adjective "full," is used only twice in connection with the Holy Spirit. One is the important verse "Be filled with the Spirit" (Eph. 5:18). The present tense of the verb, denoting a continuing action, and the fact that it is a command indicate that Spirit-baptized Christians need continually to stir up or kindle afresh the gift of God that is in them (2 Tim. 1:6). There would be no need for such a command if every believer remained permanently full of the Holy Spirit after receiving the baptism. (For further discussion, see the comment on Ephesians 5:15–21.)

The other relevant verse is Acts 13:52, which may be translated, "And the disciples continued to be filled with joy and the Holy Spirit." Here the verb *pleroo* is in the imperfect tense, describing a continuing condition in past time. In spite of persecution and the departure of Paul and Barnabas to Iconium, the joy of the new converts did not disappear, because they continued to be filled with the Spirit.

Later Paul reminded these Galatians that joy, the true and deepest joy, was the fruit of the Spirit, not the result of circumstances (Gal. 5:22). In like manner, the Thessalonian Christians received the gospel in much tribulation but with the joy inspired by the Holy Spirit (1 Thess. 1:6). Being continually saturated and overflowing with the Spirit, as these disciples were, are the goal and privilege of believers in Christ at all times and in every situation.

## Prayer for Boldness to Witness—Acts 4:29–33

Chapters 3 and 4 of Acts describe in detail one of the many apostolic signs and wonders mentioned in Acts 2:43 and the consequences of this particular miracle of healing. Going to the temple one afternoon to pray, Peter and John met a beggar lame from birth. When he asked for money, Peter responded, "Silver or gold I do not have, but what I have I give you" (3:6, NIV)—a gift of healing! So Peter commanded him in the name of Jesus Christ of Nazareth to walk. The moment Peter took the man's hand and raised him up, his feet and ankles were strengthened, and he entered the court of the temple leaping and praising God.

In a short time an amazed crowd of worshipers gathered. Peter used this opportunity as another occasion to bear witness to the healing power and saving grace of Jesus. He urged the people to turn from their wicked ways, saying:

> Repent therefore and turn to Him, so that your sins may be blotted out, in order that times of respite from judgment may come from the presence of the Lord; and that He may send Jesus, the Messiah appointed for you, whom heaven must receive until the period for the establishing of all the things which God has spoken by the mouth of His holy prophets from of old.
> —ACTS 3:19–21, AUTHOR'S TRANSLATION

Because judgment often took the form of drought and famine, "times of respite from judgment" (*kairoi anaphyxeōs*) in verse 19 includes the idea of times of refreshing or renewal.

In verse 21 Peter was not promising "universal restoration" (see NEB, JB) in the sense of ultimate salvation for all beings, but the establishing (*apokatastasis*) of all that God had announced by means of the Old Testament prophets. Israel would be restored to the Promised Land (Deut. 30:3–5; Isa. 11:11–12), and the theocracy would be restored under David's son (2 Sam. 7:16; Jer. 23:3–8; Ezek. 37:21–28; Zech. 14; note the use of the corresponding verb *apokathistēmi* in Matthew 17:11 and Acts 1:6).

Peter's term also includes the liberation of the whole creation from the bondage of corruption when Christ returns and the children of God are revealed in glory with Him (Rom. 8:19–23; Col. 3:4; 2 Thess. 1:7–10). That will be the period of the "regeneration" when the Lord Jesus will sit on the throne of His glory (Matt. 19:28). Then the new creation will reach its fullness or consummation. Through Christ, God will reconcile all things to Himself (Col. 1:20). Again, this does not mean the universal salvation or ultimate reconciliation of all humanity and of the devil and his angels, but that all rebellion will be quelled and the whole universe will be brought into peaceful harmony with God's perfect will.

Peter was calling upon the whole nation of Israel, as he did on the Day of Pentecost, to reverse their cry to crucify Jesus and instead to acknowledge Him as Messiah. F. F. Bruce has commented:

> Had Israel as a whole done this during these Pentecostal days, how different the course of world history and world evangelization would have been! How much more swiftly (we may imagine) would the consummation of Christ's kingdom have come![19]

Many believed the message, but the Jewish authorities had Peter and John arrested for teaching that Jesus had been raised from death. The controversy only tended to prove to the populace that the doctrine of the resurrection of the dead was true, contrary to the teaching of the Sadducees (Acts 4:1–4; compare 23:6–8).

When the apostles were tried before the Sanhedrin the next day, the ruling elders and leading priests (who were Sadducees) recognized them as men who had been with Jesus because of their bold and authoritative manner of speaking. Since the man who had been healed was standing there with Peter and John right before their very eyes, they could not deny the miracle. They could do nothing but release them and command them not to speak or teach at all in the name of Jesus (Acts 4:13–22).

As soon as they were discharged, Peter and John returned "to their own company" (Acts 4:23, KJV), that is, to the place where their fellow apostles were. How many other Christians were present we cannot be sure. The place could not have been the temple courtyard, for they had just come from the council chamber of the Sanhedrin, which was on the west side of the temple area. Because of surveillance by the temple police, the apostles almost certainly were gathered inside a private building, not in an open field near Jerusalem. Therefore, it does not seem likely that all five thousand male believers (Acts 4:4) were present or that all those converted subsequent to the Day of Pentecost took part in the prayer meeting. It was not a time when new believers met to receive the baptism in the Holy Spirit.

What followed is one of the most remarkable prayers of the Bible. Moved by a common impulse, all who heard the report of Peter and John raised their voices in unison to God. The prayer was unrehearsed, yet it was with one accord.

What they said consisted more of praise than of petition. They prayed to God as "Sovereign Lord" (*despota,* Acts 4:24, RSV, NIV), acknowledging His absolute control as creator and ruler of all history. They recognized where they stood in terms of prophetic revelation, that is, in the events of Psalm

2:1–3. Instead of begging for protection from persecution, however, they prayed for more power and boldness to witness: "And now, Lord, take note of their threats, and grant that Thy bond-servants may speak Thy word with all confidence" [or, boldness, Greek *parrēsia*] (v. 29). Note that they did not specifically pray to receive the Holy Spirit. When they finished, the assembly place was shaken, and "they were all filled with the Holy Spirit" (v. 31).

Because the apostles were certainly among those who prayed and consequently who were filled with the Spirit, this filling cannot have been the initial baptism in the Holy Spirit. They had asked for boldness; the Holy Spirit filled them all afresh and sent them forth to speak the word of God with renewed confidence (v. 31) and great power (v. 33). They were enabled to continue their public preaching openly and freely in spite of the threats of the Sanhedrin. (See the comment on Acts 4:8 for a discussion of "filled with the Holy Spirit.")

Three reasons for the powerful, victorious witness of the early Christians may be noted in this passage. As T. L. Osborn has pointed out, apostolic preaching was based on God's Word (v. 29), depended on the authority of the name of Jesus (v. 30), and was empowered by the Holy Spirit (v. 31).[20]

The Greek term *logos* occurs about thirty-five times in Acts in the sense of the Word of God. His Word convicted and convinced the most hardened hearts.

The term *onoma*, as used for the name of Jesus Christ, is found thirty-three times in Acts. When asked for credentials, the apostles gave the name of Jesus (Acts 4:7–13). The Christians wielded it against diseases, demons and difficulties, so that religious and political leaders were caused to tremble. The *onoma* of Jesus is not a magic formula but implies a faith relationship and full commitment to that name. What Christ has done and will do, and what He means to us now, can never be separated from His name.

The word *pneuma*, as used for the Holy Spirit, occurs at least fifty-four times (with various modifiers) in Acts. These three terms—the Word (*logos*), the name (*onoma*) of Jesus, and the Spirit (*pneuma*)—are the keys which unlock the door to the application of Acts in our lives today.

Those early disciples depended entirely on the Holy Spirit to work through their lives. So whatever the opposition or trial—whether determined unbelief (Acts 9:27–29; 19:8–9) or intense bitterness (13:44–45; 14:2) on the part of their persecutors or prolonged imprisonment such as Paul experienced (28:16, 30–31)—the Christians spoke out boldly in the name of the

Lord. Because of such courage and steadfastness, they endured. Acts 14:3 is typical of their attitude and experience: "They spent a long time there speaking boldly with reliance upon the Lord, who was bearing witness to the word of His grace, granting that signs and wonders be done by their hands."

## Obedience and the Gift of the Holy Spirit—Acts 5:32

In Acts 5:32 Peter and the other apostles were again on trial before the Jewish Sanhedrin. They had been given strict orders not to continue teaching in the name of Jesus and were now being accused of filling Jerusalem with such teaching (Acts 5:27–28). Peter stepped forward to answer the charges:

> We must obey God rather than men! The God of our fathers raised Jesus from the dead—whom you had killed by hanging him on a tree. God exalted him to his own right hand as Prince and Savior that he might give repentance and forgiveness of sins to Israel. We are witnesses of these things, and so is the Holy Spirit, whom God has given to those who obey him.
>
> —ACTS 5:29–32, NIV

The issue at stake, said Peter, was which group truly obeyed God—the Jewish rulers or the apostles. The leaders of the Jews had laid violent hands on Jesus and in effect murdered Him, inflicting the utmost disgrace on Him by having Him hanged on a tree (see Deuteronomy 21:23). On the other hand, God not only reversed the effects of their crime by raising Jesus from the dead but honored Him by exalting Him to His right hand. Furthermore, He invested Him with the authority of prince (or leader, *archēgos*) and Savior.

Who was right? Whose authority should the apostles obey? Peter's final argument that the Christians were the ones who obeyed God, and not the chief priests and elders, was that God had given the Holy Spirit to the followers of Jesus, not to the Sanhedrin.

Is obedience a necessary condition for receiving the baptism in the Spirit? Frederick D. Bruner has wrongly argued that the obedience spoken of in verse 32 is not a condition but the result of the gift of the Holy Spirit. He interpreted the text to mean that the Spirit has been given to those who are *now* obeying God. Thus "obedience is the present *result* of the *prior* gift of the Spirit."[21]

No one will deny that the gift of the Holy Spirit should make us better, more obedient Christians. Bruner's interpretation, however, is based on a misunderstanding of the present tense Greek participle *peitharchousin*, translated "obey." There is no participle in the imperfect (past) tense in Greek. The present participle expresses simultaneous action relative to the main verb, which in verse 32 is "has given," an aorist (past) tense. The present participle may even be used to suggest antecedent time relative to the main verb.[22]

Therefore, Peter's statement means that those who were truly obeying God were the ones who received the Spirit on the Day of Pentecost. And it was obvious that day on whom the Spirit had been poured out, for the 120 believers in Christ spoke in other languages when they were filled with the Spirit.

But in what does obedience to God consist? A contrast with the attitude and customs of the high priest, elders and scribes may help clarify the matter. Those men scrupulously observed the Law of Moses and the traditions of the fathers. They followed religious observances, and many were zealous and devout in their prayers, sacrifices and daily moral life. Yet, as Paul points out in Romans 9:30–10:5, they did not pursue the righteousness of the law by faith. They sought to establish their own righteousness and did not subject themselves to the righteousness based on faith in the promised Messiah.

The attitude of the Jewish leaders was wrong, loving the praise and approval of others rather than the approval of God (John 12:43). They had no spiritual hunger or conviction of their spiritual barrenness. Like the Laodiceans they felt they had need of nothing, when in God's sight they were "wretched and miserable and poor and blind and naked" (Rev. 3:17).

Like the self-righteous Pharisee who went to the temple to pray (Luke 18:9–14), they had no humility, no sense of personal unworthiness, no cry of repentance. They did all their deeds to be noticed by others and loved the chief seats in the synagogues. They were meticulous tithers but neglected the weightier matters such as justice, mercy and faithfulness. In short, Jesus said that while they outwardly appeared righteous to others, inwardly they were full of hypocrisy and lawlessness (Matt. 23:5–7, 23, 28).

Their lawless and hypocritical attitude toward God's perfect will culminated in disobedience to God's Son. In a word, this disobedience took the form of unbelief. "He who believes in the Son has eternal life; but he who does not obey the Son shall not see life, but the wrath of God abides on him" (John 3:36).

The expression "he who does not obey" is one word in Greek, *apeithōn*, which literally means "disobeys." In the view of early Christians the supreme disobedience was a refusal to believe the gospel, so the word came to mean an unbeliever (see KJV, TLB at John 3:36).[23] Such people do not obey Christ because they refuse to believe in and submit themselves to Him. Therefore, they reject Christ because they are not willing to come to the light lest their deeds be exposed (John 3:18–20).

The fundamental act of obedience to God today is to believe in Him whom God has sent. This was Jesus' own answer to those who asked Him what they might do to work the works of God (John 6:28–29), because it indicates a willingness to obey God's will in every matter. Paul said the purpose of his preaching was to bring about "the obedience of faith among all the Gentiles" (Rom. 1:5). He urged people to yield themselves to the belief of God's saving message, which is the highest of all obedience.

True faith, saving faith, is faith that works by love in serving one another (Gal. 5:6, 13). It eventuates in loving obedience to the known will of God. And full belief in Christ will not stop short of believing in and receiving God's promised gift of the Holy Spirit.

The one essential condition for receiving the gift of the Spirit, then, is to be a true believer in Jesus Christ, a born-again Christian. Such a person is obedient to the gospel and to the faith (Acts 6:7; 2 Thess. 1:8).

The converts of the Day of Pentecost continually devoted themselves to the apostles' teaching and to prayer (Acts 2:42). Their repentance was thoroughgoing, and as John the Baptist had required, they brought forth fruits in keeping with their repentance (Luke 3:8). True conversion means commitment to Christ as the new Lord of our life. The true believer says, "Jesus is Lord," by the indwelling Holy Spirit (1 Cor. 12:3).

As we continue to believe in Jesus as our Lord, we keep on obeying Him, and such obedience results in righteousness (Rom. 6:16–17). As we yield the members of our body to righteousness, it makes for a holy life—a life "unto holiness" (KJV) or sanctification (Rom. 6:19). Those who belong to Christ Jesus have crucified the flesh with its passions and selfish desires (Gal. 5:24).

Paul insisted in his epistle to the Galatians that Christians do not receive the gift of the Spirit by the works of the Law. The Living Bible brings this out clearly:

> Let me ask you this one question: Did you receive the Holy Spirit by trying to keep the Jewish laws? Of course not, for the Holy Spirit came upon you only after you heard about Christ and trusted Him to save you. Then have you gone completely crazy? For if trying to obey the Jewish laws never gave you spiritual life in the first place, why do you think that trying to obey them now will make you stronger

> Christians? ... I ask you again, does God give you the power of the Holy Spirit and work miracles among you as a result of your trying to obey the Jewish laws? No, of course not. It is when you believe in Christ and fully trust Him.
> —GALATIANS 3:2–3, 5

Doing the works of the Law can never justify us in God's sight (Gal. 2:16), because even if we could keep the letter of the Law, we offend when it comes to the true intent of the Law as the expression of God's holy will. Jesus explained this in the Sermon on the Mount when He taught, for example, that everyone who even looks on a woman to lust for her has committed adultery with her already in his heart (Matt. 5:28). Therefore, Christian obedience is a product of the inner heart, not of outward duty. It springs from gratitude for grace already received (Rom. 12:1–3), not from the desire to gain merit and to justify ourselves in the eyes of God.

The danger of a substandard Pentecostal experience is present in charismatic circles today. People may desire, or be encouraged by others, to seek for a manifestation of tongues. If they speak a few unintelligible syllables, they are told that they have been baptized in the Holy Spirit. But it may be a Pentecost without repentance, a Pentecost without Christ.

If they bypass obedience to Christ and His cross, if there is no repentance and remission of sins, the experience they receive may very well be counterfeit. Babbling in "tongues" to achieve status in a certain group may be prompted psychologically by their "flesh" or self-nature, or even be activated by an evil spirit. (See the warning under "R—Repent" in the comment on Acts 2:38–40.)

Our motive in seeking a Pentecostal experience is thus all-important. Is it the motive of love—love for Christ and love for other members of His body? (See the comment on 1 Corinthians 13.) We must keep our eyes on the Giver and not on the gifts. We must be concerned about the gifts we can render to Him—our time, our possessions, our very selves—in short, our obedience.

## The Laying On of Hands—Acts 6:6

Acts 6:6 is the first reference in the Book of Acts to the laying on of hands. Here the account tells how seven qualified men were selected and set apart to the special task of administering the business affairs of the congregation in Jerusalem. In the New Testament, the gesture of laying on of hands was used in three ways: in the healing of sickness, in connection with the baptism in the Spirit, and in consecration or ordination to the ministry.

The touch of the human hand has been considered symbolic from the earliest times. It was often looked upon as a means of transferring powers or qualities from one individual to another. The head was usually the part touched, because it was viewed as the noblest member of the body.

In the Old Testament, Jacob laid his hands on the sons of Joseph to convey his blessing (Gen. 48:13–20). On the Day of Atonement the high priest placed his hand on the head of the scapegoat and confessed the sins of the people over it, thus symbolically transferring all their iniquities to the goat (Lev. 16:21–22). The worshiper always laid his hand on the head of the animal he was offering as a sacrifice, in order to identify himself with the animal dying in his place (Exod. 29:10; Lev. 1:4; 3:2; 4:4).

When Levites were ordained to perform the service of the Lord, the Israelites laid hands on them to be their representatives (Num. 8:5–19). Moses invested Joshua with some of his authority by the laying on of his hand when he commissioned Joshua in the sight of the whole congregation (Num. 27:18–23).

Jesus Himself laid His hands on children to impart blessing to them by His touch (Mark 10:13–16). More often we read that He laid his hands on the sick and touched them when He healed them (Mark 6:5; 8:23; Luke 4:40; 13:13; compare Mark 5:23; 7:32–33).

We should not be surprised to learn that the early Christians frequently laid hands on the sick, and many were miraculously healed. Ananias placed his hands on the blinded Saul, and the latter immediately regained his sight (Acts 9:17–18). On the island of Malta, Paul laid his hands on the father of Publius and healed him of fever and dysentery (28:8). Of course, Peter touched the lame beggar sitting by the temple gate when he grasped the man's right hand and raised him to a standing position (3:7).

Other references to miracles performed "by the hands of the apostles" and other Christians suggest that the laying on of hands may have been practiced on these occasions (Acts 5:12; 14:3; 19:11). Anointing the sick with oil may be considered a specialized application of the laying on of hands for the purpose of ministering healing in the name of Jesus Christ (see the comment on James 5:13–20). Paul found that he could extend his ministry of miraculous healing by sending to sick persons pieces of cloth which he had touched (Acts 19:11–12). The practice of anointing prayer cloths to take to absent sick persons has developed from this, and it may be used effectively if done with pure motives.

The laying on of hands was also employed after water baptism with prayer for reception of the Holy Spirit (Acts 8:14–19; 19:5–6). It was not *necessary,* however, for an apostle or any other Christian to lay his hands on a believer that he or she might be baptized in the Spirit. Obviously, at Pentecost and in Cornelius's house the ascended Lord Jesus baptized them in the Holy Spirit (compare John 1:33) without the ministration of human hands.

The third function of the laying on of hands in the New Testament was to ordain a person to a certain office or assignment in the service of the Lord. The meaning of this ceremony is clearly stated in Acts 13:2–3: to set apart individuals from the local church body where they had received training in ministry and for (*eis*) the special work to which the Holy Spirit had already called them. The church at Antioch heard the voice of the Spirit, perhaps through a prophecy, that God had chosen Barnabas and Paul to perform a specific mission. The believers fasted and prayed a while longer to be certain this was the Lord speaking and then acknowledged the divine commission by laying their hands on the two men.

In this manner the local congregation associated itself with the Holy Spirit in commissioning them and in delegating to them the authority of the entire body. Since the members of Christ's body act as His ambassadors, their authority was actually His authority. Paul continued to recognize his membership in and responsibility to the church in Antioch (15:35) and felt duty-bound to report to the Christians there after a missionary journey (14:26–28; 18:22–23).

In both epistles to Timothy, Paul reminded his spiritual son of his ordination service in order to encourage him. Paul and the local elders, perhaps of the local church at Ephesus, had laid hands on the young man to consecrate him to the Christian ministry. On this occasion Timothy had received a charismatic gift to equip him further for his special task (1 Tim. 4:14; 2 Tim. 1:6). Paul also recommended that Timothy not be too hasty in laying hands on anyone (1 Tim. 5:22). Since this verse occurs in a section about elders who fall into sin (5:19–22), it seems to refer to the ordination of elders rather than to the restoration of backsliders to church fellowship with a sign of blessing, as some have explained the verse.

In light of these three functions of the laying on of hands we may understand the statement in Hebrews 6:2, which says that the doctrine of the laying on of hands was included among the foundational Christian teachings in the early church.

## *The Pentecostal Outpouring in Samaria—Acts 8:5–25*

The early church father Tertullian once said, "The blood of the martyrs is the seed of the church." The persecution beginning with Stephen's bloody death served only to spread the fires of revival beyond the city limits of Jerusalem. Philip, the deacon, is an example of the many refugees who preached the gospel as they were scattered throughout the districts of Judea and Samaria.

Philip went to the city of Samaria, the site of the old capital of the Northern Kingdom of Israel in Old Testament times. Herod the Great had renamed the city Sebaste in honor of the Roman emperor who was reigning when Herod rebuilt the city in a lavish way. As Philip proclaimed Christ, crowds listened intently because of the miraculous signs he was performing. Many demon-possessed persons were set free, and many others who were paralyzed or lame were healed. The result was that numbers of people, both men and women, believed Philip's message and were submitting to Christian baptism (Acts 8:12, 16).

We have no reason to doubt that they were genuinely converted. Even Simon, a clever magician and a great celebrity in that region, was amazed by the miracles taking place. He too made a profession of faith and was baptized. The news of the revival in Samaria soon reached the church in Jerusalem, forty miles by road to the south. The apostles felt responsible for the new believers in Samaria and delegated Peter and John to go there to give any necessary supervision and teaching. (The practice of a representative of the Jerusalem body going to a new Christian community was repeated when Barnabas was sent off to Antioch, Acts 11:22.)

The journey from Jerusalem to Samaria takes two days on foot. Thus a bare minimum of about five days elapsed, and probably a longer period, between the first conversions and the arrival of the two apostles. There was, then, a definite interval between the regenerative work of the Spirit in the lives of the Samaritan converts and their baptism in the Holy Spirit.

Peter and John realized at once that the Pentecostal gift of the Holy Spirit had not been extended to Philip's converts. They had received baptism in water but not the baptism in the Spirit. Therefore the apostles prayed for them to receive the promised gift of the Father. "Then they began laying their hands on them, and they were receiving the Holy Spirit" (v. 17). Williams's translation, on the basis of the Greek imperfect tense of the verb *elambanon*, suggests that they received the Spirit "one by one."

Luke does not directly describe the accompanying phenomena. But as F. F. Bruce commented, "The context leaves us in no doubt that their reception of the Spirit was attended by external manifestations such as had marked His descent on the earliest disciples at Pentecost."[24]

A number of Bible commentators have agreed that what Simon the sorcerer "saw" or observed was the new converts speaking in tongues when hands were laid on them. For example, Johannes Munck wrote: "Simon . . . was struck by the apostles' ability to make the baptized prophesy and to speak in tongues by the laying on of hands."[25] Simon wanted to buy the ability or authority to impart the Holy Spirit with such evidence, for he knew he could not match it with his repertoire of magic arts. All of Philip's miracles of healing and exorcism had not impressed him as this sign had!

A clue in the Greek text that tongues indeed were in evidence at Samaria may be found in 8:21. In rebuking Simon for his wicked thought that he could obtain the gift of God with money, Peter exclaimed, "You have no part or portion in this matter, for your heart is not right before God." The word for "matter" is Greek *logos*, "word," "speaking" or "kind of speaking" as in 1 Corinthians 1:5 where Paul says the Corinthians were enriched "in all your speaking" (NIV).

Simon could have no part in this kind of speaking, because his heart was obviously crooked in holding such a materialistic view of the Holy Spirit and His gifts. What an object lesson regarding right motives in asking for the baptism in the Spirit and in desiring spiritual ministries! (See the comment on 1 Corinthians 13.)

The fact that apostolic hands were laid on the Samaritan Christians and those at Ephesus (Acts 19:6) to bestow the Holy Spirit does not establish a precedent. There was no imposition of hands at Pentecost or in Cornelius's house. In the case of Paul, the man who laid hands on him was not an apostle (Acts 9:17). Paul does not include the power to impart the Spirit in the list of charismatic gifts in 1 Corinthians 12:4–11.

Perhaps the Samaritans, who were usually despised by the Jews of Jerusalem, needed to be assured by the apostles "that they were fully incorporated into the new community of the people of God."[26] The laying on of hands was as much a token of fellowship and solidarity as it was a symbol of the impartation of the gift of the Spirit (see the comment at Acts 6:63).

## The Conversion of the Ethiopian Eunuch—Acts 8:26–39

Philip's experience with the Ethiopian eunuch provides an outstanding example of how the Holy Spirit helps in soul-winning. Philip was in such close contact with God that he could get the message from an angel (compare Acts 5:19–20; 12:7–10) where to go. He was obedient to this prompting and soon met a man whose heart was already prepared.

In spite of being intimidated by the man's high rank and his fine vehicle, Philip listened to the Spirit, who said, "Go up and join this chariot" (8:29). Philip sensed the man's need when he saw him reading the Scriptures and asked, "Do you understand what you are reading?" (v. 30). The section happened to be Isaiah 53:7–8 about the suffering Servant of the Lord, a passage which people have interpreted in many different ways. But Philip opened his mouth, and the Spirit filled him and led him as he explained the Word and preached Jesus to the foreign official. Philip must have taught him the great doctrines about Christ and salvation, as well as the importance of the ordinance of baptism, judging from the eunuch's eagerness to be baptized (v. 36).

When the eunuch was immersed, he evidently received the gift of the Spirit, for "he went on his way rejoicing" (v. 39). The joy that filled his heart was undoubtedly the joy of the Holy Spirit (Rom. 14:17; 1 Thess. 1:6; compare Acts 13:52). In fact, we might note a curious addition that several Greek manuscripts and early church fathers inserted in verse 39. With the added words, it reads, "The Spirit of the Lord fell upon the eunuch, and the angel of the Lord snatched Philip away." F. F. Bruce comments that the "effect of the longer reading is to make it clear that the Ethiopian's baptism was followed by the gift of the Spirit. However, even with the shorter reading it is a safe inference that he did receive the Spirit."[27]

## The Conversion and Baptism of Saul—Acts 9:1–22

Where and when was Saul (Paul) actually converted? Was it when he heard the voice of the Lord outside the city of Damascus, or was it in Judas's house on the street called Straight when Ananias came to him several days later?

Two facts clearly point to the earlier time. First, in relating the details of his conversion later on, Paul stated that, after the one speaking from heaven had identified Himself as Jesus the Nazarene whom Paul was persecuting, he himself responded, "What shall I do, Lord?" (Acts 22:10). Paul was immediately convinced by the glorious theophany who Jesus really was—the Messiah, true deity, the Lord of glory.

Even though he was a strict Jew, Paul at once confessed Jesus as Lord. This is tantamount to conversion, as Paul later wrote: "If you confess with your mouth Jesus *as* Lord, and believe in your heart that God raised Him from the dead, you shall be saved" (Rom. 10:9).

Second, when Ananias came to the blinded man, he called him "Brother Saul" (v. 17). Because of the reputation of the Jew of Tarsus as a persecutor of the church, Ananias was at first afraid when the Lord told him in a vision to go to Paul. He never would have entered the house and addressed him as "brother" if he had not been fully assured that Paul was already a true believer in Christ.

During the three days of blindness, therefore, Paul was fasting and praying as a Christian. Only then did Ananias come and lay his hands on him and say, "Brother Saul, the Lord Jesus . . . has sent me so that you may regain your sight, and be filled with the Holy Spirit" (v. 17). At once his eyes were healed, and he arose and was baptized. Without a word to the contrary, we may assume that, as so often happened in the early decades of the church, Paul was filled with, or baptized in, the Holy Spirit at the same time of his baptism in water.

We should note that the human agent who mediated the infilling of the Spirit to Paul was not an apostle, but simply an otherwise unknown believer, and one in Damascus, not from the mother church in Jerusalem. As Howard Ervin has pointed out, it was not apostolic prerogative but the authority of Jesus' name that validated the laying on of Ananias's hands. He acted in obedience to Christ's commission in Mark 16:15–18, which included authorization to lay hands on the sick, and the Lord wonderfully healed Paul and filled him with His Spirit.[28]

The text does not specifically mention whether Paul spoke in tongues on this occasion. Thus we cannot be dogmatic as to whether this manifestation followed immediately or afterward. But that he did have the usual evidence is clear from his own testimony: "I thank God, I speak in tongues more than you all" (1 Cor. 14:18). We do know that right away Paul received power to witness and to proclaim Christ in the synagogues, saying, "He is the Son of God" (v. 20). The purpose of the Pentecostal experience (see the comment on Acts 1:4–8) began to be fulfilled without delay in this outstanding convert.

## *The First Outpouring of the Spirit on Gentiles—Acts 10:44–48*

On the Day of Pentecost, Peter had quoted Joel's prophecy in which God says, "It shall be in the last days . . . that I will pour forth of My Spirit upon all mankind" (Acts 2:17). On that occasion Peter had been the key to the salvation of thousands of Jews. Six or eight years later he became God's agent to open the door to the blessings of the new birth and Pentecost for all the Gentiles as well.

The first mission to the Gentiles was an event of fundamental importance in the fulfillment of Christ's command to preach the gospel to all nations. It is apparent that God acted sovereignly in the conversion and Spirit-baptism of Cornelius and his household. The Lord first of all acted to prepare the Roman centurion and the Jewish apostle for their meeting. He gave each a vision, and He spoke to one by an angel and to the other by the Spirit.

The long-standing and deep-seated Jewish prejudice against Gentiles was entrenched in Peter. Therefore, he had to be absolutely convinced that in Christ God truly was abolishing Jewish ceremonial laws. The Lord made His will so clear to Peter that he gave lodging to the Gentile servants of Cornelius without any hesitation or misgivings and went with them the next day to Caesarea. Peter was made to realize that "God is no respecter of persons" (KJV), that He "does not show favoritism" (NIV) but welcomes anyone who fears Him, regardless of his nationality or race (Acts 10:34–35).

When Peter arrived in Cornelius's house, he found many people already assembled. There were relatives and close friends of the centurion (Acts 10:24, 27), in addition to slaves and devout soldiers (Acts 10:7). Cornelius and his household were "God-fearers," semi-proselytes to Judaism who stopped short of circumcision, but who were "attracted by the simple monotheism of Jewish synagogue worship and by the ethical standard of the Jewish way of life."[29]

Here was a large group of people who already believed in God and were acquainted with the doctrines and prophecies of the Old Testament. Living only fifty miles from the Sea of Galilee and only a little more from Jerusalem, they had heard much about the ministry of Jesus of Nazareth (Acts 10:37).

Peter's speech is undoubtedly summarized for us. He touched upon Jesus' baptism, miracles, crucifixion, resurrection and commission to His disciples. Then Peter began to press for a decision: "Of Him all the prophets bear witness that through His name every one who believes in Him receives forgiveness of sins" (10:43). The prepared, eager hearts immediately accepted the word with saving faith.

Before Peter could finish his sermon, Pentecost was repeated! The Holy Spirit fell upon all those who were listening to the message. This verb (*epipiptō*), describing the action of the Spirit, suggests that He gripped them and took possession of them even as fear is said to "fall upon" people (Luke 1:12; Acts 19:17; Rev. 11:11). This is not a normal description of His coming in regeneration, but of the Pentecostal baptism in the Spirit for power. It was unmistakable!

The six Jewish believers with Peter from Joppa (compare Acts 11:12) were amazed, "because the gift of the Holy Spirit had been poured out upon the Gentiles also" (10:45). How did they know? Because "they were hearing them speaking with tongues and exalting God" (v. 46).

Obviously someone in the group knew one or more of the foreign languages. The content was very similar to that of the messages in tongues at Pentecost when the 120 were speaking "the wonderful works of God" (Acts 2:11, KJV). The Gentiles were manifesting the same sign of the baptism in the Spirit that had electrified the crowds at the Feast of Pentecost (see also the comment on 1 Corinthians 14).

Peter at once recognized that the Gentiles had truly been saved and should receive the sign of the New Covenant for the remission of sins. He therefore ordered Cornelius and his companions to be baptized in the name of Jesus Christ. Because of the suddenness of the Spirit's descent, in this case baptism in water followed baptism in the Holy Spirit. We should note that the apostle did not consider the reception of the Spirit a substitute for water baptism.

Afterward, Peter had to explain his conduct before the Jerusalem congregation. They accused him of having broken the ban on social intercourse with "unclean" foreigners, saying, "You went to uncircumcised men and ate with them" (Acts 11:3). Peter defended himself by giving a straightforward account of his experience. When he reached the climax of his story, he said,

> And as I began to speak, the Holy Spirit fell upon them, just as He did upon us at the beginning. And I remembered the word of the Lord, how He [said], "John baptized with water, but you shall be baptized with the Holy Spirit." If God therefore gave to them the same gift as He gave to us also after believing in the Lord Jesus Christ, who was I that I could stand in God's way?
>
> —ACTS 11:15–17

The Jerusalem leaders then calmed down and praised God that He had obviously granted to the Gentiles repentance that leads to life (11:18).

Peter remained thoroughly convinced that when the Gentiles in Cornelius's house heard the gospel they believed, and God cleansed their hearts by faith before baptizing them in the Spirit. This was his argument ten or twelve years later at the Jerusalem council, which convened to discuss the necessity of circumcising Gentile converts. Peter's proof that they were saved purely through the grace of the Lord Jesus, without any additional works of the Law, is given in these words:

> And God, who knows the hearts, bore attesting testimony to them by having given them the Holy Spirit even as also to us. And He made no distinction at all between both us and also them, in answer to their faith having cleansed their hearts.
> —ACTS 16:8–9, WUEST

The gift of the Spirit was God's seal that they had already believed in Christ (see the comment on Ephesians 1:13–14).

When Peter spoke of God's having purified their hearts by faith (Acts 15:9), he almost certainly had in mind his trance that day in Joppa. In it God had revealed to him that He was cleansing the ritually unclean so that they were no longer to be considered unholy (Acts 10:15). Therefore Peter was referring to the forgiveness of sins by the blood of Christ (1 John 1:7) and to cleansing as aspects of justification, rather than to a further step of sanctification.

Repentance as an integral part of conversion along with faith is a necessary condition for receiving the promised gift of the Holy Spirit, "but there is no suggestion that this blessing was promised on condition of a holy life, nor will its immediate result be a state of entire sanctification."[30] We conclude, then, that a person may be baptized in the Spirit immediately after believing in Christ, regardless of his or her spiritual maturity. He or she must be fully justified (not wholly sanctified) to receive the gift of the Spirit. (Regarding sanctification, see the comment on 1 Corinthians 6:11.)

## Divine Guidance—Acts 16:6–10

How does God lead His children? Acts 16:6 describes two methods which the early Christians knew and that God still uses in this age of the Holy Spirit.

On his second missionary journey Paul, along with Silas, revisited the Galatian churches to give further instruction and to strengthen them in the faith. Then they planned to travel due west into the province of Asia, undoubtedly to begin a ministry in Ephesus, the chief city. But in God's plan

Ephesus was not yet ready for Paul, nor Paul for it. So they were forbidden by the Holy Spirit to preach the word in Asia (v. 6). Next, Paul and his group tried repeatedly to go northward into the province of Bithynia along the Black Sea, but "the Spirit of Jesus did not permit them" (v. 7).

Luke did not tell how the Holy Spirit gave Paul and his companions these directions. But, as F. F. Bruce suggested, in the first case He may have spoken through a prophet in the church at Lystra.[31] For example, as Paul was nearing Jerusalem on his third journey, different Christians ministered to him in the Spirit to warn him of the danger of setting foot in that city (Acts 21:11). They received a word of knowledge (21:4) and a prophecy (21:11) for Paul, but he bore the responsibility of what God wanted him to do with this knowledge. In that case he kept on with his plans.

The comforting word which the Lord brought to Paul in the Jerusalem prison (23:11) proves that he had not been disobedient to the Spirit. Probably in Acts 21:4 the disciples added their own interpretation to the word of knowledge which revealed imminent danger for Paul, and concluded that he should not go up to Jerusalem.

In 16:7 we should note that nearly all early Greek manuscripts and many ancient versions have "the Spirit of Jesus." This is the only occurrence of this striking expression in the New Testament, although it is closely paralleled by "the Spirit of Christ" in Romans 8:9 and 1 Peter 1:11; "the Spirit of Jesus Christ" in Philippians 1:19; and "the Spirit of His Son" in Galatians 4:6. Verses 6–7 of Acts 16, taken together, are especially important in establishing the fact that the two terms "the Holy Spirit" and "the Spirit of Jesus" refer to one and the same Spirit, the same third Person of the Trinity.

Just why Luke made a change in phraseology in referring to the Spirit in these two instances is not clear. Again F. F. Bruce's comment is helpful: "Possibly the methods used to communicate the Spirit's will on the two occasions were different; it may be that on the second occasion the communication took a form closely associated with the exalted Christ."[32]

During His earthly ministry Jesus rebuked demons He was exorcizing and "would not allow them to speak" (Luke 4:41; the verb *allow* and the verb *permit* in Acts 16:7 are the same in the Greek). We may surmise, then, that the Lord Jesus Christ as head of His church issued one or more sharp commands by His Spirit to Paul not to enter Bithynia. The Lord seems to have revealed His will on this occasion in a more direct fashion than by adverse circumstances, but whether by a word of wisdom, by a prophecy or by tongues and interpretation, we do not know. Whatever its form, the guidance that Paul received is an example of the promise in Isaiah 30:21, "And your ears will hear a word behind you, 'This is the way, walk in it,' wherever you turn to the right or to the left."

God's strategy for world evangelization was Europe before Asia. Bithynia would have its chance later on. In fact, within fifteen years Peter took the gospel to that area, according to the salutation of his first epistle (1 Pet. 1:1).

By the beginning of the next century Christianity was flourishing there, as we discover in a fascinating exchange of letters between Pliny, the Roman governor of Bithynia, and the emperor Trajan. Pliny described the worship services of the Christians in his province and their oath to abstain from all criminal acts and breaches of trust, and how their "contagious superstition" only spread further as he sought to bring individuals to trial.[33]

It was wise for Paul to make plans for the next part of his journey—and usually his plans were sensible and right. But, like him, we must be ready to lay our plans aside when God sends a new revelation of His will. We should be orderly and systematic (see Paul's daily routine for two years at Ephesus, Acts 19:8–10) and use the wisdom of common sense, but be sensitive to the voice of the Spirit and subject to His change.

The other means of divine guidance to be found in these verses is by vision. In a vision a person becomes oblivious to his or her natural surroundings. The Spirit of God so controls the person's senses that he or she seems actually to see, hear and feel what is revealed in the vision.

The recipient of the vision may be awake (Dan. 10:7; Acts 9:3, 7; 10:3), in a trance (Acts 10:10, 17; 11:5) or dreaming (Job 4:13; 33:15; Dan. 4:5–13; 7:1). Paul had a number of visions (2 Cor. 12:1). He described the appearance of Christ to him on the Damascus road as a heavenly vision (Acts 26:19), and the Lord spoke to him one night in Corinth by a vision (Acts 18:9). That young men should see visions is one of the characteristics of the Pentecostal outpouring of the Spirit (Acts 2:17).

The vision that came to Paul that night at Troas is often termed the Macedonian call. We must note carefully that this was not the time when he was called to serve the Lord. He began to preach the gospel in Damascus a few days after his conversion, as soon as he had been healed and filled with the Spirit (Acts 9:17–22).

We do not need a vision or any other special divine guidance to call us to obey the great commission of our risen Lord (see the comment on Matthew 28:18–20). Paul had already been serving God as a teacher, evangelist and apostle for a number of years, and he was now on his second missionary tour. This vision was given him to provide positive direction after the series of divine prohibitions.

The Lord also guides us by His written Word. "Thy word is a lamp to my feet, and a light to my path" (Ps. 119:105). In addition, His direction may come in the form of an inner "voice" or strong impression of what to do in a certain situation. Furthermore, He permits circumstances beyond our control to alter our course. For instance, God used the famine to bring Jacob and his sons to Egypt (Gen. 45:4–11; 46:2–4; 50:20).

Nevertheless, God also expects us to seek wise human counsel (Prov. 11:14; 12:15; 15:22; 19:20; 20:18). He has created human beings with minds that can think and reason and plan, and He does not bless mental laziness on our part. Purposeful ignorance and slipshod organization bring no glory to God. We are commanded to seek wisdom and pray for it (Prov. 2:1–12; James 1:5), for by wisdom we may walk in upright paths, and our steps will not be impeded (Prov. 4:11–12).

God will not leave His children without direction. Being led by the Spirit of God is a charismatic mark of a true son of God (Rom. 8:14). He is our Redeemer, Yahweh our God, who leads us in the way we should go (Isa. 48:17). Because He is our shepherd, He acts in compassion to lead us in paths of righteousness for His name's sake (Isa. 49:10; Ps. 23:1–3). In answer to our prayer He will teach us His will and His way (Ps. 5:8; 25:4–10) as we commit ourselves completely into His hand (Ps. 31:3, 5; Rom. 12:1–2; see the comment on Romans 8:14–17).

### Tongues at Ephesus—Acts 19:1–7

The third occasion when tongues are specifically mentioned in the Book of Acts took place at Ephesus some twenty years after Pentecost. This incident suggests quite clearly that the Pentecostal experience is extended to include all believers in Christ.

Early in his third missionary journey, the apostle Paul returned to the chief city of the Roman province of Asia and happened on about a dozen men who were "disciples." In Luke's writings, when this term is not further qualified, it always designates disciples of Jesus. That they were Christians in some sense is borne out by Paul's reference to faith on their part—"when you believed" (v. 2). The verb "believe" is used about twenty times in Acts with no direct object. In every case the context indicates that believing in Christ for salvation is meant.

Paul noticed, however, an obvious lack of power in their lives. God's evident seal or stamp of ownership, which is the Holy Spirit, was not upon them at this point (compare Ephesians 1:13–14). So Paul asked them a question, the very asking of which implied that it was possible to "believe" without thereby receiving the Spirit in Pentecostal fullness. "Having believed, did you receive the Holy Spirit?" (v. 2, literal translation).

The Greek here does not employ a temporal conjunction such as "after" or "when" to indicate the time relationship between believing in Christ and receiving the Spirit. But the aorist participle *pisteusantes*, "having believed," is the same as in Ephesians 1:13. There the context more clearly brings out the fact that the gift of the Holy Spirit comes to us as a consequence of our believing in Christ, but that it is not necessarily coincident with our conversion. On the other hand, the New Testament consistently teaches that the fullness of the gospel message embraces the news of the coming of the Spirit and that normal Christian faith includes as one of the fundamentals the reception of the Holy Spirit.

In questioning the disciples, Paul discovered that their knowledge of Christianity was incomplete. They told him that they had been baptized into John's baptism. Their experience was very similar to that of Apollos before Priscilla and Aquila "explained to him the way of God more accurately" (Acts 18:26). Apollos already knew the Old Testament Scriptures and had been instructed in the way of the Lord, the teachings of the Lord Jesus. Enthusiastic and fervent in his spirit, he was able to speak and teach accurately the things about Jesus' life and to present Him as the Messiah, even though he was acquainted only with the baptism of John (18:25).

In addition to knowing Old Testament references concerning the Spirit of God, disciples of John the Baptist would have known that he had spoken of a coming baptism in the Spirit (see the comment on Matthew 3:11–17), so that they could hardly have been ignorant about the existence of the Holy Spirit. These dozen men, however, like Apollos, had not known that the outpouring of the Spirit was an accomplished fact. Therefore their reply in verse 2 should be interpreted as in the margin of the NAS: "No, we have not even heard whether the Holy Spirit has been given." The same Greek grammatical construction occurs in John 7:39, where the translator must also supply the word "given" to make good sense in English.

Thus these men had not yet heard that Jesus had fulfilled His mission after His crucifixion, resurrection and ascension by sending the Holy Spirit. Consequently, they had an incomplete knowledge of the gospel. Furthermore, their pre-Pentecost type of baptism (simply as the mark of their repentance) was no longer adequate after Peter on the Day of Pentecost had proclaimed baptism in the name of Jesus. John the Baptist himself had recognized that his baptism was only temporary, "telling the people to believe in Him who was coming after him, that is, in Jesus" (Acts 19:4).

The order of the next events at Ephesus is very clear. It is the usual New Testament pattern of the baptism in the Holy Spirit. When the twelve men heard from Paul the whole truth about Jesus, they believed and received Christian baptism from him. If they had not been regenerated by the Spirit of God prior to Paul's arrival, certainly they were before they were baptized in water and before the Spirit fell upon them. Then Paul laid his hands on them, and they were baptized in the Spirit in Pentecostal fashion: "The Holy Spirit came on them, and they began speaking with tongues and prophesying" (v. 6).

In the early church the Spirit was normally communicated in His fullness at the time of a person's baptismal ceremony. The disciples at Ephesus followed essentially the same instructions that Peter gave in Jerusalem—repent, be baptized and receive the gift of the Holy Spirit (Acts 2:38).

The speaking with tongues and prophesying were outward and visible signs of the presence and power of the Holy Spirit. Validation by means of these signs was just as important for these twelve disciples as for the believers on the Day of Pentecost. Their experience of manifesting the overflowing presence of the Comforter by speaking in tongues was consistent with that of the 120 at Pentecost and of Cornelius and his household, and probably of the Samaritan converts and of Saul of Tarsus as well.

## EIGHT

# *The Work of the Holy Spirit Explained: The Epistles*

### *Love Poured Out—Romans 5:5*

The first unmistakable mention of the Holy Spirit in Paul's great doctrinal epistle to the Romans is found in 5:5. There the apostle described the benefits that come to Christians because we have been justified by faith.

Paul said that, in addition to being accounted righteous through faith in Jesus (Rom. 3:21–31; 5:1), we have peace with God as a settled fact. Also through Jesus our Lord, we have received the right of access into the very presence of God our king, because we stand before Him in a state of grace, not in our own merit (Rom. 5:2a). Furthermore, we can even rejoice in our afflictions, because we know that our troubles and trials are producing patience or perseverance. The chain reaction continues so that perseverance produces proven character, and this in turn strengthens our hope of seeing and sharing the glory of God (Rom. 5:2–4).

Paul went on: "Nor will this hope let us down, because God's love is poured out in our hearts through the Holy Spirit who has been given to us" (v. 5, Bruce).[1] Because of our wonderful present experience of God's love, we know that our hope of future glory is not illusory. His love has been "shed abroad" (KJV) in our hearts, or better, "poured out," the very same Greek verb (*ekcheō*) used to describe the copious outpouring of the Spirit at Pentecost and in Cornelius's home (Acts 2:17–18, 33; 10:45; also Titus 3:6).

According to the perfect tense of this Greek verb, not only has the Holy Spirit poured God's love into our hearts, but He continues to flood us and comfort us with that love and to give us assurance of it. For Paul, God's boundless love for us, which was demonstrated supremely in Christ's death in our behalf (Rom. 5:5–8), was also demonstrated by the gift of the Holy Spirit to us (end of v. 5).

Historically, the Spirit was sent publicly to the corporate church at Pentecost for all time and for all believers (Acts 2:33). Individually, however, He is given to each Christian in virtue of his or her faith to receive the promised Holy Spirit (Gal. 3:2, 5, 14; 4:6; 1 John 3:24; 4:13). Though the Spirit was given to all (Acts 2:38–39), each must receive Him personally—just as Jesus died as a ransom for all (1 Tim. 2:4–6; 4:10) and rose from the dead once for all time (Heb. 9:25–28a). Yet each one must believe in Christ and receive Him personally as Savior and Lord (John 1:12).

We may note this duality of the corporate and the individual throughout both the Old and New Testaments. Most of the promises are corporate promises to be appropriated by the individual as well.

Many can testify to a new realization and appreciation of God's love for them after the baptism in the Holy Spirit. Furthermore, they experience in a new way a divine flow of love through them to others who are in need.

### Life by the Spirit—Romans 8:1–13

Romans 8 has been called—rightly or wrongly—Paul's Pentecost. While it barely touches on the charismatic empowering, it is the greatest single chapter in the Bible about the inner working of the Holy Spirit in the life of the believer. This passage brings to a climax Paul's teaching on sanctification and therefore is the peak of his major doctrinal epistle. The Holy Spirit is mentioned no fewer than seventeen times in the course of the thirty-nine verses.

In the sixth chapter the apostle taught that positionally the Christian died with Christ to sin and is alive to God in Christ Jesus (6:1–11). In the seventh chapter he stated that we have "died" to the Law's demands in our being identified with Christ's death on the cross (7:4). Therefore we have been released from the condemnation of the Law and now serve God in the new way of the Spirit instead of attempting to serve Him in the old way of the written code (7:6, NIV) with all of the inevitable failures.

Then Paul described the fierce inner struggle that he as a born-again Christian experienced between his flesh (his old fallen human nature) and his mind (his new real self as a regenerated man). The cause of this conflict continued to exist throughout this present life, but God's provision for victory was proclaimed in chapter 8. A life of righteousness could now be an actuality through the sanctifying power of the indwelling Holy Spirit.

There is a new law, in the sense of a principle or dominating force, at work in the believer (8:2). Like every human being since Adam's fall, Paul was caught in the inevitable principle of sin and death. He could not keep from sinning, and he would eventually die (Rom. 5:12). He was not only legally condemned, but morally corrupt in the eyes of his righteous and holy Creator-Judge.

But now in Christ Jesus his sentence of condemnation had been revoked (8:1), and a higher principle was operating in him to set him free from the stranglehold of sin. Sin had been choking off his life and causing certain death. The power of sin was like the force of gravity pulling him down to destruction unless a greater force intervened to hold him up.

That new force, Paul said, is the Holy Spirit. He enters the hearts of believers to supply the life of Christ. He effects the "life of Christ Jesus" by keeping vital the union of believers with Christ. This may be likened to the union of a branch grafted into a tree.

Paul insisted that the Spirit is in believers to reverse the direction of their "walk" and their thinking. In their natural state, they can only "set their minds on the things of the flesh" (8:5). That is, they can only live by the dictates and promptings of their old selfish natures and think the thoughts that come naturally to them.

But now believers can live in the sphere of the Spirit, because the Spirit of God dwells in them (8:9). Therefore the Spirit is prompting them to think His thoughts. Their whole attitude becomes spiritual under the Spirit's control, because their minds are in tune with Him. Such a basic attitude of submission to God's law, instead of the old hostility, means life and inward peace (8:6–7).

This new life in the Spirit is bound to have consequences for our whole being. Verses 10–11 describe how we are freed from the law of death (v. 2). No doubt the body is still subject to death and can be counted on to die some day because of the aftermath of sin. Yet because of the Spirit who has His home within us, our mortal bodies will one day be quickened (8:11, KJV).

The obvious meaning of the word "quicken" in this context is to restore to physical life by resurrection (as in John 5:21; 1 Corinthians 15:22). At Jesus' second coming, Christians who have died will be raised from the dead just as He was raised in His first advent. Those who are still alive and remain

(1 Thess. 4:15) will suddenly receive new resurrection life in their mortal bodies. That will be the glorious day when "this mortal will have put on immortality" (1 Cor. 15:54).

A mortal body, however, is one that is subject to death but has not yet died. This meaning is evident, for instance, in the command not to let sin reign in these mortal bodies (Rom. 6:12). Paul uses the term "mortal" again in 2 Corinthians 4:7–11 when he states that our weak bodies are like earthen vessels, so that when the life of Jesus is manifested in our mortal flesh, the surpassing greatness of the power may obviously be of God and not from ourselves. We glorify our God, then, when we implore Him to strengthen and heal our mortal bodies when there is need, as a foretaste of the resurrection.

In Romans 8:12–13 the apostle summarized what he had been teaching from verse 5 onward. We are not under obligation to the old nature, he said, to live habitually under its control. He implied that our obligation is now to the Holy Spirit.

The paraphrase of F. F. Bruce aids us in understanding verse 13: "If you live in conformity with the desires of the old nature, you are bound to die. But if by the Spirit you treat the body's former activities as dead, you will live."[2]

The Spirit is ever present to supply us with the power and determination to say no. It is the Spirit of Christ within who enables us to deny ourselves daily and take up our cross and follow the Lord Jesus. He motivates us to keep on mortifying the former deeds of the body as we exercise self-control.

To illustrate the necessity of disciplining ourselves, Paul in another letter reminded the sports-minded Corinthians of how athletes even buffet their bodies (1 Cor. 9:24–27). For this cause God has given us the Holy Spirit, who in turn gives us a spirit of discipline or self-control (see the comment on 2 Timothy 1:6–7).

From Romans 8:1–13 we can clearly conclude that the victorious life in Christ is more than a matter of mere self-control. It is living by an entirely different principle of being. It is *life by the Spirit.*

This explains why healing and other miracles can occur. A different order of creation is in effect. It is life in the realm of the Spirit.

## The Guidance and Witness of the Spirit—Romans 8:14–17

Living by the Spirit includes being led by the Spirit. The continual guidance of the Holy Spirit is one of the clearest marks of being a child of God. "For all who are being led by the Spirit of God, these are sons of God" (v. 14).

The blessed Holy Spirit not only guides us into all the truth that is in Jesus (John 14:26; 16:13), but His leading also affects the practical business of daily living. God the Father wants us, as sons and daughters, to know His will at first hand and in detail. Samuel Chadwick once said, "Nothing is too trivial for omniscience. Come straight to God. Lay all questions naked before Him and He will make it plain to you what is His will."[3]

The Book of Acts furnishes many specific instances of the Spirit's guiding in the hour of crisis and decision for the sake of the gospel (see the comment on Acts 16:6–10). But is there in addition a general direction in which the Holy Spirit is daily leading all Christians? There certainly is.

Our common destination is holiness. "Follow peace with all men, and holiness, without which no man shall see the Lord" (Heb. 12:14, KJV). "For this is the will of God, even your sanctification" (1 Thess. 4:3, KJV; see the comment on 1 Corinthians 6:11).

God has appointed the Holy Spirit to be the agent of our sanctification. Thus it is His duty to lead us away from sin. He leads us in paths of righteousness, for He is the Spirit of Christ, our good shepherd. He directs the obedient child of God to abandon the deeds of the flesh and to put down roots in the orchard of grace.

There under the Holy Spirit's expert care the believer will bear His fruit (Gal. 5:22–23). The Spirit is ever leading us to fellowship with the Father through Jesus Christ, and by the Spirit we have our right of access through Christ into the Father's presence (Eph. 2:18).

How does the Spirit lead? Often it is by His "still, small voice" appealing to the conscience (1 Kings 19:13; see comments on "Elijah, the Model Prophet"). On the other hand, sometimes the believer may be gripped by the Spirit and almost impelled against his or her will or better judgment. Luke says of Jesus that after His baptism He was led by the Spirit (Luke 4:1)—the same verb as in verse 14. But as Mark writes about that incident, he makes this striking statement: "Immediately the Spirit impelled Him to go out into the wilderness" (Mark 1:12).

With pressure like jet propulsion, the Spirit may drive the Christian from within. To be sure, He may also draw the believer from without by external circumstances or by the advice of other members of the body of Christ. He may plant suggestions in the mind. But on occasion He may lead by a strong inner compulsion that is as distinct as an audible voice. His direction, however, never leaves us in a state of anxiety or frustration, but produces a sense of inner peace.

Another assuring factor in the leading of God's Spirit is that there is a ring of certainty to it. In connection with His guidance is His inner witness with our spirit. Now one of the marvelous transformations that occurs in salvation is the change in attitude of the human spirit. Jesus Christ died to redeem us that we might receive the adoption as sons and daughters (Gal. 4:6; Eph. 1:5). This means that by a divine act God legally placed us as children in His household. We were given this status at the moment of our conversion, not as a result of special understanding or spirituality.

Through the new birth wrought in us by the Spirit of God, we became children of God with a new nature. By adoption we were made children of God with new rights and a new inheritance. As a result, our own spirits have a new outlook.

In the second instance where the word *spirit* occurs in Romans 8:15 (*pneuma huiothesias*) it should have a capital S, as in the KJV and NIV: "but ye have received the Spirit of adoption" (KJV) or "the Spirit of sonship" (NIV). There is no longer a slavery spirit to bring us back into a state of fear (compare 2 Timothy 1:7), but the Holy Spirit who makes us so aware of our being a son or daughter that we want to cry out, "Abba, Father!" It is also by the Holy Spirit that we truly call Jesus "Lord" (1 Cor. 12:3).

Paul explained this cry more fully to the Galatians: "And because you are sons, God has sent forth the Spirit of His Son into our hearts, crying, 'Abba! Father!'" (Gal. 4:6). Thus there is a joint testimony of the Holy Spirit with our own renewed spirits that we are children of God (Rom. 8:16). He is constantly bearing this inward witness so that in any and every situation we may *know* that we are saved.

The apostle John has much to say about this inner conviction in his epistle: "We know . . . that He abides in us, by the Spirit which He has given us" (1 John 3:24). As God's love is perfected in us when we love one another, we know we are abiding in Him and He is abiding in us, "because He has given us of His Spirit" (1 John 4:13; see also the comment on 1 John 5:6–12; John 20:21–23).

The Spirit of God touches the human spirit in a mysterious but intensely personal way. He who inspired the holy Scriptures uses the Word of God to bring the revelation of God about His Son to our inner consciousness. Then this same Spirit comes to provide an inner confirmation of the objective revelation.

Thus when we believe, the truth of the gospel is sealed in our hearts by the Holy Spirit. As Bernard Ramm wrote, "We not only believe, but we have a conviction in our hearts that we have believed the truth."[4] The Spirit develops within the believer a spiritual perceptivity which is an intuitive ability to recognize God, understand His truth and value His promises. The inner voice of the Holy Spirit, of which His witness with our spirits is one aspect, then becomes His chief means of leading Christians in their daily walk.

## *The Intercession of the Spirit—Romans 8:23–27*

The verses leading up to Romans 8:23–27 describe the present sufferings of this creation. Christians inevitably experience grief and pain, and they groan along with everyone else (Rom. 8:23). But even before the day when they will be glorified with Christ, they enjoy a number of advantages over other suffering human beings.

First, believers are joint heirs with Christ because they have already been adopted as sons and daughters into the family of God (8:15–17). So they can pray, act and speak from a position of authority in the spiritual realm. Second, they have a wonderful hope that an end will come to the groaning and suffering that now prevails in the present created universe (8:18–25). And third, although they still have reason to groan much as does the creation around them, they have "the first fruits of the Spirit" (v. 23).

Believers are now with perseverance waiting out the time until their present adoption will be revealed (v. 25). That will happen on the day they receive the redemption of their bodies (v. 23), at the second coming of Christ and not before (1 Cor. 15:22–23, 35–54; Phil. 3:20–21; 1 Thess 4:13–17). The manifestation or "revealing of the sons of God" (Rom. 8:19, that is, of all true believers) will occur at the same time that the created world is set free in the new creation from its groaning and slavery to corruption (8:20–23). We are elsewhere told that our formal recognition will come when Christ returns and is revealed in glory (Col. 3:4; 2 Thess. 1:7–10). Therefore, any doctrine which claims there is a special group of "manifested sons of God" during this present age is in error.

Although they may be suffering, believers already possess the Holy Spirit as the first fruits of that final, completed stage of their salvation. Paul's word for "first fruits" (*aparchē*) appears frequently in the Septuagint as the first part of a harvest. Thus the term was familiar to the Jews in the congregation in Rome. Here Paul seemed to be referring intentionally to the outpouring of the Spirit at Pentecost, which was the feast of the first fruits of wheat harvest (Exod. 34:22; see the comment on Acts 2:1–4).

The Holy Spirit is the sample of the future crop of glory and whets our appetites for what is yet to come. As A. Skevington Wood so beautifully put it in his treatment of Romans 8, "The Holy Spirit adds incentive to the life of holiness by introducing us to a taste of heaven on earth."[5] In writing to other predominantly Gentile churches with their interests more along commercial lines, Paul refers to the "earnest" or first installment of the Spirit (2 Cor. 1:22; 5:5; see the comment on Ephesians 1:13–14).

During this period of weakness and infirmity before we receive resurrected bodies, the Spirit is dwelling in us to help us (Rom. 8:26). The verb for "help" is a composite word (*sunanti-lambanetai*), which suggests that He as the Comforter or Paraclete shares our burdens with us by taking our place. Wuest translated it this way: "The Spirit lends us a helping hand with reference to our weakness."

Here it is particularly in the matter of prayer that He comes to our aid, "for we do not know"—even after becoming Christians—"how to pray as we should" (NAS) or "what we ought to pray" (NIV). Christ as our ascended high priest is praying for us in the sense that He makes us the object of His praying (Rom. 8:34; Heb. 7:25). The Holy Spirit, however, prays for us in the sense that He makes us the vehicle of His praying. There appears to be no suggestion in the Bible that the Holy Spirit ever prays except through the believer.

The Spirit, therefore, makes intercession for us and through us. Our very sense of helplessness and unworthiness before God is the first essential in true prayer. Only then do we let the Spirit intercede. He does so "with groanings which cannot be uttered." This translation represents the two Greek words *stenagmois alalētois*. The latter term describes the groanings or sighs as being inarticulate, not able to be expressed in understandable words.

The context of this passage includes our waiting for our deliverance from present bondage into full stature as sons and daughters (8:23 with v. 15). Our groaning within ourselves (v. 23) may well reflect the groaning of the Israelites in Egypt (Acts 7:34; compare Exod. 3:7). The Jews understood the Exodus event to be God's deliverance of His "son" Israel (Exod. 4:22) from slavery to the freedom of the Promised Land (Hos. 11:1). The groanings of Romans 8:26, as George Montague suggested, "may be the prayers of God's sons and daughters of this dispensation voiced by the Spirit and winning the assurance that God *knows* their plight... and will soon bring about the consummation of their deliverance."[6]

Furthermore, by introducing verse 26 with the Greek term *hōsautōs,* "in the same way" (that the Spirit helps our weakness), Paul implies that the Spirit is also working in every aspect of the new creation to bring cosmos out of chaos—order and harmony out of the present frustration, decay and groaning (8:20–23, NIV).

Does Paul's terminology in verse 26 refer to or include praying in tongues? The Lutheran Bible commentator R. C. H. Lenski wrote, "Later writers state that the charisma of tongues was a speaking in non-human language and either identify these 'groanings' with this non-human language or conceive of them as a parallel to it."[7]

Even more telling are the following comments written by Frederic Godet in the nineteenth century, before the modern Pentecostal movement:

> In every particular case, he who is the object of this assistance feels that no distinct words fully express to God the infinite good [for] which he sighs. The fact proves that the aspiration is not his own, but that it is produced in his heart by the Spirit of Him of whom John said, that "He is greater than our heart" (1 John 3:20). We here find ourselves in a domain analogous to that of the *glossais lalein, speaking in tongues,* to which 1 Corinthians 14 refers; compare verses 14 and 15, where Paul says: "When I pray in a tongue, my spirit (*pneuma*) prayeth indeed, but my understanding (*nous*) is unfruitful." The understanding cannot control, nor even follow the movement of the spirit, which, exalted by the Spirit of God, plunges into the depths of the divine. Thus, at the moment when the believer already feels the impulse of hope failing within him, a groan more elevated, holy, and intense than anything which can go forth even from his renewed heart is uttered within him, coming from God and going to God, like a pure breath, and relieves the poor downcast heart.[8]

It would be too much to claim that only when the child of God is consciously praying in tongues can the Holy Spirit make intercession from within. For surely the indwelling Spirit has interceded for Christians down through the centuries who have not known about this charismatic gift. But there is no doubt that praying in a tongue removes certain intellectual blocks by which the mind constricts the human spirit so that the Holy Spirit has greater freedom to pray within the believer.

To be effective, we should always pray "in the Spirit." No matter whether it is in English, in a tongue or in an unuttered secret groaning, every prayer must be inspired by God's Spirit for it to reach heaven. Such prayers can never fail to be answered, because the Holy Spirit "intercedes for the saints according to the will of God" (v. 27). We pray in the Spirit when we do not ask selfishly or wrongly, to consume it on our passions (James 4:3). The Holy Spirit enables us to align our wills with God's, so that whatever we ask, it is for His glory and not to gain our own ends (John 14:13).

## Gifts That Differ—Romans 12:3–8

Romans 12:3–8 is one of the key passages in the New Testament describing the charismatic gifts. The Greek word for "gifts" in verse 6 is *charismata*, the same as in 1 Corinthians 12:4, 9, 28, 30–31 and 1 Peter 4:10 (see comments on those passages). Paul had previously mentioned his desire to impart or share some "spiritual gift" (*charisma pneumatikon*) with the believers in Rome so that they might be established (Rom. 1:11).

While it is not within the scope of this study on the Holy Spirit to examine Romans 12:1–2 in detail, we should give heed to Paul's great exhortation here in order to minister successfully in the spiritual gifts. We must present or yield our bodies, our very selves (NEB), as a living and holy sacrifice so that the Holy Spirit may control us completely. This is our "reasonable service" (12:1, KJV), our "spiritual service of worship" (NAS). We must offer ourselves to God in complete dedication before we attempt to perform service to one another. Such a sacrifice is typified by the Old Testament whole burnt offering (Lev. 1:3–9), which was completely consumed on the altar.

Furthermore, we must continue to be transformed (the Greek verb is in the present tense) by the renewing of our minds so that we may be able to discern the will of God and approve it as being good and acceptable and perfect (12:2). According to Titus 3:5 (see the comment there), such renewing is the work of the Holy Spirit. This renewal is the necessary spiritual preparation for a balanced and continuing charismatic ministry.

Using the illustration of the human body, as he does also in 1 Corinthians 12, Paul goes on to remind us that its many members or parts do not all have the same duty or function (Greek *praxis*, "activity, action," Rom. 12:4). Likewise, in the body of Christ and in the local Christian communities, we have charismatic gifts "that differ according to the grace given to us" (v. 6). The gifts under discussion seem to be sovereignly and supernaturally imparted. Even the measure of faith, which enables each of us to receive and exercise a charismatic gift, is in itself an allotment from God (v. 3).

As Michael Griffiths, the principal of London Bible College, has reminded us, "Gifts are not so much possessed as exercised, and are supremely the operation of God's grace upon the congregation."[9] Therefore, Christians should avoid the feeling of self-importance because of the gifts they have and instead cooperate with the other members of their church in mutual humble service.

In recent years some Bible teachers have explained the *charismata* of Romans 12:6–8 as motivational gifts rather than manifestations of the Spirit, as in 1 Corinthians 12:7–11. The gifts of Romans 12 are thought to be habitual rather than individual acts of the Spirit to meet specific needs. Each of these motivational gifts is considered to be a continuing inner deposit of divine energizing which motivates the recipient of the gift to keep on performing that kind of ministry in the body of Christ.

George Selig and Alan Arroyo at Regent University, for instance, believe that everyone is born with the gifts described in Romans 12. Functional gifts, as they explain, either remain latent or are used selfishly and carelessly until the person is converted. Then the Holy Spirit can begin to empower and control the gifts at a higher level of motivation.[10]

Here is a list of seven representative gifts from God, with brief instructions as to how they should be exercised:

*Prophecy*—the ability to speak forth under divine prompting something which the Spirit has revealed to the one having this gift. It should be exercised "according to the measure of the faith" (*kata tēn analogian tēs pisteōs*, v. 6, author's translation), in agreement with the teaching of the Christian faith. The one prophesying should exercise the gift within the parameters set by sound doctrine "and not pretend that the Spirit could be truly inspiring anything that went counter to that deposit of faith."[11]

*Ministry or service*—the Greek word *diakonia*, which can refer either to the dispensing of the Word of life (Acts 6:4) or to the administering of the temporal affairs of a local congregation (Acts 6:1–3). Gifts of serving are one of the two main categories of charismatic gifts in Peter's short discussion of this subject (see the comment on 1 Peter 4:10–11). A charismatic gift is surely in operation when we can keep on ministering to the saints with love and hard work (Heb. 6:10) until we fulfill that ministry (Col. 4:17).

*Teaching*—not simply systematic instruction (2 Tim. 2:2), but a manifestation of the Holy Spirit in the ability to make plain the meaning of the Word of God which He has inspired. As the British Pentecostal leader Donald Gee wrote, "The main function of a true teacher is to impart the knowledge that is the ground for wisdom." Someone who has the gift of teaching may often manifest a word of knowledge, a flash of insight into truth that penetrates beyond the operation of his or her own unaided intellect.[12]

*Exhortation*—the ministry of speaking words of comfort and encouragement (*paraklēsis*) under the guidance and anointing of the Paraclete Himself (1 Tim. 4:13; Heb. 13:22; Phil. 2:1, "consolation," KJV). This gift usually accompanies preaching (compare Acts 13:15 with Paul's sermon that follows), teaching (1 Tim. 4:13; 6:2; Titus 1:9; 2:15) and prophesying (1 Cor. 14:3). Paul was careful to explain that his exhortation never was based on a desire to mislead and never made use of flattery (1 Thess. 2:3–5).

*Giving*—the exercise of private benevolence and sharing what we have. Giving should be done with "simplicity" (v. 8, KJV) in the sense of sincerity and singleheartedness, that is, with no self-seeking or ulterior motive. Or as the RSV and NAS render the word, giving should be done with "liberality." In 2 Corinthians 8:2 and 9:11, 13 Paul uses this term to commend the Macedonian Christians for giving generously and cheerfully.

A ministry of giving also needs wisdom and guidance from the Holy Spirit so that we do not contribute to unworthy causes or to selfish, grasping people. Here again, a sudden word of wisdom or of knowledge may be the Spirit's way of alerting the donor.

*Leadership*—a gift which implies ability to rule, manage or administer in a church. Elders and deacons must have this ability, as proven first of all in their own household (1 Tim. 3:4–5, 12). Some elders were especially able along this line and were worthy of double honor (1 Tim. 5:17). The members of their congregations were to obey them, submit to them (Heb. 13:17) and show due appreciation (1 Thess. 5:12).

This seems to be the same as the gift of governments (KJV) or administrations (NAS), which Paul lists in 1 Corinthians 12:28. Here in Romans Paul tells the leader to rule with diligence; or perhaps he means to cultivate the gift of leadership diligently. Certainly ruling elders will often need a charismatic word of wisdom in order to perform their task efficiently.

*Showing mercy*—probably the same as the gift of helps (1 Cor. 12:28).

Every Christian in the local church, whether a leader or not, may have this gift of compassion and exercise it with cheerfulness. A person's special ministry may involve visiting the poor, the sick or the sorrowing; it may be helping behind the scenes. In any case we should do this work cheerfully. A person of a grudging or despondent mood obviously does not have the charismatic endowment for showing mercy to others.

In conclusion, we should note that Paul did not include the gift of tongues in this list in Romans. Since he encouraged the Corinthians to desire rather to have the gift of prophecy (1 Cor. 14:1), and since that gift is listed here, it seems that speaking in tongues is not an essential ministry gift in a local congregation. When accompanied by the gift of interpretation of tongues, however, it may be used to edify others (1 Cor. 14:4–5).

## Aglow With the Spirit—Romans 12:11

Commentators and modern translations differ over the meaning of the three words "fervent in spirit" found in the KJV at verse 11. It may refer to the human spirit, as in the case of Apollos in Acts 18:25, where the same Greek expression occurs; or it may mean the Holy Spirit, as in the translation in the above title, which is taken from the RSV. The Greek participle *zeontes* literally means "boiling." In either case, "the spiritual temperature is to be high in the Christian community."[13] It is certainly the Holy Spirit who lights the fire within each believer, as Henry Alford, Anglican dean of Canterbury (1857–1871), pointed out long ago.[14]

This exhortation of the apostle appears in a series of short commands concerning Christian behavior (Rom. 12:9–21). These are to characterize the life of a Spirit-filled believer in his or her relation to other Christians.

Paul's first word has to do with Christ's great commandment to His followers, to love one another with God-given love (Greek *agapē*, v. 9a). I have paraphrased verses 9–12 to bring out the meaning of several important expressions:

> Let your Christian love be unhypocritical, always turning in horror from what is evil, joining yourselves to what is good. In your brotherly love to one another, be tenderly affectionate; take the lead in showing honor and respect to one another. In earnest diligence, never be lagging behind; be aglow with the Spirit, rendering service as a slave to the Lord. By the blessed hope of Jesus' return, keep joyous and cheerful, enduring steadfastly in the time of trouble and persecution, and persevering in your prayer-life—constantly devoting yourself to prayer.

## The Quintessence of the Kingdom of God—Romans 14:17

What is the kingdom of God like in its present phase, before the Lord Jesus Christ comes again to rule in person? Until His return the rule of God on earth is effective only among those who have been delivered from the dominion of darkness and transferred into the kingdom of God's well-beloved Son (Col. 1:13). God's kingdom exists today where Christians are formed into a community of redeemed people who live in subjection to the will of God. His kingdom does not consist in mere words or talk (1 Cor. 4:20, RSV) but is an actual demonstration of His Spirit moving in moral and spiritual power (1 Cor. 2:4) to change lives and conform them to the image of Christ.

Therefore, as Paul argued in Romans 14 and 15, the kingdom of God is not a matter of getting what you like to eat and drink without considering your brothers and sisters and their consciences (Rom. 14:13–17). Rather it is a matter of righteousness, peace and joy in the Holy Spirit. Paul was saying that the reign of God is seen in Christian living—in uprightness of conduct, in peace and harmony with other believers, and in joy inspired by the Holy Spirit (compare 1 Thessalonians 1:6). This is the joy which comes from the indwelling of the Spirit of God in the community of Christians as He produces unity, fellowship, gladness and sincerity of heart (compare Acts 2:42–46).

Paul was evidently combating the materialistic ideas which the Jews held concerning the expected messianic kingdom. Similarly, the Moslem conception of paradise taught in the Koran is a luxuriant garden where the faithful recline on soft brocaded couches while they dwell with dark-eyed virgins, and immortal youths serve them from silver dishes filled with wine and choice foods.

But Paul was describing a *now* kingdom, a kingdom where righteousness prevails. Jesus our Lord commands us to seek it (Matt. 6:33; Luke 12:31–32). Paul's prayer at the close of this section gives assurance of God's grace for such kingdom living: "May the God of hope bring you such joy and peace in your faith that the power of the Holy Spirit will remove all bounds to hope" (Rom. 15:13, JB).

## Not Lacking in Any Spiritual Gift—1 Corinthians 1:4–9

The apostle Paul began his first epistle to the members of the church at Corinth with a word of thanksgiving to God on their behalf. He was especially thankful that they had been enriched with all (forms of) utterance or speech and with all (gifts of) knowledge (v. 5). He continued, "Because in you the evidence for the truth of Christ has found confirmation" (v. 6, NEB). He went on: "So that you are not lacking in any spiritual gift, as you wait for the revealing of our Lord Jesus Christ" (v. 7, RSV). He wrote to them as though every one of them was spiritually gifted (see the comment on 1 Corinthians 12:13).

The word for "gift" or "spiritual gift" (RSV) in verse 7 is *charisma* and refers in this context to a special gift freely and graciously given by God to His children. Specific teaching regarding the Christian's charismatic gifts may be found in Romans 12:3–8; 1 Corinthians 12–14; and 1 Peter 4:10–11. Here the term shows what Paul meant by "all speech" and "all knowledge" in verse 5.

"All utterance" evidently referred to the various charismatic or spiritual gifts of speech, such as prophecy, tongues and interpretation of tongues, as well as teaching and preaching the gospel. "All knowledge" would cover the gifts of revelation, such as the word of wisdom, the word of knowledge and the discerning of spirits.

The Corinthian believers lacked none of these gifts (see also 2 Corinthians 8:7, where Paul said they abounded in faith and utterance and knowledge, as well as in earnestness and love). Paul expected them to keep using the *charismata* until the coming again ("the revelation," NAS, or "revealing," RSV) of our Lord Jesus Christ. This is a clear indication that he did not believe the gifts of the Spirit would cease before Christ's return.

In these opening lines of greeting and thanksgiving Paul beautifully expressed his love for the Christians at Corinth and his confidence that God would go on confirming them to the end. When we also read Luke's account of the Spirit's work at Corinth (Acts 18:1–18, 27–28) and Paul's second letter to the Corinthians, we get the impression that in spite of their divisions, worldliness and other disorders, they were a church dear to the heart of God. After the trouble in the synagogue at Corinth, the Lord had told Paul in a night vision, "I have many people in this city" (Acts 18:10).

It would be unfair to judge the Corinthians as the worst of the churches simply because the apostolic correctives for their problems were given in writing and have been preserved for us in fuller measure than for other congregations. To their everlasting credit, we may note that they did heed Paul's stern reprimands and repented (2 Cor. 7:5–16). It is necessary to say all this lest some tend to despise the church at Corinth and then to disparage the gifts it possessed—in effect, a form of guilt by association.

Clearly, the basic problem at Corinth was not so much a misuse or misunderstanding of the gifts of the Spirit as it was disunity, pride and even immorality or incest. Carnal weaknesses manifested themselves in almost every area. Because Paul did not deal with spiritual gifts until late in his letter, we may be sure that any abuse of these gifts was a result and not the cause of the Corinthians' more serious problems.

### The Spirit Reveals God's Wisdom—1 Corinthians 2:10–16

Cultured, intellectual people tend to indulge in the speculations and vain reasonings of human philosophy (Rom. 1:21; 2 Cor. 10:5; Col. 2:8). Paul resisted this temptation to pride when he came to Corinth and instead stuck to a message which seemed foolishness to the highly civilized Greeks (1 Cor. 1:18–25). He preached Christ crucified—the Christ who is both the power of God and the wisdom of God (1 Cor. 1:24, 30). Rather than using a show of oratory and persuasive words of human wisdom, he depended on the demonstration of the Spirit and the power of God to produce conviction (1 Cor. 2:4–5).

Not that Paul opposed all wisdom in itself—not at all! He opposed *pride* in wisdom, philosophy and human knowledge (Col. 2:8, 18, 23). When he was among spiritually mature believers, he spoke about a wisdom from God that once was hidden from human understanding but is now revealed. This wisdom is God's "secret purpose framed from the very beginning to bring us to our full glory" (1 Cor. 2:7, NEB). It covers things that humankind can never learn through scientific investigation—all the things that God has prepared for those who love Him (2:9).

In order for us ever to be able to know these wonderful things, it was necessary for God to *reveal* them to us through His Spirit. Thus Christianity is a *revealed* religion, not a natural religion. There are objective, absolute truths about God, made known by Him during the course of history, for the Christian to learn. The theologians call this "propositional revelation."

While God has revealed Himself in nature and in His mighty acts in history (for example, in the Exodus), His objective revelation that we may receive today is primarily and fundamentally verbal communication—the written Word of God. His greatest revelation of Himself in history, however, has been in Christ, His Son (Heb. 1:3), the living Word (Greek *logos*, John 1:1–18). In its present aspects, this revelation is chiefly personal and subjective as the Holy Spirit makes Christ known to us (John 16:13–15).

Looking again at 1 Corinthians 2:10, we find Paul explaining that just as it takes a person's own spirit to perceive his or her inner thoughts and reveal them by putting them in words, so it takes the Holy Spirit to search out and make known the "deep things of God" (KJV, NIV). This expression designates the very essence or nature of God and also His attributes, His will and His plans.[15] Therefore no human being can comprehend the thought of God and all the things that pertain to Him apart from the help of God's Spirit (vv. 10–11).

In his book on the internal witness of the Holy Spirit, Bernard Ramm made this statement: "The Spirit establishes the direct connection from the mind of God to the mind of the Christian." He reminded us that the reformer John Calvin maintained that the same Spirit who spoke through the prophets must "penetrate into our hearts" and *repeat* the message to us, convincing us of its divine origin. "The objective revelation, the testimony of God, is revealed in our hearts directly by the Holy Spirit, who is the actual effector, the actual executive of that inward illumination which finds its originating impulse in God the Father."[16] Calvin and other theologians called the Spirit's inward revelation or illumination the *testimonium* (see the comment on Romans 8:14–17).

How does the Holy Spirit impart His revelation to humanity? F. F. Bruce has paraphrased verses 12–16 for us and in so doing has cleared away most of the difficulties in understanding this important passage about the work of the Spirit:

> And the Spirit we have received is not the spirit of the world but the Spirit of God, that we may know the things which God by His grace has bestowed upon us. So, when we speak of these things, we do not use words taught us by human wisdom, but words taught us by the Spirit, giving a spiritual form to spiritual truth. The unspiritual man cannot take in the things which the Spirit of God imparts; they are folly to his way of thinking, and he is unable to apprehend them because they are assessed by the spiritual faculty. But the spiritual man is able to assess everything, while he himself is subject to no one's assessment. For "who has come to know the Lord's mind, so as to give Him instruction?" [quoted from Isaiah 40:13]. But we— we who have received the Spirit of God—possess the mind of Christ.[17]

This passage throws light both on the matter of the inspiration of the Scriptures and perhaps also on the guidance that the Holy Spirit gives in prophesying, teaching and other manifestations of a gift of utterance even today. The latter must be included unless the "we" and "us" pronouns of verses 10–16 are limited to refer only to the apostles and prophets who wrote the Old Testament and the New Testament. But this way of interpreting these verses is against Paul's argument that all Christians have received the Spirit so they can know God's wisdom.

Verse 13 is perhaps the clearest text in the Bible to show that the Spirit guided Paul and the other writers of Scripture in the choice of the very words when they were writing the Bible—what we call the doctrine of verbal inspiration. They were inspired or superintended by the Spirit at the unique level of perfection in their writing. At the same time He who is the bringer of spiritual freedom (2 Cor. 3:17) respected the personality of each writer, so that the individuality and writing style of the biblical authors shine through the process of divine inspiration (see the comment on 2 Peter 1:19–21).

But 1 Corinthians 2:13 also may describe charismatic Christians who are speaking under an anointing of the Holy Spirit. They speak, perhaps by prophecy or by a word of knowledge, to explain spiritual truths in words taught by the Spirit. Frederic Godet phrased it aptly: "The same Divine breath which lifted the veil to reveal, takes possession also of the mouth of its interpreter when it is to speak."[18]

Here we must humbly recognize that any given utterance by the Spirit's power may be less than perfect, depending on the degree of yieldedness of the one speaking. Furthermore, Paul specifically said that at present our knowledge is incomplete (only "in part"), and so is our prophesying (1 Cor. 13:9). We must state forthrightly that no genuine charismatic utterance will ever oppose or supersede the written Word of God, for the Holy Spirit is the author of both, and He will never contradict Himself. God's revelation in the Bible is final. His word to us through the spiritual gifts is only supportive or corroborative.

### God's Temple—1 Corinthians 3:16–17

Beginning with the last words of 1 Corinthians 3:9, Paul described the Corinthian believers as God's building. He was sounding a warning to the various workers engaged in its construction. He himself had laid the foundation, which is Jesus Christ (1 Cor. 3:10–11), and others had been building upon what he had started.

Their work, in the sense of their teachings, was of three types. Some employed enduring materials such as "gold, silver, precious stones"—the wisdom of the gospel that is divinely revealed truth. Others built with flammable materials such as "wood, hay, stubble" (or, sticks, grass, straw)—mere human wisdom, perhaps coupled with worldly church practices. Still others tended to destroy God's temple by causing division within the local congregation.

We would be wise to take a careful look at verses 16 and 17. The Amplified Bible is a valuable aid here:

> Do you not discern and understand that you [the whole church at Corinth] are God's temple (His sanctuary), and that God's Spirit has His permanent dwelling in you—to be at home in you [collectively as a church and also individually]? If any one does hurt to God's temple or corrupts [it with false doctrines] or destroys it, God will do hurt to him and bring him to the corruption of death and destroy him. For the temple of God is holy—sacred to Him—and that [temple] you [the believing church and its individual believers] are.

In connection with how someone might wreck a local church, R. C. H. Lenski's comment on verse 17 is suggestive:

> We shall not go far wrong when we say that, if the Corinthians themselves are God's sanctuary because of the indwelling of the Spirit, he destroys this sanctuary, be he teacher or layman, who by lies and deceptions drives the Spirit out of the hearts of the Corinthians and fills them with the spirit of the world.[19]

God's temple (Greek *naos*, the sanctuary itself, as contrasted with the *hieron*, the overall temple with its courts and gates) is a figure in this passage representing the local congregation at Corinth, but also the local manifestation of the one true "temple" of God, the church universal, composed of all true believers in Christ. The same meaning is attached to the figure of the temple in 2 Corinthians 6:16; Ephesians 2:20–22; and 1 Peter 2:5, 9.

In 1 Corinthians 6:19, however, Paul likened the body of each individual believer to "a temple of the Holy Spirit" (not "the temple," KJV). Each Christian, therefore, must keep his or her own body pure and holy, especially from the sin of sexual immorality. Fornication, more than any other sin, desecrates the very sanctuary of God because of the physical union consummated in its act. Yet Christ and the Christian have a mystical spiritual union, or as Paul describes it, "The one who joins himself to the Lord is one spirit with Him" (6:17). Therefore Christians should never join themselves to a harlot (vv. 15–18).

The church as the body of Christ and as the temple of God is unique in God's dispensations or periods of governing His creation. It is in this age alone that God dwells on earth only in the *hearts* of His believing people by His Spirit, both corporately and individually. In the past He dwelt in the tabernacle and in the temple among His people, and in the future there will again be a temple in Jerusalem when Jesus Christ returns in person to reign as king (Isa. 2:2–4; Ezek. 37:24–28; Zech. 6:12–13).

## Sanctified by the Spirit—1 Corinthians 6:11

To sanctify is to make holy. To be holy as God is holy is the goal of the Christian. Jesus and the apostles emphasized this over and over again: "Be perfect, therefore, as your heavenly Father is perfect" (Matt. 5:48, NIV). "He chose us in Him . . . that we should be holy and blameless before Him" (Eph. 1:4). "For this is the will of God, your sanctification" (1 Thess. 4:3). "That we may share His holiness" (Heb. 12:10). "Strive for peace with all men, and for the holiness without which no one will see the Lord" (Heb. 12:14, RSV).

God commands us to be holy, because He originally made humankind in His likeness, and holiness is the basic attribute or characteristic of His being. In the new creation His purpose is to conform us to the image of His Son (Rom. 8:28–29); and Jesus Christ is the holy Son of God (Luke 1:35), the sinless, spotless Lamb of God (1 Pet. 1:19).

Holiness is to be the characteristic mark of the believer. For holiness is more than goodness or innocence or freedom from sin. Holiness is something infinitely higher because it is godliness—Godlikeness and Christlikeness. As we shall see, holiness is possible only through having the Holy Spirit. It should never be considered apart from the sanctifying work of the Holy Spirit (1 Pet. 1:2). This is the greatest sin of all: trying to be good without God. This was the problem of the Pharisees.

Basically, the word *sanctify* means "to set apart, to consecrate, to reserve something or someone for sacred use." Therefore sanctification in the Bible has both a negative and a positive side (2 Cor. 6:16–18). We must be separated from sin, from the world, from our old selfish ways (the negative side); we must be set apart to God, to Christ to serve Him, to a life of holiness and moral purity (the positive side). But because we are born with a sinful nature, and sin has such a grip on us, none of us can make ourselves holy. Praise God, however, for He is performing His work of sanctification in each Christian, and He will not stop until the day we see Jesus (Phil. 1:6; 2:13).

God's work of sanctification, like the salvation of which it is one aspect, operates in three stages. It has three tenses—past, present and future: imputation of divine holiness; progressive growth in personal holiness; entire holiness in spirit, soul and body. A number of Scripture passages clearly teach that positionally the believer in Christ has already been sanctified.

For example, Paul considered that the Corinthian Christians were already saints ("holy ones"), for they had been sanctified in Christ Jesus (1 Cor. 1:2, past tense, the Greek perfect tense). Yet the rest of the epistle deals with sins and problems in their lives, showing that Paul could only mean by this a positional sanctification.

God considers Christians as already holy and free from the defilement of sin because He identifies them with His Son. In this sense, at the moment of our conversion we receive both sanctification (in its objective, external sense) and justification (in which God accounts us righteous from condemnation by the Law). We were sanctified by the blood of Jesus, the blood by which He ratified the New Covenant (Heb. 10:29). Therefore, because Jesus Christ has washed us from our sins by His blood (Rev. 1:5) and has sprinkled our hearts clean from an evil conscience (Heb. 10:22; compare 9:14), we as Christians are entitled to forget our past sins.

Similarly, Paul wrote to the believers at Thessalonica that "from the beginning God chose" you "to be saved through the sanctifying work of the Spirit and through belief in the truth" (2 Thess. 2:13, NIV). It is in this sense that Paul told the Christians at Corinth, most of whom were converted out of deep sin (1 Cor. 6:9–11a), that they had already been washed, sanctified and justified "in the name of the Lord Jesus Christ, and by the Spirit of our God" (v. 11).

Therefore, as Kenneth Prior has written, "because of Christ's death Christians may regard themselves as on the Godward side of the gulf which separates God from human sin."[20] Thus sin has lost its power to separate and condemn believers. But it has not lost its power to plague and torment them.

The Holy Spirit's work in us is far more extensive than convicting us (John 16:8–11), bringing us to a saving relationship with Jesus Christ and regenerating us (John 3:5). He is also the member of the Trinity who effects the present-tense stage of our sanctification. This is to make our eternal status in Christ an inward reality.

The Spirit is the sanctifier, while Christ is our sanctification, our holiness. In the current process of making us holy, the Spirit remains in the background, yet directs and energizes the entire work. His part is disclosed in 2 Corinthians 3:18: "And we, who with unveiled faces all reflect the Lord's glory, are being transformed into his likeness with ever-increasing glory, which comes from the Lord, who is the Spirit" (NIV). Paul meant that the Lord, specifically the Spirit in this case, is the divine agent of the work going on within us that transforms us into Christ's very likeness.

This process takes place as we keep our eyes fixed on Jesus, our glorious Lord (Heb. 12:2). We must remember that the Spirit makes much of Jesus Christ, for He was sent to glorify the Son (John 16:14). The Spirit continually imparts the resurrection life and the *agapē* love of Christ to us.

Sanctification is God's gracious work whereby our whole nature is being renewed or renovated into the image of God through Jesus Christ, and we are enabled to put to death the tendency to sin so we can instead live to righteousness. Paul described this as putting off the old man and putting on the new (Eph. 4:22, 24). The "old man" (*palaios anthropos*) is the "old self" (NIV), the corrupt human nature with which every human is born; it is the old pattern of life, the capacity we have to please self, to commit sin freely and to be enslaved to Satan. By "putting off the old man," Paul does not mean destroying it, but displacing it from its control center, putting it out of the driver's seat.

The "new man" is the "new self" (NIV), the new person (with a new way of life) that we become through the new birth, created by God "in righteousness and true holiness" (Eph. 4:24, KJV). It is the seat of the Spirit in the regenerated person, the inner sanctuary where the Spirit dwells within the believer's body as His temple. The "new man" is the capacity that the Christian has to love and serve both God and others and to practice righteousness.

But we must "put on the new man" in the sense of consciously exercising the graces of which this new nature consists (Col. 3:12–13). The "new man" is more than a mere capacity, however. It is inextricably united with Christ living His life through our whole being (Gal. 2:20). The *agapē* love evident in the "new man," for instance, is Christ loving the unlovable through our personalities and our service.

In order to grow in grace and to progress in holiness, the children of God need freedom and power. We must be liberated from sin's bondage and dominion over us in order to be free for Jesus to rule and lead us. But we must also have the power to resist further temptations, to say no to sin's enticements, to stand against the attacks of the devil.

This is where the work of the Spirit becomes so important. Paul could shout triumphantly: "The law of the Spirit of life in Christ Jesus has set you free from the law of sin and of death" (Rom. 8:2). The written law could no longer condemn him, for he was in Christ Jesus, justified, pardoned and accounted righteous (8:1). The unwritten law or principle of sin and death could no longer hold him in its vicious circle, because the new dominating principle of the Holy Spirit—the principle of that life that was his in Christ Jesus—had set him free.

Satan does his utmost to hide from believers the fact of this deliverance. But "where the Spirit of the Lord is, there is liberty" (2 Cor. 3:17). It is by the Holy Spirit as He empowers, teaches and leads us that this freedom from sin's dominion becomes our actual possession.

Our part in progressive sanctification is that of faith and obedience. We believe the truth about God's provision (2 Thess. 2:13); we have faith in Christ (Acts 26:18); and we practice obedience resulting in righteousness (Rom. 6:16). For as we present our members as slaves to righteousness, the end result is sanctification or holiness (Rom. 6:19).

It is the Spirit of God by His indwelling life who enables us to overcome our fleshly, selfish nature in our inner spiritual struggle (Gal. 5:17). Our responsibility is to "be filled with the Spirit," to "walk in the Spirit" and to "pray in the Spirit." Then our victory over self will come spontaneously, just as the ascending sap in the tree pushes off the dead leaves that cling to the branches all winter.

Yet progress in holiness is not inevitable or automatic. We can grieve the Holy Spirit by complacency, yielding to temptation and heeding the desires of the old nature. Following Christ and walking in the Spirit day by day are the only path of holiness. This means we must deny ourselves, forget ourselves, give up all right to ourselves, "leave self behind" (Matt. 16:24, NEB). As the Living Bible paraphrases Romans 8:5–6:

> Those who let themselves be controlled by their lower natures live only to please themselves, but those who follow after the Holy Spirit find themselves doing those things that please God. Following after the Holy Spirit leads to life and peace, but following after the old nature leads to death.

You as a believer are under obligation, not to the old nature to live according to its desires, but to the Holy Spirit. "For if you are living according to the flesh, you must die; but if by the Spirit you are putting to death the deeds of the body, you will live" (Rom. 8:13). Paul said categorically in Galatians 5:16, "Walk by the Spirit, and you will not carry out the desire of the flesh." You will not yield to self-indulgence, nor will any other deeds of the flesh become evident if the Spirit is in control and producing a harvest of love, joy, peace and the other fruit (see the comment on Galatians 5:22–23).

Through constant submission to the Lord as His willing bondservants, we are set free from all lesser masters and may experience a practical victory over former sinful appetites and habits, haunting fears and hateful thoughts. For the Holy Spirit is actively engaged in renewing our minds and giving us right attitudes (Titus 3:5; Rom. 12:2; Eph. 4:23). He implants the mind and attitude of Christ in us, which is the attitude of humility (Phil. 2:5–8). He is ever faithful in His task of conforming us to the image of Christ. In training us in righteousness, He makes much use of the Scriptures (2 Tim. 3:16), for we are sanctified and cleansed through heeding the truth of God's holy Word (John 17:17; 15:3).

And when will His task be completed? When will God have sanctified us wholly? Our spirits, souls and bodies will be preserved complete, without blame, *at the coming of our Lord Jesus Christ.* And God will bring it to pass, because He is faithful (1 Thess. 5:23–24).

He will make us stand in the presence of His glory blameless and with great joy (Jude 24). Then the bride of Christ will be holy and blameless, having no spot or wrinkle (Eph. 5:27). This is our ultimate sanctification—Paul called it our glorification (Rom. 8:30)—when we shall be like Christ, pure as He is (1 John 3:2–3). Then our personal spiritual state will be brought up to the level of our present standing in Christ; our actual practice will be in perfect accord with our position that we already enjoy as members of His body.

## Concerning Spiritual Gifts—1 Corinthians 12–14

Chapters 12–14 of this epistle comprise one of the units in Paul's discussion of the various problem areas in the life of the Christians at Corinth. Beginning with chapter 7, he apparently was answering questions that they had asked him, perhaps in a letter brought by the men he named in 1 Corinthians 16:17. He introduced his reply to each question by the expression, "now concerning" (Greek *peri de*) or "now" (see 1 Corinthians 7:1, 25; 8:1; 11:2; 12:1; 15:1; 16:1).

Linking chapters 12–14 with chapter 11, we have Paul's discussion of problems relating to the public worship of the church. So if we consider his instructions regarding the Lord's Supper (1 Cor. 11:17–34) to be relevant to modern church life, we cannot logically relegate the question of spiritual gifts to the first century only, as some try to do.

The following outline and brief discussion of these three key chapters will provide a helpful overview of the gifts of the Spirit in the local church before we study the text in greater depth.

*(1) The test of spiritual gifts* (12:1–3). In the worship of their pagan gods, the Greeks were sometimes carried away in a frenzy by demonic forces. These were the real powers behind the dumb idols (compare 1 Corinthians 10:19–21). The demons often seized people by their evil power, even prophesying or speaking in tongues through the priests and priestesses, as in the oracle at Delphi. So the proper test of the genuineness of a spiritual gift is the acknowledgment of Jesus as Lord by the person manifesting the gift. Only those who truly express from their hearts genuine submission to Christ are operating in the power of the Holy Spirit (see the comment on 1 John 4:1–6).

*(2) The common source of the various gifts* (12:4–11). While we note the diversities of charismatic gifts, we must recognize that they all come from the same triune God. All these gifts are the work of one and the same Spirit, who distributes to each individual Christian just as He wills (v. 11).

*(3) The analogy of the body* (12:12–26). The relation of Spirit-baptized believers to one another and to Christ as the head is illustrated by the human body with its many parts. Every member is essential to its proper functioning, so there should be no division or jealousy within the body.

*(4) The order of the gifts* (12:27–31a). We must be willing to recognize that our individual place and function in Christ's body is a matter of God's appointment. Three ministries are listed in order of importance, but there is a question whether the gifts which follow are ranked in any particular order.

In verse 31 Paul spoke of "the best gifts" (KJV), which should be translated as "the higher gifts" (RSV) or "the greater gifts" (NAS, NIV). Nearly all English translations and Bible commentators follow the KJV, which interprets the verb *zeloute* in verse 31a as an exhortation or command: "But covet earnestly the best gifts." This may be incorrect, however, because the Greek imperative verb form can also be translated as an indicative: "But you are striving after—zealous for—the greater gifts" (compare NIV margin).

Paul's whole argument in this chapter was that God decides which gift to give to each member of a church and that no member should think of himself or herself as greater or more important than the others. But some of the Corinthians seem to have wanted to be an apostle or a prophet or a teacher. They were also apparently seeking the gifts of a more miraculous nature: the working of miracles, gifts of healings, speaking with tongues and interpretation (vv. 29–30).

Arnold Bittlinger of Germany has pointed out that apparently they were not interested in the less dramatic gifts of helps and governments listed in verse 28, [21] which are not mentioned again in verses 29 and 30. As Michael Harper explained it:

> Paul is not encouraging the Corinthians to grade the gifts, but rather he is rebuking them for doing so, and so neglecting "the more excellent way" of manifesting them. Clearly the gift of tongues was high on the list in the estimation of the Corinthians, and Paul wants to put it in its proper place, and urges them to desire all the gifts, especially the ones which edify others. [22]

*(5) The incomparable way of love in conjunction with using the gifts* (12:31b–13:7). Paul next described that most excellent way of life (Greek *hodos*) in which the spiritual gifts could function properly and fulfill their purpose of edifying others in the church. He was showing that love is the only true course of conduct, the only correct route to follow (compare 14:1, "Follow the way of love," NIV) in using spiritual gifts. Love is the perfect way for all of life, including the ministry of our gifts. This led him to the most beautiful portrayal of love in all of literature (13:1–7).

*(6) The duration of spiritual gifts* (13:8–13). Christians have differed widely in their beliefs about whether or not the spiritual gifts and ministries of 12:28–30 and 13:8–9 continued after the apostolic age and down to the present. Obviously, the office of apostleship has been withdrawn in the primary sense. There is no warrant given in Scripture for an apostolic succession beginning with the original twelve apostles of Jesus. In the secondary sense of "apostle" found in the New Testament (Eph. 4:11), however, many missionaries and others have founded churches or done other pioneering work, manifesting extraordinary gifts and blessing from God.

Again, the gift of prophecy in its specialized sense of speaking forth and writing down the inspired, infallible Word of God has been sovereignly withdrawn. But believers may still bring forth insights revealed to them by God when they are under an anointing of the Spirit. [23]

Here Paul taught that whereas love will never fail, charismatic manifestations will stop "when the perfect comes" (v. 10). Prophecies, tongues and (utterances of) knowledge (compare 12:8, 10; 13:1–2) will come to an end, not because they are "imperfect" (RSV) but because they reveal only "in part" (*ek merous*) now. The complete understanding, the totality of knowledge, will be given us in the future age.

Some have taught that by *to teleion*, "the perfect," Paul meant the completed canon of holy Scripture. Paul's statement in verse 12, however, which says that then we shall see face to face and know fully even as now we are fully known, indicates that he was looking forward to the perfect state of things at the final consummation when God would be "all in all" (1 Cor. 15:24–28).[24] A study of church history reveals that many of the charismatic gifts continued to be manifested long after the New Testament was written and the apostles were all dead.[25]

*(7) The relative value of the gifts of tongues and of prophecy* (14:1–25). The apostle pointed out the several purposes of speaking in an unknown tongue and its limitations in a meeting of the congregation. Prophesying is preferable, because the one who prophesies edifies the church (see the separate comment on 1 Corinthians 14).

*(8) The proper ministration of spiritual gifts* (14:26–35). Paul issued careful instructions regarding the orderly exercise of the gifts of utterance in church meetings in order to promote edification and to prevent confusion. Women were not to interrupt meetings by being among those who weigh or pass judgment on prophetic messages. Instead they were to keep silent at the time and address their questions to their own husbands at home.

*(9) Final instructions on church order* (14:36–40). The apostle indignantly asked the Corinthians whether they supposed that they, in contradistinction to all other churches, had the right to maintain such irregularities as women wearing unsuitable hairstyles in defiance of their position, gluttony and drunkenness at the Lord's Supper, speaking in tongues without interpretation, prophets refusing to give place to one another, and women speaking out to ask questions. Paul then insisted that what he was writing was by divine command (v. 37).

In verse 39 Paul summarized chapter 14: "Desire earnestly to prophesy, and do not forbid to speak in tongues." Verse 40 then acts as an overall conclusion to chapters 11–14: "But all things should be done with regard to decency *and* propriety *and* in an orderly fashion" (AMP).

## Spiritual Gifts Described—1 Corinthians 12:4–11

### Definitions

A spiritual gift is a supernatural capacity or power bestowed on a Christian by the Holy Spirit to enable that person to exercise his or her function as a member of the body of Christ. These gifts are not to be thought of as natural abilities nor as permanent possessions but are supernatural (and often sudden) manifestations of the Spirit Himself (v. 7, 11). A gift is not given primarily to benefit the one through whom it is manifested but is "for the common good" (v. 7), for the profit of the whole congregation in a local church.

Spiritual gifts are not to be confused with spiritual graces or fruit of the Spirit—aspects of Christ's character that every Christian is to cultivate (Gal. 5:22–23). Nor are the gifts identical with spiritual offices in the churches. Persons filling such positions may practice spiritual or temporal oversight of the local church affairs (elders, deacons, 1 Timothy 3:1–13), or they may minister both within and beyond the confines of the local assembly (apostles, prophets, evangelists, pastor-teachers, Ephesians 4:11). God appoints only certain believers to these spiritual offices (1 Cor. 12:28–29) in line with specific spiritual gifts already manifested in their lives. These persons are Christ's gifts (*domata*) to His church (Eph. 4:8).

In 1 Corinthians 12–14 three Greek words are translated as "gifts" or "spiritual gifts." The first is *pneumatika* (12:1; 14:1; see also Romans 1:11, *ti charisma pneumatikon*, "some spiritual gift"). Literally it simply means "spirituals," a term that always bears the connotation "supernatural" in the epistles of Paul, according to a careful study made by Howard Ervin.[26] So we can be certain that the spiritual gifts are supernatural powers or manifestations of the Holy Spirit, not natural abilities. The *pneumatika* are "gifts which exceed the natural and may, therefore, be freely bestowed on members of a church irrespective of natural talents."[27]

A second word translated "spiritual gifts" is *pneumata* (1 Cor. 14:12), literally "spirits." This term also draws attention to the fact that the gifts are manifestations of the Spirit. Therefore, both of these terms emphasize that their source is the Spirit (*pneuma*).

The most frequently used term in these chapters and in the New Testament for the gifts of the Spirit is *charismata,* usually translated as "charismatic gifts" (the word has also been taken directly into English as "charismata"). Since our English adjective "charismatic" (as it appears in such expressions as the "modern Charismatic Renewal") stems from this word, we should examine it closely.

The Greek noun *charisma*, sometimes translated as "charism" or "charisma" in English, occurs seventeen times in the New Testament. It is related to the noun *charis*, "grace," and the verb *charizomai*, "to give freely" (for example, Romans 8:32; 1 Corinthians 2:12). In general, *charisma* refers to any gift of divine grace, whether of salvation and eternal life (Rom. 5:15–16; 6:23) or of the covenant privileges of the Israelites (Rom. 11:29; compare 9:4–5); or to a special "grace" given to an individual, such as the gift of continency enabling a person to remain unmarried in order to perform a specific work for God (1 Cor. 7:7); or to a miraculous deliverance from great peril ("blessing," RSV, "gracious favor," NIV, in 2 Corinthians 1:11).

The current religious usage of our English adjective *charismatic* is derived, however, from the technical sense of *charisma*, especially as it is found in 1 Peter 4:10 and, in the plural, in Romans 12:6 and five times in 1 Corinthians 12 (in vv. 4, 9, 28, 30–31). The charismata are "grace gifts," special gifts of a nonmaterial sort, freely conferred by the grace of God on individual Christians.

This word emphasizes that the spiritual manifestations are gifts and not rewards or wages. As Michael Harper said, "They are not prizes or badges given for special merit. They are freely bestowed upon the people of God according to the sovereign will of the Holy Spirit."[28]

Charismatic gifts enable individual believers, when needs arise, to minister to other members of the body of Christ, as well as to people who are not saved, in ways beyond mere human capability and ingenuity. It is a manifestation of God's presence when an ordinary human can suddenly have illumination of unknown facts and wisdom about how to meet a difficult problem; discern what an evil spirit is; believe for a miracle; administer healing to a person with an incurable disease; or speak forth a message from the Lord in the individual's own language or in one he or she has never learned, or interpret an utterance given in an unknown language.

The Lord permits every congregation to experience needs from time to time that will require the exercise of the various charismatic gifts. These will be operative wherever the exalted Christ is present in power and freedom. Sometimes they are not recognized; many times they are not wanted or are even blocked. Lack of unity and lack of faith can inhibit the gifts that God has provided for His church. False doctrine, indifference, and racial and denominational pride or divisions may often be holding back the manifestation of charismatic gifts.

The *charismata* were not isolated phenomena occurring only in the Corinthian church. Paul instructed the Roman believers to make full use of their charismatic gifts (see the comments on Romans 12:3–8) and urged Timothy not to neglect his *charisma* (see the comment on 1 Timothy 4:14) but to stir it up (see the comment on 2 Timothy 1:6–7). Peter likewise exhorted each reader to manifest his or her charismatic gift for the benefit of someone else, as a good steward of God's manifold grace (see the comment on 1 Peter 4:10–11). The entire early church knew the power of the Spirit of God (for example, Galatians 3:5; Titus 3:6; Hebrews 2:4). This same Spirit is restoring His gifts to the church today wherever members of Christ's body are willing to receive them.

In addition to the three terms translated "gifts" or "spiritual gifts," the apostle Paul used three other Greek words to reveal various facets of their nature. First, in 1 Corinthians 12:5 we read that there are varieties of "ministries" (Greek *diakoniōn*). Translated "administrations" in the KJV, this term means "services" (as in RSV, NIV) in the sense of opportunities to serve or to minister to others. Paul is saying there are different kinds of ministries in which the gifts become real in practice.

Second, we read in verse 6 (KJV) that "there are diversities of operations." Here the Greek word *energēmatōn*, "energies" or "effects," signifies the activities or results produced by God's imparted spiritual energy. It is the same word translated "effecting" (NAS) or "working" (KJV, RSV) in verse 10 in the phrase "effecting/working of miracles."

In this sense the gifts are not regular, permanent abilities. Instead they are momentary powers to effect a miracle, to bring healing, to know something in a flash. And it is the same God who energizes or activates all these gifts, both in those who act as agents and in those on whom the effect is produced.

The third descriptive word revealing the nature of the spiritual gifts is *phanerōsis*, "manifestation," in verse 7. When a gift is displayed, it is a manifestation of the Holy Spirit. It is a visible act that can be seen or heard or felt, not an invisible grace like the fruit of the Spirit. In each believer, then, the Holy Spirit can be expected to manifest Himself. It is not to be only for that person's own spiritual advantage but "to profit withal" (KJV) for the common good, for the benefit of others.

### The Purpose of the Gifts

God evidently has several reasons for the continuing manifestation of the gifts of the Spirit from the first century until now. First, the gifts manifest the power of God in the body of Christ on earth. People in every generation must be confronted with the reality of the invisible God. When the secrets of a person's heart are disclosed through a prophecy or word of knowledge, that person is bound to declare "that God is certainly among you" (1 Cor. 14:25). God's purpose is to confound all mere worldly wisdom (1 Cor. 1:27; 2:6–10). That is why Paul was led to repudiate his training in Judaism and his natural advantages (1 Cor. 2:1–5; Phil. 3:3–8) and to tell only what Christ had accomplished through him in the power of signs and wonders (Rom. 15:18–19).

Second, the gifts aid in carrying out the great commission. Before His ascension the Lord Jesus promised that supernatural signs would give confirmation to the gospel wherever His believers would go to preach it (see the comment on Mark 16:9–20). The apostles combated heathenism, not by convincing oratory and superior education, but by gifts of healings and miracles (Acts 14:8–18; 16:16–18; 19:11–20; 28:1–10).

Third, the gifts edify and perfect the church. The members of the local church are edified, exhorted and consoled by gifts of inspired utterance such as prophecy (1 Cor. 14:3, 12, 26; Acts 9:31). Each individual also may edify himself or herself through speaking in tongues privately (1 Cor. 14:4).

Fourth, the gifts effect the deliverance of God's people. God's purpose in this messianic age is beautifully summed up in the prophecy of Zacharias, the father of John the Baptist: "To grant us that we, being delivered from the hand of our enemies, might serve Him without fear, in holiness and righteousness before Him all our days" (Luke 1:74–75). Jesus was sent and anointed with the Spirit of the Lord in order to "preach the gospel to the poor" and to proclaim deliverance (or release) to the captives (Luke 4:18). He baptizes us in the same Holy Spirit in order to carry on His work.

It is thus our responsibility to rescue the lost as well as our brothers and sisters in Christ from the grip of Satan and his demons (Acts 26:18). Such was the ministry of Philip at Samaria, where many who had unclean spirits were set free (Acts 8:5–7). By a word of knowledge or the gift of the discerning of spirits we may detect the subtle devices of the unseen foe and expose the "angels of light" (2 Cor. 2:11; 11:13–14), as Peter did regarding Ananias and Sapphira in Acts 5:1–11.

In all these ways, God's purpose in bestowing charismatic gifts is that through their operation Christians might be the functioning body of Christ on earth.

### Classification and Description of the Gifts

Paul himself may have listed the gifts in verses 8–10 in three uneven groups, by starting the third and eighth items (faith and tongues) with a different Greek word for "to another" (*heterō*). In his outstanding commentary Gordon Fee has suggested this classification: the first two, wisdom and knowledge, were especially admired in Corinth (1 Cor. 1:17–2:16; 8:1–11); the next five were a random listing of obviously supernatural manifestations; and the list closed with the "problem child" and its companion, tongues and interpretation.[29] The significance of *heterō* is not certain, however, and Christians have grouped the gifts in numerous ways.

One traditional Pentecostal view adopted by many suggests a threefold classification. First are the *discerning gifts*—gifts of revelation (the power to know). These include a word of wisdom, a word of knowledge and the discerning of spirits.

Second are the *dynamic gifts*—gifts of power (the power to do). These are the gift of faith, gifts of healings and the working of miracles.

Third are the *declarative gifts*—gifts of inspired utterance (the power to speak). These include prophecy, tongues and the interpretation of tongues.

The discerning gifts are given to Christians to enable them to know what to say or do in specific situations. Jesus manifested a word of wisdom when, to the Pharisees who were intent on trapping Him with their question about paying a tax to Caesar, He gave His famous reply: "Render to Caesar the things that are Caesar's; and to God the things that are God's" (Matt. 22:21). He promised us similar wisdom in times of emergency, "For the Holy Spirit will teach you in that very hour what you ought to say" (Luke 12:12; see the comment on Matthew 10:16–20).

Acts 6:1–7 is an outstanding example of the need of a word of wisdom to settle particular problems that arise in governing a church congregation. The answer of the twelve apostles manifested wisdom of the highest degree—deep spiritual principles coupled with sound common sense. The Spirit's blessing was evident in that their statement found approval with the entire congregation and enabled the Word of God to keep on spreading so that many more became obedient to the faith.

James, acting as moderator of the first church council at Jerusalem, manifested a word of wisdom (Acts 15:13–21) in interpreting an Old Testament prophetic passage (Amos 9:11–12) to show God's plan to save Gentiles. James's word was accepted by all, and it settled the controversy regarding legalism.

The possibility of receiving a word of wisdom, however, should never cause us to stop seeking wisdom for life in general (James 1:5). We cannot depend on this charismatic gift for every situation because it is only a *word* of wisdom. As Donald Gee wrote, it is "a spoken utterance through a direct operation of the Holy Spirit at a given moment, rather than an abiding deposit of supernatural wisdom."[30]

Dennis Bennett provided this definition of a word of knowledge:

> A supernatural revelation of facts past, present, or future which were not learned through the efforts of the natural mind. It may be described as the Mind of Christ being manifested to the mind of the believer, and is given when needed in a flash of time (1 Cor. 2:16). This gift is used to protect the Christian, to show how to pray more effectively, or to show him how to help others.[31]

A word of wisdom often is given in conjunction with the word of knowledge in order to show how to apply the information God has revealed. For example, in Old Testament times Nathan the prophet received a word of knowledge regarding David's affair with Bathsheba, as well as wisdom to know how to bring the king to repentance (2 Sam. 12:1–14). The prophet Elisha knew in his heart about Gehazi's greedy act and therefore was able to expose his hypocrisy (2 Kings 5:20–27). Our Lord Jesus knew the evil thoughts of the scribes (Matt. 9:2–6) and the marital history of the Samaritan woman (John 4:17–19).

A word of knowledge enabled Peter to rebuke Ananias and Sapphira for their lying wickedness (Acts 5:1–9). And Paul commended the Roman Christians that, because they were "filled with all knowledge," they were competent to admonish (*nouthetein*, instruct, counsel) one another (Rom. 15:14).

The word of knowledge is also a teaching gift in the church, as Paul suggested in his list of manifestations that edify a congregation (1 Cor. 14:6). Donald Gee has stressed this point in his books.[32] By comparing the list of gifts in verses 8–10 with the lists of offices and gifts in 1 Corinthians 12:28 and Romans 12:6–8, we soon realize that the commensurate spiritual gift for the office of apostle is the word of wisdom and that the gift corresponding to the office of teacher is the word of knowledge.

In this sense a word of knowledge may be manifested when the teacher receives a new insight into the knowledge of God or of the Christian faith and at the same time is given new ability to express it and explain it to others. This aspect of the word of knowledge seems to be what Paul had in mind when he talked in 1 Corinthians 13:2 of knowing or coming to understand all mysteries and all knowledge (compare 1 Corinthians 2:10–11).

In Ephesians 1:17 Paul prayed that God would give each Christian a spirit able to receive wisdom and revelation in the sphere of a fuller knowledge of Himself. By a word of knowledge, teachers may be quickened upon occasion to impress on their hearers the knowledge of the hope of God's calling, of the glorious riches of God's inheritance in the saints and of the surpassing greatness of God's power toward the believer (vv. 18–19).

The third gift which operates by a direct revelation from God is the "distinguishing of spirits" (v. 10, NAS margin). It goes without saying that this is not a critical spirit in the natural or even the true intellectual discernment of the child of God that is developed through Christian fellowship and through study of the Bible. Of course, it is essential for us to partake of the word of righteousness and to train our senses or faculties to discern good and evil— that is, to make moral decisions (Heb. 5:13–14). But the spiritual gift of discernment does not come through training. Instead it is imparted in the moment when it is needed. As the Living Bible paraphrases: "He gives someone else the power to know whether evil spirits are speaking through those who claim to be giving God's messages—or whether it is really the Spirit of God who is speaking."

The Greek word for "discernment," *diakrisis*, literally means a "judging through," a seeing right through to the inner reality with a judgment based on that insight. Dennis Bennett has suggested that by this gift the believer is enabled to know immediately what is motivating a person or situation.[33]

Those responsible for the orderly progress of a meeting of believers need to know whether a person is operating under the inspiration of the Holy Spirit, whether the person is expressing his or her own thoughts or feelings, or whether the person is controlled by a wrong spirit. The Holy Spirit will manifest Himself by this gift through those who pass judgment on the messages of the prophets in the assembly (1 Cor. 14:29). Usually the discerning of a false or evil spirit brings a sense of heaviness, unrest or even sickness;

whereas, the sense of the presence of the Holy Spirit is one of joy, peace and love. This gift is the gracious provision of Christ, the head of the church, to arm it against the subtle deceptions of the enemy.

A striking example of the gift of discerning of spirits in operation is found in Acts 16:16–18. A slave girl having a spirit of divination met Paul and his party in Philippi, evidently desiring to follow them to the place of prayer. Even though her shouts to the crowds about Paul seemed lofty and spiritual, yet Paul detected the true nature of the motivating spirit and at last commanded it to come out of her. Probably he waited until the day she was ready to be saved so that when he exorcized the demon it would have no right to reenter her.

The three dynamic gifts provide extraordinary powers to effect changes in the lives and circumstances of both saints and sinners. The gift of faith is not saving faith, which people exercise when on the basis of God's Word they trust in Christ to redeem them. Nor is it the "faith" of Galatians 5:22, one of the fruits of the Spirit, which develops in the believer as faithfulness or fidelity.

Instead, the gift of faith, according to Dennis Bennett, is "a sudden surge of faith, usually in a crisis, to confidently believe without a doubt, that as we act or speak in Jesus' name it shall come to pass."[34] This is the wonder-working faith that Jesus said can move mountains (Mark 11:22–24; compare 1 Corinthians 13:2). As R. C. H. Lenski explained, by means of this *charisma*, things that are otherwise impossible are actually accomplished in the course of our service to the Lord.[35]

This gift frequently operated through Elijah and Elisha in the Old Testament. Think of Elijah's faith when he prepared for the fire to fall from heaven and when he announced that rain would come (1 Kings 18:22–38, 41–45)! Daniel had the gift of faith when he "shut the mouths of lions" (Heb. 11:33; Dan. 6:22). George Mueller's orphanages at Bristol, England, for two thousand children and Hudson Taylor's gathering of one hundred missionaries to evangelize the interior of China are modern-day examples of the gift of dynamic faith in action.

The next two gifts appear in the Greek as plurals: literally "charismatic gifts of healings" and "workings of powers." The plurals indicate that all healings and all miracles are in each separate case a supernatural operation of the Spirit. As Arnold Bittlinger, a German theologian of evangelical Lutheran persuasion, has said: "Every healing is a special gift. In this way the spiritually gifted individual stands always in new dependence upon the divine Giver."[36]

Lenski observed: "In each instance a specific intimation came to them [the disciples] from the Spirit that the act should be performed; and not until that moment did it occur, but then it always took place without fail."[37] Peter and John, for instance, had passed the lame beggar at the Gate Beautiful many a time, but not until a certain day did the Spirit prompt them to extend healing to him (Acts 3:1–8). This principle explains why a Spirit-filled Christian cannot go into a hospital and administer healing to every sick person he or she sees.

The plural nouns also indicate the different kinds of diseases and afflictions, requiring different sorts of healing. The implication may be that a certain person is especially used in bringing healing to those suffering from a certain disease or a group of diseases.

Dennis Bennett made an important clarification regarding the matter of healing as a spiritual gift. He said:

> A Christian does not have to have the baptism with the Holy Spirit in order to pray for the sick, nor is the fact that a person has prayed effectively for the sick a sign that he or she has received the baptism with the Holy Spirit. Jesus said: "These signs shall follow them that believe . . . they shall lay hands on the sick, and they shall recover" (Mark 16:17–18, KJV). Any believer can pray for the sick and see them healed by the power of Jesus. Generally speaking, however, it is after the baptism in the Holy Spirit that increased faith for healing comes, and the Christian begins to minister to the sick. Like the other gifts, healing seems to be released with a far greater intensity and reality after the receiving of the Holy Spirit.[38]

(For the prayer of faith and anointing the sick with oil, see the comment on James 5:13–20.)

The "working of miracles" covers those wonderful works that are not strictly healings. Included under the category of miracles would be the exorcizing of demons and the restoring of persons from death, such as Dorcas and Eutychus (Acts 9:36–41; 20:6–12). Quite a number of authenticated cases of the raising of the dead have taken place recently in Africa and Indonesia, as well as in America. The creation of new bodily parts or organs might better be explained as an instance of this gift in operation instead of one of the gifts of healings. In bestowing this gift of miracles, the Spirit of Jesus enables His followers to do His works and even greater works (see the comment on John 14:12–14).

The third group of spiritual gifts is those through which God may declare Himself when the Holy Spirit prompts Christians to speak forth publicly. Here in chapter 12, the apostle is listing gifts that are used within a church meeting to minister blessing to one another. Therefore in this list and in 1 Corinthians 12:28–30 the gift of speaking in various kinds of tongues is to be considered from the standpoint, not of its private devotional value, but of its function to edify the other members of the congregation when followed by the twin gift of interpretation of tongues.

The gift of prophecy or prophesying is not the same as a God-given ability to preach and teach the gospel effectively. The New Testament has a number of distinctive words that refer specifically to preaching and proclaiming the known word of God, as differentiated from speaking forth a new revelation from the Lord. The most important are *kerysso*, to proclaim or announce a message as a herald does (used sixty-one times); *euangelizo*, to tell good news, to evangelize (over fifty times, and the noun *euangelion*, gospel, over seventy times); *katangello*, to tell thoroughly or proclaim clearly (fifteen times); *laleo ton logon*, to speak the word (six times); *martureo*, to bear witness, to testify (over sixty times); and *didasko*, to teach (about ninety times).

Preaching, then, is telling and explaining what we already know, what we have learned. Christian prophesying in the churches, however, is bringing fresh insights revealed by the Lord under the prompting of the Holy Spirit and not originating in our own thoughts. The gift of prophecy is one to be greatly desired (1 Cor. 14:1, 39; see the comment on 1 Corinthians 14 for further discussion of the gifts of prophecy and tongues).

### Reception of the Gifts

Every Christian must recognize that spiritual gifts are sovereignly manifested. The Spirit divides or distributes them to each person individually as *He* wills (12:11b). As the word *charisma* indicates, such a manifestation of the Spirit is freely given and cannot be earned or purchased (as Peter so bluntly told Simon the sorcerer, Acts 8:18–23). God's plan is to equip us with all we need (Heb. 13:20–21, TLB) in order to enable us to perform the specific ministry to which God has called us and for which He has placed us in the church.

On this matter it is worthwhile to listen to the advice of Gordon Lindsay, who was one of America's foremost full-gospel Bible teachers:

> In these days, too often we see men trying to copy the ministry of another. The attempt to wear Saul's armor can never make for a satisfying ministry. We believe

that every young minister who feels the call of God should first of all, by waiting on God in prayer and fasting, and with heart open, seek to learn what ministry God has set him in the Church to accomplish. *The great question then is not how we shall use God, but how can God use us* (italics his).[39]

On the human side the ministration of the gifts is primarily dependent on our faith. Paul instructed the Roman believers that they were to exercise their various gifts according to the measure of the faith God had given each of them (Rom. 12:3–6a; see the comment on Romans 12:3–8). As members of Christ's body, we have a right—even an obligation—to desire earnestly to receive and manifest the gifts of the Spirit (1 Cor. 14:1, 13, 39).

We should long to be spiritual heirs of the early Christians, just as intensely as Elisha wanted to be Elijah's successor (2 Kings 2:9–15). Such earnest desire is evidence of an active faith. In some instances, as in the case of Timothy, the individual's faith to receive a spiritual gift was strengthened through the laying on of hands (see the comments on 1 Timothy 4:14; Acts 6:6).

We must consider other important factors as well if the gifts are to operate smoothly and for the glory of God. First, we should receive the gift of God's Spirit and keep filled with Him (see the comment on Ephesians 5:15–21). The baptism in the Holy Spirit is vital to a normal operation of the gifts. Even Jesus Christ, the Son of God, did not perform His mighty works until He was baptized with the Spirit.

Since pride is the greatest peril for those who have been the channel for gifts of the Spirit to flow out to others, we must continually humble ourselves at the feet of our Lord. God has chosen the weak things of the world to shame the things that are strong, so that no one should boast in the sight of God (1 Cor. 1:26–29). Moses was a very humble man (Num. 12:3), and he wrought many miracles; but when he lost his temper and intimated that he and Aaron were the ones whose power could bring forth water out of the rock, he lost the full blessing of God (Num. 20:10–12).

The example of the apostles and other early Christians was one of total dedication of themselves to the Lord. Barnabas was said to have been a good man and full of the Holy Spirit and of faith (Acts 11:24). Elsewhere we read of how he gladly shared his possessions with the rest of the church in Jerusalem (Acts 4:36–37). The prophets and teachers at Antioch, including Barnabas and Paul, were obedient to the voice of the Holy Spirit when He spoke to them (Acts 13:1–4). Thus it is not surprising to read that later on in a moment of crisis

Paul was filled with the Spirit, so that he discerned the spirit in Elymas and wrought a miracle of judgment to blind the wicked sorcerer (Acts 13:8–12).

Christians in that first century were uncompromising and willing to pay the price, as Stephen was, even of a martyr's death (Acts 7:55–60). Therefore the Spirit gave them a holy, supernatural boldness and confidence to proclaim the Word of God (Acts 4:8, 29–31). Their consecration, while not a sinless perfection, displayed balanced holiness that gave evidence of Christ in them along with His gifts operating through them.

## Baptized in One Spirit—1 Corinthians 12:13

Verse 13 of chapter 12 is the key verse in rightly understanding the doctrine of the baptism in the Spirit. Yet English-speaking Christians have misunderstood it for centuries because of the faulty translation in the KJV and all those modern versions that have followed in its tradition. The problem lies primarily in the incorrect rendering of the prepositions, especially the first one, which is "by" in the KJV ("For by one Spirit ...").

Before looking further into the context and meaning of verse 13, we might look at an original literal translation: "For in *one* Spirit also we were all baptized with reference to (the) *one* body, whether Jews or Greeks, whether slaves or freemen—yes, we were all given the *one* Spirit to drink" (author's translation and italics).

By taking verse 13 out of its context, many Bible expositors have taught that it is descriptive of our conversion experience, telling how the Holy Spirit incorporates us into Christ's body through the sacrament of water baptism and the new birth. In chapter 12, however, the apostle was not giving instruction about salvation and how to enter the New Covenant. He was discussing the functioning of supernatural gifts in the church. So he had no need to make a statement about how to receive Christ or how someone is to get into the body.

Instead, Paul was emphasizing the unity of the Spirit, the giver of the various spiritual gifts. In verse 13 he was explaining the *relation*—that is, the unity or common bond—which pertains to the one-and-the-same Spirit for all who are already believers. Paul's statement suggests the continuing seal of the New Covenant that is for all members of Christ's body in order to identify them as truly belonging to Christ (see the comment on Ephesians 1:13–14). The baptism in the Spirit is the great unifying factor in a body of such diverse members. In the entire chapter Paul was talking about the oneness in diversity of the church.

In this passage (12:13) we find the last of the seven verses in the New Testament that specifically mention baptism in the Spirit. Four of the verses record the prophecy of John the Baptist—Matthew 3:11 (see the comment on Matthew 3:11–17); Mark 1:8; Luke 3:16; and John 1:33 (see the comment on John 1:29–34). The other two passages are Acts 1:5 (see the comment on Acts 1:4–8) and 11:16. That Paul was referring here to the Pentecostal baptism in the Spirit, and not to some other type of baptism by the Spirit, is evident; for he alluded by his words, "whether we be Jews or Gentiles, whether we be bond or free" (KJV), to the term "all flesh" (or "all mankind") with its various categories, including bondslaves, in Joel's prophecy. Joel foretold the baptism in the Holy Spirit, the universal outpouring of God's Spirit, which began at Pentecost (see the comment on Acts 2:14–21).

Even some of those who oppose the doctrine of a baptism in the Spirit subsequent to conversion may be of help to us in correctly interpreting certain aspects of verse 13. Such a one is the Anglican rector John R. W. Stott of London, who has presented a clear but simple exegesis of the verse. He wrote:

> The Greek expression is precisely the same in all its seven occurrences, and therefore a priori, as a sound principle of interpretation, it should refer to the same baptism experience in each verse. The burden of proof rests with those who deny it. The natural interpretation is that Paul is echoing the words of John the Baptist as first Jesus and then Peter had done (Acts 1:5; 11:16). It is unwarrantable to make Jesus Christ the Baptizer in six instances, and the Holy Spirit the Baptizer in the seventh.... If it is because the words en heni pneumati ("by one Spirit," RSV) come at the beginning of the sentence, the reason for this is surely that Paul is stressing the oneness of the Spirit in whom we share, not that the Spirit is the baptizer.[40]

Stott went on to explain that four things can be said about every kind of baptism: its subject (the baptizer); its object (the baptized); the element with or in (Greek en) which the baptism takes place; and the purpose for or with reference to (Greek eis) which the baptism takes place. (See the chart on page 308 explaining the occurrences in the New Testament of the Greek verb baptizō in connection with the prepositions en and eis.)

When the preposition eis appears with the verb baptizō in the New Testament, it normally defines the relationship to which baptism introduces the person.[41] Therefore, in these verses it should be translated "in relation to" or "with reference to" rather than "into."

For instance, in 1 Corinthians 10:2 we read that all the Israelites "were baptized into (*eis*) Moses in (*en*) the cloud and in (*en*) the sea." Paul was referring to a relationship to and identification with Moses as their deliverer from Egypt and as their mediator of the Sinaitic covenant. But their connection to Moses *had begun* when they obeyed the Passover instructions by faith and shed the blood of the lamb (Exod. 12:6–13, 21–28) and then left their homes to follow him out of Egypt. Their shared experiences both of going through the Red Sea ("in the sea") and of continually being sheltered and led by the pillar of cloud ("in the cloud"; see chapter one) only sealed this already existing relationship to Moses.

Similarly, we are saved through faith in the atoning benefits of Christ's death; and baptism in water is the subsequent visible sacramental sealing of our relationship to Jesus that actually began when we first trusted Him.[42] But we also continue to be identified as Christ's followers and members of His body by the presence of His Spirit upon us, the result of our having been baptized in the Spirit.

No baptizer is mentioned in Acts 1:5 and 11:16 or in 1 Corinthians 12:13 because the verb *baptizō* is passive. So the emphasis lies on either the people who receive the baptism or on the one Spirit with whom they are baptized. It is clear that, although Jesus Christ is not named in verse 13, He must be regarded as the baptizer. Stott asks:

> If [in v. 13] the Holy Spirit were Himself the Baptizer, what would be the "element" in which He baptizes? That there is no answer to this question is enough to overthrow this interpretation, since the baptism metaphor absolutely requires an "element," or the baptism is no baptism. Therefore, the "element" in the baptism of 1 Corinthians 12:13 must be the Holy Spirit, and (consistently with the other verses) we must supply Jesus Christ as the Baptizer. Similarly, at the end of the verse, it is the Holy Spirit of whom we drink, and consistently (with John 7:37ff.) it must be Christ by whom we are "made to drink" of Him. . . . The being baptized and the drinking are clearly equivalent expressions.[43]

In verse 13 two aspects of the gift of the Holy Spirit are indicated in the two verbs "baptized" and "made to drink." The sovereign, divine act of giving is depicted in Christ's having baptized us in the one Spirit; whereas, the human act of receiving the gift by faith is intimated in the picture of our drinking the Spirit (see the comment on Acts 2:38–40). The Greek verb *epotisthēmen*, usually translated in verse 13 "made to drink" in the more literal versions, is better rendered "given to drink" (NIV).

The idea in the verb *potizō* is that a drink is offered to someone, but that person must either drink it or reject it (as in Matthew 10:42; 25:35; Romans 12:20; 1 Corinthians 3:2). When our Savior was about to die on the cross, He was given a drink of sour wine soaked in a sponge (Matt. 27:48). This He received (John 19:29–30), although He had earlier refused to drink wine mingled with gall after tasting it (Matt. 27:34). The verb "given to drink" in verse 13 points to a conscious, voluntary reception of the Spirit on the part of each Spirit-baptized Christian, not something that automatically happens to him or her.

Bittlinger confirmed this interpretation of verse 13 when he observed:

> The expression "baptize" always means "to be dipped or immersed into something." The Spirit surrounds and covers the believer as water does at baptism. The expression "drink," however, gives the impression that the believer receives the Spirit into himself as he does the bread and wine at the Lord's Supper.... In both cases the form of the verb in Greek suggests that receiving the Spirit is a single experience which happened at a specific time in the past.[44]

If verse 13 speaks of Spirit baptism and not of the new birth, then how are the two occurrences of the expression "we all" in this verse to be interpreted? Many commentators hold that these words refer to all true believers and that therefore the verse teaches that every Christian enters both the new life and the church by means of baptism by the Spirit.

John Baker of Cheltenham, England, replied most convincingly to that view by pointing out that the question of how we become Christians is irrelevant to the subjects under consideration in 1 Corinthians 12–14. He wrote:

> In prosecuting his subject in chapter 12, the Apostle centers his thoughts around two points, the unity of the Body of Christ, and the diversity of its members with their differing gifts and ministries. He has described these gifts as differing manifestations of the same one Holy Spirit (verses 4–11), and he is about to explain their varied exercise within any one church in terms of the different functions of the various different organs or "members" in the human body (vv. 14ff.). In verses 12 and 13 he is underlining the thought of the unity both of the Body of Christ, and of the Spirit who animates, inspires and fills its many members in the exercise of their differing ministries and gifts. Therefore, the emphasis of the Apostle's thought in verse 13 is not at all concerned with how we *become* Christians, but with the unity or oneness of those who *are* Christians, as members of the one Christ, empowered and filled by His one Spirit, to function effectively in His one Body

here on earth. So the object of verse 13 cannot be to assert how many of the Corinthians have been baptized in the Spirit and how many have not, but to emphasize that *all* who were so baptized, were baptized in the same one and only Holy Spirit, who produces all these different manifestations, within the one Body of Christ.[45]

The words to be emphasized in reading the verse are not "we all" but "one Spirit" and "one body." Note Paul's stress on the oneness of the body in verse 12.

At the same time, we do well to remember that it was normal in the apostolic age for every believer to be baptized in the Spirit, to receive the gift of the Holy Spirit soon after his or her conversion. Peter had cried out to the multitude of worshipers on the Day of Pentecost that the promise of the Spirit was for all, "as many as the Lord our God shall call" (see the comment on Acts 2:38–40). The full package of salvation was seldom shortchanged in those days, so that the convert to Christ received not only life but power (see the comment on 1 Corinthians 1:4–9).

The experience at Ephesus reveals that it was unusual for a professing disciple not to have the marks of the Spirit on his or her life (see the comment on Acts 19:1–7). In the early church it no doubt frequently happened that, when new converts arose from the water of baptism, the Holy Spirit came upon them, so that they were baptized in water and in the Spirit at the same time (for example, Saul of Tarsus; see the comment on Acts 9:1–22). Thus Christian baptism and baptism in the Holy Spirit could have been spoken of as one event (see the comment on Ephesians 4:3–6).

## The Incomparable Way of Love—1 Corinthians 13

Love is not a gift. Love is the motivation for giving: "God so loved . . . that He gave." Love is an act of the will, an act of self-surrender and the giving of ourselves to others. Edward J. Carnell said that love is fellowship between persons.[46] So love has always existed, even before creation, within the Trinity.

The Bible never gives a theological definition of God's love. Instead God chose to demonstrate His love in Christ (Rom. 5:8) and told us love's attributes. In this famous love chapter we find only two adjectives which describe love positively. "Love is patient, love is kind" (v. 4). And in the Greek these two descriptive terms are verbs, suggesting that love is active, not static. This sort of love was the antidote that Paul prescribed for the disease of carnality infecting and dividing the church at Corinth.

The ancient Greeks used four different words for love: *eros*, sexual desire or sensual longing (not used in the New Testament but found in the Septuagint at Proverbs 7:18); *storgē*, natural affection or mutual love of family members or friends for one another (Rom. 1:31; 2 Tim. 3:3); *philia*, love, friendship, fondness (James 4:4; compare "friend," Acts 19:31); and *agapē*. In 1 Corinthians 13 we find *agapē* only. This was a more or less neutral word in classical Greek into which the Spirit poured the meaning of the unique quality of God's love.

Because love is long-suffering or patient, it harbors no jealousy. It would not envy another's spiritual gift. It does not allow us to brag about ourselves nor let us exaggerate or become conceited about our own gifts or inflated with pride because of how the Spirit has used us. Thus love never acts arrogantly, rudely or unbecomingly (as some Corinthians were doing at the Lord's Supper, 1 Corinthians 11:17–34, and by speaking out of turn in the meetings, 14:26–40).

Love never tests the patience of others. It does not seek its own; that is, it does not insist on its own way or its own rights, for such insistence is selfish, a "work of the flesh" (Gal. 5:19). In the exercise of spiritual gifts, the loving person seeks to edify others, not to gratify himself or herself. Love is never provoked ("easily" in v. 5 of the KJV is not represented in the Greek text), meaning that it is not irritable, touchy or quick to take offense.

Love thinks no evil; that is, it "keeps no record of wrongs" (NIV) nor does it nourish resentment or try to get even. When love forgives, it forgets and begins afresh with every new encounter.[47] Love does not rejoice in unrighteousness or when injustice befalls someone else but rejoices when truth prevails. It finds no pleasure in seeing another person "get what's coming to him" and never says, "It serves him right."

Because love is kind, it bears (*stegei*) all things—it conceals the faults of others and throws a cloak of silence over what is offensive in another person.[48] Love believes all things, without doubting God. Love hopes all things—for love, there are no hopeless cases. It endures all things, without weakening or retaliating or becoming critical. Such love never fails. It abides on and on forever.

No wonder that Paul wrote to the Galatian believers that love is the fruit of the Holy Spirit (Gal. 5:22). Only the Spirit of God can produce love in us, because love is what God is in His nature. Therefore love is the evidence of divine, eternal life, of genuine, abundant life, lived by the Spirit in us. Love is not a spiritual or charismatic gift, for the *charismata* are what God *does by His power.*

Understanding what love is assists us in interpreting 1 Corinthians 12:31. The last half of that verse is the transition to chapter 13, which describes the correct way of life, the proper atmosphere, for the gifts of the Spirit to operate attractively and efficiently. Some have thought Paul's statement "And yet shew I unto you a more excellent way" (KJV) implies that love supersedes the gifts, rendering them unnecessary.

A more accurate translation, however, dispels this misunderstanding. The text really says, "And furthermore (*kai eti*) I am going to show you [the] way par excellence (*kath' huperbolēn*)." He was about to further his discussion of spiritual gifts by explaining to the Corinthians the incomparable way of love, rather than offering love as a superior alternative to charismatic gifts.

Nor in chapter 13 itself did the apostle say that if we have love, it displaces the gifts. He did not question whether the manifestations themselves are genuine gifts of tongues, prophecy, (words of) knowledge and faith even if a person shows no love (vv. 1–2, 8). The deficiency is not in the gifts or in the Spirit, but in the person endowed with the gift.

Paul did not say that the gifts are nothing or that charitable deeds do not help the recipients but that "I am nothing" and "it profits me nothing." As Godet said, "What such a man has done may be of value to the Church; to himself it is nothing, because there was no love in it."[49]

Paul did not propose love without gifts. It is rather love plus the gifts of the Spirit, for he concluded in 1 Corinthians 14:1 with this exhortation: "Make love your aim, and earnestly desire the spiritual gifts" (RSV). Keep on pursuing *(diōketē*, present tense imperative) love, "and in that context eagerly desire the things of the Spirit, especially those gifts that are intelligible and will thus edify the community."[50]

Love is the best safeguard against pride in Christian service. Desiring the gifts in order to bless and help others will enable the believer to conduct his or her charismatic ministry in a humble way. Humility and love go hand in hand. In fact, they are like a coin: Love is the obverse side and humility the reverse. Display of love rather than of power should be the goal of our ministry in the gifts of the Spirit. Since God is love, this will be the most characteristic sign of His presence and His working.

## Tongues or Prophecy?—1 Corinthians 14

An important issue in the church at Corinth which Paul addressed concerned the phenomenon of speaking in tongues. Evidently some of the members of that church did not recognize that there are distinct ministries of tongues, not all of which are intended for the assembly meetings. For instance, someone might interfere with the worship of others by uttering praise and prayer to God aloud in his unknown tongue, instead of speaking silently to himself and to God (see v. 28). Some of them showed no concern if their utterances in tongues were not interpreted (see vv. 5, 13). They seemed less interested in the value of the gift of prophecy and using it to edify the congregation than in being free to voice their worship in tongues audibly.

Others in the church reacted strongly against such excesses and evidently tried to forbid speaking in tongues (see v. 39). Perhaps these were members of the Gnostic-style faction who were alarmed at the threat of exposure through the operation of the revelatory gifts (words of wisdom and knowledge, discerning of spirits). If they were concerned that their own wrong beliefs and attitudes regarding superior wisdom might be uncovered, they may have been looking for an excuse to rule out the gifts altogether.[51]

### The Nature of Tongues

What is speaking in tongues—which is also called glossolalia (from *glōssa*, "tongue," and *laleō*, "to speak")? Paul employed the Greek term *glossa* throughout his discussion in 1 Corinthians 12–14. He said there are various kinds of tongues (1 Cor. 12:10, 28). In nearly every case in the New Testament, these seem to have been languages never learned and thus unknown to the speaker.

In mentioning the tongues "of men and of angels" (1 Cor. 13:1), however, Paul may have been suggesting both existent spoken languages and ecstatic utterances unintelligible anywhere on earth. In another letter he alluded to personal ecstatic experiences, but only in his privacy with God: "For if we are beside ourselves [*exestēmēn*], it is for God" (2 Cor. 5:13).

On the Day of Pentecost the 120 believers upon whom the Holy Spirit had just been outpoured spoke in "other tongues" (*heterais glossais*). The Greek means "different languages." These were known human languages, different from their own Hebrew, Aramaic and Greek spoken in Galilee.

Jews of the Diaspora (Dispersion), who had come to Jerusalem for the annual Feast of Weeks, recognized these "other tongues" to be their native languages or dialects (Acts 2:4–11). Each of the Jews in the temple area, where the 120 Christians had faithfully assembled for the Mosaic observances, suddenly heard his or her own native language or tongue (*dialektos* in both verse 6 and verse 8). Luke gave a list of fourteen different peoples and countries to show that the disciples spoke in at least that many different languages.

The Greek word *dialektos* refers in every case to a language of a nation or a region.[52] Luke also used *dialektos* to describe the Aramaic name Aceldama (Acts 1:19, KJV); to tell how the ascended Christ spoke intelligibly to Saul of Tarsus on the Damascus road (Acts 26:14); and to say how Paul defended himself "in the Hebrew tongue" (Acts 21:40; 22:2, KJV; see the comments on Acts 2:1–4; 2:14–21; 2:38–40).

We can safely conclude that whenever an utterance in an unknown tongue was given audibly in an assembly under the prompting of the Holy Spirit, it was in a human language. S. Lewis Johnson Jr. of Dallas Theological Seminary explained that since Luke was a close companion of Paul and wrote the Book of Acts after Paul had written his Corinthian epistles, it would seem logical for Luke to have noted the distinction between the tongues at Pentecost and those in Corinth, if any existed. "In other words, 1 Corinthians should be interpreted by Acts, the unknown by the known, a good hermeneutical principle. . . . It is quite unlikely that the phenomena, described by the two writers in identical terms, would be dissimilar."[53] In modern times, utterances in tongues on various occasions have been understood by those standing near who knew the foreign language in question.

To understand the nature of genuine speaking in tongues by the Spirit, we need to study 1 Corinthians 14:2 in conjunction with verse 5. Verse 2 describes speaking in a language unknown to the speaker or any listeners without interpretation following. Paul said those who speak in a tongue in this way speak to God, not to others. They are using a language that they themselves do not rationally understand, in order to communicate the deep thoughts and feelings of their spirits to God.

In their spirits they speak "mysteries," mysterious things not understood by their minds or by those who may overhear them. As Godet long ago stated it, speaking in a tongue is a sort of spiritual soliloquy.[54] Therefore, speaking in a tongue is a supernatural manifestation of the Holy Spirit whereby Christians speak in a language that they have never learned and that express their innermost thoughts and feelings, a language that God hears and understands.[55]

In verse 5, however, the apostle placed speaking in tongues followed by the gift of interpretation on a parallel with prophesying as far as its value in edifying the church is concerned. Now prophecy edifies, because through this gift God is giving a revelation and speaking to the church. Therefore, we may conclude that also in tongues with interpretation God is speaking to people. Occasionally, however, the tongues speaker may be praising God or praying to Him, as the interpretation makes clear. This public manifestation of tongues is apparently what Paul refers to in chapter 12:10, 28 as the charismatic gift of tongues for the ministering of one member of the body to the others.

### The Extent of Tongues

The charismatic gift of tongues was a new manifestation of the Spirit never displayed by any of the Old Testament prophets and saints. Isaiah 28:11, quoted by Paul in verse 21, is not primarily a prophecy foretelling the Pentecostal gift. In its own context Isaiah's verse refers to the seemingly "stammering lips" (KJV) and alien tongue of the Assyrians and their mercenary troops of various nationalities, whom God would bring to "speak" to His people as a divine judgment. The people of Judah had refused to listen to God's prophets when He had offered His rest and refreshing (Isa. 28:12), so they were to be hardened in their unbelief by the tongues of the foreign invaders.

Likewise, in the church at Corinth tongues were a "sign" to "them that believe not" (KJV) or "unbelievers" (RSV, NAS, NIV—the *apistoi*) and to the "unlearned" (KJV—the *idiotai*, vv. 22–24). The *apistoi* were probably not only unsaved outsiders but perhaps were even false teachers who professed to be Christians and whom the Corinthian believers were admitting to their services. The *idiotai* would then have been novices untutored in Christianity who gullibly listened to the false teachers, not "ungifted" Christians as the NAS implies.

These outsiders were in the habit of accusing the tongues speakers of being "mad," hardening their own hearts in unbelief and disobedience in the very process of mocking. While tongues without interpretation could only be a sign of God's displeasure with their unbelief (and not a means to their salvation), prophecy could disclose the secrets of their hearts and bring some of them to repentance (vv. 24–25).[56]

Thus the point of Paul's use of Isaiah 28:11 was to draw a parallel between the hardening of hearts in ancient Israel and in his own day—not to imply that Isaiah was saying God would speak to His people by glossolalia. Even

Joel's prophecy fulfilled at Pentecost (Joel 2:28–32) did not specifically foretell tongues but promised other forms of spiritual revelation, such as prophesying, visions and dreams. So to speak with "new tongues" was an unprecedented experience for Spirit-anointed men and women of God. It is a miraculous sign unique to the church age—"they will speak with new tongues" (Mark 16:17).

Even if the last verses of Mark's Gospel are not original to him but were added early in the second century A.D., they are primary evidence that the practice of tongues was not limited to the first few decades of the church (see the comment on Mark 16:9–20). So the gift of tongues extends throughout the Church Age and will only cease or come to an end "when that which is perfect is come" at the final consummation of Christ (1 Cor. 13:8–10; 15:24–28).

Speaking in tongues is reported to have occurred not only at Pentecost but also on many later occasions. The Holy Spirit was poured out upon Cornelius and his household (Acts 10:45–46), and Peter claimed later that the Spirit had fallen upon the Gentiles at Caesarea "just as" (*hosper kai*) He did at Pentecost (Acts 11:15), intimating that the Gentiles also spoke in one or more tongues recognizable as languages (see the comment on Acts 10:44–48). Tongues were in evidence again at Ephesus when Paul laid his hands upon twelve newly baptized disciples (see the comment on Acts 19:1–7).

Many commentators believe that glossolalia also happened at Samaria when the recent converts were receiving the Holy Spirit (see the comment on Acts 8:5–25). Paul sooner or later spoke in tongues and continued to do so (1 Cor. 14:18). His initial experience may have taken place when he was filled with the Holy Spirit in Damascus (see the comment on Acts 9:1–22).

The term "speaking in tongues" does not appear in any epistle other than 1 Corinthians. Certain expressions, however, indicate that the gift of tongues was not confined to the church at Corinth. Paul's instructions in 1 Corinthians 14 evidently were meant for "all the churches of the saints" (14:33–34). He urged the Ephesian and the Colossian believers to worship God with "spiritual songs" (Eph. 5:19; Col. 3:16). These are Spirit-given songs, identified by many with Paul's "singing with the Spirit," that is, singing in tongues. Yet the absence of glossolalia in the list of charismatic gifts in Romans 12:3–8 (see the comment there) shows that we cannot claim Pauline authority for tongues as a *necessary* part of the public ministry in every local church.

### The Purposes of Tongues

In the New Testament, glossolalia does not seem to have been an instrument of evangelism. On the Day of Pentecost, the disciples were heard speaking "the wonderful works" (KJV, *ta megaleia*, "the greatnesses,") of God (Acts 2:11). In Cornelius's house they likewise were praising and magnifying (*megalunontōn*) God (Acts 10:46). In neither case did they proclaim the gospel, nor did interpretation accompany the manifestation of tongues. It was Peter's sermon in a language commonly known by all the assembled Jews (in Aramaic or Greek) that wrought conviction in the hearts of the three thousand who were converted at Pentecost.

The following uses of tongues seem apparent in the New Testament (verses without book and chapter reference are in 1 Corinthians 14):

*(1) A sign of the promised outpouring of the Spirit and the believer's consequent reception of Him, known as the baptism in the Holy Spirit.* The one common immediate consequence of the coming of the Spirit in power in Jerusalem, Caesarea and Ephesus was speaking in tongues. Speaking with "new tongues" is listed as one of the signs that would accompany those who have believed the apostolic message (Mark 16:17). This initial speaking in a tongue following the baptism in the Spirit is not proof, however, that a person has received the *gift* of tongues for public use in the congregation.

*(2) A devotional exercise* (1 Cor. 14:2, 4, 14–18, 28). In this use, glossolalia becomes a means of personal edification through the communication of our spirits with God in praise and prayer. This is an act of spiritual worship not controlled or limited by our intellect.

This use of glossolalia was practiced in great measure by Paul himself (vv. 14–15, 18), and he wanted all his readers to be speaking in tongues in this way (v. 5, RSV). Praising God was the purpose that the 120 disciples had on the morning of Pentecost; although at the same time, the miracle served as a sign to the hearers (see above). Paul stressed, however, that usually this function of tongues should be performed in private or under our breath (vv. 13–19, 28).

Some have linked the intercession of the Spirit "with groanings too deep for words" (Rom. 8:26–27) and "praying in the Spirit" (Eph. 6:18; Jude 20) to praying in tongues. But these passages cannot be limited to glossolalia (see the comment on Romans 8:23–27).

Many are discovering that praying in tongues opens the door for the Holy Spirit to deal with our spirits in the area of subconscious attitudes and desires. So here is an aid in bringing every thought of our minds captive to the obedience of Christ (2 Cor. 10:5).

*(3) Congregational worship in spiritual songs* (Eph. 5:18–19). This is the beautiful, unrehearsed, extemporaneous singing in the Spirit by all or many of the believers assembled in worship. Often it takes the form of singing praise to God in various tongues, which need not be interpreted because all are participating in the adoration. If only one person sings aloud in a tongue, then an interpretation should follow, perhaps also in song.

*(4) A message to fellow believers* (vv. 5b, 13, 26–27). This use is the gift of tongues *per se,* listed in 1 Corinthians 12:10, 28 as one of the charismatic gifts, all of which are to be used to minister to other members of the body of Christ. Whereas Paul wanted all to speak in tongues devotionally (vv. 2–5a), not all speak with tongues to the congregation of the church (12:30).

Usually in this function Christ is speaking by His Spirit to the assembled people. For the message from God in an unknown tongue to edify the church, the gift of tongues must operate with the companion gift of interpretation. The one who interprets may be the one who has spoken in the tongue (vv. 5, 13), or it may be another person (vv. 27–28).

The interpretation is not necessarily an exact translation of the utterance in tongues but may be a rendering in the vernacular of the main content of the message in the unknown language.[57] The response in English may seem longer, because the interpretation itself may have been followed by words of prophecy. Or it may be that the speaking in tongues was actually a prayer, and the presumed interpretation an answer by prophecy.[58] The tongues utterance plus the interpretation may edify the church equally as much as prophesying (v. 5b), lending a distinct note of the supernatural to the meeting.

*(5) A sign to strangers and unbelievers* (vv. 20–25). Speaking in tongues may be either praise *to* God or a message *from* God. In either case, at the same time it may act also as a sign in one of several ways. First, it may serve as a sign of God's presence when the language is identified and understood. Second, when the tongue is not understood, it may nevertheless be recognized as evidence of the living God at work. Third, the tongue may even be a sign of unbelief when it is mocked and its divine character is denied.

The tongues at Pentecost that produced amazement in the Jews from other lands are an example of the first type. The glossolalia served to get their attention, so that they might listen with open ears to Peter as he preached the gospel. In some cases of recent record, a message has been given directly to a person of foreign birth in his or her mother tongue. The result is often that the heart of the hearer is convicted and melted, and he or she receives Christ as Savior and Lord.

The speaking in tongues by Cornelius and his associates may not have been understood by Peter and the Jews with him, but they knew the tongues were exalting God (Acts 10:44–46). This anecdote would illustrate the second type of sign.

In cases of the third type, unbelieving critics and scoffers may consider glossolalia to be mere gibberish and become hardened in their attitude. Their very mockery of tongues becomes the sign of their unbelief (vv. 22–23; see the discussion of Isaiah 28:11 above under "The Extent of Tongues").

### The Regulation of Tongues

Paul's discussion implies that there were at least a few in the church at Corinth who were using the gift of tongues in a thoughtless, unloving way. Therefore, along with pointing out the values of speaking in tongues, he set forth certain principles and guidelines for their proper use. Remember that at the beginning of his epistle he had complimented the congregation as a whole for their full participation in all the gifts of utterance as well as the gifts of knowledge (see comment on 1 Corinthians 1:4–9).

No one, he said, should boast that the more dramatic gifts are more supernatural or more important than other less conspicuous ones (1 Cor. 12). The only right motive for desiring the gifts, including tongues, and the only right attitude in which they function profitably, is love (1 Cor. 13). A message in tongues must be followed with an interpretation; otherwise the one manifesting the gift of tongues should remain silent (1 Cor. 14).

Only two or at the most three should speak in tongues in any given meeting, and these in turn (14:28–29). These instructions were given to prevent glossolalia from dominating the entire meeting and thus hindering persons with other gifts from ministering to the church.

### The Nature of Prophecy

Prophecy is one of the charismatic gifts manifested in Christians by the power of the Holy Spirit (1 Cor. 12:10–11). Much can be learned about the gift of prophecy through a study of the Old Testament prophets (see chapter four). The oracles that the classical prophets delivered were the actual, infallible, authoritative words of God to His people. But, as Graham Houston has pointed out, there were some occasions in the Old Testament when prophecy was not so much a revelation from God as a powerful sign of His presence with His people.[59]

An example of this is found in Numbers 11:4–30 (see the comment there) where it is said that the seventy elders whom Moses appointed all prophesied when the Spirit rested upon them (v. 25). No messages from God are recorded here, but the experience nevertheless was a clear sign that the Spirit of God was among them. While the elders did not prophesy again, Moses longed for the time when all the Lord's people would be prophets with His Spirit upon them (v. 29).

This is obviously a different kind of prophecy from that of being directed to proclaim the very words of God (as in Deuteronomy 18:15–22). Whatever words of praise or encouragement the seventy elders spoke had only general significance, but they were a blessing to God's people by confirming His presence with them.

In 1 Corinthians 14 all Christians are encouraged to engage in this secondary type of prophesying. Michael Griffiths has confirmed this differentiation:

> The very fact that prophesying is not to be regarded as automatically authoritative but is to be carefully weighed suggests that the kind of prophecy referred to in 1 Corinthians 14 cannot be regarded as in the same class at all as the direct words of God through the Old Testament prophets.[60]

One result of the Pentecostal outpouring of the Spirit during the church age is that *all* of God's children might be able to prophesy in this secondary sense (see the comment on Acts 2:14–21). Paul evidently believed that every Spirit-baptized Christian potentially can have a manifestation of the gift of prophecy, as the Spirit wills, for he wrote, "Now I wish that you all spoke in tongues, but even more that you would prophesy" (1 Cor. 14:5). Therefore, he ended his entire discussion on the spiritual gifts by exhorting, "Desire earnestly to prophesy" (14:39).

Paul considered prophecy to be the most important of the gifts of utterance, and perhaps of all the gifts (v. 1). Of course he recognized that not all members of Christ's church have the *ministry* of prophet (1 Cor. 12:28–29).

Indwelt and empowered by the Spirit of God, believers of this dispensation since Pentecost may receive an inner revelation and be prompted to speak by the Holy Spirit without the aid of a dream or vision. When they are yielded to the Spirit's control and realize that a few thoughts or words of inspiration are coming to their minds, they should act on faith and give forth these words as an utterance of God to the church (1 Pet. 4:11), expecting that the Spirit will supply the rest of the message even while they are speaking.

### The Purpose of Prophecy

Over and over in 1 Corinthians 14 Paul stated that the purpose of the gifts of utterance is to edify the other members of the church. According to verse 3, prophecy ministers to Christians in three ways: edification, exhortation, and comfort or consolation.

The first Greek term, *oikodomē*, means "building up," as in building a house (*oikos*) with strong, good materials. The words of God spoken in prophecy, like the written "word of His grace" (Acts 20:32), serve to establish and strengthen the church and to add new members to it.

The second term, *exhortation,* is the Greek *paraklēsis,* from the same root as paraclete ("Comforter"), Jesus' expression for the Holy Spirit (see the comment on John 14:15–18 and others). Thus through the gift of prophecy the Spirit can carry out His work of comforting, encouraging and counseling in the local church.

The third term, *consolation* (Greek *paramuthia*), is closely related to the second. It refers specifically to the solace afforded by love (Phil. 2:1), often at the time of bereavement, as in the case of the Jews' coming to console Mary and Martha (John 11:19, 31). It means to calm and pacify. Thus prophecy can calm our doubts and fears and help us to rest in the presence of Jesus.

Another result of prophecy may be the conversion of an unbeliever or deluded Christian, as seen in verses 24–25: "But if all prophesy, and an unbeliever. . . enters, he is convicted by all, he is called to account by all; the secrets of his heart are disclosed; and so he will fall on his face and worship God, declaring that God is certainly among you."

Here is an instance of the gift of knowledge functioning together with the gift of prophecy to reveal the condition of sinners' hearts and to turn them from the error or delusion of their way (James 5:19–20).

## The Regulation of Prophecy

In addition to the rules for the use of tongues in a meeting, the Lord gave through Paul two main instructions regarding the gift of prophecy: "Let two or three prophets speak, and let the others pass judgment" (v. 29).

Only two or three prophets were to speak during a worship service so that the meeting did not become unbalanced with charismatic utterances, with no time left for singing, prayer, teaching and preaching the Word. When one person gave a prophecy, he or she evidently stood up. If another member who was seated received a fresh revelation, that second person was to stand up to indicate this. Then the first person (who perhaps by then was going beyond the Spirit's anointing into his or her own words) was to become silent and sit down.

Each member had the right and the potential in the Spirit to prophesy, so that every other member might learn and be exhorted. All could have an opportunity if they prophesied one by one in successive meetings, no more than three to a service.

The other regulation was to test each prophetic utterance: "the others should weigh carefully what is said" (v. 29, NIV). Prophets had to be tested, because prophesying is the cooperative working together of the Holy Spirit with the human spirit. While the Spirit of God prompted and superintended, the spirit of the human being was alive and free and therefore responsible for the rational thoughts of the mind and the words of the tongue.

All were to judge, but especially those with the gift of the discerning of spirits were to be alert to detect any trace of false teaching. There was to be a witness of the Spirit in the hearts of the other brothers and sisters that the message was right and in agreement with the authoritative Scriptures. Prophecy was never to contradict the written Word of God. All believers, not only the elders, were responsible to be on guard against false prophets and teachers; these might arise even from within the congregation, "speaking perverse things, to draw away the disciples after them" (Acts 20:28–30).

Finally, order was to be maintained in the meeting by the observance of good manners and consideration of others. Paul forthrightly said, "The spirits of prophets are subject to prophets" (v. 32). This reminds us, said Dennis Bennett, that the gifts of the Spirit come by inspiration, not compulsion, and provide no excuse for erratic behavior.[61] If the Holy Spirit was truly in control, the meeting would be peaceful, loving and orderly; "for God is not the author of confusion, but of peace" (v. 33a, KJV).

The final question that some have asked about Paul's comments here is, Tongues or prophecy—which is preferable? According to Paul, however, it is not a matter of tongues versus prophecy, but of both practiced in humility as the Spirit wills and as each member is in subjection to the others in the local church. "Therefore, my brethren, desire earnestly to prophesy, and do not forbid to speak in tongues" (v. 39). There is no statement in any of Paul's epistles in which he belittled the gift of glossolalia *per se.*

## The Earnest of the Spirit—2 Corinthians 1:21–22

In the first chapter of 2 Corinthians Paul was explaining to his readers that he was not a vacillating person, though he had been prevented from visiting them sooner. His own word was consistent, not a *yes* today and a *no* tomorrow. His model was Christ Jesus, the Son of God, in whom *yes* means *yes.* For all the promises of God, who is ever true and faithful, receive the answer of *yes* in Christ (2 Cor. 1:15–20).

Paul then described God as the one who is constantly establishing our position in Christ and who gave us the earnest of the Spirit in our hearts: "It is God who gives us a firm standing in Christ, along with you; it is God who has anointed us for our service, who has set His seal upon us and given us His Spirit in our hearts as His sure pledge" (vv. 21–22).[62]

According to Paul, our present common experience as Christians is confirmed by the three simultaneous and decisive acts of anointing, sealing and receiving the Spirit that took place in the past. But when? At regeneration? At the baptism in the Holy Spirit? If the time of any one of these acts can be determined, it will set the time of all three.

We must begin by examining the first of these three acts. Paul's statement, "anointed us," means that God made us like the anointed One, Christ, in the sense that both Christ and we are anointed with the same Spirit. But we were anointed with the Spirit—we received the anointing from the Holy One (see the comment on 1 John 2:20, 27)—when we received the promised gift of the Holy Spirit. According to Acts 2:38–40 (see the comment there), the gift of the Spirit, in the sense of His enduing the believer with power, is offered to the Christian subsequent to conversion. The reception of this gift by faith is known as the baptism in the Spirit.

Anointing, sealing and giving the Spirit, therefore, in the sense of verses 21 and 22, all occur in a single event, when the Christian disciple is baptized in the

Holy Spirit. The "anointing" points to the power of the Spirit to perform the works of Christ (Isa. 61:1; Acts 10:38) and to the capacity given to believers by the Spirit to know the truth (1 John 2:20, 27). The "sealing" emphasizes the gift of the Spirit as the seal of the New Covenant that God has made with His people through Christ, the mediator. The seal also serves as a sign of ownership, for by sealing believers with His Spirit, God marks them as His very own. He did this by "giving" the Spirit "in our hearts" when we were filled with the Spirit.

It is true that the Holy Spirit first entered our being as Christ's agent to bring us His resurrection life. The New Testament, however, never equates our new birth with God's *gift* of His Spirit to us. Jesus made it clear that not until after He would return to the Father would He send the Spirit of truth as Helper to abide in them (John 16:5, 7; 14:16–17; 15:26; see the comment on John 14:16–18). He fulfilled this promise on the Day of Pentecost, ten days after His ascension to the right hand of the Father. Therefore, when Paul wrote in verse 22 that God *gave us* the Spirit in our hearts, he was referring to the baptism in the Spirit and not to conversion.

The Greek word *arrabōn*, translated "earnest" in the KJV, means the first down payment by which the recipient is assured of final payment in full. It is derived from the Hebrew word ʿ*ērābôn*, which appears in Genesis 38:17–20 as the pledge that Tamar demanded of Judah. In modern Greek, *arrabōn* means an engagement ring, the token of future marriage from the lover to his prospective bride.

The Spirit Himself is this earnest, pledge (NAS), guarantee (RSV) or deposit (NIV). Paul says again in 2 Corinthians 5:5 that the Spirit is a deposit, guaranteeing what is to come (NIV). The Spirit is God's pledge to us of our inheritance (Eph. 1:13–14; see the comment there), even of that full and perfect knowledge of God and of His Son, Jesus Christ, which is eternal life (John 17:3). The Spirit is a fitting seal, pledge and down payment, because He is a *present* experience. He is God's way of saying, "See, this is what I am talking about!"

## The Ministry of the Spirit—2 Corinthians 3:6–8, 17–18

Every Christian is a servant of Jesus Christ. As servants of Christ, we are servants or ministers of the New Covenant instituted by Christ. Whereas the ministry of the Old Covenant or Law of Moses was a ministry which tended to death—glorious as it was with the Lord's presence at Mount Sinai—the ministry of the New Covenant is a ministry of the Spirit (2 Cor. 3:6–8). We do not serve under the old written code but in the new life of the Spirit (Rom. 7:6, RSV). Therefore, the ministry of this present dispensation, from Pentecost until the return of Christ, is under the authority and direction of the Holy Spirit.

The chief characteristic of this ministry is that the Spirit gives life (2 Cor. 3:6). The Holy Spirit is the life-giver (John 6:63). By His quickening power, life from above is planted in a person, and he or she is born again (John 3:5). At the same time that person is united with Christ in His resurrection (Rom. 6:4–6).

Having imparted spiritual life to us—the new life of Christ—the Spirit's subsequent and continuing work is to change us into the very image or likeness of Christ, from one degree of glory to another (2 Cor. 3:18). In 2 Corinthians 3:16 Paul paraphrased Exodus 34:34 to read, "But whenever a man turns to the Lord, the veil is taken away." He likened the veil that hid the fading glory on Moses' face from the Israelites to the mental block that had prevented Jews from recognizing the inadequate character of the Old Covenant (3:13–15). Nor had they understood much of God's truth about their spiritual condition and His plan of salvation by faith in Christ.

In 3:17 Paul explained that the term "the Lord" must be interpreted as the Spirit, in making application of that passage to an individual seeking God during the present dispensation. He then added that wherever the Spirit of the Lord is present, there is liberty. Human souls are set free. The NEB translation enables us to understand the rich meaning of the words in 3:18: "And because for us there is no veil over the face, we all reflect as in a mirror the splendour of the Lord; thus we are [being] transfigured into his likeness, from splendour to splendour; such is the influence of the Lord who is Spirit."

Only the Spirit of Christ dwelling within us can change us into the likeness of our precious Lord and Savior. It is not possible for the believer to become conformed to the image of Christ by external imitation of Him. A. J. Gordon, a Baptist clergyman in Boston during the nineteenth century, explained the divine process in a beautiful way: "Christ, who is 'the image of the invisible God,' is set before [the believer] as his divine pattern, and Christ by the Spirit dwells within him as a divine life, and Christ is able to image forth Christ from the interior life to the outward example."[63]

As the Comforter makes us more and more like Christ, He imparts to us the fruit of the Spirit (Gal. 5:22–23), which really consists of various aspects of Christ's holy character. This is His continuing work of sanctification in its present stage (see the comment on 1 Corinthians 6:11).

Another phase of the Spirit's ministry is to make us competent ministers of the New Covenant (2 Cor. 3:6). We are not adequate or qualified in ourselves. We are not capable on our own initiative of conceiving a single wise thought or performing a single helpful deed that would benefit Christ's kingdom; our adequacy is from God (3:5).

It is the Spirit of God who teaches us, directs us, empowers us and distributes His gifts to us. In this way He equips us to be able to perform our duties as servants of Christ. Paul recognized this enabling once again in his list of characteristics of the ministry of reconciliation (2 Cor. 6:6).

A century ago the saintly Andrew Murray of South Africa pointed out that the power of the ministry on the divine side is the Spirit, while on the human side it is faith.[64] Paul said that he had the same "spirit of faith" that the writer of Psalm 116 had (2 Cor. 4:13). He was not referring directly to the Holy Spirit but to the human spirit that is in fellowship with the divine Spirit and therefore is characterized by the attitude of faith. This spirit or attitude of faith—a fruit of the Holy Spirit—sustained Paul in his severe trials and afflictions (2 Cor. 4:8–11).

Faith is necessary throughout the entire Christian life. Whatever is of the Spirit is by faith on our part. Through weakness or severe trials God brings us to the death of self—that is, to the end of trusting in ourselves—so that the resurrection life of Jesus may be manifested in our mortal flesh. Andrew Murray concluded his teaching from 2 Corinthians 4 by saying:

> And this is the Ministry of the Spirit, when faith glories in infirmities, that the power of Christ may rest upon it. It is as our faith does not stagger at the earthiness and weakness of the vessel, as it consents that the excellency of the power shall be, not from ourselves, or in anything we feel, but of God alone, that the Spirit will work in the power of the living God.[65]

## Receiving the Spirit Through Faith—Galatians 3:2–5, 14

Paul wrote the epistle to the churches he had founded in Galatia in order to teach them the correct way to live the Christian life. The error of Jewish legalism that was subverting the faith of the Galatians pertained as much to the means of their sanctification as to the means of their justification. They had known clearly how to be saved. Paul had taught them what he and the apostles in Jerusalem had agreed upon, namely, that neither Jew nor Gentile is justified by the works of the Law but through faith in Christ Jesus (Gal. 2:16). But

Jewish Christians had come after he left, teaching that believers could not enjoy the covenant blessings given to Abraham unless they submitted to circumcision (5:2–12) and observed the Jewish feasts and special days (4:10).

The key to the entire book of Galatians is the question in 3:3. Paul asked the believers why, since they had begun their new life as Christians in the Spirit, they were now trying to be made perfect by the flesh, by human effort (NIV). They would readily admit, he knew, that they had been saved by an operation of the Spirit through faith on their part. Why should they expect to be brought to spiritual maturity by dependence on the flesh and by performing works of the Law? Here Paul was using the term *sarx*, "the flesh," to refer to human nature in its weakness and fallibility carried over from the unregenerate state.

Because living the Christian life obviously requires the continued working of the Spirit, Paul centered their attention on how they received the Holy Spirit, not on how they received Christ. That is why he asked in verse 2, "Did you receive the Spirit by the works of the Law, or by hearing with faith?" Did they receive the Spirit on the grounds of their having kept the Law of Moses or as a result of their hearing the gospel accompanied by faith on their part? Obviously the latter. (See the comment on Acts 5:32.)

Verses 5 and 14, taken together, show that when the apostle was talking about their receiving the promised gift of the Spirit (v. 14) he was referring to their being baptized in the Holy Spirit. The word "miracles" (from *dunamis*) in verse 5 indicates, even to non-Pentecostal writers, that Paul had in mind "the charismatic manifestations of the Spirit evidenced by some outward sign, such as speaking with tongues or prophesying." This was the observation of Ernest DeWitt Burton, a Baptist professor of biblical and patristic Greek at the University of Chicago.[66]

In verse 14 the expression "the promise of the Spirit" is the same as that which Peter used in his Pentecost sermon (Acts 2:33). Peter was referring to the great outpouring of the Holy Spirit when the ascended Lord Jesus began to baptize the members of His church.

According to verse 5, the experience that the Galatians had with the Holy Spirit extended beyond the initial reception: "He who supplies the Spirit to you and works miracles among you" (RSV). The verb *supplies* (RSV), *provides* (NAS), *ministereth* (KJV) is *epichorēgōn*, a participle in the present tense that means "he who is continually supplying in bountiful measure."

In Philippians 1:19 Paul employed the corresponding noun, *epichorēgia*, in the phrase "the provision of the Spirit of Jesus Christ" either to mean "the help given by the Spirit of Jesus Christ" (NIV) or "the Spirit of Jesus Christ given [to Paul] for support" (NEB). The verb *works* (*energōn*) in Galatians 3:5 is also a present participle and indicates that God was continuing to perform miracles by His Spirit (see 1 Corinthians 12:10) through those Galatians who were still walking in faith and had not reverted to legalistic forms. Therefore it appears that the first great outpouring of the Spirit among the Galatians was accompanied with various spiritual gifts such as those described in 1 Corinthians 12–14. Although these manifestations had been checked by the undermining of the Judaizers, they had not entirely ceased.

From Paul's discussion we learn that the baptism in the Holy Spirit is received by faith and that we keep receiving fresh supplies of the Spirit and His power as we continue to look to the Lord in faith (see the comments on Luke 11:5–13; Acts 2:38–40; Ephesians 5:15–21).

We also learn that we encounter many temptations to retreat from the new freedom that Christ has given to us by His Spirit (Gal. 5:1, 13; John 8:32, 36; 2 Cor. 3:17–18). As Romans 6–8 teaches, the Holy Spirit ministers freedom from the bondage and oppression of sin and the flesh. But the price we must pay for this freedom is constant yieldedness to the Spirit's control and complete dependence on His guidance.

Sad to say, many Spirit-baptized people are not willing to keep on living and walking in this intimate relationship with the Lord on a moment-by-moment basis. They do not "take time to be holy," as the old hymn puts it. Instead they find it more convenient or comfortable to submit to someone else's religious system or to some outstanding human leader and to live by adhering to certain standards or "works of the law."

Christians, as well as the unregenerate, fear the sovereign unpredictability of the Holy Spirit. The full freedom of the Spirit, with its consequent necessity for utter obedience and its responsibility to be available to His prompting at all times, can be very frightening to some persons. So even in "full gospel" churches, the order of worship often becomes an elaborately structured non-structure. This is in accord with human nature, for most people seek to escape, not from slavery, but from freedom.

## The Fruit of the Spirit—Galatians 5:22–23

Paul's lovely passage on the fruit of the Spirit is itself like a choice fruit. We may not only admire it, but we should also eat it and benefit from it. It appears in a section of Paul's epistle to the Galatians explaining the right way to use our Christian liberty or freedom (Gal. 5:13–26).

Verses 13–15 declare that our freedom from bondage to the Law (5:1) must not become an excuse for selfishness. We should not abuse our liberty by permitting the flesh, our old selfish nature, to have its way. We should not use our freedom as a cover-up for evil (1 Pet. 2:16, NIV). Instead we should practice liberty in love: "through love serve one another" (Gal. 5:13).

The flesh, or selfishness and self-will, is the capacity to sin that persists in believers. It is the enemy inside us that would destroy our freedom in Christ and bring us into even worse bondage. Therefore, each child of God needs a helping and restraining hand to guard against our own evil nature.

We find this help in the divine Paraclete (the "Comforter") dwelling within us. By the Spirit we can keep walking step by step, day by day, and have strength not to fulfill the lust of the flesh (5:16, KJV). The Holy Spirit can so control us that we will not yield to self-indulgence and gratify the cravings of the old nature. By means of the Spirit we can put to death and rise above the negative attitudes and evil deeds that are the natural activities of our self-nature (Rom. 8:13).

If we truly belong to Christ Jesus, we have made the decision to consider the "old man" (Rom. 6:6, KJV) or flesh, with its passions and desires, as a crucified thing (Gal. 5:24). Our old unregenerate self, what we once were, can never be converted. The change takes place only when the "new man" becomes dominant.

The indwelling Holy Spirit and the "flesh" or godless human nature in a Christian are antagonistic to each other. Each has a strong desire to suppress the other. They are locked in continual combat. They are entrenched in an attitude of mutual opposition to each other so that the Christian is prevented from doing what he or she wants to do. This fact is developed at greater length by Paul in Romans 7:14–25, telling of his own early Christian experience.

When the Spirit enters us at the moment of our conversion, it is like the Allied invasion of Normandy in World War II. God has returned to occupy what is rightfully His. The more the new believer, like the local French inhabitants of Normandy, cooperates with the "Invader," the sooner the territory once held by the enemy may be reclaimed and fully liberated.

After listing many of the hideous practices of the flesh (Gal. 5:19–21), Paul painted for us a marvelous contrast. It is like finding a vine laden with luscious grapes or a tree covered with ripe, red apples growing in the midst of a thicket of briars, weeds and dense underbrush. "But the fruit of the Spirit is love, joy, peace, patience, kindness, goodness, faithfulness, gentleness, self-control" (vv. 22–23).

In verse 22 the term "fruit" is singular, which tends to emphasize the unity and coherence of the personality of those who walk in the Spirit. Because the Holy Spirit is guiding and controlling them, their lives are integrated, wholesome and abundant. In contrast, the term "works" or "deeds" in 5:19 is plural, stressing the disorganization and instability of a life lived under the dictates of the flesh. The unregenerate life is fragmented and at odds with itself.

Paul always used the word *fruit* (*karpos*) as a collective noun in the singular, except in 2 Timothy 2:6. So we do not have to consider love as the only fruit that is being described in its various aspects by the eight following words. Nevertheless, some may prefer to consider the fruit of the Spirit as one cluster with its individual grapes, or as a single orange with its distinct segments.

Love is beautifully described in 1 Corinthians 13 (see the comment there). *Agapē* love is the intelligent and purposeful love that is an act of the will more than of emotion or feeling. It is the inner force that energizes and activates our faith and motivates it to work: "faith working through love" (Gal. 5:6). It reveals itself in serving others (5:13). Such love must be supplied to us from its only source, which is God (1 John 4:7–8). He has poured out His love within our hearts through the Holy Spirit (Rom. 5:5; 2 Tim. 1:7).

Joy is the opposite of pessimism. True joy that persists in the midst of sorrow and calamity is bestowed by Christ as He answers our prayers (John 15:11; 16:24) and is mediated by the Holy Spirit (Rom. 14:17; 1 Thess. 1:6). Our joy in the Lord is our strength (Neh. 8:10).

Peace is shared with us by Christ Himself through His Spirit. It is *His* peace (John 14:27), and we may have it only in Him (John 16:33). This peace is the opposite of strife (KJV) and disputes and dissensions (NAS), which are listed among the works of the flesh in Galatians 5:20. It consists both of inward repose because of our consciousness of our right relationship with God (Phil. 4:7) and of harmonious relations with others. Christ gives us His peace in order to settle our questionings and to act as arbiter or referee in our hearts (Col. 3:15, NAS margin). It comes to us as we set our thoughts and desires on the things of the Spirit (Rom. 8:5–8).

Long-suffering or patience is manifested when we refuse to retaliate for a wrong done to us. When it is the true fruit of the Spirit, it shows forbearance to others along with joyfulness (Col. 1:11). It is one of the chief attributes of love in 1 Corinthians 13:4.

Gentleness or benevolent kindness (Greek *chrēstotēs*) is the mark of a sweet spirit, one that is kind and mild and full of graciousness. It is the characteristic of God's nature that He delights in showing to humankind (Eph. 2:7; Titus 3:4; Rom. 2:4). It is the other positive characteristic of love noted in 1 Corinthians 13:4. Jesus acted with this type of kindness to the fallen woman of the street who slipped into the banquet hall to wash His feet (Luke 7:37–50). This fruit makes a person easy to get along with and thoughtful of the needs and wishes of others.

Goodness is a personal integrity of character and uprightness of soul that abhors evil. A good person is honest in his or her motives as well as conduct. Goodness is also generosity; it does good to others.

Faith as a *fruit* of the Spirit means fidelity (as the word *pistis* is translated in Titus 2:10, KJV, RSV) and faithfulness to Christ and His cause (Matt. 25:21; Acts 16:15; Col. 1:7; 1 Tim. 1:12). It shows itself in trustworthy stewardship for God (1 Cor. 4:2) and in reliability that qualifies a person to teach others (2 Tim. 2:2, NIV). Faith as a *gift* of the Spirit enables us to trust God for a miracle (see the comment on 1 Corinthians 12:4–1).

Meekness (*praütes*) is based on humility and self-denial. It is humble tolerance of others, not pushing ourselves forward. It does not press its rights or threaten vengeance; yet it is not cowardly. It is gentle but strong and patiently endures injuries with no spirit of resentment. It is not self-assertive and does not depend on personality or reputation. The person of the world says, "Blessed are the aggressive, for they shall rule the world with their cunning, courage and competitiveness." Jesus said, "Blessed are the meek, for they shall inherit the earth" (Matt. 5:5, KJV). In His only description of Himself, our Lord said, "I am meek and lowly in heart" (Matt. 11:29, KJV). How do we achieve meekness? It is a fruit of the Spirit of Jesus!

Temperance is better translated self-control or self-restraint. It enables us to control the self-life, a clear indication that at its deepest level it is a product of the Spirit. It is mastery of our tempers and all carnal appetites and therefore is opposed to the drunkenness and carousings of Galatians 5:21. Later Paul would speak to the debauched Roman governor Felix about righteousness, temperance and the judgment to come (Acts 24:25). No wonder, because for his third marriage Felix had taken Drusilla, another ruler's wife. He was treacherous and cruel and could commit all kinds of evil with impunity.

The best fruit grows where the soil is fertile and cultivated and when the branches are pruned regularly. So we must break up our fallow ground (Hos. 10:12) and submit to the cleansing and pruning action of the word of Christ (John 15:2–3).

The Holy Spirit is the life-giver who causes the sap of divine life to flow through us from Jesus the vine, its only source. The fruit will develop if we do not impede the flow of that sap. And the fruit will bear marked resemblance to those same virtues so perfectly exhibited in the life of our Lord, for they are the result of His life in us.

Every Spirit-baptized Christian should heed the warning of Jesus: "By their fruit you will recognize them" (Matt. 7:20, NIV), not by their charismatic gifts and miraculous works (Matt. 7:22). The proofs of being filled with the Holy Spirit are far more convincing in the area of His fruit than of His gifts.

## Sealed With the Holy Spirit—Ephesians 1:13–14

The first mention of the Holy Spirit in Ephesians, Paul's magnificent epistle about the doctrine of Christ's body, the church, concerns His work that seals Christians in that body. The time when this sealing takes place is said to be after we have believed the gospel. "In Him, you also, after listening to the message of truth, the gospel of your salvation—having also believed, you were sealed in Him with the Holy Spirit of promise" (v. 13). The sealing corresponds to the baptism in the promised Holy Spirit, not to the Spirit's coming in regeneration nor to water baptism as such (see the comments on Acts 1:4–8; 1 Corinthians 12:13; 2 Corinthians 1:21–22).

In those days owners often stamped their signet into the still-soft clay of a newly made storage jar or of the clay lid (jar stopper). The impression left by the signet "sealed" the jar, clearly marking it and its future contents as the possession of the person making the impression. The seal, however, did not cause ownership; it only recognized ownership.

Similarly, Christ sent His Spirit to come upon His disciples and to endue them with the same supernatural power that characterized His own ministry, thus making them His witnesses (Luke 24:49; Acts 1:8). The Spirit, therefore, in one or more of His various manifestations (as in 1 Corinthians 12–14) is the immediate divine evidence that Christians belong to the Lord. They are marked as His "peculiar people" (KJV), meaning His very own special possession (Titus 2:14; 1 Pet. 2:9).

As Stanley Horton has said, the seal is not an invisible designation; it is certainly something more than the inward act of believing. Because baptism in the Holy Spirit was the normal experience of Christians in New Testament times, Paul saw all believers as having had that experience and as therefore sealed with the Spirit.[67]

Perhaps the twelve Ephesian disciples of Acts 19:1–7 were among those who heard this epistle read aloud when it reached the church in Ephesus. The Greek word *pisteusantes*, "after that ye believed" (Eph. 1:13, KJV), would have reminded them of the same word in Paul's initial question to them eight or ten years earlier: "Did you receive the Holy Spirit after you believed [*pisteusantes*]?" (Acts 19:2, author's translation). They would have remembered how Paul had instructed them to believe in Jesus and had baptized them in the name of the Lord Jesus.

They would have also remembered how, when Paul had laid his hands upon them, the Holy Spirit had fallen on them, and they had spoken in tongues and prophesied (see the comment on Acts 19:1–7). Their fellow Christians in the church would similarly have linked being sealed with Christ's Spirit to the time when the Spirit had come on *them*.

The Holy Spirit is given to believers as the earnest or pledge or first installment (*arrabōn*) of that full inheritance that will be ours on the day when God completes our redemption (see the comment on 2 Corinthians 1:21–22). By His continuing empowering in our lives He will be our seal until that time when even our bodies will be redeemed (Rom. 8:23), transformed to be like Christ's glorious resurrection body (Phil. 3:21). Therefore, during this present life we should not grieve Him (Eph. 4:30) nor act in any way out of harmony with Christ's mark of ownership upon us.

### The Unity of the Spirit—Ephesians 4:3–6

According to Paul, our duty as those who have been called to God in Christ is to keep or maintain the unity of the Spirit in the bond of peace. The apostle said in 4:3–6 that we must be diligent, we must do our very best to preserve the oneness that the Spirit produces by the peace that binds us together. The seven "ones" of verses 4–6 state what the unity of the Spirit consists of—or, to put it another way, what makes this oneness possible: Our unity is based on the fact of one body, one Spirit, one hope, one Lord, one faith, one baptism and one God and Father.

There is only one true spiritual *body*, the body of Christ, the church universal. It is one, even though it has many members. Jew and Gentile are made into a single new people by the reconciling work of Christ, so that all are fellow members of the one body (Eph. 2:14–19; 3:6; 4:12, 16; Col. 2:19; 3:15; Rom. 12:4–5; 1 Cor. 10:16–17; 12:12–26). In one sense the spiritual "body" is physical in that it is made up of people. People are visible and tangible. Thus the bodies of true believers are the physical manifestations of Christ in our space and time.

There is only one *Spirit*, the Holy Spirit. All Christians are regenerated by the same Spirit. He is the Comforter for all believers. Christ baptizes us in only one Spirit (1 Cor. 12:13). And the Holy Spirit is the same guarantee for all Christians of their future perfection and inheritance (Eph. 1:13–14).

There is only one *hope*, the blessed hope of the glorious return of our Lord and Savior, Christ Jesus (Titus 2:13). All Christians have this hope set before them when God calls them by His grace—the hope of sharing the glory of Christ, of relief from this present suffering and of the final redemption or resurrection of our bodies (Rom. 8:18–25).

There is only one *Lord* for all Christians, the Lord Jesus Christ (1 Cor. 8:5–6). Christ Himself has certainly never been divided (1 Cor. 1:13). He is the one head of the body (Eph. 1:22–23; 4:15; Col. 1:18; 2:19), the one commander-in-chief, who does not issue contradictory commands to His various servants. He is the one way to the Father (John 14:6; Eph. 2:18), and no one can be saved apart from Him (Acts 4:12).

There is only one *faith*. Subjectively, faith may denote the act and attitude of believing coupled with obedience (Rom. 1:5; 16:26; Heb. 5:9; 11:8; 1 Pet. 1:2). Objectively, it may mean what we believe, the substance of our belief. In the first sense, to be saved and become a Christian, each one must place his or her trust in Jesus Christ as Savior and Lord (Acts 16:31). In the second sense, there is only one faith by which God justifies both Jew and Gentile (Rom. 3:30), "the faith which was once for all delivered to the saints" (Jude 3).

There is one common *baptism* for all believers. It is true according to Hebrews 6:2 that Christians were given instructions regarding various baptisms (or washings, NAS). In Ephesians 4:5, however, Paul was obviously referring to

Christian baptism. During the apostolic period, the concept of one baptism probably included both water baptism and Spirit baptism, for no doubt these often occurred at the same time. One baptism, but with two aspects: baptism in water in the name of Jesus Christ (Acts 10:48), the humanly administered seal with reference to repentance and forgiveness of sins; and baptism in the Holy Spirit, the divinely administered seal with reference to Christ's one body (2 Cor. 1:21–22; Eph. 1:13–14; see the comment on 1 Corinthians 12:13).

F. F. Bruce, the outstanding British Bible scholar, has written some helpful notes on this matter:

> The baptism of the Spirit which it was our Lord's prerogative to impart took place primarily on the day of Pentecost when He poured forth "the promise of the Father" on His disciples and thus constituted them the Spirit-baptized fellowship of the people of God. Baptism in water continued to be the outward and visible sign by which individuals who believed the gospel, repented of their sins, and acknowledged Jesus as Lord, were publicly incorporated into this Spirit-baptized fellowship—"baptized into Christ" (Gal. 3:27). It must be remembered in New Testament times repentance and faith, regeneration and conversion, baptism in water, reception of the Holy Spirit, incorporation into Christ, admission to church fellowship and first communion were all parts of a single complex of events which took place within a very short time, and not always in a uniform order. Logically they were distinguishable, but in practice they were all bound up with the transition from the old life to the new.[68]

There is only one *God and Father* of all believers. Christian belief in the Trinity—one God eternally existing in three Persons—does not contradict the Old Testament doctrine of one God (Deut. 4:35, 39; 6:4; Mal. 2:10). Elsewhere in the New Testament, Christians from pagan backgrounds, who had formerly sacrificed to the idols of many gods, are reminded that there is no God but one, and that "for us there is but one God, the Father, from whom are all things, and we exist for Him" (1 Cor. 8:4–6).

Verses 4–6 may very well have been a primitive confession of faith. In it are the basic elements of true Christianity, the common ground of all Christians. In this context of oneness, there exists already a living fellowship in the spirit and by the Holy Spirit (2 Cor. 13:14; 1 John 1:3). This we are to maintain, even though all Christians have not yet "come in" (KJV; that is, attained to, arrived at) the unity of the faith (Eph. 4:13). We are to experience the living, vital unity of the Spirit with all true Christians now, even before we can agree on all points of doctrine.

We preserve the unity of the Spirit by giving careful attention to our own moral and spiritual behavior. We are to walk in a manner worthy of our having been called by God to be Christians. We are to conduct our lives "with all humility and gentleness, with patience, showing forbearance to one another in love" (Eph. 4:2).

## Grieve Not the Holy Spirit of God—Ephesians 4:30

The Bible warns of several ways in which people sin against the Holy Spirit. Some of these sins may be committed by Christians, while others are of such serious nature that they reveal the hopelessly lost condition of the person. They fall into three general categories according to the three areas of ministry of the Spirit of God regarding human beings—*with, in* and *upon*.

First, the Holy Spirit is *with* unregenerate human beings to restrain them and convict them of sin (John 16:8ff.) and to draw them to Christ. Those who balk at the tug of God in their hearts, because they love their darkness more than the light (John 3:19–20), try to turn off the convicting influence of the Spirit. They *resist* the Holy Spirit as the Jewish leaders did who heard Stephen make his magnificent defense of the faith (Acts 7:51). Those men were "cut to the quick" (NAS)—terribly convicted—and they gnashed their teeth at Stephen (7:54).

Others may go a step further and *insult* ("do despite unto," KJV) the Spirit of grace as they make fun of the blood of the covenant and "trample under foot the Son of God" (Heb. 10:29). Some may even go so far as to *blaspheme* against the Holy Spirit (Mark 3:29) by attributing the miraculous works of the Spirit of God to Satan, thus rejecting the evidence of His power. Such sin is unpardonable (see the comment on Matthew 12:22–37).

Second, the Holy Spirit is *in* believers to witness with their spirits that they are children of God (Rom. 8:14–17) and to develop the new nature of Christ in them. The Spirit of God dwells in the body of the believer—just as the Ark of the Covenant, which signified God's presence, remained in the inner sanctuary of the tabernacle, and later, of Solomon's temple. The work of the Holy Spirit in this respect is one of sanctification (see the comment on 1 Corinthians 6:11), for the temple of God must be kept holy in the New Testament dispensation as well as in the Old Testament.

The oracle room (1 Kings 6:19), also known as the inner sanctuary or the holiest of all (KJV), the most holy place (NIV) or the holy of holies (RSV, NAS, Heb.

9:3 and Exod. 26:33), was a quiet, private, holy place. No defiling thing was permitted to mar its beauty and sacredness as God's dwelling on earth.

The danger now is that the Christian can *grieve* the Holy One residing in His newly claimed temple (Eph. 4:30). The Holy Spirit is a person who is gentle as a dove and has feelings just as you and I do. As the Spirit of Christ in us (Rom. 8:9), He can be grieved, just as Jesus was grieved by the hardness of human hearts (Mark 3:5).

In Ephesians 4 and 5, Paul warned about certain specific forms of sin that disrupt the unity of the Spirit in the one body of Christ (4:3). All of these sins grieve the Holy Spirit and prevent our being filled and fully controlled by the Spirit (Eph. 5:18). They fall into three categories: *sins of speech*, or what we say; *sins of action*, or what we do; and *sins of attitude*, or what we think and feel.

*(1) Sins of speech.* We must put away lying or falsehood (Eph. 4:25) and speak the truth in love (4:15), for the Holy Spirit is the Spirit of *truth*. These commands obviously prohibit gossip and the spreading of rumors. No foul talk or rotten, unwholesome words should come out of our mouths, but only words that will edify (4:29). We must get rid of all clamor or quarreling, and slander or abusive language (4:31). We should never be accused of dirty stories, silly or flippant talk, or questionable jokes with a barb in them (5:4).

*(2) Sins of action.* "Do not participate in the unfruitful deeds of darkness, but instead even expose them" (Eph. 5:11). Stealing can no longer be a part of the Christian's life (4:28), and this includes robbing God of His tithe (Mal. 3:8–10) and of His glory (Isa. 42:8; 48:11), as well as stealing from others. Any type of sexual immorality or prostitution has absolutely no place (Eph. 5:3), as Paul makes clear again and again (compare 1 Corinthians 6:13–20; 1 Thessalonians 4:3–8). Drunkenness and dissipation such as the loose living of the prodigal son (Luke 15:13) also prevent the filling of the Holy Spirit (Eph. 5:18).

*(3) Sins of attitude.* Bitterness and malice (Eph. 4:31) certainly grieve the Spirit, named as they are immediately after Paul's command in 4:30. Resentment, spite and grudges come under this category. A Christian husband can become embittered against his wife (Col. 3:19). With or without realizing it, he may project on her the frustrations and hostilities that he feels toward his life situation and "take it out" on the one he married. The Spirit is grieved, and they can no longer pray together effectively (1 Pet. 3:7).

Paul includes here wrath and anger—and hot tempers (Eph. 4:31)! Covetousness or greed (5:3) is a distinct problem for us today because we live in a materialistic society. It is a common manifestation of selfishness, which is the essence of sin. And if we grieve our Christian brothers and sisters in our lack of concern about their feelings and scruples, we are not walking according to love (Rom. 14:15). Therefore we grieve the Spirit and destroy the relationship of unity.

In the Old Testament we are told that the children of Israel grieved the Holy Spirit (Isa. 63:10). When they rebelled against the Lord's leading them through the hot Sinai desert, they grieved (offended; "vexed," KJV) His Spirit. They quickly turned their hearts against the Lord, even though He had so recently saved them from their bondage in Egypt and redeemed them in His love and compassion (63:7–9).

The lesson is obvious for us: We can stubbornly refuse to follow God's guiding hand even though we are known as His people today. Furthermore, just as the Israelites often complained, grumbled and lusted after the fleshpots back in Egypt (Exod. 16:2–8; Num. 11:1–6), so Christians may live "after the flesh," under the control of the old, selfish nature, rather than submitting to the control of the Spirit (Rom. 8:5–8).

Third, the Holy Spirit is *upon* Spirit-baptized believers to empower them for witness and ministry. Paul issued another specific command that applies to this aspect of the Spirit's work: "Do not quench the Spirit" (1 Thess. 5:19; see the comment there). To quench means to stifle or suppress, or to put out a fire.

We may quench the Spirit in ourselves when we stifle His inner voice prompting us to witness. God has built into us a sensitivity to Him that can be quenched. We put out His fire if we neglect to stir up the charismatic gift He has placed within us (see the comment on 2 Timothy 1:6–7), perhaps through lack of faith to trust the Spirit to use us.

Similarly, we quench the Spirit by not employing our charismatic gift to serve one another (see the comment on 1 Peter 4:10–11) or by abusing the gifts in not using them to edify one another (see the comment on 1 Corinthians 14). Another form of this sin is the neglect of praying in the Spirit (see the comment on Romans 8:23–27). Finally, believers may quench the Holy Spirit's moving upon them by not worshiping by the Spirit of God (Phil. 3:3) and serving in His power, but instead worshiping and serving in dead works (Heb. 9:14), works performed in their own strength and ability.

We also quench the Holy Spirit if we hinder someone else who is manifesting Him as He operates charismatically through that individual. Many have sinned against God's Spirit by teaching that spiritual gifts such as speaking in tongues and healing are not meant for this period of church history. Certainly the Spirit is quenched when His good gifts are called psychological aberrations or satanic counterfeits.

To sum up, we should not grieve the Holy Spirit with whom we were sealed while we await the day of our completed redemption. We must not profane this seal or sign of the New Covenant, being warned by Israel's example who through disobedience and idolatry kept on profaning the sabbath sign of the Old Covenant with impunity (Ezek. 20:12–13, 16, 21, 24; compare Isaiah 56:2, 6).

## Be Filled With the Spirit—Ephesians 5:15–21

Paul's command in Ephesians 5:15–18 is one of the key principles for victorious Christian living: "Be filled with the Spirit." It is not merely a teaching or an exhortation, but a precept for the believer's daily conduct. We find it embedded among other precepts and rules directing our walk in love and self-control, so these five words should never be construed as an excuse for loosing the Christian life from the moorings of all holy restraints and disciplined order under the guise of "being free in the Spirit."

The command to be filled with the Spirit comes after the seventh occurrence of the verb "walk" in this epistle. Paul had written that Christians are created in Christ Jesus for good works that we should *walk* in them (Eph. 2:10), insisting that his readers should *walk* in a manner worthy of their Christian calling (4:1), not *walk* as the Gentiles *walk* with darkened minds (4:17–19), *walk* in love (5:2), and *walk* as children of light (5:8; see also 2:10). He had just penned the command to be careful how they *walk*, not as unwise men and women, but as wise (v. 15).

They were to redeem the time, or as the NEB renders it, "use the present opportunity to the full" (v. 16). They were to understand (gain insight into) what the will of the Lord was (v. 17). Certainly His will included being filled with the Spirit!

In verse 18 Paul intentionally contrasted the artificial and degrading stimulation of drunkenness with the divine enthusiasm of the Spirit. Perhaps he had in mind that on the Day of Pentecost the disciples, who were newly baptized in the Holy Spirit, were scoffingly accused of being drunk (Acts 2:13). Intoxication was common in Greek and Roman society, and these pagans sometimes went to the extreme of confusing its accompanying excitement of emotion and wit with divine inspiration, as in the frenzied worship of Dionysius or Bacchus. The Christian, however, was to seek a loftier inspiration!

Recklessness and self-abandonment accompany intoxication, and this leads to the involuntary stimulation of the sensual and passionate elements of the old nature. But the Holy Spirit produces self-control and appeals to the new nature without forcing us against our own will. Wine in excess debases and destroys; the Spirit of God ennobles and edifies. Instead of dissipation (see also Titus 1:6; 1 Peter 4:3–4), as in the case of the prodigal son (Luke 15:13), the Spirit brings holiness and Godlikeness.

The word for "excess" or "dissipation" is *asōtia*, the character of one who is un-savable (from an old form of the verb *sōzō*, to save, deliver). In their despair, alcoholics seem unable to be saved or delivered; they are often incorrigible. But the Holy Spirit effects deliverance of all areas of our lives to make us whole persons.

As Jonathan Edwards, the great Reformed theologian of colonial America, said in a sermon on this verse, there may be excess in wine, but we cannot be too filled with the Spirit! Likewise, there may be undue emotionalism in some charismatic meetings. But this is a human reaction, not the direct working of the Holy Spirit; for He produces self-control in all things, including worship and praise.

In discussing the exact meaning of the words "be filled with the Spirit" (Greek *plērousthe en pneumati*), some scholars believe Paul meant "to be filled in one's human spirit" in contrast to being intoxicated in mind and body. But Paul used the phrase *en pneumati* ("in the Spirit," without the definite article in Greek) three other times in this letter (Eph. 2:22; 3:5; 6:18) and once in Colossians (1:8). These verses show the phrase means that the personal working of the Holy Spirit is in view, that is, what the Spirit produces. Therefore it means "by the Spirit" in the sense of the work of the Spirit as a personal agent—not "with the Spirit" in the sense of the Spirit's being a substance like a liquid beverage.

People are said to be filled with wine when they are completely under its influence. Similarly, the Bible says they are filled with or rather by the Spirit when He controls all their thoughts, feelings, words and actions. Therefore verse 18 commands the believer to be controlled by the Spirit, to live and walk always under His influence.

Handley C. G. Moule, the warmhearted Anglican bishop of Durham in the early years of this century, explained that the fullness of the Spirit is a super-natural thing: "It is a state of man wholly unattainable by training, by reasoning, by human wish and will. It is nothing less than—God in command and control of man's whole life, flowing everywhere into it, that He may flow fully and freely out of it."[69] (For further discussion of the meaning of "filled," see the comment on Acts 4:8.)

We should note four grammatical characteristics of the Greek verb *plērousthe*, "be filled." First, it is an imperative, a command, not an optional matter. Second, it is plural, indicating that the command is meant for all, universal in application. It is not a privilege to be enjoyed by a few elite Christians but is the duty of every believer.

Third, it is passive, showing that we cannot fill ourselves with the Spirit—we must let Him fill us. Yet we are not purely inactive in receiving the Spirit's fullness, anymore than in getting drunk. A person gets drunk by drinking; even so, we receive the Spirit by drinking (see the comment on John 7:37–39).

Finally, the verb is in the present tense, teaching us that being filled with the Spirit is a continuous (or repetitive) process. We were baptized and sealed in the Spirit once; we are to be continually controlled by the Spirit at all times. This means that we must continually yield to His direction and control and repeatedly appropriate His supplies of grace and power.

We can benefit from comparing verse 18 with the parallel passage in Colossians 3:16. Paul wrote both these epistles while he was under guard in his rented quarters in Rome (Acts 28:30), and they display interesting similarities and differences of expressions.

In Colossians, instead of commanding, "Be filled with the Spirit," Paul wrote, "Let the word of Christ richly dwell within you." The remainder of Colossians 3:16 is similar to Ephesians 5:19–20. So we may conclude that an integral part of being filled with the Spirit is to know especially the New Testament thoroughly and to memorize as much as possible of it so that the Holy Spirit can use the Word He inspired to guide us.

In verses 19–21 four clauses follow the command about the Holy Spirit. In each the verb or verbs appear as a participle: speaking, singing and making melody, giving thanks, and submitting yourselves. These are evidences or results of the fullness of the Spirit. The *continual* evidence of His filling is moral, seen in the fruit of the Spirit (see the comment on Galatians 5:22–23). The *occasional* evidence is miraculous, seen in the gifts of the Spirit that He distributes only when a need arises. (See the comments on 1 Corinthians 12–14 and 1 Corinthians 12:4–11. One of the best discussions of verses 19–21 is to be found in the booklet by John R. W. Stott entitled *The Baptism and Fullness of the Holy Spirit;* many of the following thoughts are from his writing.)[70]

The consequences of being filled with the Spirit are to be found in intelligent, controlled, healthy relationships with God and with other Christians. The Spirit's control results in genuine worship of God and in spiritual fellowship with our brothers and sisters.

The first of the four evidences stated in this passage is "speaking to yourselves in psalms and hymns and spiritual songs." This does not refer to talking to ourselves, rather to conversing with one another—that is, having Christian fellowship. As Stott reminds us, however deep and intimate our communion with God may seem, we cannot claim to be filled with the Spirit if we are not on speaking terms with our Christian acquaintances.

Even so, such fellowship centers around the Lord. The Living Bible paraphrases the clause in this way: "Talk with each other much about the Lord, quoting psalms and hymns and singing sacred songs." Note how God takes delight in our having such fellowship together according to Malachi 3:16: "Then those who feared the Lord spoke to one another, and the Lord gave attention and heard it."

In the centuries prior to the invention of the printing press and the mass distribution of inexpensive Scriptures in the languages of the people, often the only portions of God's Word that Christians of even average means knew were those they had learned in the music of the church. Words and phrases from their psalms, hymns and spiritual songs would season their speech like salt (compare Colossians 4:6). Thus even in their everyday conversation with other Spirit-filled believers, as well as in times of actual worship, their talk would be that of spiritual devotion and thankfulness.

The parallel part of Colossians 3:16 is enlightening: "With all wisdom teaching and admonishing one another with psalms and hymns and spiritual songs." This reveals that the speech of early Christians—and ours today—was to be good for edification according to the need of the moment, that it might impart grace to those who hear (Eph. 4:29).

The "psalms" were almost certainly the canonical Old Testament psalms sung to instrumental accompaniment. The "hymns" may denote Christian compositions sung with or without music. "Spiritual songs" (*ōdais pneumatikais*) were those inspired on the spot by the Holy Spirit, unpremeditated words with unrehearsed melodies sung "in the Spirit," whether in tongues or in the language of the congregation. Writing before the twentieth century, when the Lord has been restoring charismatic singing in churches of the West, the Scottish theologian S. D. F. Salmond concluded that there were also *Christian* psalms:

> [These were] psalms which the Holy Spirit moved the primitive Christians to utter when they came together in worship (1 Cor. 14:15, 26), as He moved them to speak with tongues (Acts 2:4; 10:46; 19:6). It is probable, therefore, that these are intended here; especially in view of what has been said of being "filled by the Spirit."[71]

The origin of chants in the church before the time of Constantine may well lie in this type of "singing in the Spirit."

The second evidence of the Spirit's fullness is "singing and making melody in your heart to the Lord" (Eph. 5:19, KJV; compare NIV). The rendition of the RSV, "making melody to the Lord with all your heart," brings out the proper idea here. The Holy Spirit came to glorify the Lord Jesus and so manifests Him to His people that they delight to sing His praises.[72]

The early Christians knew what it was like to worship under persecution. The younger Pliny, as the Roman governor of Bithynia, was ordered by the emperor Trajan to stamp out the Christians there. In a letter (written A.D. 112) he reported that they were in the habit of assembling on an appointed day (Sunday) before sunrise and singing responsively "a song to Christ as to God." Writing in North Africa around A.D. 200, Tertullian described the Christian love feast as a time when "each is invited to sing to God in the presence of others from what he knows of the holy scripture or from his own heart."[73]

The third evidence of Spirit-filled believers is that they are "always giving thanks for all things in the name of our Lord Jesus Christ to God, even the Father." Paul himself was an outstanding example of one who thanked God for *all* things, manifesting joy as he did in prison and in all his afflictions. So his exhortations to "rejoice in the Lord" (Phil. 4:4), "rejoice always," and "in everything give thanks" (1 Thess. 5:16, 18) cannot be easily dismissed as beautiful but impossible idealism.

Such thankfulness *is* possible when the Spirit fills us. But whenever we start grumbling and complaining, it is proof positive that we are *not* filled with the Spirit.[74]

The fourth mark of the Spirit's fullness refers again to our relationships with one another. The first was speaking to one another; now it is being "subject to one another in the fear of Christ" (v. 21). In the following verses, the apostle went on to describe in detail the submission of a wife to her husband, children to their parents, and slaves to their masters (5:22–6:9). But here he listed the attitude of sweet yieldedness to others in the church as the hallmark of a Christian filled with the Spirit.

In this passage Paul listed some of the wholesome results of the fullness of the Spirit in everyday living. If we are filled with the Spirit, we shall be praising and worshiping the Lord Jesus and thanking the Father for everything and speaking helpfully and submitting to one another. These right relationships with God and others are lasting evidences of the Spirit's control.

Do you ask how to be filled with the Spirit, how to maintain such fullness or how to receive a fresh empowering by the Spirit? The answer must be, as for every aspect of the Christian life and walk, *by faith.* Paul made it clear to the Galatian believers that just as they had received the promised Spirit by faith (Gal. 3:2, 14), so they were continually supplied with the Spirit by faith, even for the working of miracles in their midst (3:5; see the comment on Galatians 3:2–5, 14). The continual filling of the Holy Spirit, as well as our initial reception of Him, is based on our believing God that He *does* fill and control us by His Spirit.

At the same time, we must recognize that the Holy Spirit is a person. This means that we must consciously yield to His control, just as we deliberately submit to one another. He who continually indwells us as believers responds from within us to fill us at our daily—yes, moment by moment—invitation. Praise is an excellent way to activate our wills to desire and seek for His constant supervision.

Again, we need to realize that all the fullness is to be found in Christ (Col. 1:19; 2:9–10; John 1:16). It is Jesus our Lord who fills His body with His fullness (Eph. 1:23). So our attention must remain centered on Him and should not be diverted by an unbalanced interest in the Holy Spirit. Jesus said that the Spirit of truth would not come to speak of Himself or on His own authority (RSV) or initiative (NAS), but to glorify the Son (John 16:13–14). The more we are in love with our precious Lord, the more filled we are with His Spirit.

## The Sword of the Spirit—Ephesians 6:17

The only weapon listed in the description of the Christian's armor in Ephesians 6:10–20 is a sword. All the other pieces are for our protection against the powers of darkness. "The sword of the Spirit," which Paul explained as being the Word of God, is the only combat equipment included for striking a blow to defeat the devil.

This sword is one that the Spirit of God supplies. Therefore, it is not "carnal" or physical, not a material weapon. Since He is the one who provides it and enables us to wield it, this sword is invincible. It is one of our divinely powerful weapons for the destruction of Satan's fortresses (2 Cor. 10:4).

Yet we must look to the Lord to train our hands in how to use this sword and to teach our fingers how to fight (Ps. 18:34; 144:1). We need to become proficient in spiritual warfare, even as David's mighty men (1 Chron. 12) and Solomon's royal bodyguard were experts in military warfare (Song of Sol. 3:7–8).

What is the meaning of the figurative expression "the sword of the Spirit"? Paul said it is "the word of God" (*rhēma theou*). This term differs in Greek from the same English expression in a somewhat similar statement in Hebrews 4:12: "For the word of God (*ho logos tou theou*) is living and active and sharper than any two-edged sword." Did the writers of the New Testament recognize a clear-cut difference in meaning between *logos* and *rhēma,* as many contemporary Christians teach?

First of all, the concept of the spoken word as a weapon appears a number of times in the Bible. Isaiah predicted that the Servant of the Lord (Christ) would say, "He made my mouth like a sharpened sword" (Isa. 49:2, NIV). Paul foretold the defeat of the "man of lawlessness," "whom the Lord will slay with the breath [or "Spirit," *pneuma*] of His mouth" (2 Thess. 2:8; compare Isaiah 11:4).

Again, in the Book of the Revelation the exalted Lord Jesus was seen in His role as judge, "out of [whose] mouth came a sharp two-edged sword" (1:16). In 2:16 He warned the church in Smyrna about false teachers: "I will make war against them with the sword of My mouth." And in chapter 19 He is pictured as returning from heaven on a white horse, "and from His mouth comes a sharp sword, so that with it He may smite the nations" (19:15).

In Hosea 6:5 Yahweh earlier had described in this way His actions against those who violated His covenant (v. 7): "Therefore I have hewn them in pieces by the prophets; I have slain them by the words of My mouth." Prophetic messages of judgment were undoubtedly in view here, which the Septuagint translation sums up collectively by the singular Greek expression "the word (*rhēma*) of My mouth." We can conclude from the foregoing verses that on occasion God's spoken word acts as a sword, "because it bears the power of His Spirit."[75]

In the New Testament *rhēma is* used mostly for individual spoken utterances (for example, John 5:47; 6:63; Acts 10:44; 28:25). But it can refer to each Old Testament passage as though proceeding from the mouth of God Himself: Jesus said, "It is written, 'Man shall not live on bread alone, but on every word [*rhēma*] that proceeds out of the mouth of God'" (Matt. 4:4, citing Deuteronomy 8:3). The word *rhēma* is found in Luke 3:2 as the same word-event formula that occurs over 120 times in prophetic passages of the Old Testament: "the word of God came to John [the Baptist]" (Greek *egeneto rhēma theou epi Ioannen*).

Peter revealed another use of *rhēma*. After writing that we have been born again through the living, enduring word (*logos*) of God, he quoted Isaiah 40:6ff. from the Septuagint, ending with the line, "But the word [*rhēma*] of the Lord abides forever." Then he explained: "That word [*rhēma*] *is* the good news which was preached to you" (1 Pet. 1:23–25, RSV). Peter seemed to be using *logos* and *rhēma* as synonymous terms to refer to the gospel.

Continuing with a study of *rhēma* in the New Testament, we read in Hebrews 11:3 (NIV) that the universe was formed "at God's command" (or, "by the word of God," *rhēmati theou*). All of the creative command statements of God in Genesis 1 were summed up as one *rhēma* of God. The Son of God is said in Hebrews 1:3 to uphold all things by the word of His power (*tō rhēmati tēs dunameōs autou*).

Paul cited Deuteronomy 30:14, "The word [*to rhēma*] is very near you, in your mouth and in your heart," and explained that this word is the word of faith (*to rhēma tēs pisteōs*) that he was proclaiming (Rom. 10:8)—namely, how to be saved (10:9–10). Later in the same chapter the apostle stated that faith comes from hearing the message, and the message is heard through the word (*rhēma*) of Christ (10:17, NIV)—that is, the gospel concerning Him.

In Ephesians 6:17 the term *rhēma theou* may designate either the gospel message that God has given; the entire prophetic word that is found in both the Old and New Testaments; the divinely powerful creative word; the dynamic sustaining word that God sends forth from His mouth and that does not return to Him unfulfilled (Isa. 55:11); or a short declaration coming from

God through prophesying. In this last sense the *rhēma* would be a specific rebuke of the enemy as spoken by the Spirit through the mouth of a Christian.

An utterance from God supplied directly and immediately by the Holy Spirit becomes the sword that can rout the devil and his demonic forces. Also, the gift of prophecy, manifested through the power of the Spirit, can reveal the secrets of a person's heart and humble him or her before God (1 Cor. 14:24–25). A word of wisdom or of knowledge spoken in love with charismatic force can pierce the resistance of hardened sinners and bring deliverance to their captive souls (compare 2 Timothy 2:24–26).

We need to beware of making too great a distinction between *rhēma* and *logos*. Within charismatic circles in recent years some have formulated a special doctrine that makes a *rhēma* word more directive or helpful to us personally than the rest of holy Scripture (but see 2 Timothy 3:14–17). The two Greek words are sometimes used interchangeably (for example, Acts 16:36 uses *logos* and 16:38 uses *rhēma*). The *logos* word is also living and active and incisive (Heb. 4:12), and it, too, often refers to spoken words (for example, Matthew 8:8; 22:46; Luke 7:7; John 2:22; 18:32; 1 Corinthians 4:19; 1 Thessalonians 1:5).

We must recognize as well that the usage of *logos* and *rhema* in the Septuagint translation of the Old Testament is what primarily informed the early Christians about the similar theological meaning of the two words. In the Septuagint there seems to be no special distinction in the theological uses of the terms. Since the terms are largely interchangeable when referring to the Word of God, we should not claim that any part of holy Scripture is a special *rhēma* word to us as opposed to the more general Word (*logos*) of God.

The important thing to remember is that whether "the word of God" in Ephesians 6:17 is a specific charismatic utterance or a portion of the entire written Word (the Bible), it becomes effective against the devil only when we direct it at him in the authority of Christ and in the power of the Spirit (see the comment on Revelation 12:9–11).

Martin Luther made this fact vivid in his hymn "A Mighty Fortress Is Our God" (excerpts from verses 3 and 4):

> The prince of darkness grim,
> We tremble not for him;
> His rage we can endure,
> For lo! his doom is sure,
> One little word shall fell him.

That word above all earthly powers,
No thanks to them, abideth;
The Spirit and the gifts are ours
Through Him who with us sideth.

## Do Not Quench the Spirit—1 Thessalonians 5:19

Paul's command not to quench the Spirit is given in the midst of a number of brief directives that all Spirit-filled Christians should follow: They should continually manifest joy (1 Thess. 5:16), which is a fruit of the Spirit (Gal. 5:22). They can pray without letup (1 Thess. 5:17), both in their native language and in tongues (1 Cor. 14:14–15). In addition, the Spirit enables them to pray when they do not know how to pray as they should (Rom. 8:26–27). And another mark of being filled with the Spirit is to give thanks in everything (1 Thess. 5:18; Eph. 5:18, 20).

For charismatic believers 1 Thessalonians 5:19–22 are especially pertinent verses because it is possible for us to quench the Holy Spirit in ourselves or in other Christians. That is, we can extinguish the flame or put out the fire of the Spirit (see how the Greek verb *sbennumi* for "quench" is used in Matthew 12:20; Mark 9:48; Ephesians 6:16; Hebrews 11:34).

Through harsh criticism, for example, we may pour cold water on the Spirit as He is manifested through a charismatic gift in someone else. Or we may stifle or suppress the prompting of the Spirit to manifest a gift through us. Paul indicated that at Thessalonica there were some who quenched the Spirit by despising prophetic utterances (1 Thess. 5:20).

In Matthew 25:8 the Greek verb for "quench" appears in the words of the foolish virgins who said, "Our lamps are going out." Thus by neglecting to "stir up" our gift, we may simply let the fire of the Spirit die down, which had formerly been burning brightly in our hearts (see the comments on Ephesians 4:30; 2 Timothy 1:6–7).

The instructions in 1 Thessalonians 5:19–22 have a general application in all areas of the Christian walk. But they are particularly relevant to the meetings of believers when the gifts of the Spirit are manifested. We have clear-cut responsibility to "prove" or examine every manifestation of the Spirit.

Paul taught in 1 Corinthians 14:29 that, when a prophet speaks, the others are to "judge" or discern whether it is a genuine prophecy by manifesting the gift of the discerning of spirits (see also the comment on 1 John 4:1–6). If the message is in agreement with the written Word of God, it is a good prophecy, and we should hold fast to it and not quench the Spirit by ignoring it. As the NEB translates 1 Thessalonians 5:19–22, "Do not stifle inspiration, and do not despise prophetic utterances, but bring them all to the test and then keep what is good in them and avoid the bad of whatever kind."

## The Restrainer of the Man of Lawlessness— 2 Thessalonians 2:6–8

The Thessalonian Christians were wrongly being led to believe that the eschatological period known as the Day of the Lord was already present (2 Thess. 2:2). This would have meant that the Lord Jesus Christ had arrived in the first stage of His coming (Greek *parousia*, 2:1) to gather His saints to Himself (1 Thess. 4:15–17). Because the Thessalonians had not been taken into His physical presence, they were alarmed to think that they had been left behind to undergo the fearful sufferings of the Great Tribulation.

Paul corrected this error by reminding them of certain key events that had to take place in relationship to Christ's second coming. In Greek literature the word *parousia*, literally "presence," could refer both to the initial arrival as well as the subsequent presence of a person; it became the official term for visits of kings and emperors to one of their provinces.[76]

The "Day of the Lord" is not a single event, but a period when God in His wrath will judge sin far more directly than through present natural calamities, and when He will wonderfully deliver and bless His people by the return of Christ. That "day" cannot be in progress unless the "falling away" (Greek *apostasia*) as its first *event* and the revealing of the "man of lawlessness" as the next distinct event have come to pass.

While many have fallen away from the faith ever since apostolic times (Heb. 3:12; 1 Tim. 4:1; 2 Tim. 3:1–9; 4:3–4), the particular event Paul referred to here is the final and complete apostasy. This will be the deliberate and official denial of the doctrine of Christ and the worldwide suppression of all organized Christianity. As long as there are true believers on earth openly and publicly worshiping the Lord Jesus Christ together, the great apostasy has not begun.

The "man of lawlessness" ("man of sin," KJV) is further described as "the son of perdition," the man doomed to destruction (NIV, v. 3). So complete is his revolt against God that by nature he is doomed to eternal loss and ruin. "He sets himself in opposition to anyone bearing the name of God, or anything that people worship; indeed, he exalts himself above all such, going so far as to enthrone himself in the temple of God and proclaim that he himself is God" (2 Thess. 2:4, Bruce's translation).[77] He is Satan's man (2 Thess. 2:9–10), known also as the Antichrist (1 John 2:18) and the beast (Rev. 13:1–10).

At present, however, Satan is being restrained from bringing his man on the stage of history. Paul said that the Thessalonian believers knew the force that "withholds" or "restrains" the Antichrist so that he would be revealed in his own time, the time appointed by God, and not prematurely. In verse 6 (KJV), "what withholdeth" (*to katechon*) is a neuter participle; in verse 7, "he who now letteth" (*ho katechon*) is a masculine participle of the same verb meaning to restrain or hold back.

Both participles are in the present tense, indicating that the restraining force is already active. It is keeping under control the "mystery of iniquity" that is also already at work. The latter expression denotes the spirit of lawlessness, which Satan is currently promoting and which will dominate the career of the man of lawlessness.

The big question that Bible commentators have about this passage is the identification of the power that exercises the restraint at present. According to Paul's words, the restrainer is both a principle and a person; he is well known to the readers; and he is more powerful than Satan, since he is able to hold back the efforts of the devil.

Many commentators have explained the restrainer as the principle of human government—manifest in Paul's day as the Roman state and its head, the emperor. Such government maintains law and order so that the church may fulfill its great commission to evangelize the world (Rom. 13:1–7). No human government, however, is stronger than Satan himself. Furthermore, human government will not be removed during the Tribulation period, for when the Antichrist gains worldwide control he will establish a super-government, not anarchy.

Only a supernatural person can effectively thwart the supernatural operations of the devil. Therefore, the restrainer must be God Himself. In particular, the Holy Spirit is in view. The use of the neuter participle in verse 6 may be accounted for by the fact that the Greek word *pneuma* for "spirit" is neuter. Yet the masculine gender in verse 7 would point either to the Spirit Himself as a Person or to the individual Spirit-filled believer in this age, acting as the salt of the earth to preserve human society from the full effects of lawlessness (Matt. 5:13).

The restrainer will continue his work "until he is taken out of the way," literally "until he gets himself, withdraws himself out of the midst" (*heos ek mesou genetai*). The fact that the restrainer will be "out of the midst" points to one who is now "in the midst." This also suggests the Holy Spirit who is now resident in the saints on earth.

The Spirit's restraining ministry through the church will be "out of the way"—no longer "in the way" of Antichrist—after Christ returns to take His church to Himself. The Holy Spirit will continue to be present in the world until that time. Many will be convicted of sin by the Spirit and led to Christ during part of the Tribulation (Rev. 7:13–14), and He will enable believers to give answer when on trial for their faith (Mark 13:11).

Another possible interpretation of the last clause of verse 7, "until he is taken out of the way," is that the "he" refers to "the lawless one" of verse 8. He is the Antichrist, the beast who "arises out of the midst" (one possible translation of verse 7) of wicked human civilization, the "sea" of Revelation 13:1 and Isaiah 57:20. The Holy Spirit, according to this view, will continue His present work of restraining unabated lawlessness until the Antichrist "arises out of the midst" and achieves a total takeover of the world system. At that point God's Spirit will cease to restrain wickedness (see the comment on Genesis 6:3).

## Do Not Neglect the Spiritual Gift Within You—1 Timothy 4:14

Paul's command to Timothy not to neglect the gift within him is an important command to every Spirit-baptized Christian, for the word "gift" is the Greek word *charisma*. All Spirit-baptized believers are assigned at least one charismatic gift as the frequent manifestation of the Holy Spirit in their lives, and they are to use it as a good steward (see 1 Peter 4:10–11 and the comment there).

Paul reminded Timothy how he had received his spiritual ministry. It was given to him through prophetic utterance with the laying on of hands of the presbytery. The occasion may have been Timothy's ordination to the special ministry to which Paul assigned him at Ephesus (1 Tim. 1:3). His task, like that of Titus on Crete, was to help organize and supervise the work of the churches in the province of Asia, to teach sound doctrine, and to refute certain heretical teachers whose errors were threatening to corrupt the churches.

At that time various prophecies were made concerning Timothy that encouraged him to fight well in the war against wickedness and to hold firmly to the faith (1 Tim. 1:18–19). One of the prophecies to Timothy no doubt revealed the nature of the charismatic ministry being bestowed upon him and perhaps how he should exercise it.

The gift was imparted in connection with the laying on of hands by the presbytery, the local body of elders. Perhaps these were the elders of the church at Ephesus whom Paul had so lovingly addressed on his third missionary journey (Acts 20:17–38). Their hands placed on Timothy's head symbolized the fact that a spiritual ministry was being communicated to Timothy; but they did not actually confer the gift, for it was given merely "with" (*meta*), not "by," the laying on of their hands.

Paul was also present at the ceremony, because he says in 2 Timothy 1:6 that Timothy had received the "gift" of God (a *charisma* of the Holy Spirit) "through (*dia*) the laying on of my hands," indicating that Paul was the chief intermediate agent. So as the first among equals (*primus inter pares*), Paul evidently exercised the decisive role as the channel of God's power in the consecration service; but Timothy was installed with the full sanction of the local church leaders at Ephesus. (See the comment on 2 Timothy 1:6–7; for the laying on of hands, see the comment on Acts 6:6.)

We are not told what Timothy's charismatic gift was. Presumably he had much earlier spoken in tongues following his baptism in the Spirit. Here the *charisma* was probably a spiritual endowment to enable him to perform his special work as an evangelist (2 Tim. 4:5) and to oversee the churches. It has also been suggested that it was a gift of teaching (1 Cor. 12:28; Rom. 12:7) or of "government" or administration (1 Cor. 12:28; 1 Tim. 5:17) to guide the churches in Asia, or a special ability to discern the spirits of error that were motivating the false teachers (1 Tim. 4:1–3; 1 Cor. 12:10; 1 John 4:1–6).

Paul urged Timothy not to forget and leave unused this special ministry he had within him for his public ministry of reading Scripture, of exhortation and of teaching (1 Tim. 4:13). Such God-given enablement is not a charm that works automatically. It requires human cooperation for its full exercise (compare Philippians 2:12–13; 2 Timothy 1:6). To neglect such a gift of God is a sin. The Living Bible paraphrase of 1 Timothy 4:15 lets us feel Paul's concern for his son in the Lord: "Put these abilities to work; throw yourself into your tasks so that everyone may notice your improvement and progress."

## *Stir Up the Gift of God—2 Timothy 1:6–7*

The last letter we have from Paul, from a dungeon in Rome as he awaited execution, was written to his beloved spiritual son Timothy. The old veteran of the gospel was familiar with Timothy's cautious and somewhat timid temperament. He realized what a blow the news of his impending death would be to his affectionate disciple. So he exhorted Timothy not to lose heart, but to be zealous, unashamed, and loyal to the gospel as persecutions grew hotter.

Paul's very first concern was to remind Timothy to stir up the gift of God, the *charisma* that he received at the time he was set apart for his special mission at Ephesus. (For the nature of Timothy's charismatic gift and its bestowal, see the comment above on 1 Timothy 4:14.) The verb "to stir up," *anazōpurein*, occurs only here in the New Testament. It means to rekindle or fan into flame. The present tense of the infinitive indicates that Paul was telling Timothy to keep the gift blazing.

By resisting the promptings of the Holy Spirit within us, we can quench the Spirit and His charismatic manifestation (1 Thess. 5:19). Paul did not necessarily imply that Timothy had altogether stopped administering the gift, but as a father he was appealing to his son to be constantly at work manifesting it in the face of suffering and serious difficulty.

Our incentive to use our charismatic gifts with burning zeal is the Holy Spirit Himself, whom God has given us. He is not a spirit of fear, cowardice or timidity so that we shrink back and let our fire go out. "For you have not received a spirit of slavery leading to fear again" (Rom. 8:15). Instead it is His Spirit who "fills us with power, love and self-control" (2 Tim. 1:7, TEV).

The Holy Spirit supplies *power* (*dunamis*) to overcome the wicked one, to witness concerning our risen Lord to all people, and to minister to the needs of other Christians as well as those who are not yet saved. This aspect of the Spirit's work in us may be compared with the dynamic functioning of the body of Christ by means of the spiritual gifts of 1 Corinthians 12.

The Holy Spirit also supplies *love*, the *agapē* love that Paul so beautifully described in 1 Corinthians 13. It is a self-forgetting love for Christ, for fellow believers and for all people.

The third quality the Spirit produces is a *sound mind*. The Greek word here, *sōphronismos*, implies prudence, self-control, self-discipline, a sense of responsibility under pressure and opposition that enables us to keep a clear head. It is the quality that is needed to maintain balance and order, not only in our personal lives, but also in the local congregation and in its meetings when each believer may share something to edify the others (1 Cor. 14).

By aggressive energy in the face of difficulty, by self-denying love and thoughtfulness, and by self-discipline, the Spirit of God enables each Christian to overcome his or her tendency to cowardice. He strengthens the child of God to work, to endure and even to die for Christ's sake if need be. This was the supply that Paul counted on when he testified, "I can do all things through Him who strengthens me" (Phil. 4:13). "For the Holy Spirit, God's gift, does not want you to be afraid of people, but to be wise and strong, and to love them and enjoy being with them. If you will stir up this inner power, you will never be afraid to tell others about our Lord" (2 Tim. 1:7–8, TLB).

## Renewing by the Holy Spirit—Titus 3:4–7

Paul's epistle to Titus contains two beautiful descriptions of salvation as the foundation for all Christian conduct. In Titus 2:11–14 he stated that salvation is made available to every human being. It is freely provided on the basis of God's grace as shown in Jesus Christ, "who gave Himself for us, that He might redeem us from every lawless deed and purify for Himself a people for His own possession, zealous for good deeds." We are to say *no* to worldly desires while we wait expectantly for "the blessed hope—the glorious appearing of our great God and Savior, Jesus Christ" (2:13, NIV).

Paul next described how Christians ought to act toward all people (Titus 3:1–3). Godly conduct should be inspired as we recollect how we ourselves were once as bad as anyone else (3:3) and how God in His kindness and mercy saved us (3:4–5). God actively intervened in our lives.

Thus the cause for the moral and spiritual transformation in us believers is not to be found in ourselves. It is not on the basis of any deeds that we performed in the realm of righteousness. Rather salvation reaches us through the initial washing of regeneration and the continuing process of renewing by the Holy Spirit (v. 5).

The term *washing* (*loutron*) does not refer to a laver or place of washing, as some writers have suggested, but to the moral and spiritual bath at the time of conversion. It is the divine work of cleansing that accompanies regeneration. Our Lord explained this to Nicodemus as being "born of water and the Spirit" (John 3:5). The sinner is forgiven and cleansed by the blood of Christ as he or she responds to the convicting message and the promise of salvation in the Word of God. At the same time, the person is regenerated or made spiritually alive by the Spirit of God (see the comment on John 3:1–8).

In writing to the Ephesians, Paul viewed the initial cleansing from another aspect. There he stated that Christ gave Himself up for the church in order that He might ultimately and completely sanctify her, "having cleansed her with the washing of the water [symbolized in baptism] in connection with a spoken word [of confession and testimony]" (Eph. 5:26, author's translation). Paul was briefly referring to the proper human response to the justifying work of Christ: Having repented, new believers through water baptism wash away the stain on their character left by past sins (Acts 22:16), and on that same occasion they vocally confess their newfound faith in Christ.

In other passages the renewing that the Holy Spirit accomplishes in the believer seems to be a phase of His progressive work of sanctification. Paul taught that the new "man" or new nature "is constantly being renewed until it attains fulness of knowledge after the image of its Creator" (Col. 3:10, Bruce's translation), and that "our inner man is being renewed day by day" (2 Cor. 4:16).

The present tense of the command "Be transformed by the renewing of your mind" (Rom. 12:2) also suggests that the work of renewal is still going on in order to complete the good work of Christ already begun in us (Phil. 1:6). Paul likewise stated that we are being transformed into the very image or likeness of our dear Lord (including both His moral character and His mighty works of ministry), from one degree of glory to another, "even as by the Spirit of the Lord" (2 Cor. 3:18, KJV; on sanctification, see the comment on 1 Corinthians 6:11).

Returning to Titus 3:6, we are also reminded of the Pentecostal outpouring of the Spirit, for the Greek word *ekcheō* for "shed" (KJV) is the same verb translated "pour out" or "shed" in Acts 2:17–18, 33; 10:45. Here the abundance or richness of God's precious gift sent to us through Jesus Christ our Savior is brought out. God planned for the baptism in the Spirit to be an integral part of the total salvation of all believers.

Professor C. L. Holman of Regent University has shown convincingly from this passage in Titus that the Pentecostal outpouring of the Holy Spirit was experienced and taught, not only in Crete where Titus was, but throughout Christendom in the formative years of the early church.[78] In this passage we can see that all three Persons of the Trinity are active to make that wonderful salvation ours!

## God's Joint Witness—Hebrews 2:1–4

The first of the warning passages in the epistle to the Hebrews points out to professing Christians the danger of drifting away from and neglecting our great salvation. Our message, it says, is far greater than the word received by Moses, and every transgression and disobedience even of that Law received a just retribution. Whereas God gave the Sinaitic law through angels to Moses for the nation of Israel (Acts 7:53; Gal. 3:19), the gospel of salvation was spoken to human beings directly by the Lord (that is, Jesus), God Himself manifested in human flesh.

The message of salvation is also extremely important because of the unusual nature of its confirmation. At the first, it was confirmed by the evidence of eyewitnesses, by those who actually heard Christ. But God Himself joins in the witness "by signs and wonders and various miracles and by gifts of the Holy Spirit distributed according to his own will" (v. 4, RSV).

The Greek participle *sunepimarturountos* is in the present tense and literally means "jointly bearing witness," not merely with the apostles but with Christians in all centuries of church history. The Living Bible brings out this truth in paraphrase: "God always has shown us that these messages are true by signs and wonders and various miracles and by giving certain special abilities from the Holy Spirit to those who believe; yes, God has assigned such gifts to each of us."

While the word for "gifts" of the Holy Spirit is not *charismata* but *merismoi*, this latter term (literally meaning "distributions") emphasizes that the gifts are not of human appointing but are wholly according to God's pleasure (compare 1 Corinthians 12:11). In Romans 12:3, where Paul wrote that God has "dealt" or allotted to each Christian a measure of faith, the verb is from the same root as the noun *merismos*. When properly translated and understood, Hebrews 2:4 gives strong testimony to the fact that miracles and gifts of the Spirit had not ceased in the latter part of the apostolic age.

## Partakers of the Holy Spirit—Hebrews 6:4–6

Theologians have argued throughout the history of the church over whether the persons described in Hebrews 6:4–5 are truly regenerate and whether a born-again person can lose his or her salvation. The writer of this epistle was urging his readers, who were Jewish Christians, to go on from the doctrines and rituals of the Old Testament and of Judaism to maturity in Christ. But some had fallen away (v. 6)—that is, they had committed apostasy. They had become enemies of Christ; they were crucifying the Son of God again, as far as they were concerned, and were putting Him to open shame (the Greek words here are present-tense participles). As long as they persisted in their active hostility to Christ, it was morally and spiritually impossible to renew them again to repentance by any human agency.[79]

The author used strong terms to describe the former spiritual condition of the apostates. They had "once been enlightened," had "tasted of the heavenly gift," had "been made partakers of the Holy Spirit" and had "tasted the good word of God and the powers of the age to come." But then they had "fallen away" (vv. 4–6).

They had been "illuminated" (the same Greek word as in Hebrews 10:32) by the light of the gospel of Christ shining in their hearts (2 Cor. 4:4, 6). They had had a taste of the supernatural gift (*dōrea*) of salvation and life in Christ (John 4:10; Rom. 5:17).

They had even been made sharers or partners of the Holy Spirit. The Greek word *metochous* means real sharers, those who participate in the object. The same word was used in Hebrews 3:1, where the recipients of the epistle are said to be "partakers of the heavenly calling"; in Hebrews 3:14, "For we have become partakers of Christ"; and in Hebrews 12:8, which says that all true children of God are partakers of His chastening. The word was also used in the sense of associate or partner in Hebrews 1:9 ("companions") and Luke 5:7. In every case, personal involvement is indicated.

Before falling by the wayside, the apostates had also "tasted the good word of God and the powers of the age to come" (Heb. 6:5). They had experienced how good God's spoken word (*rhēma*) is in prophecy and as the sword of the Spirit in overcoming the devil (Eph. 6:17). Or perhaps the "good word of God" may simply be another expression for the "good news" or gospel message. They had also received or performed miracles, the powers that even now are a foretaste of the coming age of Christ's kingdom on earth.

Hebrews 6:6 may be taken in conjunction with the warning in Hebrews 10:29: "How much severer punishment do you think he will deserve who has trampled under foot the Son of God . . . and has insulted the Spirit of grace?" Together, the verses suggest that those people were as guilty of blaspheming the Holy Spirit as were the Pharisees who ridiculed Jesus' ministry of exorcism (see the comment on Matthew 12:22–37). Theirs was a deliberate and persistent rejection of Christ's witness, not the isolated act of a moment without premeditation.

Those who fell away seemed to be Christians. Whether they were actually born again or whether they had a superficial experience of Christianity like the "stony ground" believers of Matthew 13:5–6, 20–21, God alone knows. The remarks of Harold Lindsell are pertinent here:

> Whichever view we adopt of the apostate man prior to his apostasy, the outcome is virtually the same. That is to say, if a man openly rejects Jesus Christ, he is, in either view, to be regarded as an unregenerate, unsaved man, even though he had formerly appeared to human observers to be converted. The Arminian would say that he had lost his salvation; the Calvinist that he had never had it, but the result is identical.[80]

On the basis of their experience, the writer of the epistle to the Hebrews was warning his readers of the real danger of not holding fast their confession (4:14; 10:23) and of throwing away their confidence and shrinking back (10:35–39). He sought to awaken them to the peril of sloth and urged them to be diligent "so as to realize the full assurance of hope until the end" (6:11–12).

Andrew Murray has given some priceless remarks on the matter of our assurance in commenting on Hebrews 6:4–8:

> The only sure sign that the perseverance of the saints will be ours is—perseverance in sainthood, in sanctification and obedience. "We are His house[-hold], we are become partakers of Christ, if we hold fast, firm unto the end" [Heb. 3:6]. My assurance of salvation is not something I can carry with me as a railroad ticket or a bank note, to be used as occasion calls. No, God's seal to my soul is the Holy Spirit; it is in a life in the Spirit that my safety lies; it is when I am led by the Spirit that the Spirit bears witness with my spirit, and that I can cry Abba, Father (Rom. 8:14–16). Jesus not only gives [life], but is Himself our life. *My assurance of salvation is alone to be found in the living fellowship with the living Jesus in love and obedience* [italics his].[81]

## God's Jealous Yearning Over His Spirit—James 4:5

James 4:5 is a difficult verse to translate. The KJV, NEB, NIV and other versions give similar renderings that have the text referring to the human spirit (which God at the creation of Adam implanted and caused to live in each human being) turning to envious desires as a result of the fall of humankind. The NIV text note, the RSV and the NAS, however, bring out quite a different meaning:

"Or do you suppose it is in vain that the scripture says, 'He yearns jealously over the spirit which He has made to dwell in us'?" (RSV); and "He jealously desires the Spirit which He has made to dwell in us" (NAS). If this latter translation portrays the idea James had in mind, then verse 5 is the only passage in the Book of James that mentions the Holy Spirit.

James quoted no one verse of the Old Testament. But a number of passages speak of the Lord as a jealous God who will not permit His people to worship any other god (Exod. 20:5; 34:14; Deut. 4:24; 32:16) and speak of His jealousy for Zion (Zech. 8:2). By participating in any idolatrous practices, Christians also may provoke the Lord to jealousy (1 Cor. 10:22).

God has betrothed us to Himself (Hos. 2:19) and will tolerate no rival for our affections. According to Zephaniah (3:17), Yahweh will rejoice over His people with gladness and "rest in His love" (KJV), or better, "soothe" (TAN) or "quiet [us] with His love" (NIV). His love for us is everlasting (Jer. 31:3), and nothing can make Him forget us (Isa. 49:15, 16).

The Holy Spirit dwelling in Christians is grieved when we prove unfaithful to Christ, our bridegroom and Lord (see the comment on Ephesians 4:30). When we love the world and have friendship with it (James 4:4; 1 John 2:15–17), we show a divided allegiance and thereby offend God. He yearns over us with a deep godly jealousy to have us completely for Himself. Our Creator-Redeemer-King cannot be content with a love triangle.

### The Early and the Latter Rain—James 5:7

"Be patient, therefore, brethren, until the coming of the Lord. Behold, the farmer waits for the precious fruit of the earth, being patient over it until it receives the early and the late rain" (James 5:7, RSV).

In 5:1–11, James sought to prepare his readers for the Second Coming of Christ. First (vv. 1–6), he warned those nominal Christians who had become wealthy by cheating their employees. He mocked their accumulation of riches and said, "It is in the last days that you have stored up your treasure!" (v. 3).

Next, he urged the godly believers to exercise patience as a farmer does while they wait for the coming (Greek *parousia*) of the Lord and to establish their hearts—to strengthen and confirm them in the final certainty—for His return was "at hand," imminent (vv. 7–8). They were not to complain about each other, for the great Judge Himself is standing at the very door of heaven, waiting to come and do whatever criticizing must be done (v. 9, TLB). Instead they were to endure suffering just as Job and the prophets did (vv. 10–11).

The illustration of the farmer waiting patiently for the early and latter rain was drawn from the Palestinian agricultural scene. In that region the early or autumn rain (mid-October to mid-December) softens the ground for plowing and waters the freshly seeded fields. The latter or spring rain (late February to early April) brings the grain to full growth. Barley is harvested in April and May, and wheat in May and June.

God had made this promise to the Israelites before they crossed into Canaan if they would obey His commands: "I will give the rain for your land in its season, the early and late rain, that you may gather in your grain and your new wine and your [olive] oil" (Deut. 11:14; compare Jeremiah 5:24; Proverbs 16:15; Zechariah 10:1). A few verses before his prophecy of the outpouring of the Spirit, Joel said that God would pour down the early and the latter rain as before (Joel 2:23; see the comment on Joel 2:28–32). And in a beautiful prophecy of the coming of the Lord, Hosea exhorted God's people, "So let us know, let us press on to know the Lord. His going forth is as certain as the dawn; and He will come to us like the rain, like the spring rain watering the earth" (Hos. 6:3).

In describing the history of the church, many Bible teachers have compared the outpouring of the Spirit at Pentecost and in the succeeding years to the early rain. Likewise, a commentary published over a century ago stated, "The latter rain that shall precede the coming spiritual harvest, will probably be another Pentecost-like effusion of the Holy Ghost."[82]

The twentieth century seems to be in the time of the latter rain. The return of the Lord Jesus, therefore, must be very near; as we wait for His coming, we are privileged to engage actively in the great End-Time harvest that will complete the church. In this way we may actually hasten the coming of the day of God (2 Pet. 3:12).[83]

## The Prayer of Faith—James 5:13–20

When the Lord Jesus Christ returned to heaven, He sent the Holy Spirit to continue His work of saving the lost and healing the sick. In James 5:13–20 specific provision is made for His ministry of divine healing to be conducted in each local church. Employing this scriptural order of prayer for the sick would eliminate the opportunity for cultists and charlatan faith healers to make merchandise of God's people.

The primary intention of this passage is to provide physical healing and spiritual restoration for "anyone among you" (v. 13), for everyone who has professed faith in the Lord Jesus Christ. Other passages such as Mark 16:17–18 extend the healing ministry to help people who have not yet believed.

The two Greek words for "sick" in verses 14 and 15 indicate a serious affliction. In verse 14 the word is *asthenei*, from the root word most frequently used in the New Testament to refer to sickness. It denotes bodily weakness as a result of the infirmity and is the term used of the "impotent" man in John 5:7. He had been an invalid for thirty-eight years. Such a person has no power within himself or herself for recovery.

The word in verse 15 is *kamnonta*, suggesting a person who is worn out, wasting away and hopelessly sick. Christians who are sick, however, are to ask for prayer that they might be healed, not that they might receive a last rite administered only when a person is dying.

As we apply these instructions to today, we should keep in mind first of all that James has very clearly placed the responsibility upon the sick person. That person is to call for the elders of his or her local church to perform the service of anointing and prayer. This is a definite command, as the imperative mood of the verb in verse 14 indicates. It is not the duty of the elders to go scouting for the sick. Such a call gives evidence that the afflicted person has faith that the Lord will heal him or her.

If the sick person is bedfast, that one is to call the elders to come to the bedside. If they do not bear the title of "elder," they should be prominent leaders in the local congregation. Personal uprightness and special ability should characterize these people, since these qualifications are among those that Scripture gives for an elder.

Being members of the same church, the ones called to pray will have opportunity to know the sick person, his or her testimony, the nature of the illness, and whether personal sin is a factor in the case. Likewise, the sick person will know the elders to be ordinary people. When healing comes, the person healed will give *God* the glory. Because two or more were involved in praying, none will be able to claim they have supernatural power in themselves in order to enhance their own reputation.

Before the prayer the sick person should be given opportunity to confess any known sins ("sins," v. 15, and "faults," v. 16, are the same Greek word, *hamartias*). It is no mercy to the sufferer to omit this step in hoping to avoid embarrassment, for guilt troubling the conscience may have triggered the sickness. It is always God's will to forgive confessed sins (1 John 1:9) and to grant spiritual healing.

The practice of confessing and forsaking sins that are already known in the church and of praying for one another goes far toward clearing away hostilities and resentments and allowing healing to begin in sick bodies and souls. This practice also promotes the spiritual health of the whole Christian community.

It is important to take time to inspire in the patient expectancy and trust in the Lord before the anointing and prayer. Scripture passages about healing and personal testimonies may be shared. We can encourage the person to stand upon the promises of God's Word. And we can instruct the sick to release their faith and receive the healing when they are touched with the oil and receive the elders' prayer.

After the patients' confession and after instructing them in the Word, the elders are to anoint them with oil. This follows a practice that Jesus' own disciples used (Mark 6:13). Because olive oil is a symbol of the Holy Spirit in the Bible (see chapter one), the oil is used as an aid to faith, not for any possible therapeutic value (although some scholars believe oil was used as a salve or primitive medicine on the basis of Isaiah 1:6 and Luke 10:34).

Today, the usual custom is to touch the forehead of the sick person with the oil. The name of the Lord is the authority by which the elders are to perform this rite. Thus the healing of the believer is placed into the all-powerful hands of God. Yet the purpose of the service should not be construed to rule out medical help as the means that God will use. Paul did not forbid the services of a doctor, for he spoke of Luke as "the beloved physician" in one of his later epistles (Col. 4:14).

Having anointed the person, all the elders present are to pray, "and the prayer of faith shall save the sick, and the Lord shall raise him up" (v. 15, KJV). The Greek reads literally, "the prayer of the faith." The definite article used with the word "faith" may imply here that their prayers are inspired by a manifestation of the charismatic gift of faith (1 Cor. 12:9; see the comment on 1 Corinthians 12:4–11).

James elaborated on the prayer of faith by adding, "The effectual fervent prayer of a righteous man availeth much" (v. 16, KJV). The single Greek word for "effectual fervent" (*energoumenē*) signifies that the prayer is "energized" or wrought within each elder by the Holy Spirit. This is "praying in the Spirit" (Eph. 6:18; Jude 20). Such a prayer accomplishes much, because God is the energizer (compare Philippians 2:13).

Elijah prayed this kind of prayer, and James reminded us that he was "a man with a nature like ours." His prayers were remarkably answered, not because he was a super-saint, but because God at work in him produced powerful prayer. The elders, therefore, should wait on the Lord until He enables them to pray the prayer of faith with utmost boldness and assurance.

Along with the gift of faith, other charismatic gifts may come into operation to strengthen the prayer of faith. A word of knowledge (1 Cor. 12:8) may have revealed to one of the elders the nature of the illness or its underlying cause, even before the sick person calls for them to come. This will give the sufferer great assurance and faith to reach out and receive the healing. Even at the bedside, one of the elders may receive a word of knowledge or of wisdom to detect some forgotten sin or subconscious harmful attitude that is blocking the healing and restoration. Of course, one of the gifts of healing may also be manifested along with the anointing with oil.

When the scriptural order has been followed, the promise of healing is unconditional: "The Lord shall raise him up." All healing comes from God, no matter what aids to faith are used or who offers the prayers or what spiritual gifts are exercised. The Lord may heal with or without medical attention. He may do so instantly or over a period of time. The words "shall raise up" do not indicate how soon the healing will take place, but they do guarantee God will act (see the comment on Matthew 8:14–17).

We have no scriptural warrant to end a healing prayer with the faith-undermining phrase, "if it be Thy will." Where healing does not come, it is evidence that those involved did not follow the divinely ordained procedure or pray a Spirit-given prayer of faith or that some hidden sin has not yet been truly confessed.

The ultimate purpose in this service of anointing and prayer is suggested in verses 19 and 20. It is to reach the hearts of professing believers and deal with sins in their lives. If a Christian has erred or wandered from the truth, such a service of confession and prayer may be the means of "converting" or turning that person back from the error of his or her way and saving the person's soul from eternal death. Those ministering will invoke the blood of Christ, and the sins of the restored brother or sister will be "covered" and forgiven.

## A Holy Priesthood Offering Up Spiritual Sacrifices— 1 Peter 2:5–9

In the apostle Peter's first letter he beautifully portrayed the responsibilities and privileges of all Christians as priests of the living God. He explained in 2:4 that in our continual coming or drawing near (*proserchomenoi*, the same Greek word as in Hebrews 4:16; 10:1, 22) to Christ, the living, life-giving stone, we also as living stones "are being built up as a spiritual house for a holy priesthood, to offer up spiritual sacrifices acceptable to God through Jesus Christ" (v. 5).

Peter may well have had in mind the Lord's words to him, "You are Peter [*Petros*, a stone], and upon this rock [*petra*, a rock formation, bedrock] I will build My church" (Matt. 16:18). Note that Peter made Christ, not himself, pre-eminent in the constructing of the spiritual house that is the church universal. The apostle emphasized the corporate aspect of our Christian worship; for the "spiritual" house or temple (1 Pet. 2:5) is the *community* of believers as in Ephesians 2:20–22, not the individual as in 1 Corinthians 6:19.

God's dwelling on earth in this dispensation is not a single physical structure but a worldwide spiritual habitation in the combined body of all believers. Furthermore, there is not a select priesthood from the members of one tribe, but the entire "nation" of Christians is chosen and holy; and all believers constitute a holy, royal priesthood, "the King's priests" (v. 9, TEV). Jesus Christ has made us to be "priests to His God and Father" (Rev. 1:6), prophesied long before by Isaiah (61:6; 66:21).

During this age the church is replacing Israel as God's kingdom of priests and holy nation (compare Exodus 19:6). It is our duty to announce His salvation to all peoples and to "proclaim the excellencies of Him who has called you out of darkness into His marvelous light" (1 Pet. 2:9).

Part of our priestly function is to offer up spiritual sacrifices to God. Imperfect as our worship and service may be, they are made acceptable and well-pleasing to Him, because they are offered through Jesus Christ. They derive all their worth from our high priest who presents them to God and with whose one perfect sacrifice they are combined. According to Philippians 3:3, we worship, we render sacred service (Greek *latreuontes*), by the Spirit of God. We may sing, pray and bless God in the spirit as well as with the mind (1 Cor. 14:14–16).

Through the Lord Jesus we are to offer up a "sacrifice of praise to God continually, that is, the fruit of our lips giving thanks to his name" (Heb. 13:15, KJV;

compare Isaiah 57:19; Hosea 14:2). In the Psalms we often read about the sacrifice of thanksgiving (Ps. 50:14; 107:22; 116:17). We may sing with all our hearts to the Lord in psalms and hymns and spiritual or charismatic songs (see the comment on Ephesians 5:15–21). Acts of self-dedication and faith are also spoken of as sacrifices (Rom. 12:1; 2 Cor. 8:5; Phil. 2:17). In fact, no sacrifice can be considered spiritual without self-surrender and obedience (1 Sam. 15:22).

In addition to praise and prayer, material gifts may be sacrifices that are pleasing to God (Heb. 13:16; Phil. 4:18). Paul even included the people that he had won to Christ as an acceptable offering to the Lord. He said that God's grace had made him "a minister of Christ Jesus to the Gentiles"; his "priestly service" was the preaching of the gospel of God, and it fell to him "to offer the Gentiles to him as an acceptable sacrifice, consecrated by the Holy Spirit" (Rom. 15:16, NEB). May we as priests bring similar offerings to our precious Lord and Savior.

## Preaching to the Spirits in Prison—1 Peter 3:18–20

According to the NIV translation of 3:18, Christ "died for sins once for all . . . He was put to death in the body [*sarki*], but made alive by the Spirit [*pneumati*]." Similarly, Hebrews 9:14 speaks of Christ "who through the eternal Spirit [*dia pneumatos aioniou*] offered Himself without blemish to God." Because God is eternally the one infinite Spirit-being, the phrase "eternal spirit" may refer to Christ's truly divine spiritual nature. This nature was conjoined with His humanity, His "flesh" (*sarx*), as verses 3 and 4 of Romans 1 indicate.

Yet there is also "a dynamic identification (but not a personal identity) of the Lord Jesus with the Spirit, inasmuch as the Spirit proceeds from Jesus risen," to give George Montague's helpful explanation[84] (see the comment on John 20:21–23). The Bible says that God by His Spirit raised Jesus from the dead (Acts 2:24; Rom. 8:11). The Spirit is also the "power" enabling Christ to exercise His eternal priesthood, including the offering of Himself as the all-sufficient sacrifice (Heb. 9:11–14). Furthermore, in contrast to the first man Adam, who was given a natural or human body and soul, Christ is far superior, because He became life-giving Spirit (1 Cor. 15:45, TLB).

From this discussion and from what follows it is clear that Jesus did not "die spiritually" on the cross so that He was no longer deity, and He did not lose His dynamic identification with the Spirit of God. This teaching in some circles of the Charismatic movement claims that Jesus as a man needed to be "born again" in hell (Hades) in order to overcome Satan there. It is a modern twist of the ancient Gnostic heresy that the Christ-Spirit who descended in the form of a dove on Jesus at His baptism left Him before His crucifixion. This twist is an instance of the antichrist "spirit of error" that John condemned in his first epistle (see the comments on 1 John 4:1–6).

Verse 19 in 1 Peter 3 should be translated as follows: "at which time also He went and made proclamation to the spirits in prison" (author's translation). Who were the spirits? Verse 20 states that they were disobedient during the days when Noah was constructing the ark. Therefore, many have taught that they are departed souls of the humans who drowned in the worldwide flood. But there is no trace of evidence in the New Testament that the simple term *spirits* is ever used to connote departed human spirits. In Hebrews 12:23 the term is qualified: "the spirits of righteous men made perfect."

On the other hand, there is ample evidence, both in Jewish theology of that period and in the New Testament itself (Matt. 8:16; 12:45; Luke 10:20; 1 John 4:1; plus the many verses mentioning evil spirits, seducing spirits, and so on), that Peter could have been referring to evil spirits. The "prison" he mentioned must be the realm known as Hades, "the Abyss" where Christ commanded the evil spirits to go (Luke 8:31, NIV, also RSV, NAS, where KJV has "the deep"; in Revelation 9:1–2, 11 and 20:1, 3, the "abyss" is called the "bottomless pit" in the KJV). Elsewhere, Peter wrote about angels that had sinned, whom God cast down to hell and committed to pits of darkness, reserved for judgment (2 Pet. 2:4; compare Jude 6).

Why did Christ preach to those particular evil spirits? First of all, He did not preach the gospel to them, for the verb *made proclamation* (from Greek *kerussō*) has other meanings than "to evangelize." After He finished His twofold work on the cross of dying to save humankind from its sins and of defeating Satan (John 12:31; Heb. 2:14), Christ, the victor, descended to hell (Hades) to proclaim His universal triumph. As Paul described it, by His cross Christ "despoiled the cosmic powers and authorities and boldly made a spectacle of them, leading them as captives in his triumphal procession" (Col. 2:15, NEB margin).

According to this interpretation, the victorious Christ singled out the evil spirits who were disobedient in Noah's time, probably because they were the ones who masterminded the corruption and wickedness of practically the whole human race before the flood. That was the worst period of violence and opposition to God's rule that the world has ever seen, even up to our time.

Therefore, the spirits responsible for it were brought under condemnation along with all humanity except for Noah and his household (see the comment on Genesis 6:3).

Peter's statement does not teach that unrepentant souls will have a chance to hear the gospel of salvation preached to them after death. Hebrews 9:27 clearly says that it is appointed or destined for man to die once, and after death comes judgment.

What Peter wrote in the next chapter (1 Pet. 4:6) does not contradict this. There he said that the lascivious, idolatrous heathen will have to give an account to God who is ready to judge the living and the dead (1 Pet. 4:3–5). "But for this reason the gospel was preached [during their lifetime] to those [past members of the church] who are [now] dead, that though they were judged as [all] men are in the body [by physical death], they may keep on living eternally, as God does, in the spirit" (1 Pet. 4:6; see the NEB, AMP and NIV, which reflect this interpretation). They heard the gospel and accepted Christ as their sin-bearer while alive, so that after death they would not have to suffer eternal punishment.

## Administering Your Charismatic Gift—1 Peter 4:10–11

In many respects 1 Peter 4:7–11 is similar to Romans 12. Both passages talk about a sober, serious-minded attitude, about prayer, about genuine, fervent love (charity) and about uncomplaining hospitality. In addition, both Peter and Paul urged every Christian to exercise his or her charismatic gift, for the word "gifts" in Romans 12:6 and "special gift" in 1 Peter 4:10 (NAS) is the Greek *charisma*. Peter wrote:

> As each one has received a special gift, employ it in serving one another, as good stewards of the manifold grace of God. Whoever speaks, let him speak, as it were, the utterances of God; whoever serves, let him do so as by the strength which God supplies; so that in all things God may be glorified through Jesus Christ.

In the early church every Christian was assumed to have been baptized in the Holy Spirit concurrent with (for example, Cornelius, Acts 10:44–48) or soon after conversion (see the comments on Acts 19:1–7; 1 Corinthians 12:13) and therefore to have been given "the manifestation of the Spirit for the common good" (1 Cor. 12:7). "The Spirit's gifts . . . are the common property of the Christian community, each Christian being but a steward for the edifying of the whole, not manifesting the gift merely for his own use."[85] As fellow members of a local church, we are to administer our measure of God's grace to one another, so that the body may be built up in love and be knit together "by that which every joint supplies" (Eph. 4:16). We must not bury our talent or gift, as the slothful servant did in Jesus' parable (Matt. 25:24–30).

Peter classified charismatic gifts in two main categories, gifts of speaking and gifts of ministering or serving. He instructed the person who speaks in the Spirit, such as a prophet or someone interpreting a message in tongues or a teacher manifesting a word of knowledge in the church assembly, to speak with sincerity and dignity. He desired that what that person said be as "the very words of God" (4:11, NIV), "as the oracles of God" (KJV), as His "utterances" (NAS).

In the only other New Testament passages where this Greek term *logia theou* occurs (Acts 7:38; Rom. 3:2; Heb. 5:12), it refers to the Old Testament inspired writings, the written Word of God. Those in the congregation who hear the divinely inspired spoken message should treat it with similar seriousness. "Do not despise prophetic utterances," wrote Paul (1 Thess. 5:20).

Whoever ministers to other members of the body through miracles or gifts of healings, helps, ruling or administrating, giving, or showing mercy (1 Cor. 12:28–29; Rom. 12:7–8), let that one do so as out of the large supply of strength that God furnishes abundantly (AMP). May every precious saint who feels called by God to such a ministry, but who is hindered by bodily weakness or illness, claim this provision. God's supplies are unlimited! But all is to be done to the glory of God, the true motive for all Spirit-filled service.

## The Certainty of the Prophetic Word—2 Peter 1:19–21

As he neared the end of his life, Peter was deeply concerned about the growing spirit of lawlessness and skepticism toward Christ's second coming (2 Pet. 3:2–4). He and the other apostles had been making known "the power and coming of our Lord Jesus Christ" (2 Pet. 1:16; compare Matthew 24:30). He denied the charge that the apostles followed cleverly devised stories; for the false teachers were maintaining that the gospel miracles were only allegories or fictional tales with a spiritual truth.

No—Peter, James and John had actually been eyewitnesses at the preview of Jesus' coming majesty and glory, for they were present at His transfiguration (Matt. 17:1–8). At that time they had heard God's voice from heaven, "This is my beloved Son, in whom I am well pleased" (2 Pet. 1:16–18, KJV).

Moreover, wrote Peter, they had something even more certain and valid to counteract false teaching than the voice of God heard with the natural ear, and that was the word of prophecy in the Scripture. "And we possess the prophetic word as something altogether reliable" (v. 19).[86] The apostles uniformly agreed in holding the writings of the Old Testament prophets to be most trustworthy. Peter earlier had recognized that the Spirit of the coming Messiah working in (*en*; or "with") the prophets had predicted the sufferings of Christ and the glories that would follow (1 Pet. 1:10–11).

Montague has developed the significance of Peter's statement about the Spirit of Christ in 1 Peter 1:11:

> The glorification of Jesus in His resurrection-ascension is thus the implicit link which makes it possible to say that the Spirit of God is the Spirit of Christ and to attribute all the activities of the Spirit, even Old Testament prophecy, to the Spirit of Christ. The prophetic spirit and the spirit upon the Messiah are totally identified. The continuity of the New Testament with the Old is thus assured not only because the same God speaks in both but also because the same Spirit acts in both.[87]

The writer of the epistle to the Hebrews also recognized that it is the Holy Spirit who is speaking and teaching us in the Old Testament Scriptures (Heb. 3:7; 9:8; 10:15).

Peter therefore advised his readers to pay attention in their hearts to prophecy, as a person depends on a lamp shining in a dark, murky place. The prophetic word will continue to guide God's people to the end of the age, until the day of Christ's return dawns and the morning star arises (Rev. 2:28; 22:16; compare Malachi 4:2; Luke 1:78). "For the day has already dawned in the heart of believers; what they wait for is its visible manifestation at Christ's coming."[88]

Why are the prophecies in the Bible the most dependable revelation from God that we have available today? The answer is given in verses 20 and 21: "You must understand that no prophecy of Scripture came about by the prophet's own interpretation. For prophecy never had its origin in the will of man, but men spoke from God as they were carried along by the Holy Spirit" (NIV).

The Greek noun in verse 20 for "interpretation" is from the same root word as the verb "expound" or "explain" in Mark 4:34. The KJV phrase "of any private interpretation" implies that the interpretation of the Word of God is not a matter of our own personal explanation (see also RSV, NAS, NEB, JB, TEV). Because of the overall context in verses 16–21, however, the TLB and NIV sense seems more correct that no prophecy originated through *the prophet's* own human understanding of things.[89]

Nevertheless, we have no more right to interpret Scripture according to our whim than the prophets did to add their own ideas to what God had told them. The false teachers were already misinterpreting the epistles of Paul and the rest of the Scriptures to their own ruin (2 Pet. 3:16; compare 2 Corinthians 2:17).

We need a reliable teacher to explain God's Word correctly. This teacher, ultimately, is the Holy Spirit, who has been sent to guide us into all the truth (John 16:13; see the comment on John 14:15–18 and following). As Johann Gerhard (1582–1637) once said, "He who is the author of Scripture is its supreme interpreter."

The Spirit may give direct understanding of a passage by the anointing that enables all believers to know the truth (see the comment on 1 John 2:20, 27). Or He may use a Spirit-filled teacher to "open" the Scripture (Luke 24:27, 32, 45) as Philip guided the Ethiopian eunuch (Acts 8:30–35), as Priscilla and Aquila explained the way of God more accurately to Apollos (Acts 18:26), and as Paul expounded the kingdom of God to the Jews in Rome (Acts 28:23).

The Bible is to be understood in its natural or literal sense and in its proper context. We should not allegorize and transform events and doctrines into myths and symbols so that we evade the plain sense of the passage. Because the divine revelation in the Scriptures is cumulative and never contradictory, one passage illumines the meaning of another. The Bible is "a single book with a single Author, a perfect unity growing out of its integrating theme, Jesus Christ."[90]

The author's declaration in 2 Peter 1:21 is a forthright statement regarding the origin and authorship of the prophetic Word. The Amplified Bible helps to bring out the meaning of this verse: "For no prophecy ever originated because some man willed it . . . it never came by human impulse—but as men spoke from God who were borne along (moved and impelled) by the Holy Spirit."

The word *moved* means "carried along as a ship by the wind" (Acts 27:15, 17). Here the Spirit is the wind. The prophets spoke from God, as spokespersons of God, not by their own will. The initiative lay with God.

Verse 21 reveals that Scripture is simultaneously the product of both divine and human authorship. Peter was already recognizing Paul's letters as being part of the "Scriptures" (2 Pet. 3:15–16), so that both Old Testament and New Testament are included in this term (also for the New Testament compare 1 Timothy 5:18b with Luke 10:7). Paul declared that all Scripture is inspired by God (2 Tim. 3:16), thus asserting the plenary or complete inspiration of the writings. Here Peter asserted the inspiration of the writers.

But what does divine inspiration imply in the twin processes of revealing and recording God's Word? In what manner and to what extent did the Holy Spirit stimulate and control the human authors?

The charismatic gift of prophecy in its manifestation is illustrative to a lesser degree of the *complete* inspiration and supervision that the writing prophets experienced. Prophesying is a matter of yielding to the Spirit's guiding control, while at the same time it is a harmonious cooperation as a person uses his or her own vocabulary, grammatical style, inflection and gestures. The writers of Scripture may be compared with the first violinist or concertmaster, playing with individual style and skill in a symphony orchestra that is conducted in person by the composer of the music. A Paul retained his individuality and made use of his literary capabilities, as distinct from those of a John or a Peter.

The work of inspiration guarded the writers from any and every error in recording the direct revelation of God to them and in employing eyewitness reports (Luke 1:1–4) and historical sources such as genealogical records and court archives (for example, 1 Kings 4:1–19; 14:19). The very words that communicate to us the thoughts of God were "taught" by the Holy Spirit (1 Cor. 2:13).

Nevertheless, as explained above, by plenary inspiration of the Scriptures we do not mean mechanical dictation. Instead, the divine superintendence guarantees that the sacred writings are God's Word to humanity, without error in the original manuscripts before copying began. "Divine authorship implies complete reliability and assures us the Bible will not ultimately contradict itself."[91]

### False Prophets and Teachers—2 Peter 2:1–22

The Lord Jesus warned His disciples in the Sermon on the Mount: "Beware of the false prophets, who come to you in sheep's clothing, but inwardly are ravenous wolves. You will know them by their fruits" (Matt. 7:15–16). They may produce mighty works and a display of charismatic gifts, but what is their conduct?

Again, in His Mount Olivet discourse on future events, Jesus flatly stated concerning the events as the end of this age approaches: "And many false prophets will arise, and will mislead many" (Matt. 24:11). During the Great Tribulation, false Christs and false prophets will appear who will be able to perform such amazing signs and wonders that even God's own people could be fooled (24:24).

For that reason the children of God need to be alert and instructed in the Word so that the Holy Spirit will enable us to detect false teaching (Acts 20:28–31; see the comment on 1 John 2:20, 27). Each congregation has a duty to pass judgment on the messages that the prophets and teachers who are present may bring forth (1 Cor. 14:29). At the same time, Bible teachers must recognize their great responsibility and remember that as teachers they will incur a stricter judgment (James 3:1).

Like the elders, among whose qualifications is the ability to teach (1 Tim. 3:2), teachers need to demonstrate a godly character in their home as well as in the church. They should not be self-willed but must hold fast to the sure and trustworthy Word of God as they were taught it, so that they may be able both to give "stimulating instruction and encouragement in sound . . . doctrine, and to refute and convict those who . . . oppose it" (Titus 1:9, AMP).

The Bible gives some definite clues regarding the general character and actions of false prophets and apostate teachers. Usually several of the following categories mark any particular heretical teacher and his or her followers:

*(1) Doctrinal error.* Peter wrote that they "secretly introduce destructive heresies, even denying the sovereign Lord who bought them" (v. 1, NIV). Such people deliberately oppose God's revealed truth and are rejected by Him as regards the faith (2 Tim. 3:8). Usually their wrong teaching eventuates in a denial of the Trinity or of the deity of Christ and the full efficacy of His blood by God's grace (Jude 4; Phil. 3:18; Heb. 10:29).

The distinctive doctrine to which a teacher gives special emphasis may veil the serious underlying error. Such people will tend to accept other wrong interpretations or heresies in order to support their main teaching. The individual's pet doctrine finally becomes an obsession, for the teacher is being driven by a spirit of error to promote it. That is why Paul spoke of such teachings as doctrines of demons (1 Tim. 4:1). Religiously minded people who do not want sound doctrine but who want "to have their ears tickled" will gather to themselves one teacher after another to satisfy their own likings (2 Tim. 4:3).

*(2) Arrogant pride.* False teachers gain a following because they are forceful and dogmatic. At the same time, they lack humility and love. They are self-willed and speak arrogantly (Jude 16; 2 Pet. 2:10, 12), belittling other Christians. They claim their special doctrine makes their group superior and "more spiritual" than other churches.

They demand total loyalty to their leadership and permit no difference of opinion. They are intent on building their own kingdom. Like Diotrephes, they try to get rid of those who oppose them (3 John 9–10), or they withdraw from contact with all other groups. Thus they cause divisions in the body of Christ and may well be devoid of the Spirit (Jude 19).

Paul commanded us to avoid such people (Rom. 16:17). In some cases, the seclusive nature of the false teaching hinders all activity in evangelism and detracts from an interest in missions. While the teacher may make an undue stress on love for God and others, it is a hypocritical love (Rom. 12:9) for others outside his or her own group of disciples.

*(3) Rebellion against authority.* According to Peter and Jude, false teachers despise and reject authority (2 Pet. 2:10; Jude 8). They speak evil of and scoff at dignitaries (literally, "glorious ones," whether human rulers of the church and of government, or glorious angelic beings). They are unruly or rebellious people (Titus 1:10), not allowing themselves to be placed under the authority of any other Christians. Along with their rebellious and strongly independent spirit goes their tendency to grumble and find fault (Jude 16).

*(4) Deceit.* The Lord Jesus warned of coming deceivers (see above), and Paul also alerted his readers to "false apostles, deceitful workers, disguising themselves as apostles of Christ" (2 Cor. 11:13). Paul himself had renounced the hidden things of dishonesty, refusing to walk in craftiness or to handle the word of God deceitfully (2 Cor. 4:2). He was not like many who were corrupting the Word of God by watering down the message in order to make money from it (2 Cor. 2:17, TLB).

Peter said that the false teachers would exploit his readers with feigned (false or fabricated) words, enticing unstable souls and alluring people with fleshly desires by their great swelling words of vanity (2 Pet. 2:3, 14, 18). They often employ flattery (Jude 16) and lies (Titus 1:12; Jer. 23:25–32; 27:9–16; Zech. 13:3). Instead of rightly dividing the word of truth, handling it accurately and presenting it in a straightforward way (2 Tim. 2:15), false teachers press their favorite passages to an extreme without discussing the balancing passages of the Bible. We need to weigh all of the Scripture passages that pertain to a certain doctrine in order to keep it in balance or proper perspective with the rest of God's Word.

*(5) Greed.* False teachers are often marked by covetousness (vv. 3, 14). Like Balaam, the false prophet who was hired to pronounce a curse on Israel, they are desirous of making money by means of their spiritual gift (2 Pet. 2:15; Jude 11). They are in the ministry for the sake of "filthy lucre" (KJV) or "sordid gain" (Titus 1:11, NAS). They suppose that a showing of godliness or piety can be a money-making business (1 Tim. 6:5).

*(6) Fleshly indulgence.* While some false teachers are overscrupulous and legalistic regarding morals and ethics, others turn the grace of God into lasciviousness (Jude 4). Many people will follow their teaching that there is nothing wrong with sexual sin (2 Pet. 2:2, TLB). Their eyes are full of adultery and never cease from lusting (v. 14).

In his day Jeremiah cried out against the sins of the false prophets of Jerusalem, which included adultery with their neighbors' wives (Jer. 23:14; 29:23). Their appetite ("belly") is the god of such teachers (Phil. 3:18–19). They indulge the flesh in its corrupt desires and count it a pleasure to revel, even in the daytime (2 Pet. 2:10a, 13).

As one writer put it, "Always eager for a good dinner, they make of such occasions an opportunity for raucous mirth and continued false teaching."[92] They seek to satisfy the desire for some sort of religion without demanding abandonment of sin. Paul described such people in this way:

> They are the sort that insinuate themselves into private houses and there get miserable women into their clutches, women burdened with a sinful past, and led on by all kinds of desires, who are always wanting to be taught, but are incapable of reaching a knowledge of the truth.
>
> —2 TIMOTHY 3:6–7, NEB

Situation ethics is a modern-day example of such teaching on a large scale within the ranks of Christianity. Often false teachers begin their apostasy by covering up a sin of the flesh. When they are not truthful about an ethical matter in their own lives, they seek to justify it by twisting the Scriptures—to their own destruction (2 Pet. 3:16). They deceive themselves (2 Tim. 3:13), which in turn opens them up to further lies and deception.

How can we be sure whether a certain person is a false teacher or false prophet? God in His Word lays down some definite tests in Deuteronomy that are applicable today.

First, do these people profess to be believers in the Lord? Before the coming of Christ a prophet in Old Testament times had to be an Israelite, serving as Moses did as the representative or spokesman of the one true, living God (Deut. 18:15). Today, a true prophet or teacher must at least profess to belong to the Israel of God (Gal. 6:16), to be a born-again Christian.

Second, do these people claim that their teaching is from God, that it is the gospel of Christ? Moses said that any prophet who claims to give a message from other gods must die (Deut. 18:20). Are they "a dreamer of dreams" (Deut. 13:1), telling their own dreams (Jer. 23:25, 28, 32; 29:8); or do their words have the authoritative ring of "thus saith the Lord," because God has put the words of prophecy in their mouths by the Spirit (Deut. 18:18)?

Third, does the message of these people agree with Scripture? The Spirit will never contradict Himself. Any so-called new revelation must be in accord with the written Word of God. Even if the prophet should perform a sign or wonder (it would be a satanic miracle), if they nevertheless encourage people to follow other gods, the message is wrong (Deut. 13:2).

Today, even some prominent church people are leading others into the New Age movement or the mysteries of the occult. But all practices of witchcraft and magic—incantations, divination, the horoscope, the Ouija board, the spiritist seance—are expressly forbidden in the Word of God and will only turn the children of God away from the Lord who has redeemed them (Deut. 13:5; 18:9–14; Isa. 8:19–20). God permits false prophets and heresies to come among His people in order to prove whether the believers really love Him wholeheartedly and will remain loyal to His Word (Deut. 13:3; compare 1 Corinthians 11:18–19).

Fourth, do the prophet's predictions come true? If the thing that the prophet foretells does not happen or come true, "it is not the Lord who has given him the message; he has made it up himself" (Deut. 18:22a, TLB). A Christian should never be in bondage to such prophecies that often evoke fear or anxiety: "you shall not be afraid of him" (18:22b).

The uniform instruction of God's Word is to steer clear of all false teachers. To paraphrase Paul's warning to Timothy, avoid those who have the outward form of godliness but who deny the power of the Spirit who energizes the Christian life (2 Tim. 3:5).

## An Anointing From the Holy One—1 John 2:20, 27

The words "unction" (v. 20, KJV) and "anointing" (v. 27) translate the same Greek word, *chrisma*. It refers to anything smeared on, such as the ointment prepared by the Israelites from olive oil and aromatic herbs. Anointing oil was applied as an outward symbol of the Spirit of God in the inaugural ceremony for priests (Exod. 29:7, 21; 30:23–33; 40:15; Ps. 133:2), for kings (1 Sam. 9:16; 10:1; 16:3, 13) and sometimes for prophets (1 Kings 19:16).

In 1 John 2:20, 27 the "anointing" refers to the abiding effect of the gift of the Holy Spirit from the Holy One, that is, from Christ Himself (Mark 1:24; John 6:69; Acts 3:14; Rev. 3:7; 6:10). It is the fulfillment of the promise written in the Old Testament prophets, "They will all be taught by God" (John 6:45, NIV; compare Isaiah 54:13). The "anointing" provides each believer with the continuing capacity to know the truth about the person of Jesus Christ (1 John 2:20–23).

In many Christian circles, however, people use the word "anointing" in the sense of a filling when they pray that they or their minister may receive a "fresh anointing of the Holy Spirit." They are really asking to be filled anew with the Spirit (see the comments on Luke 11:5–13; Ephesians 5:15–21).

The words *Christ* (*christos*, anointed one) and *anointing* (*chrisma*) are from the same Greek root. As Christ was anointed with the Spirit for His ministry and office of Messiah (Hebrew *māšîaḥ*, anointed one—Ps. 2:2; Dan. 9:25–26; compare Isaiah 61:1; Psalm 45:7; Acts 10:38), so too are "Christians" little anointed ones (2 Cor. 1:21–22). Therefore John seems to have been drawing a deliberate contrast in his epistle (2:18–27) between Antichrist and his many antichrists on the one hand and Christ and His Christ-ians (anointed ones) on the other.

Toward the end of the first century, when John wrote his epistles, a heresy was developing known as Gnosticism (from Greek *gnosis*, knowledge). The Gnostics boasted that they had superior knowledge and insight into spiritual truths and claimed that the divine Christ had come down upon Jesus at His baptism and left Him before the crucifixion. Thus they denied that Jesus Himself is the Christ, one Person, the unique Son of God (1 John 2:22). This lie continues to be propagated in such erroneous religious systems as Christian Science, which teaches that Christ is a divine idea while Jesus was only a human, as well as in some Pentecostal or charismatic groups (see the comment on 1 Peter 3:18–20).

The two oldest Greek manuscripts containing 1 John indicate that the second half of verse 20 should be translated "and you all know" (RSV), or "you all have knowledge" (NEB). The baptism in the Holy Spirit was available to all Christians, so that all of them might have the Spirit promised by Jesus to teach them the truth and guard them from error (John 14:26; 16:7, 13; see the comment on John 14:15–18 and others). In genuine Christianity no select group such as the Gnostics may claim secret knowledge. The Spirit of truth teaches each person who has received the anointing to be able to discern the truth from error in all its varied forms. As the English Methodist biblical scholar George Findlay noted:

> To the true believer and faithful seeker after the knowledge of God He gives an instinct for truth, a sense for the Divine in knowledge and in doctrine, which works through the reason and yet above the reason, and which works collectively in the communion of saints.[93]

Out of the collective faith of a body of believers emerges a spiritual common sense, a Christian group opinion produced by the inner witness of the Spirit.

In verse 27 John wrote, "And you have no need for anyone to teach you." Because the Holy Spirit is an *abiding* anointing ("the anointing which you received from Him abides in you"), He is in a position to teach believers continually. He uses the Word (*logos*) of God, which He inspired and which abides in the believer (1 John 2:14), written on the heart under the New Covenant (Jer. 31:33).

His teaching is true and is not a lie, but it does not guarantee a precise agreement in every point of doctrine and practice. It covers essential truth, such as the deity of Jesus Christ, which was here in question. To edify the church as a whole and individual believers in particular, Christ has given teachers to explain His Word and apply it in given situations (Gal. 6:6; Eph. 4:11–13; Col. 1:28; 2:7; 3:16; Heb. 13:7, 17). Mutual teaching or sharing is not set aside by the Spirit's teaching but is highly valued among those who are fellow-partakers of the anointing.

To summarize John's writing in 2:18–27, as the head of His body the Lord Jesus has provided us with three vital safeguards against error: the abiding anointing of His Spirit (vv. 20, 27); the abiding in us of the message of His apostles (v. 24a with 2:7–14); and our abiding in Christ Himself, who *is* the eternal life that He has promised to us (v. 25 with 1:2; 5:11–12). The first two safeguards give us the assurance that the third, our abiding in the Son and in the Father (vv. 24b, 27b; see also 3:24), is a genuine and living fellowship which nothing else can counterfeit.

## Testing the Spirits—1 John 4:1–6

John's warning not to believe every spirit but to keep testing the spirits to see whether they are from God is intensely practical. He was not writing about some eerie situation such as a seance—although these verses apply equally well to spiritist mediums. Rather he was teaching Christians how to detect false prophets and teachers in their own ranks.

The spirits under discussion here are those who motivate and guide teachers of religion and in that sense speak through such people. There is one "spirit of the truth" (*to pneuma tēs alētheias*), the Holy Spirit (v. 6); but there are many spirits of error (vv. 1, 6) sent forth by Satan. The latter are the seducing spirits that Paul wrote about to Timothy:

> But the Spirit explicitly says that in later times some will fall away from the faith, paying attention to deceitful spirits and doctrines of demons, by means of the hypocrisy of liars seared in their own conscience as with a branding iron, men who forbid marriage and advocate abstaining from foods, which God has created to be gratefully shared in by those who believe and know the truth
> —1 TIMOTHY 4:1–3

The Old Testament also taught that a deceiving spirit speaking through the mouth of a false prophet could entice people like Ahab to their doom (1 Kings 22:19–23).

To protect a local church from false prophets, the Holy Spirit may manifest Himself through a certain member of that body with the gift of the discerning of spirits (1 Cor. 12:10). In Philippi, for example, a young woman kept following Paul and his friends to the prayer meeting day after day. She would interrupt with a message that sounded like a prophecy: "These men are servants of the Most High God, who are telling you the way to be saved" (Acts 16:17, NIV).

What she was saying was true enough, but she was speaking under the influence of Satan. When Paul discerned that it was a spirit of divination, he was grieved within. He then commanded the evil spirit in the name of Jesus Christ to come out of her, and she was set free.

Even when the charismatic gift of discerning of spirits is not manifested, Christians are responsible to examine carefully every seeming work of the

Spirit. We must not quench the Spirit or despise prophetic utterances. But we are to "prove all things"—test all messages and signs—holding fast to the genuine manifestations of the Spirit and abstaining from everything that appears to be evil (1 Thess. 5:19–22; 1 Cor. 14:29).

In 1 John 4:1–6 and in 2 John 5–7 the Lord has given us certain tests to use in "trying" the spirits. Employing standards such as these, the church at Ephesus put certain self-styled apostles to the test and found them to be false (Rev. 2:2).

First and most important, what is the spirit prompting the person to teach about Jesus? "Every spirit"—that is, the spirit of every human being under the influence of the Holy Spirit—"that confesses that Jesus Christ has come in the flesh is from God" (v. 2). The person's confession of faith is that Jesus as the Christ has arrived from a spiritual sphere outside of "flesh" in order to participate in human, physical existence and that He still remains incarnate. Thus he acknowledges the divine origin and rights of Jesus and His coming in this capacity into human bodily life.

Anyone who does not so confess Jesus is not of God but is under the influence of the antichrist spirit, that is, of Satan. Paul's watchword to test whether a person is speaking by the Spirit of God is similar; only by the Holy Spirit can one genuinely say, "Jesus is Lord" (1 Cor. 12:3), for Christ exercises total lordship over a person's life only when he or she is directed by the Spirit. John had already written that it is the anointing of the Holy Spirit that enables all the believers to know the truth about Christ (see the comment on 1 John 2:20, 27).

Second, what is the person's relationship to the world? "They proceed from the world and are of the world, therefore it is out of the world [its whole economy morally considered] that they speak, and the world . . . [pays attention] to them" (v. 5, AMP).

The true children of God do not love the world (Greek *kosmos*, the world system or prevailing order of human affairs that is hostile to God) nor the things in the world (1 John 2:15–17). Therefore, through Christ, they have overcome the world (1 John 5:4–5; John 16:33) and the evil one and his spirits (1 John 2:13–14; 4:4). Christians rest upon the absolute assurance that greater is the Holy Spirit in them than Satan, who is in the world system as its ruling spirit (1 John 4:4, John 12:31).

Third, what is the person's attitude to the apostolic testimony? Does he or she listen and pay attention to John and the other apostles ("to us," 1 John 4:6; compare 1 John 1:1–5)? The young Christian who is getting to know God has a hunger for the words that John and the other apostles have spoken and written, but the person who is not from God does not care to listen to them (or to the New Testament; 4:6). We must abide in the doctrine or teaching of Christ in order to be assured that we have both the Father and the Son (2 John 9; John 8:31).

Fourth, what is the person's attitude toward true Christians? In his second epistle (2 John 5–7) John contrasted the Lord's commandment that we love one another (John 13:34) with the many deceivers who have gone out into the world, "those who do not acknowledge Jesus Christ as coming in the flesh" (2 John 7). John said in effect that this is clearly the work of the arch-deceiver and the antichrist spirit, namely, the devil. If anyone comes to a local church or to a believer's home and does not bring the correct teaching about Christ, that person must not be welcomed and admitted or encouraged in any way (2 John 10–11; for further discussion of false teachers, see the comment on 2 Peter 2:1–22).

## The Threefold Witness to the Son of God—1 John 5:6–12

How can we know with certainty that Jesus Christ is the Son of God? And how can we be sure that having believed that Jesus is the Son of God we actually possess eternal life? The answer lies in the witness that God has borne concerning His Son, as John set it forth in this section of his epistle. We should study these verses in a modern version such as the RSV, NAS or NIV because 5:7 of the KJV was not in John's original letter.

The witness is both historical and inward or personal. The two parts of the historical witness are summed up under the terms "water" and "blood." These are evidently sacred and well-known symbols since John again referred to them with the definite article, "the water" and "the blood" (5:6b). The most satisfactory explanation is that "the water" signifies Jesus' baptism when His ministry was inaugurated in the waters of the Jordan, and He received the Father's testimony to His divine sonship; and that "the blood" signifies His crucifixion, the consummation of His ministry. The Greek preposition *dia* in the phrase "by water and blood" here suggests that by means of His baptism and death He came to fulfill His role as Messiah.

While the Gnostics who were followers of the heretic Cerinthus were willing to accept Christ's coming "by water" when the divine Christ emanation supposedly came on Jesus, they insisted that the Christ left the purely human

Jesus before Calvary and therefore did not "come by blood." But after His resurrection Jesus proved from the Old Testament prophecies that the Messiah had to suffer death in order to enter into His glory (Luke 24:25–27, 44–46). According to verse 8, the third witness is the Spirit. All three are in agreement, and together they form the united testimony or witness that God has given concerning His Son (verse 9). Whereas the first two are objective events, the two supreme manifestations of Jesus' messiahship, the Holy Spirit is a continuing subjective, inner witness. Verse 10 teaches that those who believe in the Son of God have the witness in themselves.

A literal translation of the last part of verse 6 in the KJV, TEV and NIV (verse 7 in many modern versions) states that the Spirit is "the continual witnesser." He is the one who is ever illuminating and persuading Christian believers in their innermost being. He convinces them that the objective historic facts regarding Jesus Christ are true and that they have life in the Son of God and ought to keep trusting in Him. The Holy Spirit is the effective witness or persuader, "because the Spirit is the truth" and therefore can be absolutely trusted. (Regarding the Spirit of truth, see the comment on John 14:15–18; regarding the inner witness of the Spirit to our spiritual sonship, see the comment on Romans 8:14–17.)

# NINE

# The Consummation of the Age of the Spirit: The Book of the Revelation

### The Seven Spirits Before God's Throne—Revelation 1:4

In his salutation to the seven churches in the Roman province of Asia, John the Apostle extended grace and peace from the eternal God, from "the seven spirits which are before His throne" and from Jesus Christ. What is the correct interpretation of "the seven spirits"?

Some have explained the seven spirits to be the same as the seven angels of the seven churches (Rev. 1:20). It is true that angels are ministering spirits who render service for the sake of redeemed human beings (Heb. 1:14). But Revelation 1:4–5 apparently is a greeting from the triune God; and in Revelation 3:1, 4:5 and 5:6 it seems more in keeping with the contexts to understand "the seven Spirits of God" as a symbolic reference to the Holy Spirit. In Isaiah 11:2 the manifold energies of the Spirit of God are described in this way:

> And the Spirit of the Lord will rest on Him,
> The spirit of wisdom and understanding,
> The spirit of counsel and strength,
> The spirit of knowledge and the fear of the LORD.

This is one of the prophecies of the Holy Spirit upon Messiah, the Servant of the Lord (see the comment on Isaiah 11:2).

In Revelation 3:1 "He who has the seven Spirits of God" speaks to the church in Sardis. Because the number seven often suggests completeness or perfection, the quoted expression is an Oriental way of saying, "He who has all the fullness of the Spirit, He who has the Spirit without measure" (see the comment on John 3:34). Thus Christ is perfectly prepared to know our deeds and to convict of sin.

The sevenfold Spirit of God is represented in Revelation 4:5 as seven lamps of fire burning before the throne. Like a fire He purifies the godly and consumes the wicked (see the comment on Matthew 3:11–17). The symbolism is most apparent in Revelation 5:6, which describes "a Lamb standing, as if slain, having seven horns and seven eyes, which are the seven Spirits of God, sent out into all the earth." The seven horns symbolize fullness of power, and the seven eyes, perfect insight or wisdom.

In conjunction with Zechariah 3:9 and 4:10 where the seven eyes are said to belong to the Lord and to range to and fro throughout the earth (see the comments on Zechariah 4:6; 6:8), John's strange vision represents our Savior as being omnipotent and omniscient. The seven Spirits have been sent forth into all the world, suggesting the extension of Christ's ministry by the Holy Spirit. Thus the crucified, risen Lamb of God works today in the fullness of His Spirit to make His power and wisdom known and to apply the benefits of Calvary worldwide.

## In the Spirit on the Lord's Day—Revelation 1:10

One way of outlining the last book of the New Testament is to note that the expression "I was in the Spirit" or "He carried me away in the Spirit" occurs four times (Rev. 1:10; 4:2; 17:3; 21:10). This suggests four separate visions that John had. Apparently the Holy Spirit took full possession of him, so that his spirit had immediate contact with the invisible world.

John's experiences were very similar to those of the prophet Ezekiel. For instance, both saw four living creatures that acted as guardians of God's throne (Ezek. 1:6–26; Rev. 4:6–9; 5:6; 6:1, and so on). Both were carried by the Spirit (Ezek. 3:12, 14; 8:3; Rev. 17:3; 21:10). Both books, along with the Book of Daniel, are apocalyptic in nature; that is, they contain detailed prophecies of the end time and are full of figurative language and symbols with their background in the ancient Near East.

John's first vision came to him "on the Lord's day." It is quite certain that he means Sunday, and not that he was projected in this instance into the time of Christ's Second Coming. The Greek wording here is different from that in the expression "the Day of the Lord." Furthermore, in his first vision he saw

Christ as He is now in heaven and received messages for churches already in existence in the first century.

This is the earliest mention of the term "the Lord's day." But the observance by Christians of the first day of the week for worship, the Lord's Supper and giving of offerings is implied in Acts 20:7 and 1 Corinthians 16:2. The Christians very early changed from meeting on Saturday (the Jewish sabbath) to Sunday, apparently in commemoration of Jesus' resurrection. Before his martyrdom about A.D. 107 (or 116), Ignatius, a bishop of Antioch, wrote: "Let every friend of Christ keep the Lord's day as a festival, the resurrection day, the queen and chief of all days of the week."

### Overcoming the Accuser of the Brethren—Revelation 12:9–11

The fullest description in the Bible of Satan is found in 12:9. He is the great dragon of Revelation 12–13, out of whose mouth come forth demonic spirits (Rev. 16:13–14). The concept of the seven-headed dragon (Rev. 12:3) originated in the Semitic world and is found in the Old Testament where he is called Leviathan (Ps. 74:13–14; Isa. 27:1). He is identified with the serpent of old, who tempted and deceived Eve in the Garden of Eden (Gen. 3:1; 2 Cor. 11:3).

He is called the devil (Greek *diabolos*) and Satan (from Hebrew *satan*), both meaning "adversary" or "slanderer." He is the one who opposed Job before God and accused him of unworthy motives (Job 1:6–12; 2:1–7). Later, Satan tried to accuse Joshua, the high priest, but the Lord rebuked Satan (Zech. 3:1–2). Therefore, he is called the "accuser of the brethren" (that is, of Christians as brothers and sisters in the Lord), because he accuses them before God day and night (Rev. 12:10). His strategy is to deceive the whole world, and he has a great army of wicked angels to aid him in the spiritual warfare that he wages incessantly against God and His people (12:7–9).

Victory, however, is assured to the saints of God. "They overcame him by the blood of the Lamb, and by the word of their testimony" (v. 11, KJV, NIV). Those who overcome the devil are those who place implicit trust in the redemptive work of Christ on the cross, signified by His blood which He shed as He died in their stead. Because Christ, the Redeemer, paid the debt in full for every sin of the believer, His blood answers every charge and accusation of Satan. Christ is the only one who would have a right to condemn us, but He is our intercessor and advocate (Rom. 8:33–34; 1 John 2:1). He came to destroy (from *luō*, loose, undo) the works of the devil and to render him powerless (1 John 3:8; Heb. 2:14).

The testimony of Christian believers confirms the efficacy of Jesus' death. The "word of their testimony" has a twofold significance. First, it refers to the word (*logos*) of God to which they bear witness (Rev. 1:2; 3:8), corresponding to the concept in Hebrews 4:12 which likens the word of God to a two-edged sword. Second, it refers to their faithful testimony to Jesus (Rev. 1:2, 9; 6:9; 12:17; 20:4), even to death, by which they confess themselves to be followers of the slain Lamb and not worshipers of the beast, Satan's representative (Rev. 13:15; 15:2).

Even before times of persecution and martyrdom, the Christian achieves spiritual victory over sin and Satan by the application of the cross in his or her life in the crucifixion of self (Luke 9:23–26). The Lord has also poured out His Spirit to empower and enable believers to stay true to Him even during the great tribulation (Rev. 7:14), the great and dreadful Day of the Lord (see the comment on Joel 2:28–32).

## The Spirit of Prophecy—Revelation 19:10

"The testimony of Jesus is the spirit of prophecy." These are words of explanation to John from the angel who had instructed him regarding the marriage supper of the Lamb (Rev. 19:9). John wanted to worship the angel, but he restrained the aged apostle (19:10a).

The Amplified Bible represents the view which understands "the spirit of prophecy" to mean simply that the essence of all prophetic truth has to do with what Christ has spoken:

> You must not do that! I am [only] another servant with you and your brethren who have [accepted and hold] the testimony borne by Jesus. Worship God! For the substance (essence) of the truth revealed by Jesus is the spirit of all prophecy—the vital breath, the inspiration of all inspired preaching and interpretation of the divine will and purpose
>
> —REVELATION 19:10, AMP

"The spirit of prophecy" (*to pneuma tēs prophēteias*), however, was a common rabbinic description of God's Holy Spirit.[1] The first-century Christians readily accepted this view but advanced on the imperfect Jewish understanding of the Spirit and His work. The writers of the New Testament books uniformly believed that the function of all prophecy—both past and present—is to point to Jesus as the Messiah. Only insofar as the Old

Testament could be shown as holding this interpretation was it accepted by the apostles as being inspired by God's Spirit.

Similarly, only when their message was Christ-centered could the New Testament prophets be considered as anointed by the Spirit of truth (see the comment on 1 John 4:1–6).[2] Thus every true testimony to the Lord Jesus and His saving work and coming kingdom is the result of the operation of the same Spirit of prophecy that inspired the apostles and prophets of both Old and New Testaments.

The phrase "the testimony of Jesus" (*hē marturia Iēsou*) includes not only human testimony concerning Jesus by such persons as John the Baptist (John 1:19–27; 5:33–34) and Paul (Acts 22:18) but also Jesus' own testimony about Himself and His work (John 3:11, 32; 8:14; 1 Tim. 6:13). The ascended Lord Jesus Christ also testified concerning Himself in Revelation 1:2, 9. What the glorified Jesus said to the seven churches of Asia becomes His message to all churches by the Spirit (Rev. 2:7, 11, 17, 29; 3:6, 13, 22). As Stanley Horton commented, "This shows that the risen and glorified Christ who is now at the right hand of the Father speaks to us in the Church Age through the Spirit."[3]

The exalted Lord Jesus (Rev. 22:16) is described in His present ministry as "the God of the spirits of the prophets" (22:6). The human spirit of the true prophet (compare 1 Corinthians 14:32) must always be subject to the motivating and informing power of God the Holy Spirit, the true "Spirit of prophecy," both to edify, exhort and console His people (1 Cor. 14:3) and "to show his servants the things that must soon take place" (Rev. 22:6, NIV). But always the Spirit's prophetic message will focus on Christ. All those making the claim to have the Spirit of prophecy are proven to be authentic or inauthentic by the nature of the witness to Jesus in their charismatic utterances.

A proper test for a prophetic message in an assembly of believers is to ascertain whether its testimony about Jesus corresponds to that of the holy Scriptures. The Holy Spirit, "the Spirit of prophecy," will never contradict Himself.

The context of Revelation 19:10 furthermore suggests that the Holy Spirit, the Spirit of prophecy, will direct us to worship Jesus as God's Son and Him alone, never any angels (see also Revelation 22:8–9; Colossians 2:18).

In closing, we may confidently say, "The testimony of Jesus is [always the result of the Spirit of [all true] prophecy."

## *The Spirit and the Bride Say, "Come!"—Revelation 22:17*

This is the last mention of the Holy Spirit in the Bible. The Spirit, perhaps through prophetic messages (see the comment on Revelation 19:10), inspires the church, the bride of Christ, to pray for the Lord Jesus to come back. Christ (vv. 13, 16) has promised in verses 7 and 12 that He is coming quickly (compare also v. 20). Prompted by the love for Christ, which the Spirit has poured into their hearts and filled with that same Spirit of Jesus, they love His appearing (2 Tim. 4:8) and respond to His dear voice by saying, "Come!"

The hearer of the prophecy of this book is invited to join the bride as a true believer and to take part in the call for the Lord to return. As the members of the bride pray to Jesus, "Come," so they urge all who thirst spiritually to come to Christ and drink of the living waters of salvation without cost to themselves. This becomes their first taste of the water of life.

In the regenerated heaven and earth every child of God will enjoy in full measure the life-giving waters from the river that flows clear as crystal out from the throne of God and of the Lamb (Rev. 22:1–2; see the comments on Isaiah 32:15; Ezekiel 39:29). The Scripture's final words to us about the Holy Spirit are thus a beautiful picture of comfort and hope that should remain with us always: God's perpetual giving of Himself in His Spirit will be an ever-flowing river.

# EPILOGUE

The doctrine of God's Spirit permeates Scripture. God, who is Spirit, has revealed Himself as the Spirit of God from the very beginning of creation. He continues to manifest His presence in His Holy Spirit to us today as our Comforter and guide and energizer. And He will always be the life-giving river to refresh and fructify His new creation throughout the endless ages of eternity.

The Spirit is God breathing upon the dust of the ground to create the first human being (Gen. 2:7), upon the "slain" of Israel to bring forth a remnant people (Ezek. 37:11–14) and upon the believing disciples to unite them in new resurrection life with their risen Lord (John 20:22).

The Spirit is the glorious presence of God going before His people as a cloud to lead them and protect them (Exod. 13:21; 14:19–20; Isa. 63:7–14; Rom. 8:14). The Spirit is God empowering and encouraging His servants the prophets to deliver His word to His people (Mic. 3:8; Zech. 7:12; 2 Pet. 1:21). He is God enlightening our minds to understand His truth (John 16:13; 1 Cor. 2:10–13; Heb. 9:8; 10:15).

The Spirit is God blowing as a searing desert wind to bring judgment upon rebels and idolaters (Hos. 13:15–16). He is God as fire burning up the chaff to purge and sanctify God's people (Isa. 4:4; Matt. 3:12).

The Spirit is God coming as a dove to signal life and peace in a new creation (Luke 3:22). He is God anointing His own Son to be the Servant-Messiah (Isa. 11:2; 42:1; 61:1) and enabling Christ's followers to carry on His ministry (Acts 1:8; 2 Cor. 1:21; 1 John 2:20).

The Spirit is God pouring Himself out as water to revive parched souls and to supply the vitalizing power that transforms lives (Isa. 32:15; 44:3; John 7:38) and floods them with joy (Acts 13:52; Rom. 14:17; 16:13; 1 Thess. 1:5–6).

He is the eternal Spirit, the Spirit of Yahweh, the Spirit of Christ, the promised Holy Spirit who was sent forth at Pentecost to empower the church. It is God's will that He, the third Person of the Trinity, be with you and in you and upon you both now and forever. Amen.

# Various Uses of the Greek Verb *Baptizo* in the New Testament

| Kind of Baptism<br>*References* | Subject<br>*The Baptizer* | Object<br>*The Baptized* | Element/Sphere<br>*(with Greek en)* | Relationship<br>*(with Greek eis)* |
|---|---|---|---|---|
| FIGURATIVE<br>1 Cor. 10:1–2 | God<br>(understood) | THE ISRAELITES<br>(God's people, already redeemed by the Passover blood) | IN THE RED SEA<br>(typical of burial and resurrection), *and*<br>IN THE CLOUD<br>(typical of the Holy Spirit)<br>cf. Exod. 13:21–22; Num. 10:34 | unto, with ref. to Moses their leader; to identify them with Moses and seal them unto him. In 1 Cor. 10:2 Moses is a type of Christ our deliverer and mediator. |
| SUFFERING<br>Mark 10:38–39;<br>Luke 12:49–50 | God<br>(implied) | JESUS CHRIST<br>and<br>HIS FOLLOWERS | immersed in pain, suffering and the agony of death (implied). No prepositions are used with *baptizo* in this metaphorical sense. | to purify and refine Christ's faithful disciples (implied). See comment on Luke 12:49–53 (p. 108). |
| JOHN'S<br>Matt. 3:5–11; Luke 3:1–16;<br>Acts 19:3–4 | JOHN THE BAPTIST | a) PEOPLE OF JUDEA<br>(those who had already repented)<br>b) JESUS | IN THE JORDAN RIVER<br>(IN WATER)<br>Mark 1:5; John 1:26,31<br>Matt. 3:13–15; Mark 1:9 | a) unto, with ref. to the repentance and the remission of sins that they had already been granted.<br>b) to identify Him with sinful humanity |
| CHRISTIAN<br>a) Matt. 28:19; Acts 2:38;<br>Gal. 3:27; Rom. 6:3–4 | CHRISTIAN MINISTER acting upon (*epi*) the name or authority of Jesus Christ (Acts 2:38) | THE PROFESSING BELIEVER | IN WATER<br>(implied on basis of Acts 8:36–39) | unto, with ref. to the name of the Trinity or to the name of the Lord Jesus (Matt 28:19; Acts 8:16; 19:5; cf 1 Cor. 1:13–15).<br>unto, with ref. to the forgiveness of sins (Acts 2:38) unto, with ref. to Christ (Gal. 3:27).<br>unto, with ref. to His death (Rom. 6:3–6), as the outward sign or seal that positional death has taken place—like burial in physical death. |
| b) Matt. 3:11, Mark 1:8;<br>Luke 3:16; John 1:33;<br>Acts 1:5; 11:16; 1 Cor. 12:13 | CHRIST THE BAPTIZER<br>(implied in Acts 1:5;<br>11:16; and 1 Cor. 12:13) | THE REGENERATED BELIEVER | IN THE HOLY SPIRIT<br>(IN ONE SPIRIT) | unto, with ref. to the one body, to identify those who belong to the body of Christ with a continuing seal. |

# NOTES

## Introduction

1. David B. Barrett, "Statistics, Global," pp. 812–813.
2. Fee and Stuart, *How to Read the Bible for All Its Worth*, p. 26.
3. Walter C. Kaiser, *Toward Rediscovering the Old Testament*, p. 173.
4. Fee and Stuart, p. 55.
5. Walter A. Henrichsen, *A Layman's Guide to Interpreting the Bible*, p. 38.

## Chapter 1

1. Michael Green, *I Believe in the Holy Spirit*, p. 19.
2. J. Gerald Janzen, "On the Most Important Word in the Shema," p. 287.
3. P. A. Nordell, "The Old Testament Doctrine of the Spirit of God," p. 439.
4. J. Rodman Williams, *Renewal Theology*, I, pp. 85–86.
5. Roger Stronstad, *The Charismatic Theology of St. Luke*, p. 40.
6. Babylonian Talmud *Hagigah* 15a.

## Chapter 2

1. M. R. Westall, "The Scope of the Term 'Spirit of God' in the Old Testament," pp. 31–34.
2. Lloyd Neve, *The Spirit of God in the Old Testament*, pp. 64–73.
3. George T. Montague, *The Holy Spirit: Growth of a Biblical Tradition*, p. 67.
4. Friedrick Baumgaertel in Eduard Schweizer's long article on "*pneuma, pneumatikos*" in Kittel's TDNT described the Spirit of God in Genesis 1:2 as the personal, creative power of God. He pointed out that the mention together of God's Spirit and God's word excludes any belief in divine powers controlling the universe such as those expressed in pantheism, myth and mysticism. "There are no immanent divine forces in nature. In contrast to the religious beliefs of the world around, nature is stripped of power and de-deified." (TDNT, VI, p. 366).
5. Leon J. Wood, *The Holy Spirit in the Old Testament*, p. 34.
6. Williams, RT, I, p. 345.
7. L. Wood, p. 31.
8. L. Wood, p. 16.
9. Neve, p. 100.
10. Williams, RT, I, p. 210.
11. Williams, RT, I, p. 212.
12. Williams, RT, I, pp. 213–214.

13. Charles W. Carter, *The Person and Ministry of the Holy Spirit: A Wesleyan Perspective,* pp. 44–45.

14. Speiser, "*Ydwn,* Genesis 6:3," JBL 75:126–129; see J. Barton Payne, "*rûaḥ,*" TWOT, II, p. 836.

15. John F. Walvoord, "The Work of the Holy Spirit in the Old Testament," p. 430.

16. *NIV Study Bible,* p. 68.

**Chapter 3**

1. Neve, p. 18.

2. L. Wood, pp. 93, 111.

3. Graham Houston, *Prophecy: A Gift for Today?,* pp. 35–40, 160.

4. Neve, p. 16.

5. Stanley M. Horton, *What the Bible Says About the Holy Spirit,* p. 29.

6. John Bright, *A History of Israel,* p. 162.

7. Demos Shakarian, *The Happiest People on Earth,* pp. 19–22.

8. Bright, pp. 204–205.

9. R.K. Harrison, *Old Testament Times,* p. 209.

10. Bright, p. 223.

11. Green, p. 19.

12. Morris A. Inch, *Saga of the Spirit,* p. 38.

13. Chester K. Lehman, *Biblical Theology,* p. 234.

14. L. Wood, p. 105.

15. Neve, pp. 22–23.

16. Neve, p. 26.

17. Walter C. Kaiser, *Hard Sayings of the Old Testament,* p. 120

18. *NIV Study Bible,* p. 405, note on 1 Samuel 19:24.

19. L. Wood, pp. 114–115.

20. Montague, p. 24.

21. L. Wood, p. 116.

22. David M. Howard, "The Transfer of Power From Saul to David in 1 Samuel 16:13–14," p. 481.

23. Williams, RT, II, p. 160.

24. Neve, pp. 27, 36.

25. Abraham Kuyper, *The Work of the Holy Spirit,* p. 39; L. Wood, p. 51; Rea, "The Personal Relationship of Old Testament Believers to the Holy Spirit," pp. 94–96.

26. Neve, pp. 91–94.

27. See also Rea, "Personal Relationship . . . ," pp. 92–103.

28. H. H. Rowley, *Worship in Ancient Israel: Its Forms and Meaning,* pp. 251, 256–269.

29. Horton, p. 45.

30. Aladair Heron, *The Holy Spirit,* p. 35.

31. J. W. McKay, "Elihu—A Proto-Charismatic?," p. 170.

32. Horton, p. 51.

## Chapter 4

1. Edward J. Young, *My Servants the Prophets*, p. 35.
2. Montague, p. 33.
3. Neve, pp. 35, 38.
4. Montague, p. 34.
5. Neve, p. 37.
6. Leslie C. Allen, *The Books of Joel, Obadiah, Jonah, and Micah*, p. 314.
7. Rea, "Old Testament Antecedents of Baptism in the Holy Spirit," p. 14.
8. Neve, p. 38.
9. For an excellent study of these references and all other passages about the Spirit in Ezekiel, see Daniel I. Block, "The Prophet of the Spirit: The Use of *rwh* in the Book of Ezekiel," pp. 27–49.
10. L. Wood, pp. 87, 58.
11. L. Wood, p. 120.
12. *Webster's New World Dictionary*, College Edition, 1966.
13. Horton, p. 53.
14. L. Wood, p. 82.
15. J. N. Oswalt, *The Book of Isaiah: Chapters 1–39*, p. 509.
16. Neve, p. 55, note 26.
17. Montague, p. 41.
18. Neve, pp. 55–56.
19. Montague, p. 40.
20. Edward J. Young, *The Book of Isaiah, II*, p. 400.
21. Young, *Isaiah, II*, p. 400.
22. Franz Delitzsch, *Biblical Commentary on the Prophecies of Isaiah, II*, p. 174.
23. *NIV Study Bible*, p. 1076.
24. Young, *Isaiah, III*, p. 110.
25. Neve, p. 84.
26. Neve, pp. 60, 77.
27. Young, *Isaiah, III*, p. 259.
28. Meredith G. Kline, *Images of the Spirit*, p. 126, note 121.
29. Young, *Isaiah, III*, p. 459.
30. J. Barton Payne, "Jubilee, Year of," ISBE, II, p. 1142.
31. Stronstad, pp. 26–27.
32. Daniel I. Block, "Gog and the Pouring Out of the Spirit," p. 268.
33. Montague, pp. 87–88; Horton, p. 76.
34. Gary M. Burge, *The Anointed Community: The Holy Spirit in the Johannine Tradition*, p. 92.
35. See Horton, pp. 72–76, for an excellent discussion of Zechariah's fifth vision.
36. Neve, p. 104.
37. Rea, "Joel, Book of," p. 495.
38. Theodore Laetsch, *Bible Commentary on the Minor Prophets*, p. 128.

## Chapter 5

1. For a helpful survey of this period, see "The Time Between the Testaments" in the *NIV Study Bible*, pp. 1431ff.
2. Marie E. Isaacs, *The Concept of Spirit*, pp. 49, 21.
3. Isaacs, p. 86.
4. Geza Vermes, *The Dead Sea Scrolls in English*, pp. 173, 193, 199, 197, 76, 77, 192, 78.

## Chapter 6

1. James Dunn, *Baptism in the Holy Spirit*, pp. 8–14, 190–192.
2. Howard Ervin, *Conversion-Initiation and the Baptism in the Holy Spirit*, pp. 11–13.
3. Horton, pp. 96–102.
4. Morton T. Kelsey, *Tongue Speaking*, p. 25.
5. Burge, pp. 162–165.
6. Burge, p. 84.
7. Burge, p. 192.
8. Burge, p. 194.
9. Montague, pp. 347ff.; Burge, pp. 88–96.
10. Dennis and Rita Bennett, *The Holy Spirit and You*, p. 21.
11. Finis J. Dake, *Dake's Annotated Reference Bible*, p. 112a of the New Testament.
12. Jerusalem Bible, p. 179, note r.
13. Bruce Metzger, *A Textual Commentary on the Greek New Testament*, p. 245.
14. Burge, p. 138 and note 94.
15. James Dunn, *Baptism*, pp. 178–181.
16. R. C. H. Lenski, *The Interpretation of St. John's Gospel*, pp. 1371–1372.
17. Rea, "Personal Relationship . . . ," pp. 92–94, 101.
18. As Howard Ervin so clearly shows in *Conversion-Initiation*, pp. 13–14, 18–19.
19. See Ervin, pp. 137–138.
20. *NIV Study Bible*, p. 1637.

## Chapter 7

1. Stronstad, pp. 33–35, 45–48, 49–52, 63, 71–73.
2. Fred L. Fisher, "Witness," *Baker's Dictionary of Theology*, pp. 555–556.
3. Joachim Jeremias, *Jerusalem in the Time of Jesus*, pp. 58–84.
4. Horton, pp. 140–141.
5. Maynard James, *I Believe in the Holy Ghost*, p. 48.
6. For such a proof, see Henry Alford, *The Greek Testament, II*, pp. 15–17.
7. C. C. Ryrie, *The Acts of the Apostles*, p. 19.
8. Bennett, pp. 28–29.
9. William F. Arndt and F. Wilbur Gingrich, *A Greek-English Lexicon of the New Testament and Other Early Christian Literature*, p. 101.
10. Michael Harper, *Walk in the Spirit*, p. 13.
11. F. F. Bruce, *The Book of Acts*, p. 181, note 32.

12. A. T. Robertson, *A Grammar of the Greek New Testament in Light of Historical Research*, pp. 874, 942.
13. See the chapter on this important matter, "Preparing to Receive the Baptism in the Holy Spirit," in Bennett, pp. 36–55.
14. Harper, p. 19.
15. Harper, p. 22.
16. Michael Harper, *Power for the Body of Christ*, p. 35.
17. E. H. Plumptre, "The Acts of the Apostles," in C. J. Ellicott, *A Bible Commentary for English Readers*, VII, p. 21.
18. Joseph H. Thayer, *Greek-English Lexicon of the New Testament*, p. 509.
19. Bruce, p. 92.
20. T. L. Osborn, *Three Keys to the Book of Acts*, pp. 15, 37, 54.
21. Frederick D. Bruner, *A Theology of the Holy Spirit*, p. 172.
22. Robertson, pp. 891–892; see also John 9:25; 12:17; Acts 10:7; Galatians 1:23.
23. Arndt and Gingrich, p. 82.
24. Bruce, p. 181.
25. Johannes Munck, *The Acts of the Apostles*, p. 75.
26. Bruce, p. 182.
27. Bruce, p. 190.
28. Howard Ervin, *These Are Not Drunken, As Ye Suppose*, p. 98; *Spirit-Baptism*, p. 76.
29. Bruce, p. 216.
30. Harper, *Power*, pp. 31–32.
31. Bruce, p. 326.
32. Bruce, p. 327.
33. Pliny (the Younger), *Letters and Panegyricus*, X. 96.

## Chapter 8

1. F. F. Bruce, *The Letters of Paul: An Expanded Paraphrase*, p. 197.
2. Bruce, *Letters*, p. 207.
3. Samuel Chadwick, *The Way to Pentecost*.
4. Bernard Ramm, *The Witness of the Spirit*, p. 68.
5. A. Skevington Wood, *Life by the Spirit*, p. 105.
6. Montague, p. 212.
7. R. C. H. Lenski, *The Interpretation of St. Paul's Epistle to the Romans*, p. 547.
8. Frederic Godet, *Commentary on St. Paul's Epistle to the Romans*, II, p. 102.
9. Michael Griffiths, *Grace-Gifts*, pp. 16–17.
10. W. George Selig and Alan A. Arroyo, *Loving Our Differences*, pp. 25–26.
11. Montague, p. 214.
12. Donald Gee, *Spiritual Gifts in the Work of the Ministry Today*, pp. 47, 42.
13. James Denney, "Romans," *Expositor's Greek Testament*, II, p. 692.
14. Alford, II, p. 444.
15. Frederic Godet, *Commentary on St. Paul's First Epistle to the Corinthians*, I, p. 148.

16. Ramm, pp. 54, 53.

17. F. F. Bruce, *Letters*, p. 73.

18. Godet, *Corinthians, I*, pp. 153–154. Gordon Fee has argued in favor of the NIV translation, "expressing spiritual truths in spiritual words," and against the RSV, NEB, TEV and NAS margin, which all give the idea of explaining spiritual truths to those who possess the Spirit. Fee's paraphrase reads: "explaining the things of the Spirit [as described in v. 12] by means of the words taught by the Spirit" (*First Corinthians*, p. 115). See also the Living Bible: "So we use the Holy Spirit's words to explain the Holy Spirit's facts."

19. R. C. H. Lenski, *St. Paul's First and Second Epistles to the Corinthians*, p. 148.

20. Kenneth Prior, *The Way of Holiness*, p. 44.

21. Arnold Bittlinger, *Gifts and Graces: A Commentary on I Corinthians 12–14*, p. 74.

22. Harper, Walk, pp. 68–69.

23. Houston, pp. 111–130.

24. Gordon Fee, *First Corinthians*, p. 643.

25. Adolf Harnack, *The Mission and the Expansion of Christianity*, pp. 129–146, 199–205.

26. Ervin, *These Are Not Drunken*, pp. 227–233; *Spirit-Baptism*, pp. 85–102.

27. Harper, *Walk*, p. 64.

28. Harper, *Walk*, p. 65.

29. Fee, *Corinthians*, pp. 591, 584–585, note 9.

30. Donald Gee, *Concerning Spiritual Gifts*, p. 26.

31. Bennett, p. 155.

32. Gee, *Concerning*, pp. 27–34, 110–119; *Spiritual Gifts in the Work of the Ministry Today*, pp. 33–52.

33. Bennett, p. 143.

34. Bennett, p. 134.

35. Lenski, *Corinthians*, p. 501.

36. Bittlinger, p. 37.

37. Lenski, *Corinthians*, p. 502.

38. Bennett, p. 112.

39. Gordon Lindsay, *All About the Gifts of the Spirit*, p. 25.

40. John R. W. Stott, *The Baptism and Fulness of the Holy Spirit*, p. 14.

41. George G. Findlay, "I Corinthians," EGT, II, p. 890.

42. John P. Baker, *Baptized in One Spirit*, pp. 17–20.

43. Stott, p. 17. Similarly, Fee argues that the second clause, "and we were all given one Spirit to drink," is most likely a piece of Semitic parallelism with the first clause, "we were all baptized . . . ," so that both clauses make essentially the same point (*First Corinthians*, pp. 604–605).

44. Bittlinger, p. 57.

45. Baker, *Baptized*, pp. 16–17.

46. *Baker's Dictionary of Theology*, p. 332.

47. Bittlinger, p. 86.
48. Arndt and Gingrich, p. 773.
49. Godet, *Corinthians, II,* p. 240.
50. Fee, *Corinthians,* p. 625.
51. Ervin, *These Are Not Drunken,* pp. 175–208; *Spirit-Baptism,* pp. 139–166.
52. Arndt and Gingrich, p. 184.
53. S. Lewis Johnson Jr., "1 Corinthians," *Wycliffe Bible Commentary,* p. 1253.
54. Godet, *Corinthians, II,* p. 265.
55. Laurence Christenson, *Speaking in Tongues,* pp. 22, 27.
56. See Ervin, *These Are Not Drunken,* pp. 201–208; Fee, *Corinthians,* pp. 676–688.
57. Christenson, p. 116.
58. Bennett, p. 89.
59. Houston, pp. 35ff.
60. Griffiths, p. 33. Wayne Grudem distinguishes "apostolic" prophecy, "with absolute divine authority in the actual words used," from "the ordinary functioning of the gift of prophecy in local congregations" in which prophecies must be evaluated (*The Gift of Prophecy in the New Testament and Today,* pp. 110, 109; see pp. 70–114).
61. Bennett, p. 104.
62. Bruce, *Letters,* p. 127.
63. A. J. Gordon, *The Ministry of the Spirit,* p. 114.
64. Andrew Murray, *The Spirit of Christ,* p. 247.
65. Murray, p. 250.
66. Ernest DeWitt Burton, *The Epistle to the Galatians,* p. 147. Harold D. Hunter developed at length the Pentecostal-charismatic interpretation of these verses (*Spirit-Baptism: A Pentecostal Alternative,* pp. 33–35).
67. Horton, pp. 238–239. Harold Hunter, too, has argued that a special bestowal of the Spirit is in view in Ephesians 1:13: "Sealing" by the Spirit can be a term used to describe the charismatic anointing (or endowing) of the Holy Spirit, as in 2 Corinthians 1:21. Furthermore, Ephesians 1:13 (NIV) qualifies the "seal" as being "the promised Holy Spirit" (Hunter, *Spirit-Baptism,* p. 47).
68. F. F. Bruce, *The Epistle to the Ephesians,* p. 79.
69. Handley C. G. Moule, *Ephesian Studies,* pp. 275–276.
70. See pp. 26–33 of this excellent study.
71. S. D. F. Salmond, "Epistle to the Ephesians," EGT, III, p. 363.
72. Stott, pp. 28–29.
73. Bruce, *Ephesians,* p. 111.
74. Stott, p. 29.
75. Montague, p. 227.
76. Arndt and Gingrich, p. 635.
77. Bruce, *Letters,* p. 59.
78. Charles L. Holman, "Titus 3:5–6: A Window on Worldwide Pentecost."
79. B. F. Westcott, *The Epistle to the Hebrews,* pp. 150–151.

80. Harold Lindsell, *The Harper Study Bible,* p. 1810.

81. Andrew Murray, *The Holiest of All,* p. 209.

82. JFB, p. 1459.

83. See the *NIV Study Bible,* note on p. 1903.

84. Montague, p. 190

85. JFB, p. 1480.

86. Arndt and Gingrich, p. 137.

87. Montague, p. 313.

88. JFB, p. 1489.

89. *NIV Study Bible,* note on p. 1900.

90. Clark H. Pinnock, *Biblical Revelation,* pp. 212–213.

91. Pinnock, p. 210.

92. Stephen W. Paine, "The Second Epistle of Peter," WBC, p. 1460.

93. George G. Findlay, *Fellowship in the Life Eternal,* p. 222.

**Chapter 9**

1. C. K. Barrett, *The Gospel According to St. John,* p. 386.

2. Isaacs, p. 125.

3. Horton, p. 254.

# SELECTED BIBLIOGRAPHY

Alford, Henry. *The Greek Testament: An Exegetical and Critical Commentary.* 4 vols. (4th ed., 1861) Reprint. Baker, 1980.

Allen, Leslie C. *The Books of Joel, Obadiah, Jonah, and Micah.* NICOT. Grand Rapids: Eerdmans, 1976.

Andersen, Francis I. and David Noel Freedman. H*osea.* Vol. 24 of *The Anchor Bible.* Garden City, NY: Doubleday & Co., 1980.

Arndt, W. F. and F. W. Gingrich, eds. *A Greek-English Lexicon of the New Testament and Other Early Christian Literature.* Chicago: University of Chicago Press, 1957.

*Baker's Dictionary of Theology.* Grand Rapids: Baker, 1960.

Baker, John P. *Baptized in One Spirit.* London: Fountain Trust, 1967.

Barrett, C. K *The Gospel According to St. John.* 2nd ed. Philadelphia: Westminster Press, 1978.

Barrett, David B. "Statistics, Global." *Dictionary of Pentecostal and Charismatic Movements.* Ed. by Stanley M. Burgess and Gary B. McGee. Grand Rapids: Zondervan, 1988.

Bennett, Dennis and Rita. *The Holy Spirit and You.* Plainfield: Logos, 1971.

Bittlinger, Arnold. *Gifts and Graces: A Commentary on I Corinthians 12–14.* London: Hodder & Stoughton, 1967.

Block, Daniel I. "Gog and the Pouring Out of the Spirit: Reflections on Ezekiel." *Vetus Testamentum,* XXXVII, 3 (1987), 257–270.

_____."The Prophet of the Spirit: The Use of *rwh* in the Book of Ezekiel." JETS, XXXII, 1(1989), 27–49.

Bright, John. *A History of Israel.* 3rd ed. Philadelphia: Westminster Press, 1981.

Bruce, F. F. *The Book of the Acts.* Grand Rapids: Eerdmans, 1959.

_____.*The Epistle to the Ephesians.* London: Pickering & Inglis, 1961.

_____.*The Letters of Paul: An Expanded Paraphrase.* Grand Rapids: Eerdmans, 1965.

Bruner, Frederick D. *A Theology of the Holy Spirit.* Grand Rapids: Eerdmans, 1970.

Burge, Gary M. *The Anointed Community: The Holy Spirit in the Johannine Tradition.* Grand Rapids: Eerdmans, 1987.

Burton, Ernest DeWitt. *The Epistle to the Galatians.* ICC, 1921.

Carter, Charles W. *The Person and Ministry of the Holy Spirit: A Wesleyan Perspective.* Grand Rapids: Baker, 1974.

Chadwick, Samuel. *The Way to Pentecost*. New York: Revell, n.d.

Christenson, Laurence. *Speaking in Tongues, and Its Significance for the Church*. Minneapolis: Bethany Fellowship, 1968.

Culver, Robert D. *"nabi."* TWOT, II, 544–5.

Dake, Finis J. *Dake's Annotated Reference Bible*. Grand Rapids: Zondervan, 1961.

Delitzsch, Franz. *Biblical Commentary on the Prophecies of Isaiah*. Translated by James Martin. 2 vols. in C. Keil and F. Delitzsch, *Commentary on the Old Testament*. Reprint. Grand Rapids: Eerdmans, 1949.

Denny, James. "St. Paul's Epistle to the Romans." EGT, II, 557-725.

Dunn, James D. G. *Baptism in the Holy Spirit: A Re-Examination of the New Testament Teaching on the Gift of the Spirit in Relation to Pentecostalism Today*. Studies in Biblical Theology, second series, 15. London: SCM Press, 1970; Philadelphia: Westminster Press, 1977.

——. *Jesus and the Spirit*. Philadelphia: Westminster Press, 1975.

*Early Christian Fathers, The*. Edited and translated by Henry Bettenson. London: Oxford University Press, 1956.

Ellicott, C. J. *A Bible Commentary for English Readers* (1877–84). London: Cassell, n.d.

Ervin, Howard M. *Conversion-Initiation and the Baptism in the Holy Spirit*. Peabody, MA: Hendrickson, 1984.

——. *Spirit-Baptism: A Biblical Investigation*. Peabody: Hendrickson, 1987.

——. *These Are Not Drunken, As Ye Suppose*. Plainfield: Logos, 1968.

Fee, Gordon D. *The First Epistle to the Corinthians*. NICNT. Grand Rapids: Eerdmans, 1987.

Fee, Gordon D. and Douglas Stuart. *How to Read the Bible for All Its Worth: A Guide to Understanding the Bible*. Grand Rapids: Zondervan Publishing House, 1981.

Findlay, George G. "St. Paul's First Epistle to the Corinthians." EGT, II, 729–953.

——. *Fellowship in the Life Eternal*. London: Hodder & Stoughton, 1909.

Gee, Donald. *Concerning Spiritual Gifts*. Springfield, MO: Gospel Publishing House, n.d.

——. *Spiritual Gifts in the Work of the Ministry Today*. Springfield, MO: Gospel Publishing House, 1963.

Godet, Frederic. *Commentary on St. Paul's Epistle to the Romans*, 2 vols. Translated from the French by A. Cusin. Edinburgh: T. & T. Clark, 1881.

——. *Commentary on St. Paul's First Epistle to the Corinthians*, 2 vols. Translated by A. Cusin. Edinburgh: T. & T. Clark, 1889.

Gordon, A. J. *The Ministry of the Spirit*. Philadelphia: American Baptist Publishing Society, 1896.

Green, Michael. *I Believe in the Holy Spirit*. Eerdmans, 1975.

Griffiths, Michael. *Grace-Gifts*. Grand Rapids: Eerdmans, 1979.

Grogan, Geoffrey W. "The Experience of Salvation in the Old and New Testaments." Vox Evangelica, 5 (1967), 4–26.

Grudem, Wayne A. *The Gift of Prophecy in the New Testament and Today.* Westchester, IL: Crossway Books, 1988.

Harnack, Adolf. *The Mission and Expansion of Christianity.* New York: Harper Torchbooks, 1962.

Harper, Michael. *Power for the Body of Christ.* London: Fountain Trust, 1964.

_____. *Walk in the Spirit.* Plainfield: Logos, 1968.

Harrison, Roland K. *Old Testament Times.* Grand Rapids: Eerdmans, 1970.

Hasel, Gerhard F. "Dove." ISBE rev., I, 987-9.

*Hebrew-English Edition of the Babylonian Talmud: Tractates Ta'anith, Megillah, Hagigah.* Translated into English by J. Rabbinowitz. London: Soncino Press, 1984.

Henrichsen, Walter A. *A Layman's Guide to Interpreting the Bible.* Colorado Springs: NavPress, 1978.

Heron, Aladair. *The Holy Spirit.* Philadelphia: Westminster Press, 1983.

Hiebert, D. Edmond. *The Thessalonian Epistles.* Chicago: Moody Press, 1971.

Holladay, William L., ed. *A Concise Hebrew and Aramaic Lexicon of the Old Testament.* Grand Rapids: Eerdmans, 1978.

Holman, Charles L. "Titus 3:5–6: A Window on Worldwide Pentecost." Paper presented at the 17th Annual Meeting of the Society for Pentecostal Studies, 1987.

Horton, Stanley M. *What the Bible Says About the Holy Spirit.* Springfield, MO: Gospel Publishing House, 1976.

Houston, Graham. *Prophecy: A Gift for Today?* Downers Grove, IL: InterVarsity Press, 1989.

Howard, David M., Jr. "The Transfer of Power from Saul to David in 1 Samuel 16:13–14." JETS, 32/4 (December 1989), 473–483.

Hunter, Harold D. *Spirit-Baptism: A Pentecostal Alternative.* Lanham, MD: University Press of America, 1983.

Inch, Morris A. *Saga of the Spirit.* Grand Rapids: Baker, 1985.

Isaacs, Marie E. *The Concept of Spirit: A Study of Pneuma in Hellenistic Judaism and Its Bearing on the New Testament.* London: Heythrop College, University of London, 1976.

James, Maynard. *I Believe in the Holy Ghost.* Minneapolis: Bethany, 1963.

Janzen, J. Gerald. "On the Most Important Word in the Shema (Deuteronomy VI 4–5)." *Vetus Testamentum* 37 (July 1987): 280–300.

Jeremias, Joachim. *Jerusalem in the Time of Jesus.* Philadelphia: Fortress Press, 1969.

Johnson, S. Lewis. "The First Epistle to the Corinthians." WBC, 1227–1260.

Kaiser, Walter C., Jr. *Hard Sayings of the Old Testament.* Downers Grove, IL: InterVarsity Press, 1988.

_____. *Toward Rediscovering the Old Testament.* Grand Rapids: Zondervan, 1987.

Kelsey, Morton T. *Tongue Speaking.* Garden City: Doubleday, 1964.

Kline, Meredith G. *Images of the Spirit.* Grand Rapids: Baker, 1980.

Kuyper, Abraham. *The Work of the Holy Spirit.* Translated from the Dutch by Henri de Vries (1900). Reprint. Grand Rapids: Eerdmans, 1975.

Laetsch, Theodore. *Bible Commentary on the Minor Prophets.* St. Louis: Concordia Publishing House, 1956.

Lehman, Chester K. *Biblical Theology.* Vol. 1: Old Testament. Scottsdale, PA: Herald Press, 1971.

Lenski, R. C. H. *The Interpretation of St. John's Gospel.* Minneapolis: Augsburg Publishing House, 1961.

———. *The Interpretation of St. Paul's Epistle to the Romans.* Columbus: Wartburg Press, 1945.

———. *The Interpretation of St. Paul's First and Second Epistles to the Corinthians.* Minneapolis: Augsburg, 1963.

Lindsay, Gordon. *All About the Gifts of the Spirit.* Dallas: Christ for the Nations, 1962.

Lindsell, Harold. *Harper Study Bible.* Grand Rapids: Zondervan, 1965.

McKay, J. W. "Elihu—A Proto-Charismatic?" *Expository Times,* No. 6, XC (March 1979), 167–171.

Metzger, Bruce M. *A Textual Commentary on the Greek New Testament: A Companion Volume to the United Bible Societies' Greek New Testament* (3rd edition). London and New York: United Bible Societies, 1975 (corrected edition).

Montague, George T. *The Holy Spirit: Growth of a Biblical Tradition.* New York: Paulist Press, 1976.

Morgan, G. Campbell. *The Spirit of God* (1953). Reprint. Grand Rapids: Baker, 1981.

Morris, Leon. *The Gospel According to John.* NICNT. Grand Rapids: Eerdmans, 1971.

Moule, Handley C. G. *Ephesian Studies.* London: Hodder & Stoughton, 1900.

Munck, Johannes. *The Acts of the Apostles.* Vol. 31 of *The Anchor Bible.* Garden City: Doubleday, 1967.

Murray, Andrew. *The Holiest of All: An Exposition of the Epistle to the Hebrews* (c. 1890). Reprint. New York: Revell, 1965.

———. *The Spirit of Christ.* London: Nisbet, 1888.

Neve, Lloyd. *The Spirit of God in the Old Testament.* Tokyo: Seibunsha, 1972.

*The NIV Study Bible.* Kenneth Barker, gen. ed. Grand Rapids: Zondervan, 1985.

Nordell, P. A. "The Old Testament Doctrine of the Spirit of God." *The Old Testament Student,* IV (June 1885), 433–444.

Osborn, T. L. *Three Keys to the Book of Acts.* Tulsa: Osborn Evangelistic Association, 1960.

Oswalt, John N. *"baar."* TWOT, I, 121.

———. *The Book of Isaiah: Chapters 1–39.* NICOT. Grand Rapids: Eerdmans, 1986.

Paine, Stephen W. "The Second Epistle of Peter." WBC, 1453–1462.

Payne, David F. "King; Kingdom." ISBE rev., III (1986), 20–22.

Payne, J. Barton. "Jubilee, Year of." ISBE rev., II (1982), 1142–1143.

——. "*rûaḥ*." TWOT, II, 836–37.

——. *The Theology of the Older Testament*. Grand Rapids: Zondervan, 1962.

Pinnock, Clark H. *Biblical Revelation*. Chicago: Moody, 1971.

Pliny (the Younger). *Letters and Panegyricus*. 2 vols. Translated by Betty Radice. Cambridge: Harvard University Press, 1969.

Prior, K. F. W. *The Way of Holiness*. Rev. ed. Downers Grove, IL: InterVarsity Press, 1982.

Ramm, Bernard. *The Witness of the Spirit*. Grand Rapids: Eerdmans, 1960.

Rea, John. "Joel, Book of." *Dictionary of Pentecostal and Charismatic Movements*. Edited by Stanley M. Burgess and Gary B. McGee. Grand Rapids: Zondervan, 1988.

——. "Old Testament Antecedents of Baptism in the Holy Spirit: A Key to the Understanding of God's Governance of His People." Paper presented at the 14th Annual Meeting of the Society for Pentecostal Studies, 1984.

——. "The Personal Relationship of Old Testament Believers to the Holy Spirit." *Essays on Apostolic Themes: Studies in Honor of Howard M. Ervin*. Edited by Paul Elbert. Peabody, MA: Hendrickson, 1985.

Robertson, A. T. *A Grammar of the Greek New Testament in the Light of Historical Research*. Nashville: Broadman, 1947.

Rowley, H. H. *Worship in Ancient Israel: Its Forms and Meaning*. London: SPCK, 1967.

Ryrie, C. C. *The Acts of the Apostles*. Chicago: Moody Press, 1961.

Salmond, S. D. F. "The Epistle of Paul to the Ephesians." EGT, III, 203–395.

Schweizer, Eduard, and others. "Pneuma, pneumatikos." TDNT, VI, 332–455.

Selig, W. George and Alan A. Arroyo. *Loving Our Differences*. Virginia Beach: CBN Publishing, 1989.

Shakarian, Demos. *The Happiest People on Earth*. Old Tappan, NJ: Chosen Books, 1975.

Speiser, E. A. "*ydwn*, Genesis 6:3." JBL 75 (1956), 126–129.

Stott, John R. W. *The Baptism and Fulness of the Holy Spirit*. Chicago: InterVarsity Press, 1964.

Stronstad, Roger. *The Charismatic Theology of St. Luke*. Peabody, MA: Hendrickson, 1984.

*Tanakh: A New Translation of the Holy Scriptures According to the Traditional Hebrew Text*. Jewish Publication Society, 1985.

Tari, Mel. *Like a Mighty Wind*. Carol Stream, IL: Creation House, 1972.

Thayer, Joseph H. *Greek-English Lexicon of the New Testament* (1889). Reprint. Grand Rapids: Zondervan, 1956.

Vermes, Geza. *The Dead Sea Scrolls in English*. Harmondsworth: Penguin Books, 1962.

Walvoord, John F. "The Work of the Holy Spirit in the Old Testament." *Bibliotheca Sacra*, Vol. 97 (1940), 289-317, 410–434.

Westall, M.R. "The Scope of the Term 'Spirit of God' in the Old Testament." *Indian Journal of Theology*. 28 (1977), 29–43.

Westcott, B. F. *Gospel of St. John.* London: John Murray, 1898.

——. *The Epistle to the Hebrews* (1889). Reprint. Grand Rapids: Eerdmans, 1950.

Williams, J. Rodman. *Renewal Theology, Vol. I: God, the World & Redemption.* Grand Rapids: Academie Books, Zondervan, 1988.

——. *Renewal Theology, Vol. II: Salvation, the Holy Spirit, and Christian Living.* Grand Rapids: Academie Books, Zondervan, 1990.

Wood, A. Skevington. *Life by the Spirit.* Grand Rapids: Zondervan, 1963.

Wood, Leon J. *The Holy Spirit in the Old Testament.* Grand Rapids: Zondervan, 1976.

Young, Edward J. *My Servants the Prophets.* Grand Rapids: Eerdmans, 1952.

——. *The Book of Isaiah.* 3 vols. Grand Rapids: Eerdmans, 1964–72.

# SCRIPTURE INDEX

Note: Boldface numbers indicate Scripture references with major comments.

## Leviticus

## Numbers

## 2 Samuel

## 1 Kings

## 2 Kings

## Proverbs

CHARISMA'S BIBLE HANDBOOK ON THE HOLY SPIRIT

## Mark

## Luke

## John